THE UNEXPECTED SCALIA

Antonin Scalia was one of the most important, outspoken, and controversial Justices of the past century. His endorsements of originalism, which requires deciding cases as they would have been decided in 1789, and textualism, which limits judges in what they can consider in interpreting text, caused major changes in the way the U.S. Supreme Court decides cases. He was a leader in opposing abortion, the right to die, affirmative action, and mandated equality for gays and lesbians and was for virtually untrammeled gun rights, political expenditures, and imposition of the death penalty. But both the concept and the execution of originalism, by Scalia and other originalists, have been seriously flawed, leading to decisions that are both historically incorrect and socially and politically undesirable. However, he usually followed where his doctrine would take him, leading him to write many liberal opinions. A close friend of Scalia, David Dorsen explains the flawed judicial philosophy of one of the most important Supreme Court Justices of the past century.

David M. Dorsen is Of Counsel with Sedgwick, LLP. He served as Assistant U.S. Attorney in New York under Robert M. Morgenthau and later as Assistant Chief Counsel of the Senate Watergate Committee under Senator Sam Ervin. He has taught at Duke University, Georgetown Law Center, and George Washington Law School. His book *Henry Friendly, Greatest Judge of His Era* won the Green Bag Award for Exemplary Legal Writing.

867 opinions

President Reagan listens to Anthony Scalia during the swearing-in ceremony for Chief Justice Rehnquist and Associate Justice Anthony Scalia of the U.S. Supreme Court, while Warren Burger, Natalie Rehnquist, and Maureen Scalia look on, in the East Room. Courtesy of the Ronald Reagan Library.

The Unexpected Scalia

A CONSERVATIVE JUSTICE'S LIBERAL OPINIONS

DAVID M. DORSEN

CAMBRIDGE
UNIVERSITY PRESS

CAMBRIDGE
UNIVERSITY PRESS

University Printing House, Cambridge CB2 8BS, United Kingdom

One Liberty Plaza, 20th Floor, New York, NY 10006, USA

477 Williamstown Road, Port Melbourne, VIC 3207, Australia

4843/24, 2nd Floor, Ansari Road, Daryaganj, Delhi - 110002, India

79 Anson Road, #06-04/06, Singapore 079906

Cambridge University Press is part of the University of Cambridge.

It furthers the University's mission by disseminating knowledge in the pursuit of education, learning and research at the highest international levels of excellence.

www.cambridge.org
Information on this title: www.cambridge.org/9781107184107
DOI:10.1017/9781316875407

First published 2017

Printed in the United States of America by Sheridan Books, Inc.

A catalogue record for this publication is available from the British Library.

Library of Congress Cataloging-in-Publication Data
Names: Dorsen, David M., 1935– author.
Title: The unexpected Scalia : a conservative justice's liberal opinions / David Dorsen.
Description: New York : Cambridge University Press, 2017.
Identifiers: LCCN 2016043394 | ISBN 9781107184107 (hardback)
Subjects: LCSH: Scalia, Antonin. | Judges – United States – Biography. | United States. Supreme Court – Biography. | BISAC: LAW / Jurisprudence.
Classification: LCC KF8745.S33 D67   2017 | DDC 347.73/2634 – dc23
LC record available at https://lccn.loc.gov/2016043394

ISBN 978-1-107-18410-7 Hardback
ISBN 978-1-316-63535-3 Paperback

To Kenna Dorsen and Norman Dorsen

Contents

Preface

As long as anyone can remember, himself included, Antonin Scalia was a conservative, at times vexingly so. His professorial law review articles were conservative, and his judicial opinions were conservative. These have included decisions both on issues affecting business and, probably more important in today's world, on social issues. A study in the *Supreme Court Compendium* listed the Justices with whom Scalia agreed and disagreed most. In descending order, the top correlations were with Thomas, Roberts, Rehnquist, Alito, Kennedy, and O'Connor; in ascending order, his lowest correlations were with Marshall, Brennan, Stevens, Blackmun, Breyer, and Ginsburg.[1]

Among Scalia's opinions, however, were many that qualify as liberal under the definition we shall shortly consider. In fact, the number totals 135 (listed in Appendix C) out of 867 opinions on the merits and at least twelve opinions on petitions for *certiorari*.[2] The principal question that this book tries to answer is why Scalia wrote many liberal opinions. His answer was that his legal philosophy compelled him to do so; otherwise, he said, he would have been inconsistent or worse. This book provides substantial support for his answer. Interestingly, he seemed to employ his view of the original understanding, whether or not it was consistent with the view of most historians, equally – well, almost equally – to reach liberal and conservative results. His conservative views on the Second Amendment seem ahistorical, but then, so do some of his liberal views on search and seizure.

Aside from explaining the judicial philosophy of one of the most important Justices in the past century, a goal of the book is to subject the doctrine of originalism to serious scrutiny. Originalism insists that the Constitution should be construed the same way it was understood when it was originally adopted in 1789, when it was amended to include a Bill of Right in 1791, and so on. While an amazing document for its time, the eighteenth-century Constitution would be a reactionary document today. It allowed slavery, denied women the vote, and mandated an indirect vote for President and the Senate. While those constitutional abominations have largely been eliminated, their original presence says something about the founders and their era, in which Congress could pass a law criminalizing seditious libel and executing someone for forgery. Nevertheless, 60 percent of respondents to a 2012 survey said that the Supreme Court "should base its ruling on its understanding of what the Constitution meant as it was originally written."[3]

Among my findings is that information about the understanding of the Framers, whether in the late nineteen century or in the 1860s, that are germane to present issues are so few and ambiguous that many constitutional judgments cannot be determined by resort to history. What this means, aside from its challenge to originalism as a valid approach to constitutional law, is that Scalia had had little reason to write liberal opinions. More easily, he could have written additional conservative opinions based on originalism.

This book attempts something that may be impossible, namely, to separate Scalia's judicial philosophy from his personality and style. There is no shortage of commentaries that portray him as divisive, combative, overbearing, intolerant, intemperate, bumptious, nasty, bullying, vain, rude, acerbic, narrow-minded, and, also, charming, funny, brilliant, loyal, candid, conscientious, rigorous, exacting, meticulous, willing to engage on issues, larger than life, and an excellent writing stylist. These characteristics were very much part of Scalia the man and Scalia the judge. If they had an impact on his views, they undoubtedly have had a greater impact on his influence, including his status as role model and molder of Supreme Court advocacy.

Scalia criticized his fellow Justices, sometimes mercilessly, and it is impossible to gauge the consequences of that disrespect. He said of one of Stevens's opinions: "I join the opinion of the Court except that portion which takes seriously, and thus encourages in the future, an argument that should be laughed out of court."[4] He said of one of White's arguments that it "should not be taken seriously."[5] He also said that an assertion by O'Connor "cannot be taken seriously."[6] Scalia was equally dismissive of some of Kennedy's opinions, ridiculing, for example, what he called Kennedy's "sweet-mystery-of life passage" in *Lawrence v. Texas* (2003)[7] as a ground for holding unconstitutional laws criminalizing homosexual acts. In one of his last opinions Scalia wrote: "If, even as the price to be paid for a fifth vote, I ever joined an opinion for the Court that began: 'The Constitution promises liberty to all within its reach, a liberty that includes certain specific rights that allow persons, within a lawful realm to define and express their identity,' I would hide my head in a bag. The Supreme Court of the United States has descended from the disciplined legal reasoning of John Marshall and Joseph Story to the mystical aphorisms of the fortune cookie."[8] What seemed to bother Scalia most was the perceived absence of a coherent and rigorous philosophy on the part of Stevens, O'Connor, and Kennedy.[9] He was far more tolerant and respectful of Ginsburg and Breyer.[10]

Commentators have searched for the genesis of Scalia's views in his Catholicism and Catholic schooling and in his Italian-American heritage.[11] I will leave that quest to psychologists (preferably ones with a law degree).[12] I believe that it is enlightening to separate Scalia's intellectual accomplishments and deficiencies from, for want of a better term, his personal qualities. At least, that is my assumption in this book.

I communicated in person, by telephone, and by e-mail with Scalia frequently about this book. Scalia was an old friend, dating from our overlapping year on the *Harvard Law Review*, 1958–59 (my third, his second, law school year). In recent years, starting roughly in 2003 (after my wife and I sufficiently recovered from *Bush v. Gore*), we dined together regularly and got along splendidly on a personal level. We celebrated election nights and some of each other's birthdays together. He also commented extensively on a draft of *Henry Friendly, Greatest Judge of His Era*, my prior book. When it was published, he graciously threw a book party for me at his home, attended by seven Brethren and others. But the fact that he was a friend should not be confused with whether we agreed on political and social issues. We rarely did. I am liberal, nonoriginalist, and atheist. He most definitely was none of these. Nevertheless, we had some common ground in the liberal opinions discussed in this book. Books are written all the time on people the author either agrees with or disagrees with. This is a book by a friend who disagreed with the subject's main impact.[13] The results will speak for themselves.

With rare exceptions, which I note, I have not relied on speeches not published in law reviews under Scalia's byline, his statements and questions at oral arguments, comments attributed to him, or comments to me. I accepted only what Scalia put his name on for publication, whether articles or judicial opinions. Many of his speeches were provocative, and some had an off-the-cuff quality that may not have reflected his considered thought. He may have been giving his personal views, which were not the same as his judicial views. His questions at oral arguments were often designed to provoke, not necessarily to enlighten. Scalia liked to engage listeners, even to disturb and outrage them, and this does not make for a reliable account of his jurisprudence. Judges and scholars cite judicial opinions and articles, but it is extremely rare, if not unprecedented, for them to cite statements in speeches, questions at oral argument, or the like. Relying on stray comments is not scholarship.

Scalia loved to become engaged in serious issues with those who disagreed with him, such as the meaning of the Second Amendment, whether the death penalty reduced homicide, search and seizure issues, and the role of religion. He debated many liberals and addressed hostile audiences. His well-developed philosophy left little room for persuasion on my part. My fallback position was to urge the Christian value of mercy. While a small minority of our time together, usually with our wives at one of our homes, and sometimes at wine society dinners, a baseball game, or an opera, was devoted to these issues, he and I argued about them in his chambers over a light lunch and a good bottle of wine. He never saw this book but was interested in my arguments and was happy to reply to my e-mails that asked him to explain and even defend his opinions. When I complained by e-mail that I had tried and failed to appreciate his point, he responded almost immediately: "Try harder."

Leaving to one side Scalia's vote in the dismaying *Bush v. Gore* (2000)[14] (about which I have no special knowledge), I believe that Scalia was principled,[15] although

his interpretation of Second Amendment history challenged my charitable characterization. Both are extremely difficult to defend on any ground, including originalism.
For me the key to understanding Scalia is his liberal opinions, which as a conserva-
tive he did not want to write and, moreover, sometimes took him to the left of what
history in fact required and even what the Court's liberal Justices (or I) embraced.
He was just as passionate about a violation of his liberal tenets, such as what con-
stituted a search and seizure under the Fourth Amendment and what violated the
Confrontation Clause of the Sixth Amendment, as he was about violations of the
Second and Eighth Amendments. I note that some not necessarily sympathetic to
Scalia's jurisprudence agree with my assessment;[16] many liberals do not.

Part I of the book provides a discussion of Scalia's principles of decision making,
virtually all of which predated his tenure on the Supreme Court in the form of law
review articles. It starts with the confirmation hearings on Scalia's nomination to the
Supreme Court and is followed by a more detailed examination of his views.

Part II is a nonexhaustive review of Scalia's conservative constitutional opinions
in the Supreme Court in a variety of areas based largely on the themes discussed in
Part I.

Part III is a description of Scalia's liberal constitutional opinions in the Supreme
Court, with explanations as to how they flowed from his basic principles of originalism and textualism.

Part IV deals with several areas that are difficult to classify in the abstract as liberal
or conservative, including Scalia's refusal to allow limits on political speech and his
support of asserted rights of antiabortion picketers on the ground that limitations
would restrict exercise of their First Amendment rights.

Part V is a return to originalism and its applications with a more critical and
expansive eye. The opinions in Parts II, III, and IV are reexamined in the light of
modern scholarship by historians, legal historians, and, to a lesser extent, linguists.

Part VI discusses Scalia's nonconstitutional opinions in the light of his principles,
especially textualism. While some attention is paid to his conservative opinions,
most attention is paid to his liberal opinions and how his textualism took him there.

Part VII encompasses a comparison of Scalia's positions with those of the Court's
other originalist, Clarence Thomas, and a conclusion.

On a technical level, the book makes some changes from traditional legal scholarship citation form. Almost everything quoted in this book has footnotes, and they
are uniformly deleted without mention. Emphasis and punctuation that appeared
in the original are not identified unless there may be ambiguity. I do not adhere to
the *Bluebook* on form.

Acknowledgments

I want to express my great appreciation to Sedgwick, LLP, where I am Of Counsel. The law firm and its predecessor have supported my writing career, including my prior biography of Judge Henry Friendly, by giving me an office and clerical services without accepting anything in return, except, possibly, the satisfaction of helping a lawyer, now largely removed from private practice, engage in a new career as an author of books on judges and the courts. I also want to thank George Washington Law School, where I taught as an adjunct professor more than a decade ago, for allowing me to employ its library and facilities, including its highly professional staff.

A number of people have given generously of their time and knowledge to read and comment on drafts of this book. Three members of the judiciary, present or former judges on U.S. courts of appeals, provided invaluable assistance: Judges Patricia Wald (D.C. Circuit, retired), J. Harvie Wilkinson (Fourth Circuit), and Stephen F. Williams (D.C. Circuit), who also provided assistance on my first book. I want equally to thank four distinguished professors of law: Norman Dorsen (NYU Law School), my brother, whose help and encouragement require special notice; John F. Manning (Harvard Law School and a former law clerk to Justice Scalia); and Stephen B. Presser (Northwestern Law School) – all of whom, like the judges, commented on the entire manuscript – and James J. Grudney (Fordham Law School), who reviewed my chapters on legislation. Their comments have been invaluable to me.

I relied extensively on scholarship in books and professional periodicals, and I have done my best to acknowledge my predecessors in thought. I want to thank the many scholars, primarily historians and law professors with training and advanced degrees in history or related relevant fields, who graciously answered my e-mails and provided encouragement. While I have relied on their learned and often groundbreaking books and articles in my analysis of Justice Scalia's jurisprudence, which are duly noted in the endnotes and sometimes in the text, I especially appreciated their willingness to interrupt their work to respond to my questions.

I want to express my appreciation to Cambridge University Press, especially Lew Bateman and John Berger, for publishing this book and for the assistance they provided.

Thanks are also due to Mike Aronson, who was my editor at Harvard University Press on my previous book and on this book before his untimely retirement, which did not diminish his interest and encouragement.

I also was helped by part-time law student researchers from George Washington Law School, who located hard-to-find citations and sources and did other essential work: Nicholas Sachanda (GWU '13), Joshua Champagne (GWU '14), and Douglas Strauss (GWU '16).

I want to thank the late Justice Antonin Scalia, who graciously responded to my many inquiries about his judicial opinions and views both orally and by e-mail, but who had no say in what is written on these pages and who never read the manuscript. He encouraged me to write a rigorous book. I have endeavored to represent his views accurately and fairly. I also want to thank Maureen Scalia, also a close friend, for making our many dinners together calmer as well as enjoyable.

It goes almost without saying that I take full responsibility for everything in the book.

Introduction

What Is Liberal?

Before turning to Scalia, the question must be asked, what is liberal?

Over centuries and even recent decades, what qualifies as liberal has changed considerably. For example, supporting rights to private property and a minimal government were once considered hallmarks of liberalism as framed by John Locke and Adam Smith. Scalia has been described as "hid[ing] a political ideology sympathetic to classical Manchester Liberalism. Such an ideology, as originally articulated in nineteenth-century England, emphasized limited government, faith in the marketplace and commitment to legalism, materialism, property rights, and enforcement of majoritarian morality as essential to the creation of free society."[1] Classic liberalism is related to modern libertarianism, which often finds support among conservatives anxious to insulate their property from government regulation.[2]

What about liberalism today? A 1986 book by Oxford scholar John Gray cited four elements as comprising liberalism: "It is *individualist*, in that it asserts the moral primacy of the person against the claims of any social collectivity; *egalitarian*, inasmuch as it confers on all men the same moral status and denies the relevance to legal or political order of differences in moral worth among human beings; *universalist*, affirming the moral unity of the human species and according a secondary importance to specific historic associations and cultural forms; and *meliorist* in its affirmation of the corrigibility and improvability of all social institutions and political arrangements."[3]

None of the standard philosophical concepts seems to qualify as a useful definition for purposes of this book. I have decided to forgo an overarching definition in favor of particular positions on which at least a fairly general consensus exists, recognizing that there may be anomalies, even contradictions, in particular cases. For purposes of this book, a liberal opinion is liberal when it produces liberal results, even though the standard and reasoning are neutral. For example, a ruling declining to extend the time for filing a notice of appeal is facially neutral. However, the ruling will almost always harm criminal defendants, many of whom are without lawyers, rather than corporations, so it will be viewed as conservative. As a result, my approach is undertheorized and practical. It also ignores some long-range problems and issues, such as political stability.[4] It is a public and political rather than internal and moral paradigm and contains aspects of John Rawls's concept of justice as fairness.[5] Also, some characteristics of liberalism may be in conflict in a case. The elements listed below are more specific and more numerous than many formulations.[6] A "liberal" *generally* supports

respect for and the primacy of the individual;

a broad right to free speech, freedom and protection of the press, and freedom of assembly (although generally for some restrictions on campaign spending);

the right to privacy and to be let alone, including pro-choice on abortion and right to die;

broad and enforced antidiscrimination laws;

affirmative action for disadvantaged minorities;

the removal of barriers based on class, income, nationality, gender, and sexual orientation;

a secular orientation and preference for secular rationales and arguments and a strong separation of church and state;

representative government with broad voting rights and participation, with federal government protection;

one person, one vote, with severe limits on gerrymandering;

the rule of law and an independent judiciary;

ready access to the courts, including free or subsidized access for those without funds;

pro-plaintiff in civil cases;

extensive rights for criminal defendants and others held in custody by governments;[7]

abolition of the death penalty;

strong gun control;

limited power and influence of corporations and the very rich;

government transparency, including access to information from the government;

federal, not state, government controlling entitlements;

the government, especially federal government, exercising regulatory control over businesses and property;

protection of the environment, including lenient standing rules;

limited or no immunity for wrongful governmental actions.

Yale Professor Bruce Ackerman, among others, has argued that Justices like Stevens, Souter, Ginsburg, and Breyer were not liberals but moderates. "Justices Breyer and Ginsburg are main-stream moderates, not aggressive liberals, when measured against the likes of Justices Brennan and Marshall."[8] I do not engage that question but treat decisions as liberal that meet the criteria.

One more question has to be answered: how should a Scalia opinion be treated when it is neither the most nor least liberal in the case? I include it, but note that the opinion was flanked by both a more and less liberal one. Because Scalia was a known conservative, according to some an unvarnished conservative, it seems preferable to include those opinions as liberal, both in the text and in charts included in the book.

Scalia's Judicial Philosophy

PART I.

Social and Political Philosophy.

1

The Confirmation Hearings

Scalia was an ideal candidate for the Supreme Court. He was an Italian-American who was the only child of Salvatore Eugene Scalia, who was born in Sicily, and the native-born former Catherine Panaro. The older Scalia was a professor of Romance languages at Brooklyn College in New York City, a public institution, and lived in Queens, New York. Theirs was a devout Catholic household. The younger Scalia excelled at New York's Xavier High School, an all-boys Jesuit school, where he was valedictorian. ROTC training was required, and he learned about and shot rifles. As an undergraduate at Georgetown, he graduated *summa cum laude* and first in his class; at Harvard Law School, he was an officer of the prestigious *Harvard Law Review*, near the top of his class. He married Irish-American Maureen McCarthy, and they had nine children, including a Catholic priest. The household was Catholic, conservative Catholic. Scalia's prior legal career included private practice at top law firms, professorships at prestigious law schools (Virginia and University of Chicago), high-ranking Executive Branch positions (chairman of the Administrative Conference of the United States, an independent agency in the Executive Branch, and assistant attorney general in charge of the Office of Legal Counsel), and four years as a judge on the U.S. Court of Appeals for the District of Columbia Circuit. There was no hint of scandal, or even failure, in his background.[1]

His half-day of testimony on August 5, 1986, if not a lovefest, was cordial and respectful. He carefully chose which questions he would answer, gave cautious responses, and broke little new ground. No comment on *Roe v. Wade*, for example, could be pried from him. His answer was if someone cannot follow the law, he should not be a judge. If he could not separate his personal views from his judicial obligation, he would recuse himself from the case.[2] He only minimally enlightened the Senate on his views on discrimination, affirmative action, the death penalty, and privacy.[3] He was respectful of the Constitution and of individual rights. His ability not to answer questions is illustrated in an exchange on the constitutionality of the delegation of powers to federal agencies:

SENATOR KENNEDY: Well, would I be correct in saying that you would support then a broad congressional mandate in these areas?

JUDGE SCALIA: I would support a broad congressional mandate that is not unconstitutionally overbroad, yes. [Laughter]. . . . But seriously, I am not trying to go around and around. I think I am accurate in saying that my writings do not show that I am likely to be more restrictive on that matter than others.[4]

Scalia acknowledged he was conservative but smoothed some of the rough edges. One of the first softballs lobbed to Scalia by a Republican was on his views "regarding the success of the Constitution." He responded:

I think most of the questions today will probably be about that portion of the Constitution that is called the Bill of Rights, which is a very important part of it, of course. But if you had to put your finger on what has made our Constitution so enduring, I think it is the original document before the amendments were added. Because the amendments, by themselves, do not do anything. The Russian constitution probably has better, or at least as good, guarantees of personal freedom as our document does. What makes it work, what assures that those words are not just hollow promises, is the structure of government that the original Constitution established, the checks and balances among the three branches, in particular, so that no one of them is able to "run roughshod" over the liberties of the people as those liberties are described in the Bill of Rights. If I had to put my finger on what it was that has made the difference, that is it.[5]

Later, replying to a question about the role of the judiciary relative to federalism, Scalia said that "the primary institution to strike the right balance is the Congress . . . when it enacts the laws. . . . I think what the Supreme Court cases on the subject show is that it is very hard to find a distinct justiciable line between those matters that are appropriate for the States and those that are appropriate for the Federal Government, that finding that line is much easier for a legislator than for a court, and by and large the courts have not interfered."[6] Referring to a law review article he wrote on congressional delegation, Scalia said that his view was that "the courts are just going to have to leave that constitutional issue to be resolved by Congress."[7]

He was an originalist ("I start from the original meaning"[8]), but not indelibly so, he testified. He applied *stare decisis*, but not invariably. He answered a question by Senator Kennedy with the standard answer: "I assure you, I have no agenda. I am not going onto the Court with a list of things I want to do. My only agenda is to be a good judge."[9] In response to another question from Kennedy about the weight to be given to precedents, Scalia replied:

It depends on the nature of the precedent, the nature of the issue. Let us assume that somebody runs in from Princeton University, and on the basis of the latest historical research, he or she has discovered a lost document which shows that it was never intended that the Supreme Court should have the authority to declare a statute unconstitutional. I would not necessarily reverse *Marbury v. Madison* on the basis of something like that. To some extent, Government even at the Supreme Court level is a practical exercise. There are some things that are done, and when they are done, they are done and you move on. Now, which of those you think are so woven in the fabric of the law that mistakes are too late to correct, and which are not, that is a difficult question to answer.[10]

In response to questions from then-Senator Joseph Biden, Scalia addressed the Eighth Amendment, noting that, "I cannot say that I have a fully framed omnibus view of the Constitution," but adding, "I think it fair to say you would not regard me as someone who would be likely to make use of the phrase, living Constitution," which leaves judges "with nothing to tell me what are our most profound beliefs except my own little voice inside. I do not want to govern this society on the basis of that."[11] "What I think is that the Constitution is obviously not meant to be evolvable so easily that in effect a court of nine judges can treat it as though it is a bring-along-with-me statute and fill it up with whatever content the current times seem to require. To a large degree it is intended to be insulation against the current times, against the passions of the moment that may cause individual liberties to be disregarded, and it has served that function valuably very often. . . . It was adopted by the people's acceptance of it, by their voting for it, and its legitimacy depends upon democratic adoption at the time it was enacted."[12] He acknowledged that there was room for "a certain amount of development of constitutional doctrine," and continued:

SCALIA: . . . [T]he strict original intentist, I think, would say that even such a clause as the cruel and unusual punishment clause would have to mean precisely the same thing today that it meant in 1789.

BIDEN: That it would have to mean that?

SCALIA: Yes, so that if lashing was fine then, lashing would be fine now. I am not sure that I agree with that. I think that there are some provisions of the Constitution that may have a certain amount of evolutionary content with them. . . . I have always had trouble with lashing, Senator. I have always had trouble thinking that is constitutional. And if I have trouble with that –

BIDEN: Are you being serious or being a wise guy?

SCALIA: I am being serious, no; I am being serious.

BIDEN: I just wanted to make sure.[13]

When Senator Metzenbaum asked Scalia whether "you are saying that the Constitution means what the majority says it means," Scalia answered:

A constitution has to have ultimately majoritarian underpinnings. To be sure a constitution is a document that protects against future democratic excesses. But when it is adopted, it is adopted by democratic process. That is what legitimizes it. . . . [I]f the majority that adopted it did not believe this unspecified right, which is not reflected clearly in the language, if their laws at the time do not reflect that that right existed, nor do the laws at the present date reflect that the society believes that that right exists, I worry about my deciding that it exists. I worry that I am not reflecting the most fundamental, deeply felt beliefs of our society, which is what a constitution means, but rather, I am reflecting the most deeply felt beliefs of Scalia, which is not what I want to impose on the society.[14]

Amid these exchanges were discussions of a few of Scalia's court-of-appeals opinions, including *Community for Creative Non-Violence v. Watt* (1983).[15] In violation of Park Service regulations that prohibited sleeping overnight in a national park, demonstrators camped out without a permit in Lafayette Park across from the White House to express the message that homeless persons had nowhere to sleep. Seven of the nine members of the *en banc* D.C. Circuit upheld the demonstrators on the basis that sleeping under the circumstances of the case constituted speech protected by the First Amendment and that the government interest was minimal. Scalia dissented in an opinion that viewed protected action as speech more narrowly. He explained:

> If they passed a law that allows all other sleeping but only prohibits sleeping where it is intended to communicate, then it would be invalidated.... [W]here you have a general law that just applies to an activity which in itself is normally not communicative, such as sleeping, spitting, whatever you like; clenching your fist, for example; such a law would not be subject to heightened standards of the first amendment.... Whereas, when you are dealing with communicative activity, naturally communicative activity – writing, speech, and so forth – any law, even if it is general, across the board, has to meet those higher standards.... If you want to protest, as a means of civil disobedience, and take the penalty, that is fine. But if the law is not itself directed against demonstrations or against communication, I do not think it is the kind of law that in and of itself requires the heightened scrutiny.

Immediately after Scalia's explanation, Biden said: "That is very helpful to me. I am not being smart when I say that. That puts my mind at ease a great deal."[16]

In response to a general question about his support for tuition tax credits for private and parochial schools, Scalia described Religion Clauses decisions as messy, if not irrational:

> [Y]ou get cases like the case of the Jehovah's Witness, who being a sabbatarian, wants to have Saturday off instead of Sunday, and wants to draw unemployment compensation when she's been offered a job that requires work on Saturday and turned it down. And the way the Court resolved the case was to say it violated the freedom-of-religion clause for a State not to allow her to draw unemployment compensation simply because she refused to accept a job that would require her to work on Saturday. Well yes, that does protect freedom of religion, but, on the other hand, doesn't that somehow amount to an establishment of religion to have the State make a special rule to accommodate the religious belief of this sabbatarian. That's the problem that runs throughout these cases, and that's the reason they are very hard to figure.[17]

Scalia explained that he favored "affirmative action programs for the poor and disadvantaged, even when it turned out that every one of the poor people or every one of the disadvantaged people assisted by a particular program turned out to be of a particular race. . . . What I expressed myself in opposition to, on policy grounds, was favoring a group solely on racial or ethnic grounds, and not on the basis of poverty or disadvantage."[18] One reason was "when you favor one person because of his race, you are automatically disfavoring another one because of his race." The other reason is "to an extent it deprives the members of the race who are given a special advantage of the fruits of their labors, because they are sometimes regarded as having achieved those fruits only because of affirmative action, whereas they could have made it without it."[19]

Senator Kennedy criticized Scalia on women's rights,[20] his position that independent agencies may be unconstitutional, and his position that the courts can deny "Congress the power to delegate authority of regulatory agencies."[21] Metzenbaum and Arlen Specter questioned Scalia's position on the preeminence of the Executive Branch and his restricting access to the courts by individuals.[22] Paul Simon questioned Scalia's position on affirmative action and the First Amendment.[23] Biden optimistically suggested that Scalia would not vote to overrule *Roe v. Wade*.[24] Mitch McConnell and other Republicans praised Scalia's conservatism.[25] Dennis DeConcini described Scalia as "probably one of the most evasive nominees I have ever seen."[26] That was pretty much it as far as the Senators were concerned.

Despite hostility from a range of liberal organizations,[27] Scalia was confirmed unanimously. Many factors contributed to Scalia's easy time. The Senate had just gone through the challenging confirmation of Rehnquist; the addition of Scalia would not change the ideological makeup of the Court; Scalia had excellent qualifications and his views were mainstream; he was personally engaging and charming; he had not participated in any controversial activities; he was a Roman Catholic Italian-American with a large and attractive family; and he was not Robert Bork, the main rival candidate.

2

Scalia's Principles of Decision Making

Before he was a Justice, Antonin Scalia recognized that he was not an unadulterated originalist. A few years after his confirmation-hearing testimony about flogging he said that, "even though no prior Supreme Court decision has specifically disapproved them ... I am confident that public flogging and handbranding would not be sustained in our courts, and any espousal of originalism as a practical theory of exegesis must somehow come to terms with that reality.... Having made that endorsement [of originalism], I hasten to confess that in a crunch I may prove a faint-hearted originalist. I cannot imagine myself, any more than any other federal judge, upholding a statute that imposes the punishment of flogging."[1]

Scalia publicly changed his position on flogging,[2] and as a result committed himself to the full logic of the originalist position. Or did he? In fact, Scalia's approach was not an untrammeled originalist, as some have claimed,[3] but embraced other principles that tempered and at times diverted his originalism, as we shall see. His originalism was selective, most pronounced in connection with the Seventh and Eight Amendments; present in varying degrees in his Second, Fourth, Fifth, and Sixth Amendment analysis; and essentially absent in his First Amendment Free Speech jurisprudence (except for pornography). He aggressively adhered to originalism in connection with some of the original Constitution, such as the Commerce Clause and Separation of Powers.[4] He rejected incorporation for the states via the Fourteenth Amendment of the Bill of Rights on principle, but accepted it and other decisions because of *stare decisis*. Scalia was a *qualified* originalist.

The other major component of Scalia's approach was textualism, which, in the case of statutes means that what counts are the words that Congress voted for, not unexpressed purposes or unvoted legislative history. Textualism, which also applies to the Constitution, is discussed prior to originalism. Other principles and approaches, including an emphasis on tradition and majoritarianism, follow.

TEXTUALISM

The question of textualism arises only because there are written statutes and con-stitutions. A century ago, the work of the Supreme Court largely involved common law, that is, judge-made law. With judge-made law, courts felt permitted, within reason and customary bounds, to change the law as circumstances and the level of sophistication changed. When statutes proliferated, the question arose as to the obligation of judges to follow the written word and the right of judges to interpret or even modify the written word.

The traditional approach when Scalia joined the Court was to read the statutory language, legislative history, and other sources to determine congressional intent or purpose.[5] Thus, a classic work by Harvard Professors Henry M. Hart, Jr., and Albert M. Sacks, *The Legal Process*, stated that a court's role is to interpret a statute "to carry out the purpose as best it can," subject to the caveat that it does not give the words either "a meaning they will not bear, or . . . a meaning which would violate any established policy of clear statement."[6] Legislative history was an integral part of the effort, and at times strong legislative history trumped the language of a statute.[7]

Justice Breyer explained: "At the heart of a purpose-based approach stands the 'reasonable member of Congress' – a legal fiction that applies for example, even when Congress did not in fact consider a particular problem. The judge will ask how this person (real or fictional), aware of the statute's language, structure, and general objectives (actually or hypothetically), *would have wanted* a court to inter-pret the statute in light of present circumstances in the particular case. . . . [A]n interpretation of a statute that tends to implement the legislator's will helps to imple-ment the public's will and is therefore consistent with the Constitution's democratic purpose."[8]

Judge Henry Friendly, a nontextualist nonoriginalist, wrote: "Although it is not too difficult to justify a court's drawing from appropriate legislative materials a reading that would be a bit dubious 'if one had only the words . . . to go on,' such material cannot justify a construction which apart from them would be downright impossible."[9] Judge Learned Hand said: "When a judge tries to find out what the government would have intended which it did not say, he puts into its mouth things which he thinks it ought to have said, and that is very close to substituting what he himself thinks is right. . . . Nobody does this exactly right; great judges do it better than the rest of us."[10]

In Scalia's jurisprudence the U.S. Constitution is just a special case of textualism, which brings originalism into play because of its age.[11] Textualism and originalism can diverge. Hugo Black, a progressive who supported the New Deal and similar initiatives, was generally a strong textualist, although textualism tended to be liberal in those days.[12] "The phrase 'Congress shall make no law' is composed of plain words, easily understood. . . . Neither as offered nor as adopted is the language of this amendment anything less than absolute."[13] The practice in the late eighteenth century did not concern Black. He, like Scalia, feared "the rewriting of the Constitution by judges under the guise of interpreting it."[14] Textualism in the constitutional context tends to disallow the existence of rights that are not articulated in the Constitution, *i.e.*, unenumerated rights. However, many, including Breyer, dispute applying strict textualism to the Constitution, arguing that it is not required either by the text or the Framers' plan. Also, the Ninth Amendment states that, "The Enumeration in the Constitution, of certain rights, shall not be construed to deny or disparage others retained by the people."[15]

Scalia's approach to legal texts consisted basically of strict adherence to the language of the text[16] and to the meaning of the language at the time it was enacted into law. Scalia identified himself as a "textualist-originalist."[17] "I am more inclined to adhere closely to the plain meaning of a text [than some judges]."[18] "We look for a sort of 'objectified' intent – the intent that a reasonable person would gather from the text of the law, placed alongside the remained of the *corpus juris*."[19] Context was crucial.[20] Scalia and Bryan Garner's over 500-page encyclopedia explained textualism, *Reading Law: The Interpretation of Legal Texts* (2012).

Textualism's interpretive approach is that of the "fair reading," namely, "determining the application of a governing text to given facts on the basis of a reasonable reader, fully competent in the language, would have understood the text at the time it was issued." "[I]t is simply incompatible with democratic government, or indeed, even with fair government, to have the meaning of a law determined by what the lawgiver meant, rather than what the lawgiver promulgated. . . . Men may intend what they will; but it is only the laws that they enact which bind us," Scalia stated. The *"practical* threat is that, under the guise or even the self-delusion of pursuing unexpressed legislate intents, common-law judges will in fact pursue their own objectives and desires, extending their lawmaking proclivities from the common law to the statutory field."[21]

Purpose is a legitimate consideration for Scalia, providing it is derived exclusively from the text and the context, including the prefatory materials frequently accompanying statutes. Context will be instructive on whether the word "vehicle" in a statute that prohibits bringing vehicles into a park includes airplanes, ambulances, motorcycles, bicycles, and baby carriages. An overly restrictive definition could be as unsatisfactory as an overly broad one. "A text should not be construed strictly, and it should not be construed leniently; it should be construed reasonably, to contain all that it fairly means."[22] The justifications for a strong component of textualism in the reading of statutes are substantial. First, there is the public choice; legislation is best understood as the result of compromise and textualism is the methodology that best respect compromise.[23] Second, judicial restraint; judges should follow what the public branches enact.[24] Third, judicial competence; judges construe law, not set policy. Fourth, focusing on the enacted language provides fair notice to the public.[25]

Scalia employed one major extraneous aid in construing language, namely, canons of construction that apply to the reading of all documents. Examples are "The expression of one thing implies the exclusion of others (*expressio unius est exclusio alterius*)" and "The provisions of a text should be interpreted in a way that renders them compatible, not contradictory."[26] The assumption is that canons are background that writers and readers of laws and other documents recognize, akin to grammatical rules. *Reading Law* is organized around canons.

Scalia rejected the use of legislative history on constitutional, structural, and democracy grounds.[27] Only the text of a statute is voted on by both houses of Congress and presented to the President for his signature.[28] Professor John Manning wrote: "Justice Scalia has emphasized that legislation proceeds though an intricate, constitutionally prescribed process that has implications for statutory interpretation: 'We are governed,' he said, 'by laws, not by the intentions of legislators.... The law as it passed is the will of the majority of both houses, and the only mode in which that will is spoken is in the act itself.' That is to say, Article I, § 7 of the Constitution prescribes a rather specific method of enacting laws (bicameral and presentment), and the ultimate output of that process is an agreed-upon set of words that possess a singular claim to legitimacy, at least when their semantic import is clear."[29] One scholar wrote: "Scalia defends his approach based upon a strict formal separation of powers: the constitutional role of the legislature is to enact statues, not to have intent or purposes, and the role of the courts is to apply the words and only the words, without regard to arguments of fairness or political equilibrium."[30] Scalia stated: "The greatest defect of legislative history is its illegitimacy."[31]

While Scalia's total rejection of legislative history has not been widely accepted, its use has considerably diminished.[32] Scalia relied, however, on the "legislative history" of the Constitution, such as *The Federalist*, on the ground that the sources reflect how the Constitution was understood by the ratifying generation. "I do so, however, not because they were Framers and therefore their intent is authoritative and must be the law; but rather because their writings, like those of other intelligent and informed people of the time, display how the text of the Constitution was originally understood."[33]

As early as 1990, Yale Professor William N. Eskridge, Jr., stated, "Justice Scalia's new textualism has already been a valuable intellectual contribution to theoretical statutory interpretation."[34] "Scalia's new textualism is a radical, as opposed to marginal, critique. It is a bold rethinking of the Court's role," adding that "the new textualism is a very attractive formalist theory."[35] To many, however, formalism is *un*attractive because, focusing on rules, it ignores consequences.[36]

ORIGINALISM

The prevalent philosophies of constitutional interpretation involve a flexible and evolving approach that relies on the text, structure, and goals of the Constitution, coupled with a usually strong deference to precedent, to reach solutions compatible with contemporary society. Originalism in its present forms is a relatively recent phenomenon and distinctly a minority view.[37] Many consider the ascendency, such as it is, of originalism to date from an address in 1985 by then Attorney General Edwin Meese.[38] It was a reaction to the Warren Court's liberal or even radical decisions that were unhinged from the traditional view of the Constitution (although the Warren Court strove mightily to attach their decisions to the past).[39] While there were liberal, and ahistorical, decisions before (and after) the Warren Court, as well as discussions of the intention of the Framers as the guide to constitutional interpretation,[40] the evil was the Warren Court. It decided *Brown v. Board of Education* (1954) (racial discrimination in schools unconstitutional),[41] *Mapp v. Ohio* (1961) (exclusionary rule applicable to states),[42] *Baker v. Carr* (1962) and *Reynolds v. Sims* (1964) (one man, one vote),[43] *Gideon v. Wainwright* (1963) (government-provided counsel required for all felony prosecutions),[44] *Fay v. Noia* (1963) (extended federal *habeas corpus* protection for state prisoners),[45] *Griswold v. Connecticut* (1965) (state cannot prohibit married couples from using contraception),[46] *Miranda v. Arizona* (1966) (police required to explain rights to person detained),[47] and a host of other newly identified constitutional rights for prospective and actual criminal defendants. Originalism "has been the cutting edge of the conservative attack on the federal court decisions that helped to undermine the enforcement of traditional social orthodoxies."[48]

Judge Robert Bork and others promoted original intent as the proper method of constitutional interpretation. Originalists claimed that competing approaches made decisions on the meaning of the Constitution subjective and allowed judges or Justices to say that the Constitution meant what they wanted it to mean. They argued that no principled jurisprudence was possible without originalism; indeed, originalism was inevitable given "the design of the American Republic."[49] The originalist premise is "the assumption that originalism, rightly conceived, is the best, or indeed the only, conception of fidelity in constitutional interpretation."[50]

Original intent of the drafters as the exclusive guide to constitutional interpretation foundered, however, for a number of reasons, including the problems of determining, even conceiving, collective intent and making the meaning of the Constitution depend on the unexpressed intent of a small group of people.[51] There was, moreover, insufficient evidence of what the Framers intended or understood on many issues aside from the words they used in the Constitution. Others argued that originalism should consider only "the action of the Constitutional Ratifiers... whose actions gave legal life to the otherwise dead words on paper drafted by the Philadelphia Convention."[52] Although Madison took reasonably good notes, which reveal that many provisions received scant attention, there was no verbatim transcript of the Constitutional Convention.[53]

Largely originated and led by Scalia,[54] the movement regrouped and turned to the standard of the original *meaning* of the Constitution, which rarely changed substance. "I take it to be a fundamental principle of constitutional adjudication that the terms of the Constitution must be given the meaning ascribed to them at the time of their ratification."[55] For Scalia, the Constitution was just a special case of ordinary textual interpretation.[56] "What I look for in the Constitution is precisely what I look for in a statute; the original meaning of the text, not what the original draftsmen intended." "The problem [of constitutional interpretation] is distinctive, not because special principles of interpretation apply, but because the usual principles are being applied to an unusual text," namely, by and large, an unspecific text that was designed to last for the ages.[57]

Before considering originalism in more detail, it is necessary to consider why Scalia adopted it. The first answer that comes to mind is that he thought that was what the Framers of the Constitution expected and wanted. But that answer would be incorrect. There is nothing approaching sufficient evidence of that position.[58] Additionally, Scalia rejected reliance on the Framers' unexpressed or even expressed intent.

Scalia endorsed originalism for the pragmatic reason that in his mind it produced the best results while remaining consistent with the proper role of a constitution. His defense means that there is no moral or historical legitimacy for originalism any more than any other interpretive theory; it must compete with other theories on a level playing field. He defended originalism in 1989 in an article modestly entitled, "Originalism: The Lesser Evil." "[O]riginalism seems to me more compatible with the nature and purpose of a Constitution in a democratic system. . . . The purpose of constitutional guarantees – and in particular those constitutional guarantees of individual rights that are at the center of the controversy – is precisely to prevent the law from reflecting certain *changes* in original values that the society adopting the Constitution thinks fundamentally undesirable."[59] People who choose it are knowingly selecting a theory that is generally conservative and static, primarily because of the difficulty of formally amending the Constitution. Would the country be better off if the Supreme Court were dominated by originalism? Whether originalism produces better results is a legitimate question. Indeed, for many, it may be the most important question.

Scalia framed his main complaint not against liberals who attacked originalism, but rather on the danger to liberals and conservatives alike from an unprincipled and unanchored approach to the Constitution that empowered the judiciary.[60] "It makes a lot of sense to guarantee to a society that 'the freedom of speech you now enjoy (*whatever* that consists of) will never be diminished by the federal government'; it makes very little sense to guarantee that 'the federal government will respect the moral principle of freedom of speech, which may entitle you to more, or less, freedom of speech than you now legally enjoy.'"[61] Originalism treats the Constitution as having "a fixed meaning ascertainable through the usual devices familiar to those learned in the law," by "establish[ing] a historical criterion that is conceptually quite separate from the preferences of the judge himself."[62] Changes must adhere to the formal amendment process.[63] While more coherent, its logic and results were virtually the same as original intent.

For Scalia, like Bork, anchoring the interpretation of the Constitution to its public meaning in the late eighteenth century avoided the overarching problem of subjectivity. Otherwise, they said, the Constitution would mean whatever any judge or scholar says it means with unelected and elitist judges and Justices enacting their personal values.[64] Originalism assumes that answers can be found in the Constitution as it was understood when it was ratified and they minimize the argument that while that may be true to a limited extent, *e.g.*, the Constitution does not suggest an exclusionary rule, it is not true for many other issues, *e.g.*, how should the Constitution be applied to the use of a Global Positioning System device.

Nonoriginalists conceive of the Constitution as embodying abstract moral and political principles – not merely codifying concrete historical rules or practices – and interpretation of those principles as requiring judgments of political theory about how they are best understood – not merely historical research to discover original meanings.[65] The key issue in considering originalism is whether the mostly eighteenth-century Constitution should be interpreted to preserve "not enduring values but specific eighteenth-century thoughts about how those values [should be] applied."[66] Most nonoriginalists will not subscribe to a constitutional position that the language of the Constitution will not bear, but search for reasonable interpretations that are both consistent with the constitutional text and with current values."[67] Just as there is variety among originalists, there is variety among nonoriginalists in how they approach the language of the Constitution in the context of current issues and values.[68]

Most liberals favor what has been called a living, evolving, developing, or common-law Constitution, which posits a Constitution that accommodates itself to meet the needs of a changing society, a body of law that (unlike normal statutes) grows and changes from age to age in order to meet the needs of a changing society, tempered by a respect for existing law. Harvard Law Professor Laurence H. Tribe wrote that the "Supreme Court just cannot avoid the painful duty of exercising judgment so as to give concrete meaning to the fluid constitution, because the constitutional rules and precepts that it is charged with administering lack that certainty which permits anything resembling automatic application."[69] Yale Professor Owen Fiss similarly stated that the courts should give "concrete meaning and applications" to those values "that give our society an identity and inner coherence and its distinctive public morality."[70] Proponents of this approach may start with the language of the Constitution, but rely largely on Supreme Court precedent and their logic, and extend the broad constitutional language as needed, to include a right to an abortion and protection of equal rights for lesbians and gays, among others, and restrictions on, if not abolition of, the death penalty. Nonoriginalism has an unquestionable and acknowledged normative element that equates certain types of change with progress. Inherent in its approach is the conviction that original meaning will not always, and perhaps not very often, give the best result. Nevertheless, history is important for the nonoriginalist, since it is essential for an intelligent transition from the past to the future.

Those disagreeing with originalism also point out that the founding generation and its Constitution was racist, misogynist, and pro-property owner.[71] They created a largely undemocratic document that provided for an elite group from each state to select the President and motley collections of state legislators to select each Senator. Speaking in terms of the "democratic branches" as of 1789 was a gross exaggeration.[72] Moreover, nonoriginalists challenge the power of the founding generation to limit future generations in the interpretation of the country's fundamental document. Judge Richard A. Posner put it more graphically: to be "ruled by the dead hand of the past is not self government."[73] Rejecting originalist interpretations of the Constitution, Justice Brennan stated that their approach "is not the living charter that I have taken to be our Constitution; it is instead a stagnant, archaic, hidebound document" steeped in the prejudices and superstitions of a time long past."[74] He criticized original intent as "little more than arrogance cloaked in humility. It is arrogant to pretend that from our vantage we can gauge accurately the intent of the Framers on application of principles to specific contemporary questions. . . . A position that upholds constitutional claims only if they were within the specific contemplation of the Framers in effect establishes a presumption of resolving textual ambiguities against the claim of constitutional rights."[75] He asked, "What do the words mean in our time?"[76]

For many, originalism is a rationalization for a conservative jurisprudence, namely, revert to earlier and generally less liberal legal standards when you can, and hold the line when you cannot. Justice John Paul Stevens explained in a postretirement law review article that "a jurisprudence of original intent cannot provide the correct answer to novel questions of constitutional law – questions such as whether the duty to govern impartially curtails a state's power to prohibit same-sex marriages cannot be answered by historians, or by judges who limit the scope of their inquiry to a study of history. A study of what earlier students and leaders have had to say about an issue will inform the judgment that the Court must make, but will not dictate the answer."[77] Two scholars stated, "[a]s a political practice that developed in the 1980s, originalism seeks, more or less blatantly, to alter the Constitution so as to infuse it with conservative political principles."[78] Another said: "Originalism is not a theory of constitutional interpretation. It is not a historical method. It is a historical device to win arguments. . . . Invoking the sainted Framers in constitutional debate is akin to invoking the deity in religious controversies."[79]

While Scalia and others framed the debate as between originalists and nonoriginalists, few totally reject originalist thinking. Judge J. Harvey Wilkinson said: "Originalism, or at least a watered down version of it, enjoys what perhaps no other constitutional theory can claim: widespread acceptance."[80] Everyone is interested in what the language of the Constitution means, and that sometimes requires examining what it meant when it was adopted.[81] But that meaning is not binding on nonoriginalists when it is not specific.[82] "The kinds of questions that tend to arise in constitutional interpretation, and on which historical evidence might be helpful, tend not to be the kinds of questions that can aspire to truth. . . . An honest look at those who created and ratified the Constitution requires an acknowledgment that they valued history for its contribution to their own wisdom, theory, and judgment."[83] Professor Ronald Dworkin provided a summary of his nonoriginalist view:

> Proper constitutional interpretation takes both text and past practice as its object: Lawyers and judges faced with a contemporary constitutional issue must try to construct a coherent, principled, and persuasive interpretation of the text of particular clauses, the structure of the Constitution as a whole, and our history under the Constitution – an interpretation that both unifies these distinct sources, so far as this is possible, and directs future adjudication. . . .

> If we are trying to make best sense of the Framers speaking as they did in the context in which they spoke, we should conclude that they intended to lay down abstract not dated commands and prohibitions. The Framers were careful statesmen who knew how to use the language they spoke. We cannot make good sense of their behavior unless we assume that they meant to say what people who use the words they used would normally mean to say – that they used abstract language because they intended to state abstract principles. They are best understood as making a constitution out of abstract moral principles, not coded references to their own opinions (or those of their contemporaries) about the best way to apply those principles.[84]

Whatever the content or merits of originalism, it has risen from a little-noted curiosity in the 1970s to a major discipline and factor in today's jurisprudence, largely the product of having had two avowed originalist Justices. Scalia noted the change in 2012. "In 1988, when the Supreme Court considered whether the Eighth Amendment barred the execution of someone who was under the age of 16 at the time of the offense, any Justice interested in the original meaning of the phrase *cruel and unusual punishment* would look in vain for the phrase for help from the parties or their *amici*. Briefs about child psychology – yes. Briefs about international law – plenty. But not a single brief reflecting the history of the Eighth Amendment or the practice it was understood to condemn at the time of the founding. Twenty years later, in *District of Columbia v. Heller*, the *amicus* briefing presented an array of historical material whose thoroughness would have been unthinkable earlier."[85]

Tradition

While Scalia was not unique among Justices in relying on tradition,[86] he used tradition extensively and defined it broadly, to include federal laws, state laws, and common practices and understandings.[87] *Rutan v. Republican Party of Illinois* (1990)[88] struck down as violating the Free Speech Clause long-standing patronage practices that permitted newly elected officials to fire legally unprotected government employees at will. Scalia dissented:

> The provisions of the Bill of Rights were designed to restrain transient majorities from impairing long-recognized liberties. They did not create by implication novel individual rights overturning accepted political norms. Thus, when a practice not expressly prohibited by the text of the Bill of Rights bears the endorsement of a long tradition of open, widespread, and unchallenged use that dates back to the beginning of the Republic, we have no proper basis for striking it down. Such a venerable and accepted tradition is not to be laid on the examining table and scrutinized for its conformity to some abstract principle of First Amendment adjudication devised by this Court. To the contrary, such traditions are themselves the stuff out of which the Court's principles are to be formed.[89]

"[R]ather than ask whether the police conduct here at issue shocks my unelected conscience, I would ask whether our Nation has traditionally protected the right respondents assert."[90] Scalia placed limits on the power of tradition. "Custom or practice may give content to vague or ambiguous constitutional provisions, but it cannot overcome the explicit language of the text, especially when that text is supported by historical evidence that shows it means precisely what it says."[91]

The specificity – or level of generality – of an alleged tradition was a crucial part of Scalia's analysis. A tradition of considerable generality, such as "promoting the general welfare," can be relied upon to support practically any position. The narrower and more specific the tradition the more directly it will determine the outcome of a case and reduce the power of the judge. The issue in *Michael H. v. Gerald D.* (1989)[92] was whether the biological father or the husband of the woman who gave birth to a child should be deemed the father for purposes of parental rights. A state statute fixed the husband of a woman who gave birth as the father of a child rather than the biological father. For Scalia the issue was the right of an adulterous father rather than a broader one, such as the right of a parent. His position was that the Constitution requires finding the most specific historical practice of which the Framers were aware that is analogous to the activity at issue,[93] although the Constitution is silent on the level of specificity. Writing for the Court, he upheld the statute.[94]

Intertwined with Scalia's traditionalism was his strong conservative philosophy. Conceptually, the two are distinct, since conservatism does not absolutely rule out creating new rights and restrictions. While some of his positions were libertarian, Scalia asserted that the "federal government is not bad but good. The trick is to use it wisely."[95] Traditionalism, as Scalia often used it, can be a creative escape from the rigors of originalism as well as an application of it. Since the Constitution was an ongoing creation with many gaps and uncertainties, the use of long-standing traditions allowed him to give content, albeit generally conservative content, to the often unhelpful language of the document.

Majoritarianism, Judicial Restraint, and Stare Decisis

The practice of respecting precedent, or *stare decisis*, is an integral part of Anglo-American jurisprudence. Precedent, however, poses a problem for originalists on constitutional issues. Scalia explained his rationale for *stare decisis*: "That doctrine, to the extent it rests upon anything more than administrative convenience, is merely the application to judicial precedents of a more general principle that the settled practices and expectations of a democratic society should generally not be disturbed by the courts."[96] "[S]*tare decisis* is a principle of policy and not a mechanical formula of adherence to the latest decision."[97] "Despite my misgivings about Substantive Due Process as an original matter, I have acquiesced in the Court's incorporation of certain guarantees in the Bill of Rights because it is both long established and narrowly limited."[98]

Scalia accepted a more tolerant view of precedent (or accepted a weaker brand of originalism), than many originalists, including Clarence Thomas, who has taken a more activist posture.[99] Scalia excused his departure from untrammeled originalism: "[S]*tare decisis* is not *part* of my originalist philosophy; it is a pragmatic *exception* to it."[100] Scalia wrote in 1989: "In its undiluted form, at least, [originalism] is medicine that seems too strong to swallow. Thus, almost every originalist would adulterate it with the doctrine of *stare decisis* – so that *Marbury v. Madison* would stand even if Professor Raoul Berger should demonstrate unassailably that it got the meaning of the Constitution wrong."[101] However, he felt no obligation to continue an unsupportable precedent. "We provide far greater reassurance by eliminating than by retaining such a decision."[102] Scalia explained:

> Originalism, like any other theory of interpretation put into practice in an ongoing system of law, must accommodate the doctrine of *stare decisis*; it cannot remake the world anew. . . . Where originalism will make a difference is not in the rolling back of accepted old principles but in the rejection of usurpatious new ones. . . . The demand that originalists alone "be true to their lights" and forswear *stare decisis* is essentially a demand that they alone render their methodology so disruptive of the established state of things that it will be useful only as an academic exercise and not as a workable prescription for judicial governance. . . . I cannot deny that *stare decisis* affords some opportunity for arbitrariness – though I attempt to constrain my own use of the doctrine by consistent rules. In any event, I have never claimed that originalism inoculates against willfulness; only that (unlike aspirationism) it does not cater to it.[103]

Scalia provided an explanation of how he applied *stare decisis* in unpublished speeches or in answers to audience questions:

1. How wrong was it? Compare *Roe* (even those who like the result agree it was a lousy opinion) with cases on the Incorporation Doctrine [Fourteenth Amendment incorporates Bill of Rights] (probably wrong, but close). 2. How well accepted has it been? Again, compare *Roe* (controversial from the start and remains so) with the Incorporation Doctrine (I'm not about to announce that New York is not bound by the First Amendment). 3. Most important to me, does it permit me to function as a lawyer, or does it make me a legislator. Again, compare (I have to decide what is an "undue" burden on abortion – not a lawyer's question but surely one appropriate for legislators) with the Incorporation Doctrine (I just apply the principles of law applicable to the federal government to the States).[104]

Obviously, "an originalist can accept the doctrine of *stare decisis* so long as the prior decision was made on the basis of a good-faith effort to ascertain the original meaning of the Constitution."[105] Since there have never been more than two originalist Justices, the qualifying language overwhelms the statement of support for *stare decisis*. But what is a conscientious originalist to do with precedent that conflict with the original understanding of the Constitution? One commentator wrote: "It is... not surprising that self-styled originalists are all over the map on the question of whether deference should be paid to prior judicial decisions."[106] Some commentators deny Scalia the status of an originalist because he accepts *stare decisis*.[107] However, Scalia rejected *stare decisis* in a number of crucial areas, including abortion.

Emphasizing the Court's limited role, Scalia wrote in 1979: "Congress has an authority and indeed a responsibility to interpret the Constitution that are no less solemn and binding than the similar authority and responsibility of the Supreme Court – because they spring from the same source, which is the obligation to take no action that would contravene that document. Moreover, congressional interpretations are of enormous importance – of greater importance, ultimately, than those of the Supreme Court."[108] For Scalia, the least democratic branch was subordinated to the popular branches.[109]

Scalia considered balancing, as opposed to applying rules, a method of enhancing judicial power, because it allows a judge to give weight to those considerations he thinks most important. It permits lower-court judges to do what they want when the Supreme Court tells them to come up with the best result, all things considered.[110] Sometimes, balancing requires weighing incommensurable qualities, such as Scalia's example: "It is... like judging whether a particular line is longer than a particular rock is heavy."[111] "[W]hen an appellate judge comes up with nothing better than a totality of the circumstances to explain his decision, he is not so much pronouncing the law in the normal sense as engaging in the less exalted function of fact finding."[112] Nevertheless, many judges and academics, including Justice Holmes and Judge Henry Friendly[113] believed that pragmatic balancing permitted drawing subtle distinctions and was flexible and represented an advance over strict adherence to rules.

Separation of Powers and Federalism

Scalia's originalism emphasized structural considerations: "The constitutional structure of the United States has two main features: (1) separation and equilibrium of powers[114] and (2) federalism."[115] The 1787 Philadelphia Convention was called to correct deficiencies of the Articles of Confederation, which provided for an essentially helpless national government. The danger, however, was that a strong central government would create "tyranny," a majoritarian nightmare that would destroy the rights of ordinary citizens. Protection could be achieved "through such institutional means as the multiplicity of interests present in an extended republic, separation of powers and checks and balances, and federalism."[116]

In 1982 Scalia wrote, "The Doctrine of Standing as an Essential Element of Separation of Powers."[117] "[T]he principle of separation of powers is found only in the structure of the document, which successively describes where the legislative, executive and judicial powers, respectively, shall reside. Separation of powers and federalism were critical parts of the pre-ratification discussions and debates. [N]o less than five of the *Federalist Papers* were devoted to the demonstration that the principle was adequately observed in the proposed Constitution. . . . Madison said of it, in *Federalist* 47, that 'no political truth is certainly of greater intrinsic value, or is stamped with the authority of more enlightened patrons of liberty.'"[118] Scalia also quoted Madison's "exorbitant praise" of the principle, noting that those who opposed ratification shared that view. The founders "lived among the ruins of a system of intermingled legislative and judicial power. . . . Important principles of law ought to have clear rules of application. That is particularly true of the principle of separation of power between three differently constituted, and hence differently motivated, political institutions, is bound to be the regular battleground of partisan war."[119] Scalia saw the result the protection of the individual: "The purpose of the separation and equilibrium of powers in general, and of the unitary Executive in particular, was not merely to assure effective government but to preserve individual freedom."[120]

PART II

Scalia's Conservative Constitutional Opinions

Despite, but mostly because of, his philosophy, Scalia wrote a remarkably large number of liberal constitutional and statutory opinions – 135 by my count. To some extent this is an anomaly, given Scalia's conservative views. One article alleged that "Scalia inconsistently defers to the majoritarian process, opting to defer only when he feels the process will support interests of outcomes he endorses."[1] Thus, the article argues, Scalia supported laws upholding the death penalty, outlawing abortion, protecting religious expression, protecting property rights, and reducing gay rights. But it is not that simple. Scalia's originalism encompassed both liberal and conservative views of framing-era history and did not appear to be a simple mechanism for reaching conservative results, as some have said. That is not to say that Scalia followed originalism consistently or adhered to what historians consider the most persuasive historical evidence. But, as noted, there are more examples of Scalia's following the logic of his positions to reach liberal results than many would expect.

Before considering Scalia's liberal opinions, it is important to review some of his conservative ones, which was his dominant approach. For one thing, there is an element of the comparative in the word "liberal." Someone may legitimately ask, "compared to what?" One answer is the rest of Scalia's judicial output. Another is the opinions of other Justices on the Court. Another is general understanding. All approaches are relevant. What follows is mostly about opinions, Scalia's and others. Reserved until Part V is an analysis of the serious scholarship both by historians and by legal historians in framing-era history, which is where Scalia's originalist jurisprudence is analyzed in greatest detail.

Several categories of cases that some might expect to find in this group are absent – Scalia's opinions rejecting limitations on campaign financing and his opinions rejecting restrictions on antiabortion picketing are prominent. They are discussed separately, for the reason that Scalia defended his positions on the basis of the First Amendment and claims that his was the true liberal view. The American Civil Liberties Union, the premier liberal organization, adheres to the view that freedom of speech is essential.

3

First and Second Amendments

FREE SPEECH

Scalia's core freedom-of-speech jurisprudence (other than aspects of libel and pornography) had no connection or even purported connection with the original understanding of the First Amendment, if, in fact, one existed.[2] Modern concepts of free speech did not exist until Oliver Wendell Holmes, Jr., and Louis D. Brandeis first championed the cause. Laurence Tribe described the state of speech in the Framers' era: "When the First Amendment was adopted in 1791, it was widely understood to prohibit mainly 'prior restraints' on speech, such as an insistence on preapproval of published works."[3] The government generally remained free to punish speech with a tendency to endanger public morals, health, welfare, or security. "A lot of expression that we now protect – including scandalous art, advertisements, religious blasphemy, frank expressions of sexuality, and even some political commentary – could be prohibited if we were strict originalists."[4] Professor Rodney A. Smolla wrote: "If Blackstone's view of free speech was the *real* original meaning of the First Amendment, then arguably 90 percent of modern free speech jurisprudence . . . is intellectually dishonest and historically illegitimate."[5]

Scalia's approach to pornography was largely originalist. In *FW/PBS, Inc. v. Dallas* (1990),[6] Dallas passed an ordinance that restricted the locations of sexually oriented businesses, such as adult book stores, video stores, escort agencies, nude model agencies, and massage parlors. O'Connor's opinion for a plurality balanced the interests of the city with those of the businesses and, although it identified procedural flaws that violated the Due Process Clause, upheld some of the regulations' substantive provisions. For Scalia in dissent, the First Amendment did not "require a state or municipality to permit a business that intentionally specializes in, and holds itself out to the public as specializing, in performance or portrayal of sex acts, sexual organs in a state of arousal, or live human nudity." Businesses that offer "live nudity or hard-core sexual material as a constant, intentional objective of their business" were not engaged in the communication of ideas, but were pandering, an activity traditionally not protected by the First Amendment.[7] "[N]either the merchant nor the buyer is interested in the work's literary, artistic, political, or scientific value."[8]

Barnes v. Glen Theatre, Inc. (1991)[9] upheld an Indiana statute which, among other things, banned nude dancing in public. White's plurality opinion held that nude dancing was expressive conduct under the First Amendment, but further held that the state's interest in protecting order and morality sufficed to sustain the law. Scalia concurred only in the judgment because "as a general law regulating conduct and not specifically directed at expression, it was not subject to First Amendment scrutiny at all. . . . The purpose of the Indiana statute, as both its text and the manner of enforcement demonstrate, is to enforce the traditional moral belief that people should not expose their private parts indiscriminately, regardless of whether those who see them are disedified." Scalia distinguished cases where "the government prohibits conduct precisely because of its communicative attributes."[10] Judge Posner's opinion in the court of appeals agreed: "[T]he Founding Fathers would writhe in their graves if they knew that the nude dancers of the Kitty Kat Lounge could envelop themselves with the First Amendment."[11]

ESTABLISHMENT CLAUSE

The Religion Clauses of the First Amendment read: "Congress shall make no law respecting an establishment of religion, or prohibiting the free exercise thereof." While iconoclast Jefferson believed there should be "a wall of separation between Church and State," at least as far as the federal government was concerned, the Court's attitude in recent decades has been less secular and more nuanced (or confused). For Scalia the Framers contemplated a robust religiosity in the Union that did not require the government to be neutral between religion and nonreligion, but sought only to prevent any governmental activity that discriminated in favor of one religion at the expense of another; the federal government and the states need not be neutral between religiousness and nonreligiousness, but only among various denominations of religion. Scalia dissented in *Lee v. Weisman* (1992),[12] a school prayer case:

> From our Nation's origin, prayer has been a prominent part of governmental ceremonies and proclamations. The Declaration of Independence, the document marking our birth as a separate people, "appeal[ed] to the Supreme Judge of the world for the rectitude of our intentions" and avowed "a firm reliance on the protection of divine Providence." In his first inaugural address, after swearing his oath of office on a Bible, George Washington deliberately made a prayer a part of his first official act as President. . . . In holding that the Establishment Clause prohibits invocations and benedictions at public-school graduation ceremonies, the Court – with nary a mention that it is doing so – lays waste a tradition that is as old as public-school graduation ceremonies themselves, and that is a component of an

even more longstanding American tradition of nonsectarian prayer to God at Public celebrations generally.

Scalia expanded on the theme in *Board of Education of Kiryas Joel Village School District v. Grumet* (1994):

[T]he Founding Fathers would be astonished to find that the Establishment Clause – which they designed "to ensure that no one powerful sect or combination of sects would use political or governmental power to punish dissenters" – has been employed to prohibit characteristically and admirably American accommodation of the religious practices (or more precisely, cultural peculiarities) of a tiny minority sect. I, however, am not surprised. Once this Court has abandoned text and history as guides, nothing prevents it from calling religious tolerance the establishment of religion.[13]

Other cases illustrate Scalia's views. *Edwards v. Aguillard* (1987)[14] applied the Establishment Clause to a Louisiana statute, entitled Balanced Treatment for Creation Science and Evolution Science in Public Schools Instruction Act, which forbade the teaching of evolution in public schools unless accompanied by instruction in "creation science." Seven Justices declared the statute unconstitutional. Brennan's opinion followed *Lemon v. Kurtzman* (1971),[15] declaring that to survive Establishment Clause scrutiny, the government conduct in question must have a secular purpose, was essentially neutral on religion, and did not foster an excessive governmental entanglement with religion. "While the Court is normally deferential to a State's articulation of a secular purpose, it is required that the statement of such purpose be sincere and not a sham." He concluded that the purpose of the act had nothing to do with academic freedom and everything to do with the establishment of a religious program of instruction.[16]

While the *Lemon* test has had its detractors, it was so repugnant to Scalia that he vividly described it as "some ghoul in a late-night horror movie that repeatedly sits up in its grave and shuffles abroad after being repeatedly killed and buried, *Lemon* stalks our Establishment Clause jurisprudence once again, frightening the little children and school attorneys of Center Moriches Union Free School District. . . . When we wish to strike down a practice it forbids, we invoke it; when we wish to uphold a practice it forbids, we ignore it entirely. . . . Such a docile and useful monster is worth keeping around, at least in a somnolent state; one never knows when one might need him."[17] For Scalia the test gave judges enormous discretion to vote their personal views; he wanted a bright-line test. The Court should not assume that the Louisiana legislators lied concerning the purpose of the act when they described its purpose as secular; the legislature heard considerable expert testimony and evidence. In fact, nothing in the Constitution prohibits legislatures from acting on the basis of their religious convictions.

McCreary County, Kentucky v. ACLU (2005)[18] barred as unconstitutional McCreary County's conspicuous posting of a version of the Ten Commandments at county courthouses. After challenge, the county added copies of secular historical documents, including Magna Carta. The Court held that the display still constituted an establishment of religion. Scalia's dissent argued that while the government cannot favor one religion over another where public aid or assistance is concerned, the Clause "necessarily applies in a more limited sense to public acknowledgment of the Creator." "Those who wrote the Constitution believed that morality was essential to the well-being of society and that encouragement of religion was the best way to foster morality."[19] In dozens of instances in presidential speeches, government practices, and Supreme Court cases, the deity was invoked and religion endorsed. It was therefore permissible, Scalia argued, to express favoritism toward monotheism, which included Christianity, Judaism, and Islam, all of which accept the Ten Commandments as given by God to Moses.[20] "The frequency of these displays testifies to the popular understanding that the Ten Commandments are a foundation of the rule of law, and a symbol of the role that religion played, and continues to play, in our system of government." "Historical practices thus demonstrate that there is a distance between the acknowledgment of a single Creator and the establishment of a religion."

Scalia supported school vouchers that can be used in religious schools[21]; equal access to school facilities by religious groups[22]; clergy-read prayers at public graduation ceremonies[23]; student-led prayers at football games[24]; reciting the Pledge of Allegiance in public schools[25]; eliminating state sales tax for only religious magazines[26]; creating a special school district that followed the lines of a religious community and excluded all but practitioners of the religion[27]; and removing a ban on using scholarships for study of theology.[28] Scalia summarized his creed in *Lamb's Chapel v. Center Moriches School District* (1993)[29]: "As for the asserted Establishment Clause justification, I would hold, simply and clearly, that giving Lamb's Chapel nondiscriminatory access to school facilities cannot violate that provision because it does not signify state or local embrace of a particular religious sect."

Scalia and Thomas endorsed a doctrine that would make it virtually impossible to challenge federal actions respecting religion. They would reverse *Flast v. Cohen* (1968),[30] which held that the generalized interest of a taxpayer is sufficient to create standing in cases claiming an unconstitutional establishment of religion. In *Hein v. Freedom from Religion Foundation* (2007),[31] taxpayers successfully challenged President George W. Bush's Executive Orders that favored faith-based incentives in the distribution of money to support certain programs. Scalia and Thomas argued that the interests of ordinary plaintiffs in federal government action that favor religion in general are too remote and speculative to sustain standing. Scalia elsewhere said that the Establishment Clause served to "prohibit an establishment of religion at the federal level," but also "to protect state establishments of religion from federal interference."[32] Thomas adopted the approach in *Elk Grove Unified School District v. Newdow* (2004),[33] the Pledge of Allegiance case from which Scalia recused himself. Scalia joined Thomas's concurrence in *Town of Greece v. Galloway* (2014),[34] which stated that "the Establishment Clause is 'best understood as a federalism provision,'" citing *Elk Grove*.

SECOND AMENDMENT

The Second Amendment states that, "A well regulated Militia, being necessary to the security of a free State, the right of the people to keep and bear Arms, shall not be infringed." In *District of Columbia v. Heller* (2008),[35] Scalia wrote for a five-Justice majority in striking down the District of Columbia strict gun-control law, where the Second Amendment applied undiluted because the District is a federal enclave. It was the first time in the nation's history that the Court struck down a statute on Second Amendment grounds.[36] Scalia wrote: "The phrase 'keep arms' was not prevalent in the written documents of the founding period that we have found, but there are a few examples, all of which favor viewing the right to 'keep Arms' as an individual right unconnected with militia service.... At the time of the founding, as now, to 'bear' meant to 'carry.'"[37] Perhaps most important, because the Second Amendment described "the right of the people," it provided individual rights that anyone could assert. Despite his status as an originalist, Scalia peppered his opinion with citations to earlier Supreme Court cases. So did the dissenters. But, he said, the precedents were not controlling.

Scalia concluded: "We are aware of the problem of handgun violence in this country, and we take seriously the concerns raised by the many *amici* who believe that prohibition of handgun ownership is a solution. The Constitution leaves the District of Columbia a variety of tools for combating that problem, including some measures regulating handguns.... But the enshrinement of constitutional rights necessarily takes certain policy choices off the table. These include the absolute prohibition of handguns used for self-defense in the home."[38] Scalia observed that the Second Amendment does not apply to everyone, such as felons, and did not cover all weapons, such as sawed-off shot guns, which some commentators viewed as narrow, even nonoriginalist, reading of the amendment.[39]

Scalia joined Alito's opinion and wrote a concurring opinion in *McDonald v. Chicago* (2010),[40] which applied *Heller* to the states on the basis of Fourteenth Amendment incorporation. The majority concluded that incorporation was virtually total and that nonincorporation would "adopt a special incorporation test applicable only to the Second Amendment." It also rejected as without current support the argument that the Second Amendment should mean one thing for the federal government and another for the states. "We have previously held that most of the provisions of the Bill of Rights apply with full force to both the Federal Government and the States.... Anti-Federalists and Federalists alike agreed that the right to bear arms was fundamental to the newly formed system of government.... [I]n *Heller*, we held that individual self defense is 'the central component' of the Second Amendment right.... In debating the Fourteenth Amendment, the 39th Congress referred to the right to keep and bear arms as a fundamental right deserving of protection."[41] To the argument that the Second Amendment was linguistically directed at the federal government, Scalia replied that the First Amendment was even more so. To the argument that judges are not historians, Scalia said, "whether or not special expertise is needed to answer historical questions, judges most certainly have no 'comparative... advantage' in resolving moral disputes."[42] Finally, to the argument that the majority's approach is undemocratic because it strikes down state laws, Scalia noted that that happens whenever the Court declares any statute unconstitutional.[43] Four Justices dissented.

4

Constitutional Criminal Procedure

At the end of the Burger Court in 1986, some aspects of capital punishment seemed settled. First, capital punishment was impermissible for certain classes of defendants, especially those whose crimes did not involve homicide or who were under sixteen or insane.[1] Second, capital punishment could not be conducted so as to discriminate against members of a discrete minority group. Third, certain processes were required, including demanding that the jury consider the death penalty separately from the determination of guilt and subjecting any death penalty to judicial review.

Scalia quickly established himself as an avowed originalist on Eighth Amendment jurisprudence, which meant that there were few, if any, restrictions on laws relating to the imposition of the death penalty based on the ground that the punishment was "cruel and unusual."[2] Not only was the death penalty almost routinely applied in the founding era, he argued, but the Fifth Amendment specifically referred to capital crimes. For Scalia, the Eighth Amendment barred only cruel methods of punishment that were not regularly or customarily employed when the amendment was ratified in 1791. In Scalia's view, there were no special rules for death penalty cases. Scalia simply rejected the proposition that "death is different."[3]

Scalia disagreed with the Burger Court's *Woodson v. North Carolina* (1976),[4] which declared that the Eighth Amendment prohibited a mandatory death sentence. Scalia's concurring opinion in *Walton v. Arizona* (1990)[5] stated, "The mandatory imposition of death – without sentencing discretion – for a crime which States have traditionally punished with death cannot possibly violate the Eighth Amendment." Current thinkers, Scalia said, could not reverse the founders' duly adopted Bill of Rights.[6] Scalia's Eighth Amendment jurisprudence likewise did not limit the imposition of the death penalty based on the age of the offender. In *Thompson v. Oklahoma* (1988)[7] he dissented from the Court's decision to bar the execution of a defendant tried as an adult and convicted of first-degree murder that he had committed when he was fifteen. Scalia relied on William Blackstone's *Commentaries on the Laws of England*, rather than the "evolving standards of decency that mark the progress of a maturing society," cited by the Court.[8] The best standard of what society currently believes is proper are the laws it passed and enforced; the fact that it was rarely done was not the same as saying the Constitution barred it.[9]

Scalia took a similar position when, overruling a thirteen-year-old precedent, the Court held in *Atkins v. Virginia* (2002)[10] that a national consensus had developed against execution of criminals who suffered from retardation. Scalia began his dissent: "Today's decision is the pinnacle of our Eighth Amendment death-is-different jurisprudence. Not only does it, like all of that jurisprudence, find no support in the text or history of the Eighth Amendment; it does not even have support in current social attitudes regarding the conditions that render an otherwise just death penalty inappropriate. Seldom has an opinion of this Court rested so obviously upon nothing but the personal views of its Members." "But the Prize for the Court's Most Feeble Effort to fabricate 'national consensus' must go to its appeal (deservedly relegated to a footnote) to the views of assorted professional and religious organizations, members of the so-called 'world community,' and opinion polls," which he called irrelevant, adding, "We must never forget that it is a Constitution for the United States we are expounding."[11]

In 2005 the Court, voting 5–4, upped to eighteen the age a defendant must have been at the time of the offense to qualify for execution. Dissenting in *Roper v. Simmons* (2005),[12] Scalia noted, "The Court thus proclaims itself sole arbiter of our Nation's moral standards." "In other words, all the Court has done today, to borrow from another context, is to look over the heads of the crowd and pick out its friends."[13] "[T]he basic premise of the Court's argument – that American law should conform to the laws of the rest of the world – ought to be rejected out of hand," for the reason, among others, that the Court ignores the views of other countries when it interprets many provisions of the Constitution more liberally than the laws of other countries.[14] "To invoke alien law when it agrees with one's own thinking, and ignore it otherwise, is not reasoned decisionmaking, but sophistry."[15]

Scalia's position that the Eighth Amendment barred only cruel and unusual methods of punishment as defined in 1791 led him to conclude that the Eighth Amendment also had no bearing on state death-penalty procedures. In *Booth v. Maryland* (1987)[16] a liberal 5–4 majority held that the Eighth Amendment barred the introduction at the penalty stage of a capital case of a Victim Impact Statement (VIS), which, based on interviews of family members and others, described the personal characteristics of the victims and the emotional impact of the crimes on the family and the family members' opinions and characterizations of the crimes and the defendant, often in graphic and emotional language.[17] The Court held that in the penalty phase "the jury is required to focus on the defendant as a 'uniquely individual human bein[g].'" The focus of the VIS, however, is "on the character and reputation of the victim and the effect on his family," which "creates an impermissible risk that the capital sentencing decision will be made in an arbitrary manner."[18]

Agreeing with Justice White's dissent that sentencing considerations are peculiarly questions of legislative policy, Scalia also pointed out that all crimes depend on the consequences of someone's action, for example, whether a driver of a speeding car strikes no one, strikes someone who is injured but survives, or strikes someone who is killed. "In sum, the principle upon which the Court's opinion rests – that the imposition of capital punishment is to be determined solely on the basis of moral guilt – does not exist, neither in the text of the Constitution, nor in the historic practices of our society, nor even in the opinions of this Court.... [The applicable procedure] is a question to be decided through the democratic processes of a free people, and not by the decrees of this Court. There is nothing in the Constitution that dictates the answer, nor more in the field of capital punishment than elsewhere."[19]

Scalia stated that the Eighth Amendment did not require proportionality and upheld the imposition of a mandatory life sentence for possession of 672 grams of cocaine in his plurality opinion in *Harmelin v. Michigan* (1991).[20] Largely because "excessive fines" were prohibited, but not excessive punishments, and because the death penalty was the stated punishment for felonies, Scalia refused to read into the amendment a proportionality principle for prison sentences.[21] Otherwise, the excessive-fines provision in the Fifth Amendment would have been superfluous. Abetting his originalism was his inclination to give states considerable breathing room in fashioning their legal systems, independent of Supreme Court commands.[22]

The Court, with Scalia playing a prominent role, expanded the definition of probable cause and narrowed the definition of seizure of a person. The latter permitted the police to engage a suspect without probable cause, but with, for instance, reasonable suspicion.[23] It also expanded the scope of the *Terry* "stop and frisk" exception[24] and routine auto checkpoints (as opposed to detaining individual drivers).[25] Scalia also narrowed Fourth Amendment rights of students and other insular groups,[26] and had a mixed record on the rights of government employees.[27]

Scalia rejected the exclusionary rule of the Fourth Amendment, which in order to deter law-enforcement officers from acting unlawfully required the exclusion of all evidence illegally seized. Arguably illogical and certainly antioriginalist, the Court created the rule when it concluded that other remedies, including law suits by victims and disciplinary action by superiors, were ineffective. At first a rule applied by federal courts to federal conduct in *Weeks v. United States* (1914),[28] the rule was expanded to encompass state courts via the Fourteenth Amendment in *Mapp v. Ohio* (1961).[29] Conservatives, and even some moderates like Benjamin N. Cardozo and Henry J. Friendly, criticized the exclusionary rule.[30] Cardozo famously asked rhetorically, "Should the criminal go free because the constable has blundered?"[31] Conservatives narrowed the rule, including allowing the admission of illegally seized evidence when the police acted in good faith, limiting application to direct appeals and not to petitions for *habeas corpus*, and allowing prosecutors to employ unlawfully seized evidence to impeach defendants whose testimony was inconsistent with the (reliable) unlawfully seized evidence. Scalia played an important role in this development.[32]

For the ardent originalist/textualist the Second Amendment is a walk in the park compared to the Fifth Amendment's cryptic Self-Incrimination Clause. All the preceding sections of the Fifth Amendment deal with the procedural rights of the accused at trial before reading: "nor shall be compelled in any criminal case to be a witness against himself." Scalia took a narrow view of the protections of the Clause. He dissented from the Court's decision in *Mitchell v. United States* (1999)[33] that a defendant does not waive her self-incrimination plea at her sentencing by having pleaded guilty to the crime.

> [T]he text and history of the Fifth Amendment give no indication that there is a federal *constitutional* prohibition on the use of the defendant's silence as demeanor evidence. Our hardy forebears, who thought of compulsion in terms of the rack and oaths forced by the power of law, would not have viewed the drawing of a commonsensical inference as equivalent pressure. And it is implausible that the Americans of 1791, who were subject to adverse inferences for failing to give unsworn testimony, would have viewed an adverse inference for failing to give sworn testimony as a violation of the Fifth Amendment.

Scalia urged the Supreme Court to overrule *Miranda v. Arizona* (1966),[34] an exemplar of the Warren Court's expansion of the rights of defendants and suspects, which required specific warnings before a suspect's statement made during custodial interrogation could be admitted into evidence. *Dickerson v. United States* (2000),[35] an opinion by Rehnquist for seven Justices, struck down a federal statute designed to weaken *Miranda* largely on the basis of *stare decisis*: "*Miranda* has become embedded in routine police practice to the point where the warnings have become part of our national culture."[36] The opinion noted that "the routine practice of . . . [custodial] police interrogation is itself a relatively new development."[37]

Dissenting, Scalia argued that there never has been a constitutional right to exclude foolishly made confessions, so violation of *Miranda* cannot amount to a violation of the privilege against compelled self-incrimination. Indeed, he said, the Court abandoned the idea that a violation of *Miranda* was a violation of the Fifth or Fourteenth Amendment – it admitted the fruits of a *Miranda* violation and permitted a confession taken in violation of *Miranda* to be used on cross-examination. "[H]istory and precedent aside, the decision in *Miranda*, if read as an exposition of what the Constitution *requires*, is preposterous."[38] Because the underpinnings of *Miranda* have been splintered, *stare decisis* was no bar to overruling it.

Scalia took a narrow view of the right "to have the assistance of counsel for his defense." Writing for a seven-Justice majority in *Kansas v. Ventris* (2009),[39] Scalia decided that a defendant's incriminating statement to a jailhouse informant, concededly elicited in violation of Sixth Amendment strictures, was admissible at trial to impeach the defendant's conflicting statement. The *taking* of the statement did not violate Donnie Ray Ventris's Sixth Amendment rights, which did not occur until it was introduced in evidence. "We have held in every other context that tainted evidence – evidence whose very introduction does not constitute the constitutional violation, but whose obtaining was constitutional – is admissible for impeachment."[40]

An important liberal-conservative issue has been whether the Court's constitutional rulings in criminal cases should be applied retroactively to include *habeas corpus* petitioners and whether new constitutional rules should be created in the *habeas corpus* context. Scalia rarely applied liberal changes in constitutional criminal law to petitioners seeking *habeas corpus*. He joined the Supreme Court holding in 1989 in *Teague v. Lane* (1989),[41] a nonoriginalist opinion that held that expansions of defendants' constitutional procedural rights would not apply to judgments that have become final except for cases involving fundamental constitutional violations, correction of which were "watershed" decisions.[42] *Linkletter v. Walker* (1965) decided "the Constitution neither prohibits nor requires retrospective effect" and created a rule that only the most fundamental and structural changes would be applied to defendants whose judgments were final.[43] One pragmatic reason was that giving full retroactivity would place an overwhelming burden on the state courts. Scalia followed *Linkletter*'s approach, although originalists tend to reject such arguments.[44]

In general Scalia broadly applied statutory procedural bars to *habeas corpus*, and frequently denied claims on historical, textual, and precedential grounds. In one area where *habeas corpus* figured prominently, namely, prison conditions, he questioned whether the Eighth Amendment even applied, denying any constitutional right for prisoners' access to the courts.[45] Other cases demonstrate his narrow view of *habeas corpus* relief. *Houston v. Lack* (1988) (to satisfy time requirement for filing *habeas* brief, prisoner's delivery to prison authorities is not sufficient)[46]; *Ylst v. Nunnemaker* (1991) (construing final state judgment as resting on ground unavailable for *habeas* relief)[47]; *Reed v. Farley* (1994) (rejecting claim under *habeas corpus* that 120-day speedy trial rule of the Interstate Agreement on Detainers is cognizable under the federal *habeas corpus* statute)[48]; *Schlup v. Delo* (1995) (requiring more stringent standard for ascertaining whether prisoner sentenced to death raised a claim of actual innocence)[49]; *Stewart v. Martinez-Villereal* (1998) (construing "second or successive petition" to bar petitioner's *habeas* petition)[50]; *Slack v. McDaniel* (2000) (same)[51]; *Holland v. Florida* (2010) (failure of prison authorities to file timely brief did not amount to "extraordinary circumstances" to permit equitable tolling of one-year statute for filing)[52]; *Gonzalez v. Thaler* (2012) (failure to obtain certificate of appealability is jurisdictional defect)[53]; *Maples v. Thomas* (2012) (failure of lawyers who abandoned prisoner to file timely notice of appeal did not suffice to extend filing deadline)[54]; and *Trevino v. Thaler* (2013) (finding state procedures inadequate for challenging competence of counsel).[55]

5

Privacy and Individual Rights

This chapter includes some of the most sensitive issues the Supreme Court considers, including abortion, homosexual rights, and the right to die. They fall under the heading unenumerated rights because the Constitution does not specifically mention them as protected rights,[1] in contrast to African-Americans and other blacks, who have rights that are enumerated in the Constitution, dating from the late 1860s. Originalists reject newly created rights, perhaps by definition, and it is here that the split between the originalists and nonoriginalists is the most pronounced. The modern dispute began with *Griswold v. Connecticut* (1965),[2] where the Court accepted a right of privacy that protected married couples' right to use contraceptives, and expanded with *Roe v. Wade* (1973).[3] On the eve of Scalia's appointment originalists and traditionalists prevailed in *Bowers v. Hardwick* (1986),[4] upholding a statute that made sodomy, at least between members of the same gender, a crime. Discussed first, however, are issues involving race.

City of Richmond v. J.A. Croson Co. (1989)[5] confronted the constitutionality of a plan adopted by Richmond that "required prime contractors to whom the city awarded construction contracts to subcontract at least 30 percent of the dollar amount of the contract to one or more Minority Business Enterprises (MBE's)," defined as "a business the majority of which is owned and controlled by minority group members." The Richmond City Council found no direct evidence of race discrimination and a paucity of local qualified minority businesses, but also ascertained that while Richmond was 50 percent black, less than one percent of construction contracts had been awarded to minority businesses.[6] The district court and Fourth Circuit upheld the Plan.

O'Connor's opinion for the Court concluded that the statistics were flawed. The over-inclusive gross figures had little if anything to do with demonstrating unlawful race discrimination. Needed were statistics in the Richmond area about racial discrimination against qualified minority firms. Her opinion was cautious. Brennan, Marshall, and Blackmun dissented in an opinion that broadly defended affirmative action both legally and as a social imperative, including that pervasive segregation in important occupations was inherently destructive.[7]

Scalia concurred in the judgment, but on a more fundamental ground. The Constitution is "color-blind and neither knows nor tolerates classes among citizens. . . . I do not agree . . . that despite the Fourteenth Amendment, state and local governments may in some circumstances discriminate on the basis of race in order (in a broad sense) 'to ameliorate the effects of past discrimination.'"[8] He elaborated: "In my view there is only one circumstance in which the States may act *by race* to 'undo the effects of past discrimination': where that is necessary to eliminate their own maintenance of a system of unlawful racial classification. . . . Nothing prevents Richmond from according a contracting preference to identified victims of discrimination. . . . Racial preferences appear to 'even the score' (in some small degree) only if one embraces the proposition that our society is appropriately viewed as divided into races, making it right that an injustice rendered in the past to a black man should be compensated for by discriminating against a white."[9] While discrimination and preferences based on race are unconstitutional, states are free to aid the poor and unprivileged.[10]

Fourteen years later, *Grutter v. Bollinger* (2003)[11] decided that the University of Michigan Law School could lawfully use race as a factor in student admissions. O'Connor's opinion for the Court emphasized that "the path to leadership [must] be *visibly* open to talented and qualified individuals of every race and ethnicity. All members of our heterogeneous society must have confidence in the openness and integrity of the educational institutions that provide this training,"[12]

Scalia's dissent was dismissive: "[T]he University of Michigan Law School's mystical 'critical mass' justification for its discrimination by race challenges even the most gullible mind. The admissions statistics show it to be a sham to cover a scheme of racially proportionate admissions," adding that the holding "seems perversely designed to prolong the controversy and the litigation" by its vagueness. Mocking the supposed "educational benefit" that the law school seeks to obtain, including "good citizenship," Scalia wrote: "This is not, of course, an 'educational benefit' on which students will be graded only on their law school transcripts (Works and Plays Well with Others: B+) or tested by bar examiners (Q: Describe in 500 words or less your cross-racial understanding). For it is a lesson of life rather than law – essentially the same lesson taught to (or rather learned by, for it cannot be 'taught' in the usual sense) people three feet shorter and 20 years younger than the full-grown adults at the University of Michigan Law School, in institutions ranging from Boy Scouts to public-school kindergartens."[13]

Scalia joined Roberts's majority opinion in *Shelby County, Alabama v. Holder* (2013),[14] which struck down as unconstitutional an important section of the Voting Rights Act (VRA) that imposed preclearance requirements for particular states that sought to change voting districts. Roberts's opinion relied, first of all, on the enormous changes since 1966, when preclearance went into effect, including elimination of virtually all discriminatory bars against blacks. He accused Congress of relying on old data. Contradicting the majority, Ginsburg's dissent stated: "The record supporting the 2006 reauthorization of the VRA is also extraordinary. It was described by the Chairman of the House Judiciary Committee as 'one of the most extensive considerations of any piece of legislation that the United States Congress has dealt with in the 27 ½ years' he had served in the House." To the Court's criticism that no thought and no changes went into the reauthorization, the dissent cited twenty-one hearings, studies, and reports, including congressional findings. "[C]ongress was satisfied that the VRA's bailout mechanism provided effective means of adjusting the VRA's coverage over time," citing a House report.[15]

Scalia rejected unenumerated rights. Scalia's opposition to judicially created abortion rights in all forms and in all contexts is well known. Likewise, he abhorred *Griswold v. Connecticut* (1965) (state cannot prohibit married couples from using contraception),[16] ridiculing Justice Douglas's expansion of the Bill of Rights in terms of "penumbras" and "emanations."[17] The discussion here of abortion is brief, consisting of a lengthy quotation from his dissenting opinion in *Planned Parenthood v. Casey* (1992),[18] where, largely on grounds of *stare decisis*, five Justices refused to overrule *Roe*, although modified its teaching. Scalia wrote:

> The States may, if they wish, permit abortion on demand, but the Constitution does not *require* them to do so. The permissibility of abortion, and the limitations upon it, are to be resolved like most important questions in our democracy: by citizens trying to persuade one another and then voting. As the Court acknowledges, "where reasonable people disagree the government can adopt one position or the other." The Court is correct in adding the qualification that this "assumes a state of affairs in which the choice does not intrude upon a protected liberty" – but the crucial part of that qualification is the penultimate word. A State's choice between two positions on which reasonable people can disagree is constitutional even when (as is often the case) it intrudes upon a "liberty" in the absolute sense. Laws against bigamy, for example – with which entire societies of reasonable people disagree – intrude upon men and women's liberty to marry and live with one another. But bigamy happens not to be a liberty specially "protected" by the Constitution.
>
> That is, quite simply, the issue in these cases: not whether the power of a woman to abort her unborn child is a "liberty" in the absolute sense; or even whether it is a liberty of great importance to many women. Of course it is both. The issue is whether it is a liberty protected by the Constitution of the United States. I am sure that it is not. I reach that conclusion not because of anything so exalted as my views concerning the "concept of existence, of meaning, of the universe, and of the mystery of human life." Rather, I reach it for the same reason I reach the conclusion that bigamy is not constitutionally protected – because of two simple facts: (1) the Constitution says absolutely nothing about it, and (2) the longstanding traditions of American society have permitted it to be legally proscribed.[19]

Scalia employed a similar analysis in *Cruzan v. Director, Missouri Department of Health* (1990)[20] to state his opposition to a right to die by a person in "a persistent vegetative state." Rehnquist's opinion for the Court stated that, "we do not think the Due Process Clause requires the State to repose judgment on these matters with anyone but the patient herself."[21] While Scalia joined Rehnquist's opinion, he concurred separately with a more aggressive analysis:

> While I agree with the Court's analysis today, and therefore join in its opinion, I would have preferred that we announce, clearly and promptly, that the federal courts have no business in this field; that American law has always afforded the State the power to prevent, by force if necessary, suicide – including suicide by refusing to take appropriate measures necessary to preserve one's life; that the point at which life becomes "worthless," and the point at which the means necessary to preserve it become "extraordinary" or "inappropriate," are neither set forth in the Constitution nor known to the nine Justices of this Court any better than they are known to nine people picked at random from the Kansas City telephone directory; and hence, that even when it *is* demonstrated by clear and convincing evidence that a patient no longer wishes certain measures to be taken to preserve his or her life, it is up to the citizens of Missouri to decide, through their elected representatives, whether that wish will be honored.[22]

For Scalia, "[s]tarving oneself to death is no different from putting a gun to one's temple as far as the common-law definition of suicide is concerned." The dissent's view had no logical stopping point and would require outlawing laws against suicide. Scalia added, "What I have said above is not meant to suggest that I would think it desirable, if we're sure that Nancy Cruzan wanted to die, to keep her alive by the means at issue here. I assert only that the Constitution has nothing to say about the subject."[23] No other Justice signed on.

United States v. Virginia (1996)[24] challenged under the Equal Protection Clause the men-only admissions policy of the Virginia Military Institute (VMI). The state's defense was that it would be forced to change its rigorous training requirements, which provided valuable benefits to the male participants, to society, and to the government. The Court decided that individualized admission decisions would provide substantially the same benefits. Scalia alone objected (Thomas recused himself because his son attended VMI). The exclusion of women from VMI, he wrote, was historically accepted and "substantially related to an important government objective."[25] He then turned to mostly majoritarian arguments[26] – VMI was founded in 1839 and reflected the uniform practice for government-supported military colleges. It was up to the people, not the courts, to change that policy. Of controlling importance for Scalia was the widely held view that "although males and females have significant areas of developmental overlap, they also have differing developmental needs that are deep-seated."[27] The Court, he added, ignored specific findings of fact, including that Virginia's women-only military college was an appropriate alternative to integrating VMI. He turned against the liberal majority an argument frequently employed against conservatives:

> Justice Brandeis said it is "one of the happy incidents of the federal system that a single courageous State may, if its citizens choose, serve as a laboratory; and try novel social and economic experiments without risk to the rest of the country." *New State Ice Co. v. Liebman*, 285 U.S. 262, 311 (1932) (dissenting opinion). But it is one of the unhappy incidents of the federal system that a self-righteous Supreme Court, acting on its Members' personal view of what would make a "more perfect Union" . . . (a criterion only slightly more restrictive that a "more perfect world"), can impose its own favored social and economic dispositions nationwide. . . . The sphere of self-government reserved to the people of the Republic is progressively narrowed.[28]

The remaining cases involved the rights of gays and lesbians. Compared to the laborious pace with which the rights of African-Americans have been vindicated, the gay and lesbian movement has operated at breakneck speed. It took only twenty-nine years to traverse from *Bowers v. Hardwick* (1986), where the Court wrote, "Against this background, to claim a right to engage in [homosexual sodomy] is 'deeply rooted in this Nation's history and tradition,' is, at best facetious,"[29] to *Obergefell v. Hodges* (2015),[30] where it upheld the constitutional right to marriage by same-sex couples.

In 1992 the state of Colorado amended its Constitution (Amendment 2) to prohibit all legislative, executive, or judicial action at any level of state or local government "whereby homosexual, lesbian or bisexual orientation, conduct, practices or relationships shall constitute or otherwise be the basis of or entitle any person or class of persons to have or claim any minority status, quota preferences, protected status or claim of discrimination." The amendment was in reaction to broadly based ordinances passed by several Colorado municipalities that essentially placed discrimination against gays and lesbians on a par with discrimination on the basis of race, national origin, and gender. The challenge to the constitutionality of Amendment 2 was facial, which meant that "no set of circumstances exists under which the Act would be valid."[31]

Speaking for six Justices in *Romer v. Evans* (1996),[32] Kennedy declared the amendment violated the U.S. Constitution on its face. "Homosexuals, by state decree, are put in a solitary class with respect to transactions and relations in both the private and government sphere"; the amendment "deprives gays and lesbians even of the protection of general laws and policies that prohibit arbitrary discrimination in government and private settings." Only they are deprived the opportunity to change discrimination laws by statute; they are required to follow the much more difficult task of securing a constitutional amendment. "A second and related point is that laws of the kind now before us raised the inevitable inference that the disadvantage imposed is born of animosity toward the class of persons affected."[33] "[I]t is a classification of persons undertaken for its own sake, something the Equal Protection

Clause does not permit. '[C]lass legislation . . . [is] obnoxious to the prohibitions of the Fourteenth Amendment.'"[34] The opinion barely touched history. Perhaps for that reason, one commentary said that Kennedy won the hearts and Scalia won the brains.[35]

Scalia, joined by Rehnquist and Thomas, tore into the majority, in effect denouncing its opinion as unlawful, un-American, and perhaps ungodly. "No principle set forth in the Constitution, nor even any imagined by this Court in the past 200 years, prohibits what Colorado has done here."[36] The amendment, Scalia maintained, just placed homosexuals with most of the population, including people who were obese or short, who received no special protections. "[T]he principle underlying the Court's opinion is that one who is accorded equal treatment under the laws, but cannot as readily as others obtain preferential treatment under the laws, has been denied equal protection of the laws." If merely stating this "alleged 'equal protection' violation does not suffice to refute it, our constitutional jurisprudence has achieved terminal silliness."[37] Scalia rejected the argument that the desire of the voters for the amendment reflected a "bare . . . desire to harm" homosexuals. Instead, it was "a modest attempt by seemingly tolerant Coloradans to preserve sexual mores against the efforts of a politically powerful minority to revise those mores through the use of the laws."[38] Scalia took the side of the ordinary citizen against the power elite (which included homosexuals). Law firms interviewing at law schools can refuse to offer jobs to Republicans, adulterers, eaters of snails, or fur-wearers, but not homosexuals, a policy that would bar the firm from law school campuses. "Today's opinion has no foundation in American constitutional law, and barely pretends to. The people of Colorado have adopted an entirely reasonable provision which does not even disfavor homosexuals in any substantive sense, but merely denies them preferential treatment. . . . Striking it down is an act, not of judicial judgment, but of political will."[39]

Finally, Scalia argued, even if homosexuals were disadvantaged by the amendment, it would not mean that the law was unconstitutional, because homosexuals were not a protected class. In fact, they were a disrespected class. "If it is constitutionally permissible for a State to make homosexual conduct criminal, surely it is constitutionally permissible for a State to enact other laws merely *disfavoring* homosexual conduct," assuming that is what the amendment accomplished. *Bowers v. Hardwick* (1986),[40] decided months before Scalia joined the Court, arguably alone sufficed to answer all constitutional objections.[41] Scalia turned the history of discrimination against the homosexuals to his advantage, citing a "close[] analogy," namely, the insistence by the United States and the agreement by four states as a condition for becoming states that they include in their constitutions the prohibition of polygamy.[42]

Lawrence v. Texas (2003)[43] overruled *Bowers* by a 6–3 vote, asserting that, "The liberty protected by the Constitution allows homosexual persons the right to make this [sexual relationships] choice,"[44] relying on cases including *Griswold v. Connecticut*

(1965),[45] *Planned Parenthood of Southeastern Pa. v. Casey* (1992),[46] and *Romer v. Evans* (1996). It found the historical legal status of homosexual acts far more unclear than the Court's "assumptions about history" in *Bowers*. Sexual relations between consenting adults cannot be prohibited in the face of the Fourteenth Amendment. "Liberty presumes an autonomy of self that includes freedom of thought, belief, expression, and certain intimate conduct."[47]

Rehnquist and Thomas joined Scalia's dissenting opinion in *Lawrence*, which attacked overruling a seven-year-old precedent on what he considered insubstantial grounds, particularly in view of the position taken by the majority of Justices that *Roe v. Wade* (1973)[48] should be sustained on grounds of *stare decisis*. "It is clear from this that the Court has taken sides in the culture war, departing from its assuring, as neutral observer, that the democratic rules of engagement are observed." Scalia argued that the decision would mean the end of all morals legislation, including incest, bigamy, and bestiality. Scalia concluded with a broad pronouncement and warning. People are entitled to protect their lifestyles, which can include a choice not to engage with homosexuals. "What Texas has chosen to do is well within the range of traditional democratic action, and its hand should not be stayed through the intervention of a brand-new 'constitutional right' by a Court that is impatient of democratic change." Prophetically, he added: "Today's opinion dismantles the structure of constitutional law that has permitted a distinction to be made between heterosexual and homosexual unions, insofar as formal recognition in marriage is concerned."[49]

Implicating the two strands of judicial restraint and majoritarianism was *United States v. Windsor* (2013),[50] holding unconstitutional the federal Defense of Marriage Act (DOMA), which defined marriage in more than 10,000 federal statutes as between a man and a woman. Plaintiff Edith Windsor was married to another woman who died. She paid an estate tax that would not have been due had the marriage been a traditional one, and sued for a refund on the ground that DOMA was unconstitutional. The Court concluded that the statute was "motivated by an improper animus or purpose" and burdened certain classes of people and created inequities within states in violation of "basic due process and equal protection principles applicable to the Federal Government."[51] "The federal statute is invalid, for no legitimate purpose overcomes the purpose and effect to disparage and to injure those whom the States, by its marriage laws, sought to protect in personhood and dignity."[52]

Dissenting, Scalia argued that "[t]o defend traditional marriage is not to condemn, demean, or humiliate those who would prefer other arrangements. . . . [The Act] did no more than codify an aspect of marriage that has been unquestioned in our society for most of its existence – indeed, had been unquestioned in virtually all societies for virtually all of human history." States have the right to protect their citizens, especially in the case of intimate relationships such as marriage. Scalia scoffed at the meager evidence that the motivation for DOMA was the "bare . . . desire to harm a politically unpopular group."[53] The choice by a large majority of Congress and the President to support traditional marriage was not the product of malice, but the desire to uphold a broad long-standing cultural consensus not prohibited by the Constitution.[54]

The march culminated with *Obergefell v. Hodges* (2015).[55] The dissents argued that the five-Justice majority of Kennedy, Ginsburg, Breyer, Sotomayor, and Kagan made up the right of same-sex couples to marry without reference to the Constitution, traditional values, or historical practice. There was no issue of liberty or privacy, as those terms are commonly and historically understood, the dissents argued. The majority converted the transcendent respect accorded to traditional marriage to a right to an untraditional one. Roberts and Scalia said they had no concern with the result, only the method by which it was instituted. Scalia said that "it is not of special importance to me what the law says about marriage. It is of overwhelming importance, however, who it is that rules me."[56] Scalia's originalist, textualist, and majoritarian dissent concluded: "We have no basis for striking down a practice that is not expressly prohibited by the Fourteenth Amendment's text, and that bears the endorsement of a long tradition of open, widespread, and unchallenged use dating back to the [Fourteenth] Amendment's ratification."[57] Dissenters, both originalists (Scalia, Thomas) and nonoriginalists (Roberts, Alito), decried the expansion and distortion of a concept they argued was not recognized in 1791 (or 1868). Unelected judges had no power to rewrite the Constitution in their image while rejecting its traditional meaning. The issues were for the public, not unelected unaccountable officials, to decide.

On the surface Scalia's position on abortion was inconsistent with his position on gun control. On the former it was up to the public; on the latter it was up to the Court. Scalia's resolution was a combination of originalism and textualism. He read the Constitution as creating an individual right to gun ownership; it was an enumerated right that the Court was required to protect. There was no enumerated right to abortion, so the Constitution was irrelevant and the will of the people controlled. An alternative route to a constitutional right for Scalia was a long-standing tradition. He concluded, however, that there was no long-standing tradition for abortions, either. Thus, the Court had no business interfering with the public will in defining the lawfulness of abortions. He reached the same result by the same process with rights claimed for gays, women, and persons who wanted to terminate their lives. He preferred the status quo.

6

Government Power and Regulation

Scalia generally favored businesses litigating against the government, especially the federal government. Scalia rejected the distinction made in famous footnote 4 of Chief Justice Harlan F. Stone opinion in *United States v. Carolene Products* (1938),[1] which placed the protection of economic interests below the protection of individual rights. Scalia wrote: "in the real world a stark dichotomy between economic freedoms and civil rights does not exist.... [I]t seems to me that the difference between economic freedom and what are generally called civil rights turns out to be a difference of degree rather than of kind.... Human liberties of various types are dependent on one another.... The free market, which presupposes relatively broad economic freedom, has historically been the cradle of broad political freedom."[2] Scalia furthered conservative positions in a variety of ways – taking a narrow view of the Commerce Clause; taking a narrow view of the right of individuals and groups to challenge government failure to take action; construing the Takings Clause broadly to protect some nontangible property rights; construing regulatory statutes narrowly; and reducing financial incentives to challenge government action or inaction, such as limiting class actions and reimbursement for attorneys' fees and expenses.

Aside from *Gonzales v. Raich* (2005),[3] discussed in Chapter 16, Scalia took a restrictive view of the federal government's power under the Commerce Clause in *United States v. Lopez* (1995) (regulation of firearms near schools)[4]; *United States v. Morrison* (2000) (Violence Against Women Act of 1994)[5]; and *National Federation of Independent Business v. Sibelius* (2012) (Affordable Care Act).[6] *Lopez* was the first case since 1936 in which the Court held that a federal statute exceeded Congress's powers under the Commerce Clause, the product of a new conservative majority. The federal power did not include regulation for noncommercial purposes or creation of new regulatory schemes, the Court held.

The importance of access to federal courts cannot be overestimated to protect individual rights, including economic rights. Scalia restricted access to the federal courts by persons asserting grievances against the federal government or against businesses. For Scalia, standing was an integral part of the constitutional plan, part of the requirement that courts decided only "cases" and "controversies" between adverse parties, with its roots traced back to *Marbury v. Madison* (1803)[7] and earlier. Scalia's 1983 article, "The Doctrine of Standing as an Essential Element of the Separation of Powers," argued that "courts need to give greater weight than they have in recent times to the traditional requirement that the plaintiff's alleged injury be a particularized one, which sets him apart from the citizenry at large.... My thesis is that the judicial doctrine of standing is a crucial and inseparable element of [the separation of powers principle], whose disregard will inevitably produce – as it has during the past few decades – an overjudicialization of the process of self-governance."[8] Thus, he argued, the right to challenge administrative conduct was limited to those directly harmed, and was not a general right to tell the agencies how to do their jobs through the device of a lawsuit.[9] To those who said that Scalia's restrictive concept of standing might prevent anyone from challenging a federal statute, his response was that the Constitution does not require everything to be decided by the courts, even the Supreme Court.[10]

The Endangered Species Act (ESA) limited its scope to events within the United States or on the high seas, but also gave "any citizen" the right to challenge actions taken under the statute. In *Lujan v. Defenders of Wildlife* (1992),[11] plaintiff organizations filed suit against the Secretary of the Interior for a declaratory judgment that challenged his narrow interpretation of ESA. Scalia's opinion for the Court held that the plaintiffs lacked standing. He acknowledged that a desire to use or observe an animal species was a cognizable interest for purposes of standing. "But the 'injury in fact' test requires more than an injury to a cognizable interest. It requires that the party seeking review 'be himself among the injured.' Statements by affiants that they had travelled abroad to visit the traditional habitats of certain endangered species and intended to do so again, although without specific plans to do so in the near future, 'plainly contain no facts . . . showing how damage to the species will produce imminent injury to [the affiants].'"[12] "Vindicating the public interest (including the public interest in Government observance of the Constitution and laws) is the function of Congress and the Chief Executive."[13] Congress cannot provide by statute standing to an individual unless the latter satisfies Article III, Scalia concluded. "To permit Congress to convert the undifferentiated public interest in executive officers' compliance with the law into an 'individual right' vindicable in the courts is to permit Congress to transfer from the President to the courts the Chief Executive's most important constitutional duty, to 'take Care that the Laws be faithfully executed.'"[14] A dissent disputed Scalia's opinion on almost every front.

Scalia was in the minority in *Friends of the Earth, Inc. v. Laidlaw Environmental Services* (2000),[15] a case under the Clean Water Act, which limited discharge of pollutants and provided that suits may be initiated by "a person or persons having an interest which is or may be adversely affected." Fines imposed by the courts were payable to the U.S. Treasury. The organizations submitted affidavits of some of their members that they lived near Laidlow's facility, spent time near it, wanted to use the river into which Laidlow discharged pollutants for swimming and fishing, but the river smelled and they refrained because of fear of pollutants. Joined by six Justices, Ginsburg upheld the organizations' right to sue, pointing out that the affidavits related to specific properties and demonstrated a close connection to the polluted river. The organizations' complaints could be redressed – "the civil penalties sought by FOE carried with them a deterrent effect that made it likely, as opposed to merely speculative, that the penalties would redress FOE's injuries by abating current violations and preventing future ones."[16]

Scalia dissented. Affidavits asserting "concern" and "belief" that the river was polluted do not carry the plaintiffs' burden of demonstrating that they have suffered a "concrete and particularized" injury, he maintained. The district court had found "no demonstrated proof of harm to the environment" and there can be no harm to plaintiffs without harm to the environment. Nor was redressability shown, which would require plaintiffs to seek an injunction against future pollution or damages for past injuries rather than a fine of the offender, which is too speculative to serve as the basis for finding redressability.[17] The government, not private-interest groups, should decide which companies to prosecute under federal law.[18]

Windsor, discussed above, raised an important standing and jurisdictional issue. When the suit was pending, the United States decided it would not defend the constitutionality of DOMA and both sides asked the court of appeals and then the Supreme Court to affirm the district court's decision for the plaintiff. The Court's majority held that there nevertheless was a case or controversy, quoting on Chief Justice John Marshall's statement, that "when an Act of Congress is alleged to conflict with the Constitution, '[i]t is emphatically the province and duty of the judicial department to say what the law is.'"[19]

Scalia forcefully attacked the majority's holding of a paramount or "primary" power in the judiciary to make law without a bona fide case or controversy; the implied right of courts to engage in judicial review can only be exercised in the context of an Article III case or controversy. Scalia explained:

> [D]eclaring the compatibility of state or federal laws with the Constitution is not only not the "primary role" of this Court, it is not a separate, free-standing role *at all*. We perform that role incidentally – by accident, as it were – when that is necessary to resolve a dispute before us. Then, and only then, does it become "'the province and duty of the judicial department to say what the law is.'" ... [The majority's position] is an assertion of judicial supremacy over the people's Representatives in Congress and the Executive.... [T]hose who wrote and ratified our national charter ... knew well the dangers of "primary" power, and so created branches of government that would be "perfectly coordinated by the terms of their common commission," none of which could "pretend to an exclusive or superior right of settling the boundaries between their respective powers."[20]

In a sense, the right to compensation under the Takings Clause of the Fifth Amendment is a reciprocal of the standing requirement. The latter asks what you have to demonstrate to sue in a federal court for governmental action that adversely affected your rights. The former asks what you have to demonstrate before you sue for action taken by the government that adversely affected your property. A strict requirement is conservative for standing while a low requirement is conservative under the Takings Clause. While physical takings by the government must indisputably be compensated, Scalia also wanted diminution in the value of property values extracted for the public good to be shared by everyone.

The dispute between liberals and conservatives on the Takings Clause was over the liberal position that under the Takings Clause, there is "no taking without touching," rejecting what is sometimes called regulatory taking, which denies the owner the right to modify or improve property. *Penn Central Transp. Co. v. New York City* (1978)[21] upheld the city's landmarks law, which prevented the owners of Pennsylvania Station from developing their property. Scalia disagreed. "Where the State seeks to sustain a regulation that deprives land of all economically beneficial use, we think it may resist compensation only if the logically antecedent inquiry into the nature of the owner's estate shows that the proscribed use interests were not part of his title to begin with."[22] It was a bright-line methodology that supported landowners. Dissenting in a later case, Scalia described the alleged benefit to the public as "profit to the thief."[23] Along the same lines, he unsuccessfully voted to declare rent control unconstitutional.[24] The public, not a landowner, should bear the costs of government policies.

While Scalia took an expansive view of the scope of the Takings Clause, he conceded that his regulatory takings doctrine "is not supported by early American experience" and that early constitutional theorists did not believe that the Takings Clause embraced regulation of property.[25] Scalia authored the Court's somewhat textualist, somewhat attached to precedent, somewhat libertarian, somewhat conservative, but nonoriginalist opinion in *Lucas v. South Carolina Coastal Council* (1992),[26] which granted compensation to the purchaser of two lots on the Atlantic coast when the state prohibited him from building anything on the property. Calling the historical absence of regulatory taking "entirely irrelevant," Scalia relied on a broad reading of the language of the clause:

> Justice Blackmun is correct that early constitutional theorists did not believe the Takings Clause embraced regulations of property at all ... but even he does not suggest (explicitly, at least) that we renounce the Court's contrary conclusion in [*Pennsylvania Coal Co. v. Mahon*, 260 U.S. 393, 415 (1922)]. Since the text of the Clause can be read to encompass regulatory as well as physical deprivations (in contrast to the text originally proposed by Madison, see Speech Proposing Bill of Rights (June 8, 1789), in J. Madison, *The Papers of James Madison* 201 (C. Hobson, R. Rutland, W. Rachel & Sisson ed. 1979) ("No person shall be ... obliged to

relinquish his property, where it may be necessary for public use, without a just compensation"), we decline to do so as well.[27]

As framed by Scalia writing for five Justices in *Printz v. United States* (1997),[28] the question before the Court was "whether certain interim provisions of the Brady Handgun Violence Prevention Act . . . commanding state and local law-enforcement officers to conduct background checks on prospective handgun purchasers and to perform certain related tasks, violate the Constitution." The provisions required the relevant local "chief law enforcement officer" (CLEO) to perform background checks on handgun purchasers. CLEOs contended that congressional action compelling state officers to execute federal laws was unconstitutional. "Because there is no constitutional text speaking to this precise question, the answer to the CLEOs' challenge must be sought in historical understanding and practice, in the structure of the Constitution, and in the jurisprudence of this Court."[29] Scalia rejected the Government's citation of early practice as consistent with the states' having consented to the duty imposed by federal law, and the obligation of all citizens to adhere to federal law as the law of the land. At most, the federal government could impose obligations on state judges, who were required to hear federal cases and apply federal law. Federalism and separation of powers, buoyed by contemporary documentation, including *The Federalist*, supported the states, he wrote. "Not only do the enactments of the early Congresses, as far as we are aware, contain no evidence of an assumption that the Federal Government may command the States' executive power in the absence of a particularized constitutional authorization, they contain some indication of precisely the opposite assumption. . . . It is an essential attribute of the States' retained sovereignty that they remain independent and autonomous within their proper sphere of authority."[30] Finally, he said, Supreme Court precedent did not support the statute. In 1992, while invalidating a federal statute, the Court stated: "The Federal Government may not compel the States to enact or administer a federal regulatory program."[31]

Relying both on the Eleventh Amendment and the principle that the states remained sovereign, Scalia sided with the states when sued by individuals, corporations, other states, and the federal government. In chronological order, he wrote federalist opinions in *Pennsylvania v. Union Gas Co.* (1989) (concurring in part and dissenting in part) (immunity of states is not limited by the language of Eleventh Amendment)[32]; *Blatchford v. Native Village of Noatak* (1991) (sovereign immunity extends to suits by Indian tribes and is not overcome by statutory grant of jurisdiction to federal courts in actions by Indian tribes)[33]; *College Savings Bank v. Florida Prepaid Postsecondary Education Expense Bd.* (1999) (state immunity extends to commercial enterprises of the states, in the context of suit for unfair competition under a federal statute)[34]; *Nevada Dept. of Human Resources v. Hibbs* (2003) (states enjoy immunity from suits for damages under Family Medical Leave Act of 1993 because no showing of pattern of violations; Scalia concurred separately that Nevada lacked standing since there was no showing that it violated the act).[35]

The principal merits issue in *Arizona State Legislature v. Arizona Independent Redistricting Comm'n* (2015)[36] was whether an Arizona initiative that gave exclusive power to set congressional districts to an independent commission violated the Elections Clause of the Constitution, Art. I, § 4, cl. 1: "The Times, Places and Manner of holding Elections for Senators and Representative, shall be prescribed in each State by the Legislature thereof; but the Congress may at any time by Law make or alter such Regulations." Noting that direct lawmaking by the people was "'virtually unknown when the Constitution of 1787 was drafted'" and emphasizing the evil of gerrymandering, the liberal quartet (plus Kennedy) held that "our precedent teaches that redistricting is a legislative function, to be performed in accordance with the State's prescriptions for lawmaking, which may include the referendum and the Governor's veto."[37]

Roberts wrote the principal dissent for the Court's conservatives. "The Court seems to conclude, based on its understanding of the 'history and purpose' of the Elections Clause . . . that 'the Legislature' encompasses any entity in a States that exercises legislative power. That circular definition lacks any basis in the text of the Constitution or any other relevant legal source" for the decision. Every state Constitution referred to the Legislature as a distinct multimember entity comprising representatives; so did *The Federalist* and other sources. The Constitution includes seventeen provisions referring to a State's "Legislature," including the Seventeenth Amendment, which changed the electors of Senators from state legislature to the people. Every one of those references, Roberts observed, was consistent with the understanding of a legislature as a representative body. At the Constitutional Convention, Madison, George Mason, and James Wilson used the term narrowly.[38] Finally, Roberts concluded that the Court's precedents supported the decision.

Scalia argued that the dispute between the state legislature and the Commission was not judiciable as an intragovernmental dispute, and voted to dismiss the case for want of jurisdiction.[39] Scalia concluded: "Normally, having arrived at that conclusion, I would express no opinion on the merits unless my vote was necessary to enable the Court to produce a judgment. In the present case, however, the majority's resolution of the merits question ('legislature' means 'the people') is so outrageously wrong, so utterly devoid of textual or historic support, so flatly in contradiction of prior Supreme Court cases, so obviously the willful product of hostility to districting by state legislatures, that I cannot avoid adding my vote to the devastating dissent by the Chief Justice."[40]

Bush v. Gore (2000)[41] warrants inclusion even though Scalia did not sign an opinion. The five most conservative Justices voted to halt the Florida recount in the 2000 presidential election, giving victory to Republican George W. Bush.[42] Different standards for counting or invalidating ballots at polling places in different counties violated the Clause, the Court held.[43] Rehnquist, joined by Scalia and Thomas, wrote a concurrence that rejected the procedures mandated by the Florida Supreme Court and decided the issues itself rather than remand to that court. While the decision has its defenders,[44] it was an activist and polarizing decision, where Gore supporters accused the majority of rank partisanship, theft, overreaching, and violating the Constitution.

The Court resolved the nonjusticiability claim in favor of proceeding, challenged the scope of review by the Florida Supreme Court of state law, and decided the merits of the case itself rather than remand the case to the Florida state courts, contrary to the dictates of past practice and federalism.[45] Moreover, the Court's *per curiam* opinion provided an expansive, if not unique, reading of the Equal Protection Clause, which the Court consistently held requires proof of discriminatory intent. *E.g., Arlington Heights v. Metropolitan Housing Corp.* (1977).[46] Unlike other controversial Supreme Court cases, there was no important constitutional principle involved.[47] The opinion did not even purport to give guidance to the future,[48] something Scalia often demanded. It was an opinion that advanced judicial aggrandizement.[49] Robert Post spoke for many professors when he said, "until *Bush v. Gore* I had never been embarrassed to teach a decision of the Supreme Court. Never.... I was simply stung by distrust of the Court's good faith.... [T]he Court seemed bent on achieving a blatantly extralegal objective."[50]

PART III

Scalia's Liberal Constitutional Opinions

Along with major areas in which Justice Scalia joined, and frequently directed, the Court's conservative positions, he was also the author of many liberal constitutional opinions. This legacy is surprising for a jurist whom many consider a conservative ideologue. It would be difficult to imagine, for example, a book on the conservative opinions of William Brennan or Thurgood Marshall. Yet that is effectively what we have here. The major influences in his liberal opinions, like the major influences on his conservative opinions, were textualism and originalism. To a significant extent, he followed where those creeds took him. Sometimes he fell short and sometimes he overshot the target – duly noted below. But his was generally a conscientious attempt. Scalia's liberal opinions tend to refute the refrain that "originalism does not appear to constrain Supreme Court outcomes."[1] In a sense he demonstrated the wisdom of the title of an article, "Why Conservatives Shouldn't Be Originalists."[2]

In some contexts Scalia's opinions were unashamedly liberal, such as those under the Sixth's Amendment's Confrontation Clause. In others, they constituted a single liberal opinion among a sea of conservative ones, based on a reason that he, but not some other Justices, considered dispositive, such as his opinion granting *habeas corpus* relief to an American citizen in *Hamdi v. Rumsfeld* (2004),[3] while denying relief to aliens based on his reading of 28 U.S.C. § 2241 that did not cover foreign nationals held outside of the territorial jurisdiction of federal courts.[4]

One opinion granted several constitutional rights to the plaintiffs. Writing for eight Justices, Scalia decided that the National Railroad Passenger Corporation

(Amtrak) was part of the government for purposes of the First Amendment when it censored a billboard display in Amtrak's Pennsylvania Station in New York City in *Lebron v. National Railroad Passenger Corp.* (1995).[5] Scalia reasoned that the government created Amtrak to further government objectives and was for all practical purposes part of the government. Moderate O'Connor, the sole dissenter, reasoned that "Amtrak's decision to reject Lebron's billboard proposal was a matter of private business judgment and not of Government coercion."[6]

7

First Amendment: Freedom of Speech and More

Justice Scalia's generally conservative opinions on establishment of religion contrasted with his generally liberal opinions on freedom of speech, at least speech that was historically protected (exclusions were predominantly obscenity but also libel[7]). Curiously, he did not rely much on the founders' views of the speech clause, as he had in connection with many of the other rights protected by the Bill of Rights. He told me that he recognized that most of his free-speech jurisprudence was not originalist. Discussed are four First Amendment cases. First, two cases of broad First Amendment applicability. Second, cases in which the government sought to punish certain types of speech that it deemed undeserving of protection based on the content of the speech, for example, "hate speech" or "fighting words."[8] Third, cases where the government sought to equate depictions of animal cruelty and violence with pornography. Fourth, cases under the Free Press and Petition Clauses. The opinions represented a broad commitment to freedom of speech.

The concept of overbreadth is part of constitutional law. In essence it means that a penal statute punished constitutionally protected as well as unprotected conduct. For example, a statute could punish all payments of cash to a government employee, which read literally would criminalize a mother's payment to her son if he was a government employee. A defendant indicted for bribery could not complain about the overbreadth of the statute unless the cash payment was from his mother. The rule is different in free-speech cases because of the concern that an overly broad statute might chill protected speech. *Massachusetts v. Oakes* (1989)[9] involved a statute that punished anyone who permitted a nude child under eighteen to pose for a photograph. While the case implicated overbreadth because it would punish parents who took pictures of their nude infants, there was a controlling preliminary issue. After Douglas Oakes allegedly violated the statute by taking nude pictures of his fourteen-year-old stepdaughter who was attending modeling school, the state legislature amended the statute to require "lascivious intent," which cured the overbreadth problem for the future. The question for the Court was whether it cured the overbreadth problem for prosecuting Oakes.

Four conservative Justices answered yes. "[O]verbreadth analysis is inappropriate if the statute being challenged has been amended or repealed.... Because the special concern that animates the overbreadth doctrine is no longer present after the amendment or repeal of the challenged statute, we need not extend the benefits of the doctrine to a defendant whose conduct is not protected."[10] Five Justices answered no and acquitted Oakes in an opinion by Scalia:

> The overbreadth doctrine serves to protect constitutionally legitimate speech not merely *ex post,* that is, after the offending statute is enacted, but also *ex ante,* that is, when the legislature is contemplating what sort of statute to enact.... In my view, we have the power to adopt a rule of law which says that the defendant's acts were lawful because the statue that sought to prohibit them was overbroad and therefore invalid. I do not think we have the power to pursue the policy underlying that rule of law more directly and precisely, saying that we will hold the defendant criminally liable or not, depending upon whether, by the time his last appeal is exhausted, letting him off would serve to eliminate any First Amendment "chill."[11]

When a municipality promulgated an ordinance that required registering and obtaining a permit to go on private property to canvass or solicit or face misdemeanor charges, Jehovah's Witnesses objected based on the First Amendment. Seven Justices struck down the ordinance as applied to the plaintiff on broad grounds in *Watchtower Bible & Tract Soc. of N.Y., Inc. v. Village of Stratton* (2002).[12] Rehnquist alone dissented on the ground Stratton's concern over crime justified its ordinance. Scalia's concurrence rejected the ground that a person's religious objection to applying for a permit had validity. It also rejected the Court's argument that there "are no doubt other patriotic citizens, who have such firm convictions about their constitutional right to engage in uninhibited debate in the context of door-to-door advocacy, that they would prefer silence to speech licensed by a petty official."[13] Scalia intolerant response? "If our free-speech jurisprudence is to be determined by the predicted behavior of such crackpots, we are in a sorry state indeed."[14]

Texas v. Johnson (1989),[15] decided in Scalia's third Term as a Justice, generated a higher ration of ire than any First Amendment case on which he sat. Scalia wrote no opinion, but instead joined Brennan's majority opinion, with Marshall, Blackmun, and Kennedy. Involved was a conviction for burning the American flag under a Texas statute that made it a crime when "[a] person ... intentionally or knowingly desecrates ... a state or national flag.... For purposes of this section 'desecrate' means deface, damage, or otherwise physically mistreat in a way that the actor knows will seriously offend one or more persons likely to observe or discover his action."[16] Despite a broadly based and passionate populace that condemned the conduct, the Court majority declared the statute unconstitutional.

Brennan wrote that flag-burning was expressive conduct, and while the "government generally has a freer hand in restricting expressive conduct than it has in restricting the written or spoken word . . . [i]t may not . . . proscribe particular conduct *because* it has expressive elements. . . . If there is a bedrock principle underlying the First Amendment, it is that the government may not prohibit the expression of an idea simply because society finds the idea itself offensive or disagreeable." Texas asserted "no interest in support of Johnson's conviction that is unrelated to the suppression of expression," such as preventing breaches of the peace.[17] As expected, there was no suggestion of originalist analysis in Brennan's opinion. *Johnson* relied on post–World War II cases that involved the wearing of black armbands to protest the war in Viet Nam,[18] sit-ins by blacks in "whites only" areas to protest racial discrimination,[19] and picketing regarding a wide variety of causes.[20] Brennan asked whether expression was prohibited "simply because society found the idea itself offensive or disagreeable," a bright, but fuzzy, line.[21]

Rehnquist wrote an over-heated dissent, in which he compared flag-burning to incinerating the Jefferson Memorial, ignoring, among other things, that the burned flag was only a copy not the original flag, the amount of property damage was *de minimis*, and the property was the defendant's. His opinion stressed the flag as "holding a unique position as symbol of our Nation," dating back to the Revolution, that warrants government protection.[22] Not all expressive conduct is permitted by the First Amendment, and publicly burning the flag had the potential for disturbing the peace.

Scalia's voice surfaced three years after *Johnson*, when he wrote for the Court in *R.A.V. v. St. Paul* (1992),[23] another conflagration case where the igniters lacked popular support. Teenagers burned a cross on the lawn of a black family and St. Paul had charged them under a city ordinance that prohibited the display of a symbol, "including a burning cross or a Nazi swastika, which one knows or has reason to know arouses anger, alarm or resentment in others on the basis of race, color, creed, religion or gender." The Minnesota Supreme Court had construed the statute to apply only to that conduct that constitutes "fighting words," namely, "conduct that itself inflicts injury or tends to incite immediate violence."[24]

Scalia's opinion held that "the ordinance is facially unconstitutional because it prohibits otherwise permitted speech solely on the basis of the subjects the speech addresses."[25] "[T]he government may proscribe libel, but it may not make the further content discrimination of proscribing *only* libel critical of the government." While a state may prohibit obscenity, it may not prohibit only obscenity that includes an offensive political message and while a government can ban outdoor fires, it cannot punish an outdoor fire that dishonors a flag.[26] "The First Amendment does not permit St. Paul to impose special prohibitions on those speakers who express views on disfavored subjects. . . . The dispositive question in this case, therefore, is whether content discrimination is reasonably necessary to achieve St. Paul's compelling interests; it plainly is not." Scalia added: "Let there be no mistake about our belief that burning a cross in someone's front yard is reprehensible. But St. Paul has sufficient means at its disposal to prevent such behavior without adding the First Amendment to the fire."[27] Scalia's only nod to originalism in *R.A.V.* was the statement that, while "[i]ntent-based regulations are presumptively invalid,... [f]rom 1791 to the present, however, our society, like other free but civilized societies, has permitted restrictions upon the content of speech in a few limited areas, which are 'of such slight social value as a step to truth that any benefit may be derived from them is clearly outweighed by the social interest in order and morality,'" quoting *Chaplinsky v. New Hampshire* (1942),[28] a nonoriginalist opinion.

Scalia rejected several counterarguments, including the intriguing one that since defamation, obscenity, and fighting words are not speech within the First Amendment, distinctions could be based on content. "Such a simplistic, all-or-nothing approach to First Amendment protection is at odds with common sense and with our jurisprudence as well." The communications were obviously speech, whatever had been said about them, but they constituted speech that was not "an essential part of any exposition of ideas." "The point of the First Amendment is that majority preferences must be expressed in some fashion other than silencing speech on the basis of its content."[29] Scalia's reasoning closely mirrored Brennan's.[30] Four Justices concurred in the result in three separate opinions, all of whom stated that the case should have been decided on the well-established ground "that the St. Paul ordinance is fatally overbroad because it criminalizes not only unprotected expression but expression protected by the First Amendment," rather than on constitutional grounds neither presented to the state supreme court nor briefed by the parties in the Supreme Court.[31]

In his first Term, Scalia wrote a cryptic concurring opinion that suggested that he was willing to accept sexually explicit writing as deserving of First Amendment protection. *Pope v. Illinois* (1987),[32] a prosecution of sellers of allegedly obscene magazines, involved the standard for judging the literary and artistic value of alleged obscenity, including whether the standard should include the ubiquitous "reasonable man."[33] Scalia voted to uphold the conviction, concluding that the various standards were nearly identical so the use of one rather than another amounted to harmless error. Bringing to mind Justice John Marshall Harlan's 1971 comment that "one man's vulgarity is another's lyric,"[34] he added: "I think we would be better advised to adopt as a legal maxim what has long been the wisdom of mankind: *De gustibus non est disputandum*. Just as there is no use arguing about taste, there is no use litigating about it. For the law courts to decide 'What is Beauty' is a novelty even by today's standards."[35]

Twenty-four years later, *Brown v. Entertainment Merchants Ass'n* (2011)[36] invalidated a California law imposing restrictions on violent video games sold to minors, which drew heavily on the standards applicable to obscenity, including forbidding the sale of offending games to minors unless accompanied by a parent.[37] Kennedy, Ginsburg, Sotomayor, and Kagan joined Scalia's opinion striking down the statute on its face. The dominant precedent guiding the opinions was *United States v. Stevens* (2010,[38] a case dealing with depiction of animal cruelty, which held that legislatures cannot create new categories of unprotected speech.

"No doubt a State possesses legitimate power to protect children from harm," Scalia wrote in *Brown*, "but that does not include a free-floating power to restrict the ideas to which children may be exposed.... Because the Act imposes a restriction on the content of protected speech, it is invalid unless California can demonstrate that it passes strict scrutiny – that is, unless it is justified by a compelling government interest and is narrowly drawn to serve that interest.... The State's evidence is not compelling." It does not even establish "that violent videos *cause* minors to *act* aggressively," certainly not to a significant extent.[39] Moreover, "California cannot show that the Act's restrictions meet a substantial need of parents who wish to restrict their children's access to violent video games but cannot do so." Finally, there was no long-standing tradition in the United States of restricting children's access to depictions of violence. Violence is everywhere from movies to fairy tales to serious literature. There was no more than a passing reference to early history.

All concurring and dissenting opinions were more conservative than Scalia's. Alito, joined by Roberts, concurred in the judgment of the Court, but on the ground that the California Act was void for vagueness; it did not define "'violent video games' with the 'narrow specificity' that the Constitution demanded." Disagreeing with striking down the statute on its face, Breyer responded by carving out a subclass that the statute could legitimately cover, namely, sales to minors under the age of seventeen of highly realistic, violent video games. Supporting parental authority and the state's independent interest in the well-being of its youth were compelling state interests. Breyer also identified scientific studies that found a connection between violent video games and aggressive behavior.[40]

Compared to the Freedom of Speech Clause and the Religion Clauses, core freedom of the press was tangential to the Court's efforts during Scalia's tenure. An exception was *Florida Star v. B.J.F.* (1989),[41] where a newspaper's "Police Reports" section published the full name of a rape victim, who sued the newspaper. The Sheriff's Department had inadvertently included the name in its report. B.J.F. sued the newspaper under a Florida statute making it unlawful to publish the name of the victim of a sexual offense in "any instrument of mass communications." An opinion by Marshall, in which Brennan, Blackmun, Stevens, and Kennedy joined, held for the newspaper. Applying the standard, "if a newspaper lawfully obtains truthful information about a matter of public significance, then state officials may not constitutionally punish publication of the information, absent a need to further a state interest of the highest order,"[42] the Court found no state interest of the highest order. Concurring separately, Scalia agreed: "This law has every appearance of a prohibition that society is prepared to impose upon the press but not upon itself."[43]

White's dissent concluded that the majority had undervalued the wrong committed to B.J.F. Emphasizing that the right of privacy is not absolute, he nevertheless accused the Court of "obliterate[ing] one of the most noteworthy legal inventions of the 20th century: the tort of publication of private facts. . . . The public's right to know is subject to reasonable limitations so far as concerns the private facts of its individual members."[44] A basically conservative trio (White, Rehnquist, and O'Connor, but not Scalia) favored privacy over free speech.[45]

8

Fourth Amendment: Search and Seizure

The Fourth Amendment, which is made applicable to the states by the Fourteenth, provides: "The right of the people to be secure in their persons, houses, papers, and effects, against unreasonable searches and seizures, shall not be violated, and no Warrants shall issue, but upon probable cause, supported by Oath or affirmation, and particularly describing the place to be searched, and the persons or things to be seized." Scalia's opinions in the area of search and seizure include, among many that were conservative, such as his abhorrence of the exclusionary rule at both the federal and state level and generosity to law-enforcement in construing warrants,[1] several that qualify as distinctly liberal. Scalia generally protected home and person from invasion by law-enforcement agents.[2]

All of the seven cases in this chapter involved warrantless searches. The Court said in 2009: "Consistent with our precedents, our analysis begins, as it should in every case addressing the reasonableness of a warrantless search, with the basic rule that 'searches conducted outside the judicial process, without prior approval by a judge or magistrate, are *per se* unreasonable under the Fourth Amendment – subject only to a few specifically established and well-delineated exceptions.'"[3] Scalia protected defendants by using a broad definition of search (although not what constituted a seizure of a person). He also demanded a close connection between the search and a lawful objective. However, he was less generous to special categories of persons, such as students and prisoners, largely on the ground that those groups of people had no rights at the time of the adoption of the Constitution and Bill of Rights.

STANDARD FOURTH AMENDMENT SEARCH AND SEIZURE

Scalia's vigorous dissents in 2013 and 2014 strongly supporting defendants' claims that they were subjected to illegal searches raised a number of eyebrows, but his position was consistent with his earlier opinions that took a broad view of what was a search. *Arizona v. Hicks* (1987),[4] his first opinion for the Court, considered how much police could interfere with private property before there was a search under the Constitution. After a bullet was fired through the floor of James Hicks's apartment injuring a man in the apartment below, police officers entered Hicks's apartment to search for the shooter. They found and seized three weapons, including a sawed-off shotgun, as well as drug paraphernalia and a ski mask. A policeman noticed expensive stereo equipment, which seemed out of place in the squalid apartment. Suspicious that they were stolen, the officer moved a piece of equipment to read and record its serial number. When he called in and learned that it had been taken in an armed robbery, he confiscated it. After Hicks was indicted for the robbery, he moved to suppress.

The first question was whether the officer conducted a search or seizure. Writing for the Court, Scalia said that since the officer was lawfully on the premises, his mere recording of serial numbers in plain view did not qualify. But his moving the equipment, which was separate and apart from the search for the shooter or weapons, constituted a search and seizure. Scalia said that moving an object even a few inches "is much more than trivial for purposes of the Fourth Amendment."[5] A bright line. He rejected the complaint that the police officer was essentially helpless if he lacked probable cause, pointing out that he was in the same position as had he been walking down the street and saw the equipment on a ledge inside the building just below an open window. Maybe the officer could do nothing. "But there is nothing new in the realization that the Constitution sometimes insulates the criminality of a few in order to protect the privacy of us all. Our disagreement with the dissenters pertains to where the proper balance should be struck; we choose to adhere to the textual and traditional standard of probable cause."[6] His brief discussion relied on Court precedent to support the proposition that mere inspection of the equipment would have been legal.[7] But he cited no authority that moving a chattel in plain view a few inches constituted a search under the Fourth Amendment; he did not refer to the law or practice at the time of the adoption of the Bill of Rights.

The remaining question was whether the search was "reasonable" under the Fourth Amendment, which Scalia equated with probable cause, again without reference to early practice. Precedent did not tell whether probable cause was required, but Scalia answered the question forcefully in the positive: "We now hold that probable cause is required. To say otherwise would be to cut the 'plain view' doctrine loose from its theoretical and practical moorings. The theory of that doctrine consists of extending to nonpublic places such as the home, where searches and seizures without a warrant are presumptively unreasonable, the police's long-standing authority to make warrantless seizures in public places of such objects as weapons and contraband."[8] The earliest authority Scalia cited was a 1969 Supreme Court case.[9] His was a textualist and formalist opinion.[10]

Based on his suspicion that Danny Kyllo was growing marijuana in his home in Florence, Oregon, a federal agent scanned his home from the front and from a street to the rear with a thermal imager. The agent was seeking spots of infrared radiation often associated with growing marijuana, which requires large amounts of high-intensity lamps. Relying on the scan, information from informants, and utility bills, the agent obtained a search warrant for Kyllo's home. The search revealed more than 100 marijuana plants. Kyllo moved to suppress the scan after he was indicted. *Kyllo v. United States* (2001)[11] resolved whether there was a search in a high-tech context.

Supreme Court precedent established that visual surveillance did not constitute a "search" under the Fourth Amendment, although common-law trespass was no longer required to create a search. *Katz v. United States* (1967)[12] held unconstitutional eavesdropping by means of an electronic device placed on the outside of a telephone booth. While *Katz* did not involve a traditionally protected location, the Fourth Amendment nonetheless protected Katz because he "justifiably relied" upon the privacy of the telephone booth (or had a reasonable expectation of privacy). *Kyllo* involved the prototypical protected space of the interior of one's home.

Writing for a majority of five,[13] Scalia rejected the Government's argument that thermal devices detected "only heat radiating from the external surface of the house." Just as a thermal imager captures only heat emanating from a house, Scalia pointed out, so also a powerful directional microphone picks up only sound emanating from a house. He also rejected the argument that the thermal imaging was constitutional because it did not "detect private activities occurring in private areas." He countered that the Fourth Amendment's protection of the home had never been tied to measurement of the quality or quantity of the information obtained. A test that depended on the type of information obtained would not be workable.[14] Scalia tied his test to the degree of privacy accepted when the Fourth Amendment was adopted, while acknowledging that advances in technology complicated the analysis. "We have said that the Fourth Amendment draws 'a firm line at the entrance to the house.' . . . That line, we think, must be not only firm but also bright. . . . Where, as here, the Government uses a device that is not in general public use, to explore details of the home that would previously have been unknowable without physical intrusion, the surveillance is a 'search' and is presumptively unreasonable without a warrant."[15]

Stevens's conservative dissent distinguished "off-the-wall" observations from "through-the-wall" surveillance, a pragmatic opinion that took a narrow view of precedent. "Any member of the public might notice that one part of a house is warmer than another part or a nearby building if, for example, rainwater evaporates or snow melts at different rates across its surface."[16] Stevens's dissent was both passionate and not unpersuasive. Not only was the standard hopelessly vague, Stevens argued, but it would have the perverse effect of reducing constitutional protections just when the threats of intrusive technology increased the most. Finally, there was no good reason to adopt a new rule. *Katz* worked.[17]

Later, the Supreme Court confronted "whether the attachment of a Global-Positioning-System (GPS) tracking device to an individual's vehicle, and subsequent use of that device to monitor the vehicle's movements on public streets, constituted a search or seizure within the meaning of the Fourth Amendment." The FBI and the District of Columbia Police attached the device to Antoine Jones's car for four weeks, and the information obtained helped convict him of a federal narcotics offense. Because a search warrant had expired, the attachment was viewed as a warrantless search. All nine Justices voted to reverse with five Justices (Scalia joined by Roberts, Kennedy, Thomas, and Sotomayor) adhering to one opinion and four (Alito joined by Ginsburg, Breyer, and Kagan) to another.

The first question in *United States v. Jones* (2012)[18] was whether the Government engaged in a Fourth Amendment search. Scalia's opinion reached back to the colonial period, especially a 1765 English case, and continued. "[O]ur Fourth Amendment jurisprudence was tied to Common Law trespass, at least until the latter half of the 20th century.... [O]ur law holds the property of every man so sacred that no man can ever set his foot upon his neighbour's close without his leave; if he does he is a trespasser, though he does no damage at all; if he will tread upon his neighbour's ground, he must justify it by law."[19] Since the Government physically invaded private property for the purpose of obtaining information, a technical trespass, there was a Fourth Amendment search.[20] Alito's concurring opinion concluded that "it is almost impossible to think of late-18th-century situations that are analogous to what took place in this case," so the historical analysis was not useful and the *Katz* standard should be applied directly.

Scalia's dissent in *Maryland v. King* (2013)[21] objected to the practice of swabbing the insides of the mouths of arrestees with a cotton swab or filter paper (known as a buccal swab) in order to create a DNA bank. Alonzo King was arrested in 2009 for assault for menacing a group of people with a shotgun. His DNA sample was checked against the DNA data base and it matched with DNA recovered from an unsolved 2003 rape. Over his objection that the taking of his DNA sample violated his Fourth Amendment rights, King was indicted, convicted, and sentenced to life imprisonment for the rape. A majority sustained the search.

For Scalia, the buccal swab was unconstitutional: "The Fourth Amendment forbids searching a person for evidence of a crime when there is no basis for believing the person is guilty of the crime or is in possession of incriminating evidence. That prohibition is categorical and without exception; it lies at the very heart of the Fourth Amendment."[22] The police action was tantamount to a "despised" and rejected general warrant used by the Crown during the colonial era. "The first Virginia Constitution declared that 'general warrants, whereby any officer or messenger may be commanded to search suspected places without evidence of a crime committed,' or to search a person 'whose offence is not particularly described and supported by evidence,' 'are grievous and oppressive, and ought not to be granted.'"[23] Scalia scoffed that the majority's rationale for taking the DNA was to identify King at "every stage of the criminal process." It took four months to match King's sample with the FBI national DNA database, a fact the majority ignored. Moreover, the database did not include King's identity, since the 2003 rapist was unknown. "Solving unsolved crimes is a noble objective, but it occupies a lower place in the American pantheon of noble objectives than the protection of our people from suspicionless law-enforcement searches. The Fourth Amendment must prevail.... I doubt that the proud men who wrote the charter of our liberties would have been so eager to open their mouths for royal inspection."[24]

An anonymous 911 caller reported that a truck ran her off the road, and gave the truck's model, make, and license plate number, along with location, and direction. After locating the truck, police officers followed the truck for five minutes, and stopped it for drunk driving even though they found no suspicious activity. They smelled marijuana when they approached the truck and found a large stash. The Court affirmed the conviction in *Navarette v. California* (2014)[25] on the ground that while an anonymous tip alone did not provide the required reasonable suspicion, the officer's corroboration of the truck's description, location, and direction established that the tip was reliable.

Scalia was incredulous. Neither the tip nor the corroboration tended to prove anything relating to reasonable suspicion of *drunk driving*. Moreover, the caller did not accuse the driver of the truck of drunken driving, and cars are run off the road for many reasons. The police conceded that the driving was irreproachable and unsuspicious. The suggestion of drunk driving "not only went uncorroborated; it was affirmatively undermined." Drunk drivers do not suddenly drive soberly.

> All the malevolent 911 caller need do is assert a traffic violation, and the targeted car will be stopped, forcibly if necessary, by the police. If the driver turns out not to be drunk (which will almost always be the case), the caller need fear no consequence, even if 911 knows his identity. After all, he never alleged drunkenness, but merely called in a traffic violation – and on that point his word is as good as his victim's. Drunken driving is a serious matter, but so is the loss of our freedom to come and go as we please without police interference.... After today's opinion all of us on the road, and not just drug dealers, are at risk of having our freedom of movement curtailed on suspicion of drunkenness, based upon a phone tip, true or false, of a single instance of careless driving.[26]

Scalia was the author of another liberal Fourth Amendment opinion in *Florida v. Jardines* (2013),[27] which held that sending a drug-sniffing dog onto a homeowner's porch constituted a search and seizure. The homeowner's implicit invitation did not extend to the police's bringing a trained dog to conduct a search on his porch, which is part of his home.[28] There was virtually no discussion of views or the law at the founding.

SPECIAL CASES

Three situations are discussed in the order in which Scalia encountered them, starting with workplace searches of government employees, where the government was the employer. Scalia's dissenting opinion in *National Treasury Employees Union v.*

Von Raab (1989)[29] was liberal, although not the most liberal in the case. Involved were searches of employees' excretions to ascertain whether they were using drugs or alcohol. The Court's opinion upheld mandatory drug testing through urinalysis of employees of the U.S. Customs Service who sought transfer or promotion to certain positions. "It is readily apparent that the Government has a compelling interest in insuring that front-line interdiction personnel are physically fit, and have unimpeachable integrity and judgment.... Against these valid public interests we must weigh the interference with individual liberty that results from requiring these classes of employees to undergo a urine test."[30] Marshall, joined by Brennan, dissented in a sweeping opinion, which maintained that probable cause was necessary for a search.

Scalia's narrower dissent acknowledged that "Customs Service employees can constitutionally be denied promotion, or even dismissed, for a single instance of drug use, at home or at work.... The issue here is what steps can be constitutionally taken to *detect* such drug use." "What is absent in the Government's justifications – notably absent, revealingly absent – is the recitation of even *a single instance* in which any of the speculated horrible actually occurred." In fact, the agency's head testified before Congress that there was no drug problem.[31] Scalia concluded:

> The only plausible explanation, in my view, is what the Commissioner himself offered in the concluding memorandum to Customs Service employees announcing the program: "Implementation of the drug screening program would set an important example in our country's struggle with this most serious threat to our national security."... What better way to show that the Government is serious about its "war on drugs" than to subject its employees on the front line of that war to this invasion of their privacy and affront to their dignity?... I think it obvious that this justification is unacceptable; that the impairment of individual liberties cannot be the means of making a point that symbolism, even symbolism for so worthy a cause as the abolition of unlawful drugs, cannot validate an otherwise unreasonable search.... Those who lose because of the lack of understanding that begot the present exercise in symbolism are not just the Customs Service employees, whose dignity is thus offended, but all of us – who suffer a coarsening of our national manners that ultimately give the Fourth Amendment its content, and who become subject to the administration of federal officials whose respect for our privacy can hardly be greater that the small respect they have been taught to have for their own.[32]

Terry v. Ohio (1968)[33] permits police officers to stop a suspicious-looking person and frisk him to ensure that he is not carrying a weapon, so that he can continue his investigation without fear of deadly violence; the frisk is not connected with investigating a crime. The police stopped Timothy Dickerson and ascertained he was not carrying a weapon. Nevertheless, engaging in a broader search, the officer felt a small lump, which, after squeezing and otherwise manipulating, concluded was crack cocaine in cellophane. He reached into Dickerson's pocket and retrieved a small plastic bag containing a small amount of crack cocaine. Dickerson, who was charged with possession of a controlled substance, did not complain about the stop or frisk, only the follow-up search. The Court's opinion in *Minnesota v. Dickerson* (1993)[34] said police officers may seize contraband detected during the lawful execution of a *Terry* search, along the lines of an officer's seizing contraband that is in plain view. However, the officer overstepped his powers when he continued the search after he ascertained there was no weapon.

Scalia's concurrence was originalist in approach. "There is good evidence, I think, that the 'stop' portion of the *Terry* 'stop-and-frisk' holding accords with the common law – that it had been considered reasonable to detain suspicious persons for purposes of demanding that they give an account of themselves. This is suggested, in particular, by the so-called night-walker statutes, and their common law antecedents." About the search, he stated: "I am unaware, however, of any precedent for a physical search of a person thus temporarily detained for questioning," as opposed to someone who had been arrested. "I frankly doubt, moreover, whether the fiercely proud men who adopted our Fourth Amendment would have allowed themselves to be subjected, on mere *suspicion* of being armed and dangerous, to such indignity."[35]

The warrantless search of automobiles had had a long history starting with *Carroll v. United States* (1925), which recognized "a necessary difference between a search of a store, dwelling house, or other structure in respect of which a proper official warrant readily may be obtained, and a search of a ship, motor boat, wagon or automobile, for contraband goods, where it is not practicable to secure a warrant because the vehicle can be quickly moved out of the locality or jurisdiction in which the warrant must be sought."[36] Debate over automobile searches divided those who endorsed a bright-line *per se* warrant requirement (to which exceptions were attached)[37] from those who opted for a reasonable-under-the circumstances approach.

The Burger Court held that the Fourth Amendment permitted a police officer who had made a lawful custodial arrest of an occupant of an automobile to search the vehicle's passenger compartment incident to the arrest in *New York v. Belton* (1981).[38] Considerations of safety allowed a search within the immediate vicinity to deny the person arrested access to weapons. Returning to the problem more than two decades later, the Court held in *Thornton v. United States* (2004)[39] that *Belton* applied when the officer first makes contact with the arrestee after he stepped out of his vehicle. By the time of the search Marcus Thornton was handcuffed and sitting in the back of a patrol car. Nonetheless, Rehnquist wrote for the Court: "In all relevant respects, the arrest of a suspect who is next to a vehicle presents identical concerns regarding officer safety and the destruction of evidence as the arrest of one who is inside the vehicle."[40]

Concurring in the result, Scalia denounced the Court's opinion as perpetuating a legal fiction and urged the Court to tackle head-on the difficult problem of searches of automobiles when the occupant had left the vehicle. "When officer safety or imminent evidence concealment or destruction is at issue, officers should not have to make fine judgments in the heat of the moment. But in the context of a general evidence-gathering search, the state interests that might justify any overbreadth are far less compelling. A motorist may be arrested for a wide variety of offenses; in many cases, there is no reasonable basis to believe relevant evidence might be found in the car.... I would therefore limit *Belton* searches to cases where it is reasonable to believe evidence relevant to the crime of arrest might be found in the vehicle."[41]

Scalia's concurring opinion in *Arizona v. Gant* (2009)[42] began:

> To determine what is an 'unreasonable' search within the meaning of the Fourth Amendment, we look first to the historical practices the Framers sought to preserve; if those provide inadequate guidance, we apply traditional standards of reasonableness.... Since the historical scope of officers' authority to search vehicles incident to arrest is uncertain, ... traditional standards of reasonableness govern.... In my view we should simply abandon the *Belton-Thornton* charade of officer safety and overrule those cases. I would hold that a vehicle search incident to an arrest is *ipso facto* 'reasonable' only when the object of the search is evidence of the crime for which the arrest was made, or of another crime that the officer has probable cause to believe occurred.[43]

Because Gant was arrested for driving without a license, a crime for which no evidence was likely to be found in the vehicle, Scalia judged the search unlawful.[44]

Balancing the needs of the state and of the suspect, the Supreme Court announced in 1975 that the Fourth Amendment requires a "prompt" judicial determination of probable cause as a prerequisite to an extended pretrial detention and established a "practical compromise" between the rights of individuals and the realities of law enforcement.[45] *County of Riverside v. McLaughlin* (1991)[46] considered the length of time a state could delay bringing an individual arrested without a warrant before a judicial officer. O'Connor's majority opinion rejected a requirement of an immediate judicial determination and held that a delay of forty-eight hours satisfied the requirement.[47] Marshall's one-paragraph dissent, joined by Blackmun and Stevens, stated simply that "a probable cause hearing is sufficiently 'prompt' ... only when provided immediately upon completion of the 'administrative steps incident to arrest.'"[48] There was no place in the law for balancing a defendant's interests with anything else.

Scalia's solo dissent also rejected the majority's balancing. The balance had been struck "in 1791 and has been generally adhered to by the traditions of our society ever since." An early-nineteenth-century rule required the sovereign to take an arrested person to a justice or magistrate "as soon as he reasonably can," which for Scalia was twenty-four hours. He wrote:

> While in recent years we have invented novel applications of the Fourth Amendment to release the unquestionably guilty, we today repudiate one of its core applications so that the presumptively innocent may be left in jail. Hereinafter a law-abiding citizen wrongfully arrested may be compelled to await the grace of a

Dickensian bureaucratic machine, as it churns its cycle for up to two days – never once given the opportunity to show a judge that there is absolutely no reason to hold him, that a mistake has been made. In my view, this is the image of a system of justice that has lost its ancient sense of priority, a system that few Americans would recognize as our own.[49]

9

Fifth Amendment: Criminal Applications

Scalia's philosophy contained a number of liberal patches covering a considerable area of the Fifth Amendment's application to criminal prosecution. One perennial concern of his helped liberals, namely, judicial restraint. Thus, courts could not amend indictments, the law had to advise people what conduct was unlawful, and judges had to respect constitutional mandates even when they produced illogical results. These principles led to many cases in which Scalia's liberal views contrasted with those of the majority.

DUE PROCESS CLAUSE

Scalia had to do without any company when he dissented in *United States v. Resendiz-Ponce* (2007).[1] The Court held that an indictment charging Juan Resendiz-Ponce with attempting to reenter the United States illegally was not defective for failure to allege an overt act as a substantial step toward completion of his goal; the indictment sufficiently alleged the necessary overt act when it alleged that the defendant "attempted to enter the United States" at a particular time and place.[2] Scalia described the Court's argument "as certainly irrelevant, and probably incorrect to boot." It was irrelevant because "we have always required the elements of a crime to be explicitly set forth in the indictment, *whether or not* they are fairly called to mind by the mere name of the crime.... Would we say that, in a prosecution for first-degree murder, the element of 'malice aforethought' could be omitted from the indictment simply because it is commonly understood, and the law has always required it? Certainly not."[3] Because Scalia rejected the argument on which the Government and the Court relied, he was required to decide whether the error was, on the one hand, structural error or, on the other hand, harmless error. He chose the former and dissented.

Wilbert K. Rogers was convicted of second-degree murder for having stabbed James Bowdery, who did not die until fifteen months after the stabbing. Under common law, there was no murder (only manslaughter) unless the victim died within a year and a day of the crime. On Rogers's appeal, the Tennessee Supreme Court abolished the rule and upheld the conviction because the reasons for the rule – mostly the limited ability of science to determine the cause of death – no longer existed. Rogers claimed that this action violated his right to due process. Rogers relied heavily on the Supreme Court's decision in *Bouie v. City of Columbia, Georgia* (1964),[4] where the city prosecuted blacks for trespass when they refused to leave a lunch counter when the owner ordered them to leave. The trespass statute under which they were convicted required, however, that the owner give notice to alleged trespassers *before* they entered the property. In *Bouie*, Georgia's highest court reconstrued the trespass statute by holding that the defendants' refusal to leave when ordered to do so constituted trespass. The Supreme Court reversed.

O'Connor's majority opinion affirmed the murder conviction in *Rogers v. Tennessee* (2001).[5] While the *Ex Post Facto* Clause contained in Article I did not apply to judicial proceedings, "a judicial alteration of a common-law doctrine of criminal law violates the principle of fair warning, and hence must not be given retroactive effect, only where it is 'unexpected and indefensible by reference to the law which had been expressed prior to the conduct in issue.'"[6] Many states had legislatively or judicially abolished the rule and the rule was not firmly entrenched as part of Tennessee law, O'Connor noted. Thus, Rogers was on notice that the year-and-a-day rule might be changed. "There is, in short, nothing to indicate that the Tennessee court's abolition of the rule in petitioner's case represented an exercise of the sort of unfair and arbitrary judicial action against which the Due Process Clause aims to protect."[7]

Scalia's dissent passionately and convincingly argued Rogers's side of the case on the due process ground.[8]

The Court today approves the conviction of a man for a murder that was not murder (but only manslaughter) when the offense was committed. It thus violates a principle – encapsulated in the maxim *nulla poena sine lege* – which "dates from the ancient Greeks" and has been described as one of the most "widely held value judgment[s] in the entire history of human thought." . . . Today's opinion produces, moreover, a curious constitution that only a judge could love. One in which (by virtue of the *Ex Post Facto* Clause) the elected representatives of all the people cannot retroactively make murder what was not murder when the act was committed; but in which unelected judges can do precisely that. One in which the predictability of parliamentary lawmaking cannot validate the retroactive creation of crime, but the predictability of judicial lawmaking can do so. I do not believe this is the system that the Framers envisioned – or, for that matter, that any reasonable person would imagine.[9]

Scalia's continued: "To begin with, let us be clear that the law here was altered after the fact. Petitioner, whatever else he was guilty of, was innocent of murder."

The Court retroactively changed the *elements* of a crime. "Though the Court spends some time questioning whether the year-and-a-day rule was ever truly established in Tennessee . . . the Supreme Court of Tennessee said it was . . . and this reasonable reading of state law by the State's highest court is binding upon us." Scalia continued: "Even if I agreed with the Court that the Due Process Clause is violated only when there is lack of 'fair warning' of the impending retroactive change, I would not find such warning here. The 'fair warning' to which *Bouie* and subsequent cases referred was not 'fair warning that the law might be changed,' but fair warning *of what constituted the crime at the time of the offense.* . . . *Bouie* rested squarely upon "[t]he fundamental principle that 'the required criminal law must have existed when the conduct in issue occurred.'"[10] While courts can apply the penal law to new fact patterns, they cannot engage in "a square, head-on *overruling* of prior law."[11]

Two cases involved statutes that the Court majority, over Scalia's objections, construed (or rewrote in Scalia's view) in order to find them constitutional. Scalia would have reversed both convictions on the ground that the statutes, properly construed, violated either the First Amendment in *United States v. X-Citement Video, Inc.* (1994)[12] or the Due Process Clause in *Skilling v. United States* (2010).[13] While Scalia's decisions were Constitution-based, he saw the principal vice in both cases the rampant improper rewriting of federal statutes as part of an effort to uphold convictions. The cases are discussed below in Chapter 29.

SELF-INCRIMINATION CLAUSE

Scalia wrote one liberal Self-Incrimination Clause opinion for the Court, although it was not the most liberal in the case. When Michael Blaine Shatzer was arrested for child abuse, he demanded a lawyer, he was not questioned, and he remained in custody. Two and one-half years later, the police sought to question him again in the correctional institution, and this time he responded without requesting an attorney. The issue was whether the lapse of time permitted the prosecutor to introduce the second set of answers. Building on prior cases, Scalia's opinion for the Court created a presumption that the passage of fourteen days would constitute a "break in custody" that would exempt the second questioning from the *Miranda* Rule; it would not do to have no standard.[14] Thomas wanted the two-week rule to be absolute. Stevens argued that two weeks was too short, but agreed that two-and-one-half years was a sufficient gap.

DOUBLE JEOPARDY CLAUSE

The Double Jeopardy Clause states that, "nor shall any person be subject for the same offense to be twice put in jeopardy of life or limb."[15] It bars a subsequent prosecution for the same offense (or, alternatively and more generously phrased, for the same conduct) following a disposition on the merits, and applies to dispositions both by a judge and by a jury.[16] The issues are often technical and a prosecution's mistake or miscalculation can have serious consequences.

In one of the two cases under review Alvin Dixon had been released on bail from a drug charge conditioned on his staying away from drugs. He violated the order and the judge held him in contempt and sentenced him to 180 days in jail. But when the state then brought far more serious charges under the state's drug laws, Dixon claimed violation of double jeopardy. *United States v. Dixon* (1993)[17] faced whether the clause barred prosecution of the underlying criminal charge after a defendant had been sentenced for violating a related civil-protection order, in other words, the effect of the nature of the first proceeding on the application of double jeopardy. Four Justices, led by Stevens, said that the standard was whether the two prosecutions arose out of the same conduct, and concluded that the Double Jeopardy Clause protected Dixon.[18] Four others said the clause applied only when the *elements* of the two offenses were identical, and criminal contempt required the additional element of disobedience of a judge's order.

Fully in neither camp, Scalia first concluded, along with Stevens, that the clause applied to nonsummary criminal-contempt prosecutions and that "criminal contempt, at least in its nonsummary form, 'is a crime in every fundamental effect,'" a liberal position that favored defendants.[19] But he took the textualist and conservative standard of requiring the same elements in order to sustain a claim of double jeopardy. He nevertheless concluded that Dixon met the stricter standard and freed Dixon. "Because Dixon's drug offense did not include any element not contained in his previous contempt offense, his subsequent prosecution violates the Double Jeopardy Clause."[20]

Scalia could not have picked a worse case to demonstrate the liberal aspects of his view of double jeopardy. Many, mostly liberal, commentators condemned Scalia. David M. Zlotnick accused him of "aggravated historical malpractice" for ignoring Blackstone, actions of the First Congress, and early Supreme Court cases. "[I]n a variety of ways, Scalia's *Dixon* opinion embodies the kind of judicial lawmaking that stands in opposition to his vision of a constitutional law of clear and inviolable rules." Zlotnick examined the opinion's consequences: "Because of the confusion created by *Dixon*, battered women and their allies in law enforcement and the legal community have been unable to take advantage of one of the best tools for combating domestic violence – civil protection followed by swift criminal contempt sanctions."[21] Liberal Yale Professor Akhil Amar also challenged Scalia's treatment of criminal contempt: "The mind boggles here: Contempt of court and drug pushing are somehow "the same"; a fifteen-year offense is somehow "lesser" than a six-month offense; because someone is found guilty of a small crime he must be set free on his big crime – and all this from Justice Scalia, who usually claims he believes in plain meaning and common sense."[22] But despite the unusual situation in *Dixon*, Scalia's position was certainly liberal and probably the better rule despite its occasional injustice.[23] He resisted the trap that creates bad law from hard cases. Someone should not be incarcerated or even prosecuted twice by the same sovereign for essentially the same crime. It has the potential for abuse.

No one could have imagined the next case when the Bill of Rights was adopted. A Missouri trial court convicted Larry Thomas of attempted robbery and first-degree felony murder in connection with a hold-up of an auto-parts store in St. Louis and sentenced him to consecutive terms of fifteen years for attempted robbery and for life imprisonment for felony murder, with the robbery sentence to run first. The state's supreme court affirmed his conviction and sentence on direct appeal. In a later case, however, that court concluded that the legislature had not intended separate punishments for the two crimes. The Governor commuted to time served Thomas's sentence for attempted robbery, and he began serving his life sentence for felony murder. Thomas claimed, however, that he was entitled to immediate release since he could not be required to serve both sentences, and he had completed service of the shorter sentence.

Kennedy's opinion for the Court in *Jones v. Thomas* (1989)[24] accepted that the original sentence was unlawful, but concluded that the Missouri courts had not violated Thomas's rights: "The answer turns on the interest that the Double Jeopardy Clause seeks to protect. Our cases establish that in the multiple-punishment context, that interest is 'limited to ensuring that the total punishment did not exceed that authorized by the legislature.'... Given that, in its application to the case before us, 'the Double Jeopardy Clause does no more than prevent the sentencing court from prescribing greater punishment than the legislature intended.'"[25] Kennedy distinguished two cases on which Thomas relied, which held that when a trial court improperly sentenced a defendant to both imprisonment and a fine and he had fully paid his fine, double jeopardy prevented his being required to serve his prison term.[26] Conceding that "strict application" of precedent would support Thomas, Kennedy said that the cases involved two different types of punishment for a single criminal act, but cited no authority for the distinction. For Kennedy, it was "anomalous" to make the order of imposition of consecutive sentences determinative and Thomas should not be treated better because he received consecutive sentences rather than the less severe concurrent sentences. "[N]either the Double Jeopardy Clause nor any other constitutional provision exists to provide unjustified windfalls."[27]

Scalia's liberal dissent argued persuasively that the fine+imprisonment cases were directly in point.[28] "It is difficult to imagine, however, why the difference between a credit and a refund... should be of constitutional dimensions insofar as the Double Jeopardy Clause is concerned." To Kennedy's assertion that the result provided Thomas with a windfall, Scalia responded: "The Double Jeopardy Clause is not a device designed to assure effectuation of legislative intent – but to the contrary is often the means of frustrating it." He also rejected Kennedy's confining the Clause only to the aggregate sentence.[29]

[T]he Double Jeopardy Clause is a statute of repose for sentences as well as for proceedings.... The Double Jeopardy Clause is and has always been, not a provision to assure reason and justice in the particular case, but the embodiment of technical, prophylactic rules that require the Government to turn square corners. Whenever it is applied to release a criminal deserving of punishment it frustrates justice in the particular case, but for the greater purpose of assuring repose in the totality of criminal prosecutions and sentences.... With technical rules, above all others, it is imperative that we adhere strictly to what we have stated the rules to be. A technical rule with equitable exceptions is no rule at all. Three strikes is out. The State broke the rules here, and must abide by the result.[30]

The issue in *Smith v. Massachusetts* (2005)[31] was simply stated but not necessarily easy – when is an acquittal an acquittal? Writing for the majority, Scalia held that a defendant had been acquitted on one count of a multicount indictment when a judge granted a motion for acquittal on that count and entered the acquittal on the docket, because the acquittal was final under state law.[32] While no showing of prejudice was required, "[t]he Double Jeopardy Clause's guarantee cannot be allowed to become a potential snare for those who reasonably rely on it. If, after a facially unqualified midtrial dismissal of one count, the trial has proceeded to the defendant's introduction of evidence, the acquittal must be treated as final, unless the availability of reconsideration has been plainly established by pre-existing rule or case authority expressly applicable to midtrial rulings on the sufficiency of the evidence. That requirement was not met here."[33] Originalism played virtually no role in Scalia's reasoning. Ginsburg's conservative dissent emphasized that the Double Jeopardy Clause did not generally bar trial judges from reconsidering the grant of a midtrial motion to acquit on one of several counts.[34] While Ginsburg made good points, it was Scalia, not Ginsburg, who examined the practical implications of the rule and voted for the defendant.

SENTENCING – "VIOLENT FELONIES"

This category is noteworthy because Scalia started out his liberal dissents on statutory grounds, but ended up throwing out a federal statute because it violated due process. The Armed Career Criminal Act (ACCA)[35] provided for a fifteen-year mandatory sentence for having been convicted of three violent felonies. "Violent felony" was any felony that "(i) has as an element the use, or threatened use of physical force against the person of another; or (ii) is burglary, arson, or extortion, involves use of explosives, or otherwise involves conduct that presents a serious potential risk of physical injury to another."

Alphonso James claimed that one prior felony conviction, a Florida conviction for attempted burglary, did not qualify under the residual "otherwise" clause. Affirming the enhanced sentence in *James v. United States* (2007),[36] Alito concluded for the

Court that attempted burglary was "comparable to that posed by its closest ana-
log among the enumerated offenses – here, completed burglary." Even if some
attempted burglaries do not qualify, the crime is risky because many attempted
burglaries often end with a confrontation with a police officer or someone else.
"While it may be reasonable to infer that the risks presented by the enumerated offenses involve a risk of this magnitude, it does not follow that an offense
that presents a lesser risk necessarily fails to qualify. Nothing in the language of
§ 924(e)(2)(B)(ii) rules out the possibility that an offense may present 'a serious
risk of physical injury to another' without presenting as great a risk as any of the
enumerated offenses."[37]

Scalia dissented, beginning with the criticism that the Court "utterly fails to do
what this Court is supposed to do: provide guidance concrete enough for" district
judges. (Scalia referred to the Court's "puny solution."[38]) He employed the canon of
construction, *ejusdem generis*, that the specific follows the general. "[T]he application of that principle suggests that what the residual provision means by the general
phrase 'conduct that presents a serious potential risk of physical injury to another'
is conduct that resembles, insofar as the degree of such risk is concerned, the previously enumerated crimes." The requirement that the degree of risk be similar to
that of the enumerated crimes meant that it be no less than the risk posed by the
least dangerous of those enumerated crimes," which was burglary.[39] Scalia asked,
"does attempted burglary categorically involve conduct that poses at least as much
risk of physical injury to another as completed burglary? Contrary to what the Court
says, the answer must be no."[40] Scalia cited the extra risk flowing from the fact that
the offender actually entered the building in the completed offense. Ergo, Scalia
concluded, an attempted burglary possesses a less serious risk of physical injury than
burglary, and thus cannot be a predicate "violent felony."

The cases kept coming. After Larry Begay was convicted of being a felon in
possession of a firearm, the trial judge ruled that he had three convictions for
violent felonies, including one for driving under the influence (DUI), and enhanced
his sentence. Breyer's majority opinion concluded that the listed crimes, unlike
DUI, involve purposeful, violent, and aggressive conduct, and the Court reversed.
Concurring, Scalia concluded that "the rule of lenity brings me to concur in the
judgment of the Court."[41] His opinion was less liberal than the Court's,[42] but more
liberal than Alito's dissent, which voted to affirm.

Scalia rejected enhancement when the issue was "whether the Florida felony
offense of battery by '[a]ctually and intentionally touch[ing]' another person, has
as an element the use . . . of physical force against the person of another,' and thus
constitutes a 'violent felony' under the Armed Career Criminal Act." "In the context of a statutory definition of '*violent* felony,' the phrase 'physical force' means
violent force – that is, force capable of causing physical pain or injury to another
person."[43]

Scalia threw up his hands in 2011, when the Court held that intentional flight from law-enforcement officers by vehicle was a "violent felony." "The residual-clause series will be endless and we will be doing ad hoc application of ACCA to the vast majority of state criminal offenses until the cows come home." His dissent raised a constitutional objection:

> What does violate the Constitution is approving the enforcement of a sentencing statute that does not "give a person of ordinary intelligence fair notice" of its reach, and that permits, indeed invites, arbitrary enforcement. . . . The Court's ever-evolving interpretation of the residual clause will keep defendants and judges guessing for years to come. The reality is that the phrase "otherwise involves conduct that presents a serious potential risk of physical injury to another" does not clearly define the crimes that will subject defendants to the greatly increased ACCA penalties. It is not the job of this Court to impose a clarity which the text itself does not honestly contain.[44]

When the Supreme Court refused to grant *certiorari* in a quartet of cases involving the concept of "violent felony," Scalia alone dissented: "Since our ACCA cases are incomprehensible to judges, the statute obviously does not give 'person[s] of ordinary intelligence fair notice of its reach.' . . . I would grant *certiorari*, declare ACCA's residual provision unconstitutionally vague, and ring down the curtain on the ACCA farce playing in federal courts throughout the Nation."[45]

As with the Confrontation Clause, Scalia's persistence paid off when seven Justices held the residual clause unconstitutionally vague in *Johnson v. United States* (2015)[46]:

> Two features of the residual clause conspire to make it unconstitutionally vague. In the first place, the residual clause leaves grave uncertainty about how to estimate the risk poses by a crime. It ties the judicial assessment of risk to a judicially imagined "ordinary case" of a crime, not to real-world facts or statutory elements. How does one go about deciding what kind of conduct the "ordinary case" of a crime involves? . . . At the same time, the residual clause leaves uncertainty about how much risk it takes for a crime to qualify as a violent felony. It is one thing to apply an imprecise "serious potential risk" standard to real-world facts; it is quite another to apply it to a judge-imagined abstraction.[47]

Scalia was similarly pragmatic in rejecting the pull of *stare decisis*. "The doctrine of *stare decisis* allows us to revisit an earlier decision where experience with its application reveals that it is unworkable. . . . Unlike other judicial mistakes that need correction, the error of having rejected a vagueness challenge manifests itself precisely in subsequent judicial decisions; the inability of later decisions to impart the predictability that the earlier opinion forecast. Here, the experience of the federal courts leaves no doubt about the unavoidable uncertainty and arbitrariness of adjudications under the residual clause."[48] Alito alone dissented: the statute satisfied the Constitution and, in any event, *stare decisis* should sustain it; statutes should be interpreted, if possible, to avoid constitutional problems.[49] Alito's dissent sounded like Scalia's frequent criticisms of the Justices: "The Court is tired of the Armed Career Criminal Act of 1984 (ACCA) and in particular its residual clause. Anxious to rid our docket of bothersome residual clause cases, the Court is willing to do what it takes to get the job done."[50]

10

Sixth Amendment: Right to Trial by Jury

Article III, § 2, cl. 3, of the Constitution provides: "The Trial of all Crimes, except in cases of Impeachment, shall be by Jury." The Sixth Amendment reads: "In all criminal prosecutions, the accused shall enjoy the right to a speedy and public trial, by an impartial jury of the State and district wherein the crime shall have been committed, which district shall have been previously ascertained by law." This chapter concerns the allocation of functions between the judge and jury in criminal cases.

For Scalia the right to trial by jury in a criminal case occupied a special place among constitutional rights; "When this Court deals with the content of this guarantee – the only one to appear in both the body of the Constitution and the Bill of Rights – it is operating upon the spinal column of American democracy.... The right to trial by jury in criminal cases was the only guarantee common to the 12 state constitutions and predated the Constitutional Convention, and it has appeared in the constitution of every State to enter the Union thereafter."[1] "Just as suffrage ensures the people's ultimate control in the legislative and executive branches, jury trial is meant to ensure their control in the judiciary."[2] Although juries may be tougher on defendants than judges in some situations, the position that the Constitution requires submission of the issue to the jury is classified as liberal, especially since defendants can waive trial by jury.

The first two cases involve presumptions, such as that a letter placed in a mail box is delivered within a reasonable time, which are allowed in civil cases but not in criminal cases. Presumptions tend to interfere with the requirement that juries decide the guilt or innocence of a defendant, because presumptions, especially mandatory presumptions, can put the thumb of the judge on the prosecutor's side of the scale. A California jury had convicted Eugene Carella for grand theft for failure to return a rented car after the trial judge instructed the jury that intent to commit theft by fraud is presumed if someone who rents personal property fails to return it within twenty days after the expiration of a rental agreement and that embezzlement of a vehicle is presumed if someone willfully and intentionally fails to return the vehicle to the owner within five days after the rental agreement expired.[3] After the Supreme Court reversed the conviction, the California courts decided that the instructions constituted harmless error, which meant it did not contribute to the defendant's conviction or was "unimportant in relation to everything else the jury considered on the issue in question."[4]

The Court unanimously reversed in *Carella v. California* (1989).[5] Scalia wrote a concurring opinion that emphasized a subtle but important point, namely, "that the harmless error analysis applicable in assessing a mandatory conclusive presumption is wholly unlike the typical form of such analysis. In the usual case the harmlessness determination requires consideration of the 'trial record as a whole' . . . in order to decide whether the fact supported by the improperly admitted evidence was in any event overwhelmingly established by other evidence." In the ordinary case the jury found the elements of the crime beyond a reasonable doubt. In this case the jury never decided the question of Carella's intent. "Findings made by a judge cannot cure deficiencies in a jury's finding as to the guilt or innocence of a defendant resulting from the court's failure to instruct it to find an element of a crime."[6]

Brandishing weapons, Dale Yates and an accomplice robbed a store, during which the accomplice and another person were killed. South Carolina charged Yates with felony murder. Here, too, the Supreme Court had previously decided that the instructions unconstitutionally shifted the burden of proof. On retrial the trial judge instructed the jury that to convict it had to find that Yates acted with malice, which was the intention to kill, but also charged that the "willful, deliberate, and unlawful act without any just cause or excuse" implied malice and that "malice is implied or presumed from the use of a deadly weapon." This prompted a second reversal and remand. When the state courts found the errors were harmless, the Supreme Court held in *Yates v. Evatt* (1991)[7] that the instructions permitted the jury to consider the presumptions along with the evidence of malice, and that was reversible error.

Scalia's concurrence was both more conservative and more liberal than the Court's. He first found the "deadly weapon" presumption harmless error on the basis of a somewhat different reading of the instructions, a more conservative view. The "unlawful act" presumption was not harmless error and required reversal, but on a ground that required reversal regardless of the other evidence in the case. The jury never "actually rested its verdict on evidence establishing the presumed fact beyond a reasonable doubt, independent of the presumption."[8] The amount of evidence was irrelevant because under the instruction

the jury [was] examining the evidence *with the wrong question in mind*. Not whether it established malice beyond a reasonable doubt, but whether it was sufficient to overcome (rebut) the improper presumption. . . . Given the nature of the instruction here, then, to determine from the "entire record" that the error is "harmless" would be to answer a purely hypothetical question, *viz.*, whether if the jury *had been*

instructed properly, it *would have* found that the State proved the existence of
malice beyond a reasonable doubt. Such a hypothetical inquiry is inconsistent with
the harmless-error standard.[9]

A federal jury convicted Ellis E. Neder, Jr., of various types and counts of fraud.
It was undisputed that the district court erred in refusing to submit to the jury the
issue of materiality of the alleged tax fraud, as Neder had requested. Affirming in
Neder v. United States (1999),[10] Rehnquist's opinion recognized that some errors,
but not others, automatically required reversal. "Unlike such defects as the complete
deprivation of counsel or trial before a biased judge, an instruction that omits an
element of the offense does not *necessarily* render a criminal trial fundamentally
unfair or an unreliable vehicle for determining guilt or innocence."[11] Failure of the
jury to find an essential element of the crime was not a structural error. Deciding
that "no jury could reasonably find that Neder's failure to report substantial amounts
of income on his tax returns was not a 'material matter,'" the Court ruled that
the error was harmless with respect to Neder, who had underreported his income
a total of $5 million over two years and whose summation did not argue lack of
materiality.[12]

Scalia began his dissent with the passage quoted at the start of the chapter on the
centrality of the right to trial by jury, then continued:

> The right to be tried by a jury in a criminal case obviously means the right to
> have a jury determine whether the defendant has been proved guilty of the crime
> charged. . . . The Court . . . lets the defendant's sentence stand, *because we judges
> can tell that he is unquestionably guilty.* . . . The constitutionally required step that
> was omitted here is distinctive, in that the basis for it is precisely that, absent
> voluntary waiver of the jury right, *the Constitution does not trust judges to make
> determinations of criminal guilt"* . . . [D]epriving the criminal defendant of a jury
> verdict is *structural error.* . . . Harmless-error review applies only when the jury *actu-
> ally renders a verdict* – that is, when it has found the defendant guilty of all the
> elements of a crime. . . . The right to render the verdict in criminal prosecutions
> belongs exclusively to the jury.[13]

This chapter's second subject is the role of juries in sentencing. Judges impose sentences after conviction by a jury or the judge. Traditionally, and without anyone
thinking that the process was unconstitutional, trial judges "enhanced" sentences
based on prior arrests or convictions and on information contained in reports prepared by probation officers. Scalia led the Court in attacking sentencing enhancement by judges, arguing that the enhancement factor was often part of the crime for
which sentence was imposed and, under the Sixth Amendment, was for the jury to
determine. Court liberals, and occasionally originalist Thomas, usually joined him
in ruling that the Sixth Amendment preempted state procedures. Scalia relied in
part on the pivotal role of the jury in the minds of the founding generation. Scalia's

specific references to original understanding, however, were few. He had an uphill battle to gain recognition of the importance of the jury.

The question presented in *Almendarez-Torres v. United States* (1998)[14] was whether the enhancement factor was an element of the crime for the jury or a permissible sentencing consideration for the judge. The statute, 18 U.S.C. § 1326(a), provided for a prison term of up to two years for a previously deported alien to return to the United States without permission. Added later, § 1326(b) provided for a sentence of up to twenty years if the initial "deportation was subsequent to a conviction of an aggravated felony." The district court imposed a sentence of eighty-five months following conviction based on an indictment that did not mention Almendarez-Torres's earlier aggravated-assault conviction. The largely conservative majority affirmed on the ground that Congress intended to make subsection (b) a sentencing factor rather than a separate crime. "[N]either the statute nor the Constitution requires the Government to charge the factor that it mentions, an earlier conviction, in the indictment. . . . [T]he sentencing factor at issue here – recidivism – is a traditional, if not the most traditional, basis for a sentencing court's increasing an offender's sentence."[15]

Scalia dissented. Increasing a sentence as a matter of discretion because the defendant had a prior felony conviction is not the same thing as a longer sentence for a more serious crime spelled out in the criminal statute. "[T]he *relevant* question for present purposes is not whether prior felony conviction is 'typically' used as a sentencing factor, but rather whether, in statutes that provide higher maximum sentences for crimes committed by convicted felons, prior conviction is 'typically' treated as a mere sentence enhancement or rather as an element of a separate offense. The answer to that question is the latter."[16]

A state appellate court reversed an enhanced sentence that was based in part on a conviction for assault with a deadly weapon. Relying on additional facts, the trial judge increased the sentence on resentencing. In *Monge v. California* (1998)[17] a Court majority upheld the longer sentence on the ground that the Double Jeopardy Clause did not apply.[18] Scalia, however, saw the problem as a judge's unconstitutionally displacing a jury. "I do not believe that that distinction is (as the Court seems to assume) simply a matter of the label affixed to each fact by the legislature." For example, a state could not create a crime of "knowingly causing injury to another," bearing a sentence of thirty days in prison, but subject to substantial sentencing enhancements imposed by the judge depending upon the nature of the defendant's intent and other surrounding circumstances. The Bill of Rights cannot be so easily circumvented. Although California's system is not nearly that sinister, it takes the first step down the road."[19]

The Court finally accepted Scalia's argument in *Apprendi v. New Jersey* (2000).[20] After Charles C. Apprendi, Jr., pleaded guilty to firearms charges, the sentencing judge enhanced his sentence under a statute that permitted increase upon his finding that the crime was racially motivated. Stevens's opinion reversed on the ground that the Due Process Clause of the Fourteenth Amendment required any fact increasing the penalty for a state crime beyond the prescribed statutory maximum – other than the fact of a prior conviction – to be submitted to a jury and proved beyond a reasonable doubt. What New Jersey had deemed a "sentencing factor" was in reality an element of the crime. Stevens's largely originalist opinion expounded on both the important role of the jury and the limited role of the judge in the framing era and beyond.[21]

Scalia joined Stevens's opinion and wrote a short concurrence of his own, which said that leaving enhancements to a judge may or may not give better results, but that was not the system envisaged by the Constitution:

> (Judges, it is sometimes necessary to remind ourselves, are part of the State) . . . The founders of the American Republic were not prepared to leave [criminal justice] to the State. . . . What ultimately demolishes the case for the dissenters is that they are unable to say what the right to trial by jury *does* guarantee if, as they assert, it does not guarantee – what it has been assumed to guarantee throughout our history – the right to have a jury determine those facts that determine the maximum sentence the law allows. . . . [The Constitution] means what it says. And the guarantee that in "all criminal prosecutions, the accused shall enjoy the right to trial, by an impartial jury" has no intelligible context unless it means that all the facts which must exist in order to subject the defendant to a legally prescribed punishment *must* be found by the jury.[22]

Three cases that explored the reach of *Apprendi*. *Ring v. Arizona* (2002)[23] held that *Walton v. Arizona* (1990)[24] was no longer law, and that the Sixth Amendment required the jury to find the aggravating sentencing factor that authorized the death penalty. Concurring, Scalia "favored the States' freedom to develop their own capital sentencing procedures (already erroneously abridged by *Furman* [*v. Georgia*[25]]) over the logic of the *Apprendi* principle." But he expressed concern "that our people's traditional belief in the right of trial by jury is in perilous decline. That decline is bound to be confirmed, if not accelerated, by the repeated spectacle of a man's going to his death because *a judge* found that an aggravating factor existed. We cannot preserve our veneration for the protection of the jury in criminal cases if we render ourselves callous to the need for that protection by regularly imposing the death penalty without it."[26]

Scalia's opinion in *Blakely v. Washington* (2004)[27] established that "the relevant statutory maximum is not the maximum sentence a judge may impose after finding additional facts, but the maximum he may impose *without* any additional findings." A state judge had increased a sentence beyond the statutory maximum based on his finding that the crime involved "deliberate cruelty." Scalia explained that "the judge's authority to sentence derives wholly from the jury's verdict. Without that restriction, the jury would not exercise the control the Framers intended. . . . [T]he very reason the Framers put a jury-trial guarantee in the Constitution is that they were unwilling to trust government to mark out the role of the jury."[28] Dissenting, O'Connor argued that the case spelled the death knell for sentencing guidelines, including federal, an outcome the Constitution did not require. Breyer's dissent noted that all alternatives give more power to the prosecutor, increase disparity in sentencing, or add complexity and expense.[29]

In the third *Apprendi* follow-up, *Oregon v. Ice* (2009),[30] Scalia was on the losing end of a 5–4 decision that gave the judge the power to decide whether to impose consecutive as opposed to concurrent sentences. Ginsburg's opinion for the Court decided that "historical practice and respect for state sovereignty . . . counsel against extending *Apprendi*'s rule to the imposition of sentences for discrete crimes. The decision to impose sentences consecutively is not within the jury function that 'extends down centuries into the common law,'" citing *Apprendi*.[31] Scalia's dissent called the Court's opinion "formalistic" and "artificial," creating "a strange exception to the treasured right of trial by jury." "For many defendants, the difference between consecutive and concurrent sentences is more important than a jury verdict of innocence on any single count," a nonoriginalist argument. "Any fact – other than that of a prior conviction – that increases the maximum punishment to which a defendant may be sentenced must be admitted by the defendant or proved beyond a reasonable doubt to a jury."[32] Ordinary jury practice was irrelevant; the Sixth Amendment as interpreted by *Apprendi* was dispositive.

Historically, criminal statutes specified the maximum penalties for crimes but gave sentencing judges wide leeway, which caused great disparity in sentences for similar criminal conduct and led judges to punish blacks more harshly than whites. The Sentencing Reform Act of 1984 made federal sentences almost determinate. A Sentencing Commission fixed narrow ranges for sentences based primarily on the nature and seriousness of the crime, with enhancements or reductions based on a large number of identified factors, such as whether the defendant was armed, whether he had committed a more serious crime than the one of which he was convicted, whether he was the principal figure in the crime, whether he accepted responsibility for his actions, and so on. A judge had limited power to deviate from the Guidelines and there was an appeal to the court of appeals based on failure to follow the Sentencing Guidelines.[33]

For the crime of possession of 92.5 grams of cocaine, the Sentencing Guidelines mandated a maximum sentence of ten years for Freddie J. Booker, but, taking account his criminal record, the Guidelines provided for a maximum prison sentence of twenty years and ten months. Following the conviction, however, the trial judge held a hearing and concluded by a preponderance of the evidence that Booker had possessed an additional 566 grams of crack cocaine and was guilty of obstruction of justice. He sentenced Booker to thirty years. Booker appealed the sentence. The Court held in *United States v. Booker* (2005)[34] that the Guidelines could not meet constitutional muster so long as they were compulsory, and it declared them advisory only. Relying on *Apprendi* and *Blakely*, it also held that the imposition of an enhanced sentence based on the sentencing judge's determination of a fact (other than a prior conviction) not found by the jury or admitted by the defendant violated the Sixth Amendment.[35] Four opinions ranged from upholding the act as written (Breyer for four Justices)[36]; upholding the act but requiring jury trials of the Sixth Amendment issues; holding the act unconstitutional only as applied to issues essential to the resolution of *Booker* and postponing other issues for later cases[37]; and junking the whole statute. The last view was Scalia's.

Scalia unsuccessfully tried to have the Court take other cases. For example, the jury convicted Patrick Marlowe, a prison guard, of involuntary manslaughter in the death of one of the inmates, but the trial judge determined that Marlowe had possessed the "malice aforethought" required for second-degree murder, and increased his sentence from five years to life imprisonment.[38] Scalia alone dissented from the denial of *certiorari*. In another case the jury convicted Joseph Jones and others of distributing small amounts of crack cocaine, but acquitted them of conspiracy. The trial judge, however, found they had conspired and imposed longer sentences. Scalia dissented from the denial of *certiorari*: "This has gone on long enough. . . . We should put an end to the unbroken string of cases disregarding the Sixth Amendment – or to eliminate the Sixth Amendment difficulty by acknowledging that all sentences below the statutory maximum are substantially reasonable."[39]

Article III, § 2, cl. 3, mandates that "[t]he Trial of all Crimes . . . shall be held in the State where the said Crimes shall have been committed." Under the Sixth Amendment "the accused shall enjoy the right to a speedy and public trial, by an impartial jury of the State and district wherein the crime shall have been committed." The provisions protect a criminal defendant's right not to be prosecuted in a distant locale, as sometimes happened during the colonial era.[40] In *United States v. Rodriquez-Moreno* (1999)[41] the charge was kidnapping in the course of a drug transaction, during a portion of which the victim was held at gun point in Maryland. The prosecution took place in New Jersey. The Supreme Court affirmed the conviction and the enhanced sentence.

Scalia dissented. "I disagree with the Court . . . that the crime defined in 18 U.S.C. § 924(c)(1) is 'committed' either where the defendant commits the predicate offense or where he uses or carries the gun. It seems to me unmistakably clear from the text of the law that this crime can be committed only where the defendant *both* engages in the acts making up the predicate offense *and* uses or carries the gun." Scalia used a homey analogy. "The Court quite simply reads this requirement out of the statute – as though there were no difference between a statute making it a crime to steal a cookie and eat it (which could be prosecuted either in New Jersey, where the cookie was stolen, or in Maryland, where it was eaten) and a statute making it a crime to eat a cookie while robbing a bakery (which could be prosecuted only where the ingestive theft occurred)."[42]

11

Sixth Amendment: Confrontation Clause

The Confrontation Clause provides: "In all criminal trials, the accused shall enjoy the right . . . to be confronted with the witnesses against him." The clause was not controversial. While not all of the original or early states had bills or declarations of rights, seven of the eight that had them included a Confrontation Clause with little variation – ranging narrowly from the constitutional language, with or without the addition of "accusers," to "to meet the witnesses against him face to face."[1] The states' list of rights did not mention either an obligation or a requirement of an oath on the part of the witnesses or a right to cross-examination, although the former would have been subsumed under "witnesses" while the latter may have been subsumed under "confront."

Whatever the original understanding of the Confrontation Clause, which sailed through the ratification process, the Supreme Court has not been particularly helpful in pinning it down. Scalia noted in 2004: "Although the results of our decisions have generally been faithful to the original meaning of the Confrontation Clause, the same cannot be said of our rationales."[2] The rationale *du jour* when Scalia joined the Court was stated in *Ohio v. Roberts* (1980),[3] which allowed hearsay evidence when it fell within a "firmly rooted hearsay exception" or bore "particularized guarantees of trustworthiness." Establishing trustworthiness was the objective, with only a "preference" for face-to-face confrontation at trial. Proof of unavailability was required.[4] Scalia did more than dip his toe into the murky waters of the Confrontation Clause. This subject is the most conspicuous one in which he reinforced the primacy of the originalist (or, rather, textualist) interpretation of the Constitution to enhance the rights of criminal defendants. He wrote six liberal opinions, five of them for the Court, rewriting the law and changing the terms of the debate.

Four liberals joined Scalia's first-Term opinion in *Cruz v. New York* (1987).[5] The Court had previously held that one defendant's postarrest confession was not admissible against a codefendant, as to whom it was inadmissible hearsay, and the jury was so instructed. The risk, of course, was that the jury would ignore instructions to disregard a codefendant's confession. In *Cruz*, both defendants incriminated themselves, and the state courts had permitted the jury to hear both of their confessions at a joint trial, in part because there were indicia of reliability: the confessions interlocked. Scalia objected: "In fact, it seems to us that 'interlocking' bears a positively inverse relationship to devastation [caused by their introduction]. A codefendant's confession will be relatively harmless if the incriminating story it tells is different from that which the defendant himself is alleged to have told, but enormously damaging if it confirms, in all essential respects, the defendant's alleged confession.... The law cannot command respect if such an inexplicable exception to a supposed constitutional imperative is adopted."[6] Four Justices dissented on the grounds that it was the defendant's own confession that was devastating rather than the confession of a codefendant.[7]

The context moved to the realm of child abuse. A pair of cases raised the sensitive question whether a defendant on trial for a sex crime against children had a constitutional right to confront his child accusers. The unappealing defendant in *Coy v. Iowa* (1988)[8] was convicted of sexually assaulting two thirteen-year-old girls who were camping out in the backyard of the house next to his. It was a time of widespread concern, if not hysteria, about child abuse.[9] As authorized by a state statute, the state trial court placed a screen between John Coy and the girls, which blocked him from their sight. Writing for a majority of five, Scalia observed that the "perception that confrontation is essential to fairness has persisted over the centuries because there is much truth to it.... It is difficult to imagine a more obvious and damaging violation of the defendant's right to a face-to-face encounter," citing sources, which dated from Roman times and included Shakespeare.[10] To the state's argument that the screen was necessary to prevent trauma to the minors, Scalia replied that any possible exception must involve "something more than the type of generalized finding underlying such a statute when the exception is not 'firmly...rooted in our jurisprudence.'... That face-to-face presence may, unfortunately, upset the truthful rape victim or the abused child; but by the same token it may confound and undo the false accuser, or reveal the child coached by a malevolent adult. It is a truism that constitutional protections have costs." Scalia also relied on the word's derivation: "the word 'confront' ultimately derives from the preface 'con-' (from "contra" meaning 'against' or 'opposed') and the noun 'frons' (forehead)."[11] The opinion did not categorically require confrontation.

Dissenters argued that the protected right was not absolute and should yield to other important public policies. Absence of confrontation was permitted, O'Connor said, by numerous exceptions to the hearsay rule.[12] Rehnquist and Blackmun argued that the Iowa procedure did not defeat the purposes of the Confrontation Clause; since the testimony was under oath and subject to cross-examination, the defendant and the jurors saw the witnesses, and the jury saw the defendant, thus exposing his demeanor to the trier of fact.

The six-year-old girl victim and other child victims were permitted to testify in *Maryland v. Craig* (1990)[13] under a state statutory procedure that could be invoked upon a judicial finding that her testifying in a courtroom "will result in the child suffering serious emotional distress such that the child cannot reasonably communicate." Upon the receipt of sufficient expert testimony, the judge, prosecutor, and defense counsel were located in the room with the child victim, but defendant Sandra Ann Craig observed the proceeding through a one-way mirror that prevented the witness from seeing her.[14] The Court upheld the conviction, 5–4. O'Connor wrote: "The central concern of the Confrontation Clause is to ensure the reliability of the evidence against a criminal defendant by subjecting it to rigorous testing in the context of an adversary proceeding before the trier of fact. The word 'confront,' after all, also means a clashing of forces or ideas, thus carrying with it the notion of adversariness. . . . [W]e cannot say that face-to-face confrontation [with witnesses appearing at trial] is an indispensable element of the Sixth Amendment's guarantee of the right to confront one's accusers."[15]

Joined by three liberals, Scalia's dissent began: "Seldom has this Court failed so conspicuously to sustain a categorical guarantee of the Constitution against the tide of prevailing current opinion." The majority's statement that it cannot say that face-to-face confrontation is "'an indispensable element of the Sixth Amendment's guarantee of the right to confront one's accusers' . . . is rather like saying 'we cannot say that being tried before a jury is an indispensable element of the Sixth Amendment's guarantee of the right to jury trial.' . . . [T]he Confrontation Clause does not guarantee reliable evidence; it guarantees specific trial procedures that were thought to assure reliable evidence, undeniably among which was 'face-to-face confrontation.'"[16] Scalia also argued that the Court mischaracterized the state's interest as protection of victims of child abuse. They can be fully protected by not calling them as witnesses. "The State's interest here is in fact no more and no less than what the State's interest always is when it seeks to get a class of evidence admitted in criminal proceedings: more convictions of guilty defendants. That is not an unworthy interest, but it should not be dressed up as a humanitarian one. . . . In the last analysis, however, this debate is not an appropriate one. I have no need to defend the value of confrontation, because the Court has no authority to question it."[17]

The vote was nine to zero for reversal in the landmark case of *Crawford v. Washington* (2004),[18] although Rehnquist and O'Connor objected to overruling *Roberts* as unnecessary and unwise. Michael Crawford stabbed a man who allegedly tried to rape his wife Sylvia. Sylvia did not testify at Crawford's trial for assault and attempted murder because of the state's marital privilege. Instead, the state played for the jury Sylvia's incriminating tape-recorded statement to the police, which Crawford had no opportunity to cross-examine. Among the reasons for admission were that Sylvia was not shifting blame, she had direct knowledge as an eye-witness, she was describing recent events, and she was being questioned by a "neutral" law-enforcement officer. The prosecution argued that the tape recording refuted Crawford's claim of self-defense.[19] The Washington Supreme Court upheld Crawford's conviction after determining that Sylvia's statement was reliable.

Scalia's majority opinion took nine pages to trace the history of the Confrontation Clause through English and colonial history, concluding that the clause flatly bars "testimonial statements of a witness who did not appear at trial unless he was unavailable to testify and the defendant had had a prior opportunity for cross examination." He recognized that the Constitution's text does not alone resolve this case. One could plausibly read "witness against a defendant to mean those who actually testify at trial."[20] But the conclusion became obvious in the light of "the historical background of the Clause."[21] "[T]he principal evil at which the Confrontation Clause was directed was the civil-law mode of criminal procedure, and particularly its use of *ex parte* examinations as evidence against the accused."[22] While there may have been exceptions, "there is scant evidence that exceptions were invoked to admit *testimonial* statements against the accused in a *criminal* case."[23]

Roberts, moreover, was unworkable, Scalia said.[24] Repeatedly, lower courts used contradictory qualities to support the conclusion that prior statements were reliable. "The unpardonable vice of the *Roberts* test, however, is not its unpredictability, but its demonstrated capacity to admit core testimonial statements that the Confrontation Clause plainly meant to exclude." The Sixth Amendment "commands, not that evidence be reliable, but that reliability be assessed in a particular manner: by testing in the crucible of cross-examination."[25] Scalia's approach to the Confrontation Clause reflected his preference for bright-line solutions as well as textualism. Limited exceptions to the hearsay rule provided the outer limit of exemptions from the rule's rigors.

Two years later, Scalia fleshed out *Crawford* in the majority opinion in *Davis v. Washington* (2006),[26] which decided two cases of domestic violence where neither victim-spouse appeared at the trial and the prosecution introduced earlier statements each had made to the authorities. To be admissible, Scalia said, the statements had to be nontestimonial: "Statement are nontestimonial [under the Sixth Amendment] when made in the course of police interrogation under circumstances objectively indicating that the primary purpose of the interrogation is to enable police assistance to meet an ongoing emergency. They are testimonial when the circumstances objectively indicate that there is no such ongoing emergency, and that the primary purpose of the interrogation is to establish or prove past events potentially relevant to later criminal prosecution."[27] Part of the rationale for the distinction was that people are more apt to be truthful when they are trying to control a current emergency.

When the Court applied *Crawford* to scientific evidence, law-enforcement authorities objected. Under Massachusetts law, affidavits constituted *prima facie* evidence of what they stated. In *Melendez-Diaz v. Massachusetts* (2009)[28] Scalia, Stevens, Souter, Thomas, and Ginsburg reversed a conviction because the trial court admitted a scientific report attached to an affidavit without the testimony of any live witness. Scalia confronted arguments raised by the state, including that the affiants were not "accusatory" or "conventional" witnesses, but rather witnesses who provided neutral, scientific testing. Scalia argued that they certainly were "witnesses against" the defendant and that the argument was no more than that they are reliable and allegedly neutral, similar to the arguments *Crawford* rejected. Dire predictions of chaos were dubious, especially since some states already required the appearance of analysts, and their experience has not proven disruptive. States were free to adopt procedural rules, such as requiring a defendant to give early notice of his intent to confront the analyst. In sum, the case "involves little more than the application of our holding in *Crawford v. Washington*."[29]

Kennedy dissented in a pragmatic opinion joined by Roberts, Breyer, and Alito, which said that the Court imposed enormous costs on the criminal-justice system for a negligible benefit. The dissent accused the Court of "meddling" with the Confrontation Clause, which does not mention "testimonial." The clause speaks of "witnesses," and it deals with ordinary witnesses of the sort understood at the framing, a person who perceived an event relevant to a defendant's guilt, inasmuch as expert witnesses were rare at common law and do not possess the characteristics of ordinary witnesses.[30]

The spring of 2011 brought a severe setback for Scalia in *Michigan v. Bryant* (2011),[31] when the Court rejected a Confrontation Clause objection to the admission of a statement to the police of the victim of a shooting that identified the person who shot him. Creating an "objective" test that considered several factors to ascertain the primary purpose of the police in questioning the victim, the Court concluded the police had a primary purpose to enable police assistance to meet an ongoing emergency.[32]

Only Scalia and Ginsburg dissented despite the dubious factual basis for the Court's opinion. Scalia wrote: "Today's tale – a story of five officers conducting successive examinations of a dying man with the primary purpose, not of obtaining and preserving his testimony regarding his killer, but of protecting him, them, and others from a murderer somewhere on the loose – is so transparently false that professing to believe it demeans the institution. . . . [T]oday's opinion distorts our Confrontation Clause jurisprudence and leaves it in shambles. Instead of clarifying the law, the Court makes itself the obfuscator of last resort."[33] "Looking to the declarant's purpose (as we should), this is an absurdly easy case."[34] Scalia concluded: "For all I know, Bryant has received his just desserts. But he surely has not received them pursuant to the procedures that our Constitution requires. And what has been taken away from him has been taken away from us all."[35]

Forfeiture or waiver of rights is a major and sensitive part of constitutional law. Waiver is usually done during the proceeding, such as by failing to demand a jury trial within the allotted time or answering too many questions before asserting the Fifth Amendment privilege against self-incrimination. But it can also be accomplished by out-of-court conduct. Dwayne Giles shot and killed his girlfriend Brenda Avie. He claimed self-defense. When the state sought to introduce statements that Avie had given police who responded to a report of domestic violence about three weeks earlier, the California Supreme Court concluded that Giles had forfeited his right to confront Avie because his intentional criminal act made her unavailable to testify, and affirmed Giles's conviction for first-degree murder.

In *Giles v. California* (2008)[36] the Supreme Court (per Scalia) held that the Sixth Amendment confrontation right was not forfeited. Supporting Scalia were Roberts, Thomas, Alito, Souter, and Ginsburg – four conservatives and two liberals – while Breyer, Stevens, and Kennedy – two liberals and a moderate – dissented. Both sides purported to follow originalism while coming to opposite conclusions. A common-law doctrine, Scalia maintained, "permitted the introduction of statements of a witness who was 'detained' or 'kept away' by the 'means or procurement' of the defendant."[37] Relying on dictionaries, treatises, and cases, Scalia said that "general statements were made in the context of conduct *designed* to procure the unavailability of a witness. American courts never – prior to 1985 – invoked forfeiture outside the context of deliberate witness tampering," and the Confrontation Clause is "most naturally read as a reference to the right of confrontation at common law, admitting only those exceptions established at the time of the founding."[38]

Breyer's dissent argued that the rule of forfeiture was satisfied if the defendant's wrongful conduct prevented a witness from testifying. The exception was warranted by precedent, by the rule's purposes and objectives, and by the analogy to other cases, such as life-insurance law. Now, Giles can say anything he wants at his trial about what Avie supposedly did and said without contradiction. "Rather than limit forfeiture to instances where the defendant's act has absence of the witness as its *purpose*, the relevant cases suggest that the forfeiture rule would apply where the witness' absence was the *known consequence* of the defendant's wrongful act. . . . To the extent that it insists upon an additional showing of purpose, the Court . . . grants the defendant not fair treatment, but a windfall. I can find no history, no underlying purpose, no administrative condition, and no constitutional principle that requires this result."[39]

12

Sixth Amendment: Right to Counsel

None of the three cases in this section on a criminal defendant's right to counsel involves what can be described as the traditional right to counsel. *Gideon v. Wainright* (1963)[1] established a criminal defendant's right to have assigned counsel at his trial. In *Faretta v. California* (1975)[2] the Court held that a criminal defendant has a constitutional right to proceed *without* counsel when he voluntarily and intelligently elects to do so. Self-representation was permitted since the founding. A defendant's decision should be honored out of "that respect for the individual which is the lifeblood of the law."[3] Originalism played little role in these cases, largely because the Supreme Court had taken the rights of defendants far beyond what the framing era provided or imagined. In fact, Scalia noted that, "Defense counsel did not become a regular fixture of the criminal trial until the mid-1800's."[4]

In 2006 the Court considered whether a defendant's conviction following a trial judge's concededly erroneous disqualification of the defendant's choice of attorney must be reversed even when the defendant failed to present evidence of prejudice.[5] Put differently, does the harmless-error rule apply to the erroneous disqualification of counsel in a criminal cases? Writing for the Court in *United States v. Gonzalez-Lopez* (2006),[6] Scalia rejected the conservative dissent's argument that the Sixth Amendment required assistance of counsel, not a particular counsel, and that many rules stood in the way of a defendant's choosing his lawyer, including that the lawyer must be eligible to practice in the particular jurisdiction and must be available to try the case at the time set. "[T]he right at stake here is the right to counsel of choice, not the right to a fair trial; and that right was violated because the deprivation of counsel was erroneous. . . . The right to select counsel of one's choice . . . has never been derived from the Sixth Amendment's purpose of ensuring a fair trial. It has been regarded as the root meaning of the constitutional guarantee."[7] Crucial for Scalia was that "[i]t is impossible to know what different choices the rejected counsel would have made, and then to quantify the impact of those different choices on the outcome of the proceedings." Evaluation of the effect of a lost counsel cannot be compared with the failure to object to the admission of a document or to the testimony of a witness. Scalia's bright-line rule favored defendants.

The next two cases produced libertarian more than liberal opinions. No one considered which result represented the original understanding in *Indiana v. Edwards* (2008),[8] perhaps because it was unlikely that there was any. Breyer wrote for the Court: "This case focuses upon a criminal defendant whom a state court found mentally competent to stand trial if represented by counsel but not mentally competent to conduct the trial himself. We must decide whether in these circumstances the Constitution prohibits a State from insisting that the defendant proceed to trial with counsel, the State thereby denying the defendant the right to represent himself."[9] While earlier cases involved concededly competent defendants, who could not be deprived of the right to represent themselves, Breyer concluded that the goal of affirming human dignity was not furthered by allowing a defendant who lacked mental capacity to conduct his defense. In addition, "proceedings must not only be fair, they must 'appear fair to all who observe them,'" and that would not be the case with an impaired defendant representing himself.[10]

Scalia dissented. "In my view the Constitution does not permit a State to substitute its own perception of fairness for the defendant's right to make his own case before the jury – a specific right long understood as essential to a fair trial. . . . The [trial] court did not dispute that Edwards knowingly and intelligently waived his right to counsel. . . . Until today, the right of self-representation has been accorded the same respect as other constitutional guarantees."[11] Scalia also challenged the majority's reference to the dignity of the individual and the appearance of fairness. "[T]he dignity at issue is the supreme human dignity of being master of one's fate rather than a ward of the State – the dignity of individual choice. . . . To my knowledge we have never denied a defendant a right simply on the ground that it would make his trial appear less 'fair' to outside observers, and I would not inaugurate that principle here."[12] Because of the state's action, Scalia said, Edwards was not able to present to the jury the defense that he believed was most meritorious, namely, self-defense. "[T]o hold that a defendant may be deprived of the right to make legal arguments for acquittal simply because a state-selected agent has made different arguments on his behalf is, as Justice Frankfurter wrote in *Adams* [*v. United States ex rel. McCann*],[13] to 'imprison a man in his privileges and call it the Constitution.'"[14]

When the Court held that a criminal defendant had no constitutional right to represent himself in an appeal primarily because there was no constitutional right to appeal, and, in fact, "the right of appeal itself is of relatively recent origin,"[15] Scalia disagreed. "I have no doubt that the Framers of our Constitution, who were suspicious enough of government power – including judicial power – that they insisted upon a citizen's right to be judged by an independent jury of private citizens, would not have found acceptable the compulsory assignment of counsel *by the government* to plead a criminal defendant's case."[16]

Which view treats the defendant with more respect and autonomy? In the end the answer may turn on one's view of individual autonomy. What cannot be denied is that Scalia empowered the individual criminal defendant against the state and federal governments, which many would categorize as both liberal and libertarian.

13

Seventh Amendment: Right to Jury Trial

The Seventh Amendment provides: "In all Suits at common law, where the value in controversy shall exceed twenty dollars, the right of trial be a jury shall be preserved, and no fact tried by a jury, shall be otherwise re-examined in any Court of the United States, than according to the rules of the common law."[1] Jury trial in civil cases was a recurring demand during the colonial era, appeared in the Declaration of Independence, and was perhaps the strongest argument for a Bill of Rights. Juries were seen as an important political right, which resulted in jury nullification of unpopular laws and actions. The Seventh Amendment has played a role in a variety of contexts, including whether the judge or the jury traditionally decided a case or issue,[2] but also has governed cases that had no counterpart in 1791, such as a suit for employment discrimination or for a tax refund. The language and history of the Seventh Amendment seem to demand originalist analysis.

Reformers and advocates for efficiency have bemoaned the fact that the Seventh Amendment requires jury trials in classes of cases, such as automobile personal-injury cases, that no other country in the world mandates, including England. They have pointed out that the jury system is wasteful and prevents the growth of a body of precedent created by judicial decisions that would tend to equalize recovery. The Framers had more basic concerns. Those who pressed for the Seventh Amendment wanted to protect debtors and others with limited economic power, and that rationale is still applicable. The jury represented – indeed embodied – the ideals of populism, localism, duty, and civic virtue that were the essence of the original Bill of Rights.[3] A vote in favor of expanding the reach of the Seventh Amendment must be considered a liberal vote, even though liberal Justices, including Brennan, have tended to disagree.

Scalia laid out his broad conception of the Seventh Amendment in the federal courts in three opinions. As framed by Brennan for the seven-Justice majority in *Tull v. United States* (1987),[4] the "question for decision is whether the Seventh Amendment guaranteed [Tull] a right to a jury trial on both liability and amount of penalty in an action instituted by the Federal Government seeking civil penalties and injunctive relief under the Clean Water Act," which provided for a civil penalty not to exceed $10,000 per day.[5] Tull was indisputably entitled to a jury trial on the issue of liability, since a civil penalty suit was a species of an action in debt within the jurisdiction of the law courts. Open was whether Tull also had a right to trial by jury on the amount of the civil penalty. Brennan explained that the assessment of a civil penalty is not one of the Amendment's "most fundamental elements" and that the action to recover civil penalties usually seeks the amount fixed by Congress. "The assessment of civil penalties thus cannot be said to involve the 'substance of a common-law right to a trial by jury,' nor a 'fundamental element of a jury trial.' Since Congress itself may fix the civil penalties, it may delegate that determination to trial judges."[6]

Scalia, joined by Stevens, disagreed. Finding no common-law precedent, he examined the traditionally indivisible action for damages, which included both liability and damages.

> [T]he right to trial by jury on whether a civil penalty of unspecified amount is assessable also involves a right to trial by jury on what the amount should be. The fact that the Legislature could elect to fix the amount of the penalty has nothing to do with whether, if it chooses not to do so, that element comes within the jury-trial guarantee. Congress could, I suppose, create a private cause of action by one individual against another for a fixed amount of damages, but it surely does not follow that that if it creates such a cause of action *without* prescribing the amount of damages, that issue could be taken from the jury.... Since, as the Court correctly reasons, the proper analogue to a civil-fine action is the common-law action for debt, the Government need only prove liability by a preponderance of the evidence, but must, as in any action for debt, accept the amount of award determined not by its own officials but by 12 private citizens. If that tends to discourage the Government from proceeding in this fashion, I doubt that the Founding Fathers would be upset.[7]

Excepted from Seventh Amendment coverage have been cases involving "public rights." Precedent limited the concept to suits against the sovereign, which can set conditions on waiver of sovereign immunity. Those cases can be tried before tribunals other than Article III judges, such as judges who are part of the Executive Branch appointed under Article I. Departing from precedent, Brennan wrote that the public-rights exception was broader than suits against the sovereign. It included some cases under the Bankruptcy Act not involving monetary relief where the government was not a party.[8] Scalia dissented. "It is clear what we meant by public rights were not rights important to the public, or rights created by the public, but rights *of the public* – that is, rights pertaining to claims brought by or against the United States."[9] It was a jury-empowering opinion that also endorsed a bright line.

Whether the Seventh Amendment permitted a federal appeals court in a diversity case to set aside a jury verdict and enter judgment for a lesser amount had not been decided. New York law permitted that practice, and the Second Circuit ordered a new trial in a diversity case unless the plaintiff accepted an amount substantially less than the jury verdict. Writing for the Court, Ginsburg sought to reconcile New York law on judicial review with the Seventh Amendment, which limited "re-examin[ation]" of a jury verdict to common-law practices. "[N]othing in the Seventh Amendment . . . precludes appellate review of the trial judge's denial of a motion to set aside [a jury verdict] as excessive." The federal court is capable of performing the checking function, *i.e.*, that court can apply the State's "'deviates materially' standard in line with New York case law."[10]

Conservatives Rehnquist and Thomas joined Scalia's textualist and originalist dissent, which both supported juries and favored the plaintiff.[11] Scalia quoted Rule 59 of the Federal Rules of Civil Procedure, that "'[a] new trial may be granted . . . for any of the reasons for which new trials have heretofore been granted in action at law *in the courts of the United States*.' (Emphasis added.)."[12] Scalia explained that "the practice of *federal* appellate reexamination of facts found by a jury is precisely what the People of the several States considered *not* to be good legal policy in 1791. Indeed, so fearful were they of such a practice that the Constitution prohibited it by means of the Seventh Amendment."[13] "'[R]eexamination' of the facts found by a jury could be undertaken only by the trial court, and . . . appellate review was restricted to a writ of error which could challenge the judgment only upon matters of law."[14]

14

Habeas Corpus

In venerable *Ex parte Milligan* (1866)[1] a southerner was arrested while at home and not on a field of battle. The Supreme Court rejected trial in a military court and required trial before an Article III court. *Ex parte Quirin* (1942),[2] two major wars later, distinguished *Milligan* and unanimously upheld the trial, conviction, and execution by a *military* tribunal of Herbert Haupt, an American citizen who was charged with being a German spy. The *Quirin* Court found him subject to trial and punishment by a military tribunal for those acts, and held that his American citizenship did not change the result.

Following the September 11, 2001, al Qaeda terrorist attack, Congress passed a resolution authorizing the President to "use all necessary and appropriate force against those nations, organizations, or persons he determines planned, authorized, committed, or aided the terrorist attacks" or "harbored such organizations or persons, in order to prevent any future acts of international terrorism against the United States by such nations, organizations or persons" (Authorization for Use of Military Force or AUMF).[3] After President George W. Bush ordered American troops to Afghanistan, forces hostile to the Taliban seized Afghanistan resident Yaser Esam Hamdi and turned him over to the U.S. military. Eventually, he was transferred to the U.S. naval base in Guantanamo Bay and, when it was learned that he was a U.S. citizen, to a navel brig in the United States, where he was held without formal charges or proceedings and without access to counsel. Hamdi's father filed a petition for a writ of *habeas corpus* on the ground that Hamdi's detention violated the Fifth Amendment.

Hamdi v. Rumsfeld (2004)[4] decided that due process required a U.S. citizen being held as an enemy combatant to be given a meaningful opportunity to contest the factual basis for his detention. What follows is a discussion of the four opinions, beginning with the most conservative, Thomas's, and ending with the most liberal, Scalia's. Thomas, the sole dissenter, voted to affirm on the ground that the President can "unilaterally decide to detain an individual if the Executive deems this necessary for the public safety even if he is mistaken" about the individual's guilt or dangerousness, an opinion conspicuous for its rejection of civil liberties.[5]

O'Connor wrote for herself, Rehnquist, Kennedy, and Breyer, which made hers the plurality opinion but not the opinion of the Court. O'Connor did not reach the question of whether Article II of the Constitution provided authority to detain Hamdi, because she found that AUMF authorized his detention. Citing *Quirin*, she stated, "There is no bar to this Nation's holding one of its own citizens as an enemy combatant," and proceeded to evaluate the procedure under the statute under a balancing-of-interests test.[6] She concluded "that a citizen-detainee seeking to challenge his classification as an enemy combatant must receive notice of the factual basis for his classification, and a fair opportunity to rebut the Government's factual assertions before a neutral decisionmaker."[7]

More respectful of Hamdi's rights, Souter joined by Ginsburg opined that the AUMF failed to authorize Hamdi's detention. Detention required explicit congressional authority, as evidenced, *inter alia*, by AUMF's background as a repudiation of World War II internments.[8] Since the federal government rejected all claims that Taliban detainees were entitled to prisoner-of-war status, the Court could not rely on treaties, statutes, and Executive Orders relating to prisoners of war.[9] No authority allowed Hamdi's detention.

Scalia, with Stevens, took the most expansive view of Hamdi's rights: U.S. citizens possessed a right not to be imprisoned without due process. "The allegations here, of course, are no ordinary accusations of criminal activity. Yaser Esam Hamdi has been imprisoned because the Government believes he participated in the waging of war against the United States. The relevant question then is whether there is a different, special procedure for imprisonment of a citizen accused of wrongdoing *by aiding the enemy in wartime*."[10] Relying on Blackstone's *Commentaries*, the two Justices concluded the Constitution gave the government two and only two options to deal with a citizen who wages war against the United States – either prosecute him for treason or, if circumstances warrant, employ the Constitution's Suspension Clause, Art. I, § 9, cl. 2 ("The Privilege of the Writ of Habeas Corpus shall not be suspended, unless when in Cases of Rebellion or Invasion the public Safety may require it"), to remove the right to *habeas corpus*.

To the plurality opinion's assertion that "captured enemy combatants have traditionally been detained until the cessation of hostilities and then released," Scalia responded that the practice applied only to enemy aliens. "The tradition with respect to American citizens, however, has been quite different. Citizens aiding the enemy have been treated as traitors subject to the criminal process."[11] Scalia's historical discussion began in 1350 and ended with the treason statute, 18 U.S.C. § 2381. *Quirin* was a poorly reasoned decision hastily rendered in a *per curiam* order the day after oral argument, followed by executions of all defendants, including Haupt, one week later. "In my view [*Quirin*] seeks to revise *Milligan* rather than describe it."[12] Scalia conceded that he could not tell whether his formulation provided the proper tradeoff between safety and freedom, but that was not the point. "Whatever the general merits of the view that war silences law or modulates its voice, that view has no place in the interpretation and application of a Constitution designed precisely to confront war and, in a manner that accords with democratic principles, to accommodate it."[13] It was a powerful statement of the limitations of government power against a citizen.

Subsequent *habeas corpus* petitions arising out of hostilities in Afghanistan and Iraq were brought on behalf of *aliens* who were held in the American enclave at Guantanamo Bay, Cuba. Scalia voted against granting *habeas corpus* when the petitioner was an alien held outside the United States.[14] Scalia confined relief to U.S. citizens.

15

Separation of Powers and Federalism

A position leaning toward a strong or weak application of separation of powers says little about placement along the liberal-conservative spectrum, unlike many other constitutional rights. A possible exception is standing, denial of which tends to work in favor of corporate defendants. For that reason standing was considered earlier. Nevertheless, Scalia's strong application of separation of powers frequently operated to produce liberal outcomes. The most significant were those that related to statutory special prosecutors or, more formally, independent counsel, a position created in the wake of the Watergate scandal. But first, a case from Scalia's initial Term in which he alone relied on separation of powers.

Louis Vuitton, S.A., a French leather-goods manufacturer, sued for trademark infringement and obtained an injunction prohibiting infringement. When Vuitton uncovered violations of the injunction, its attorneys secured appointment as special counsel to prosecute a criminal-contempt action for violation of the injunction, which led to the conviction of several defendants, whom the judge sentenced to prison terms of up to five years. The Supreme Court reversed the judgment in *Young v. United States* (1987)[1] and held, first, that "the initiation of contempt proceedings to punish obedience to court orders is part of the judicial function. . . . Courts cannot be at the mercy of another Branch in deciding whether such proceedings should be initiated."[2] "While contempt proceedings are sufficiently criminal in nature to warrant the imposition of many procedural protections, their fundamental purpose is to preserve respect for the judicial system itself."[3] However, the prosecutor must be independent. "Private attorneys appointed to prosecute a criminal contempt action represent the United States, not the party that is the beneficiary of the court order allegedly violated."[4] The four most liberal Justices voted to affirm the conviction on the ground that any error was harmless, a position that strains credulity.[5]

Scalia's concurred. "Prosecution of individuals who disregard court orders (except orders necessary to protect the courts' ability to function) is not an exercise of '[t]he judicial power of the United States,' U.S. Const., Art. III, §§ 1, 2. . . . The judicial power is the power to decide, in accordance with law, who should prevail in a case or controversy. . . . It is accordingly well established that the judicial power does not generally include the power to prosecute crimes."[6] Judges have inherent power to prosecute individuals for contempt only when necessary to protect the court's ability to conduct proceedings before it. Scalia cited *The Federalist* No. 78 and Supreme Court cases going back to 1812 and 1821. With the exception of one discredited line of cases that included *In re Debs* (1895),[7] "no holding of this Court has ever found inherent power to punish those violating court judgments with contempt, much less to appoint officers to prosecute such contempts."[8] No Justice joined his sensible concurrence.[9]

Under the popular post-Watergate Ethics in Government Act the Attorney General, upon receipt of information suggesting that a senior government official violated the law, was required to conduct a limited investigation and, if there were reasonable grounds to warrant further investigation, was required to apply to a division of the federal courts (the Special Division) for the appointment of an independent counsel (or, as some called her, a special prosecutor). The independent counsel would have the powers of the Attorney General and Department of Justice. Only the Attorney General could remove the independent counsel and then only for cause. Finally, there was a provision for congressional oversight and an obligation to provide reports to Congress.[10] Virtually every important liberal and many others supported the Act.[11] When independent counsel Alexia Morrison subpoenaed Theodore B. Olson, then Assistant Attorney General for the Office of Legal Counsel, to produce records, Olson refused and moved to quash the subpoena on the ground the Act was unconstitutional. The Court upheld the Act 8–1 in *Morrison v. Olson* (1988).[12]

While the case presented fundamental issues of executive power and separation of powers, the majority barely nodded to historical origins. Rehnquist's formalistic opinion rejected Olson's claim that "the powers vested in the Special Division by the Act conflicted with Article III of the Constitution. . . . [T]he power itself derives from the Appointments Clause, a source of authority for judicial action that is independent of Article III." Article II's Appointments Clause provides for the President to appoint "Officers of the United States," but "Congress may by Law vest the Appointment of such Inferior Officers, as they think proper, in the President alone, in the Courts of Law, or in the Heads of Departments."[13] While there may be a requirement that there can be no "incongruity between the functions normally performed by the courts and the performance of their duty to appoint," none was present.[14] Independent counsel had limited duties and limited jurisdiction.[15] The final issue was "whether, taken as a whole, the Act violates the separation of powers by reducing the President's ability to control the prosecutorial powers wielded by independent counsel." Relying heavily on *The Federalist* Nos. 47–51, eight Justices said no. The Attorney General must request the appointment of independent counsel and his power is defined on the basis of facts submitted by the Attorney General. "Most importantly, the Attorney General retains the power to remove the counsel for 'good cause,' a power that we have already concluded provides the Executive with substantial ability to ensure that the laws are 'faithfully executed' by an independent counsel."[16]

Scalia was not only unimpressed, he was offended by the majority's analysis, including its rejection of sources that he considered almost sacrosanct. Among them was *The Federalist* No. 73, that "the great security against a gradual concentration of the several powers in the same department consists in giving to those who administer each department the necessary constitutional means and personal motives to resist encroachment of the others. The provision for defense must in this, as it all other cases, be made commensurate to the dangers of attack. . . . That is what this suit is about. Power."[17] "The fundamental separation-of-powers principles that the Constitution embodies are not to be derived from some judicially imagined matrix, but from the sum total of the individual separation-of-powers provisions that the Constitution set forth. Only by considering them one-by-one does the full shape of the Constitution's separation-of-powers principles emerge. It is nonsensical to interpret those provisions themselves in light of some general 'separation-of-powers principles' dreamed up by the Court, . . . [but] must be interpreted to mean what they were understood to mean when the people ratified them."[18] The doctrine must be enforced when failure causes a distortion of the structure of government. "The executive Power shall be vested in a President of the United States," which, he explained, "does not mean *some of* the executive power, but *all* of the executive power. . . . The Court devotes most of its attention to such relatively technical details as the Appointments Clause and removal power, addressing only briefly and only at the end of its opinion the separation of powers. As my prologue suggests, I think that has it backwards."[19]

> [T]he decision of the Court of Appeals invalidating the present statute must be upheld on fundamental separation of powers principles if the following two questions are answered affirmatively: (1) Is the conduct of a criminal prosecution (and of an investigation to decide whether to prosecute) the exercise of purely executive power? (2) Does the statute deprive the President of the United States of exclusive control over that power? Surprising to say, the Court appears to concede an affirmative answer to both questions, but seeks to avoid the inevitable conclusion that, since the statute vests some purely executive power in a person who is not the President of the United States, it is void.[20]

The power to remove independent counsel for "good cause" has traditionally been considered an impediment to effective presidential control, Scalia argued.[21] The Attorney General's alleged discretion on whether to refer a matter to the Special Division was a chimera: "He had a duty to [refer] unless he could conclude that there were '*no reasonable grounds to believe*' not that prosecution was warranted, but merely that '*further investigation* was warranted.'" Morrison was the only person in the Executive Branch the President cannot fire at will. Also, everyone has limited duties, but within her sphere she has the full powers of the Department of Justice.

"Inferior" ordinarily means "subordinate" to a superior officer, and independent counsel are in practice subordinate to no one. That is a necessary, but not sufficient, condition.[22] "Balancing tests" have no place in separation-of-powers analysis, Scalia maintained. Nor, obviously, does deference to the political branches that are accused of upsetting the constitutional balance.[23] The Act weakened the President and, particularly, with his relations with Congress.[24] Moreover, the majority position had no principled limiting ground.[25] "As far as I can discern from the Court's opinion, it is now open season upon the President's removal power for all executive offices. . . . The Court essentially says to the President: 'Trust us. We will make sure that you are able to accomplish your constitutional role.' I think the constitution gives the President – and the people – more protection than that."[26]

Scalia's final point was that the Court's opinion would undermine individual freedom. His main source was a memorable speech given by then Attorney General Robert Jackson to United States Attorneys in 1940.[27] Jackson described the great importance of prosecutors with limited resources deciding which cases to bring and the dangers of targeting defendants; with the large number of crimes on the books it was always possible to find at least a technical violation. Moreover, there were many institutional restraints on regular prosecutors, such as a practice of not prosecuting minor infractions. Scalia observed that the primary check against prosecutorial abuse was political. Federal prosecutors are subject to removal by the President if they do their jobs badly or discriminatorily. With independent counsel, there was absence of accountability. Also, there was no uniform application of the law and no tradition to follow in the office. "Today's decision on the basic issue of fragmentation of executive power is ungoverned by rule, and hence ungoverned by law."[28] It was largely a functional and pragmatic analysis, but it illuminated the reason separation of powers was important to the Framers.

The tyranny that a special prosecutor or counsel could (and did) create is the main basis for describing Scalia's position as liberal.[29] Checks and balances often make for inefficiency. But they exist to prevent over-hasty and unchecked exercises of power, including circumventing accountability to the electorate.[30] While Scalia might not have anticipated the full scope of subsequent abuses of special counsel, he recognized that unconstrained power was often harmful if not tyrannical. The Act was allowed to expire in 1999 largely for political reasons, although those reasons were intertwined with constitutional ones.[31]

The Sentencing Reform Act of 1984 imposed binding Sentencing Guidelines promulgated by the U.S. Sentencing Commission for convicted federal criminal defendants. The Commission consisted of legislators, judges, and others appointed by the President with the advice and consent of the Senate. Many liberal and good-government groups applauded the Act and Commission. Eight Justices rejected defendant John M. Mistretta's claim that the Sentencing Commission violated separation of powers. *Mistretta v. United States* (1989)[32] concluded that differentiated government power was pragmatic and flexible and that "the Framers did not require – and indeed rejected – the notion that the three Branches must be entirely separate and distinct." "[J]udicial rulemaking, at least with respect to some subjects, falls within [a] twilight area is no longer an issue for dispute," and was the same as other nonadjudicatory activities vested by Congress within the Judicial Branch, such as the promulgation of rules of procedure. "[T]he placement of the Sentencing Commission in the Judicial Branch has not increased the Branch's authority."[33] Service of three judges on the Sentencing Commission did not, for instance, "threaten, either in fact or in appearance, the impartiality of the Judicial Branch" or its constitutionally assigned functions.[34] Moreover, neither constitutional text nor historical practice barred service of active federal judges on independent commissions. Jackson served as prosecutor at the Nuremberg trials and Warren presided over the commission investigating the assassination of President Kennedy. "The Act does not, and could not under the Constitution, authorize the President to remove, or in any way diminish the status of Article III judges, as judges."[35]

Scalia's dissent was popular with the defense bar because the Guidelines tended to make sentences longer, even though its announced goal was to reduce arbitrary disparities in sentences. Unlike *Morrison v. Olson*, he did not discuss any negative operational consequences flowing from the composition of the Commission; his objection was more formalistic. Scalia concluded: "Today's decision follows the regrettable tendency of our recent separation-of-powers jurisprudence . . . to treat the Constitution as though it were no more than a generalized prescription that the functions of the Branches should not be commingled too much – how much is too much to be determined, case-by-case, by this Court. The Constitution is not that."[36]

The Eleventh Amendment bars the use of federal judicial power "in any suit in law or equity, commenced or prosecuted against one of the United States by Citizens of another State, or by Citizens or Subjects of any Foreign States." *Virginia Office for Protection & Advocacy v. Stewart* (2011)[37] considered whether the Eleventh Amendment barred a suit for prospective (injunctive) relief brought against state officials by another agency of the state. Its human context was an effort by plaintiff VOPA to obtain state records in order to improve community services, such as medical care and job training, for individuals with developmental disabilities. Over the dissents of Roberts and Alito, Scalia's opinion held that suit was not barred. The seminal case of *Ex parte Young* (1908)[38] created an exception to state sovereign immunity for suits against state officials to their stop ongoing violations of federal law. Although states were entitled to considerable deference and respect, not every offense to a state's dignity constituted a denial of sovereign immunity, Scalia concluded. His opinion both limited states' immunity and expanded assistance to the disabled.

16

Commerce Clause and Other Provisions

It is axiomatic to view Scalia as conservative on the scope of the Commerce Clause. That was confirmed by his dissenting opinion in *National Federation of Independent Business v. Sibelius* (2012) (*Affordable Care Act Case*).[1] Only one Scalia Commerce Clause opinion can be counted as liberal, *Gonzales v. Raich* (2005).[2] The federal Controlled Substances Act (CSA), enacted in 1970 as part of a comprehensive reordering of drug-abuse prevention, listed marijuana as a Schedule A drug, which indicated that it had no significant medical use. Medical users of marijuana brought an action to bar enforcement of the CSA against them. The liberal plurality framed the issue: "The question presented in this case is whether the power vested in Congress by Article I, § 8, of the Constitution '[t]o make all Laws which shall be necessary and proper for carrying into Execution' its authority to 'regulate Commerce with foreign Nations, among the several States,' included the power to prohibit the local cultivation and use of marijuana in compliance with California law." The plurality endorsed a broad Commerce Clause: "Our case law firmly establishes Congress' power to regulate purely local activities that are part of an economic 'class of activities' that have a substantial effect on interstate commerce."[3]

While the four most liberal Justices probably preferred virtually no limits on the federal government's power under the Commerce Clause, they were forced to bow to precedent. They distinguished cases, including *United States v. Lopez* (1995),[4] which invalidated the Gun-Free School Zones Act of 1990, on the ground that it "was a brief single-subject statute making it a crime for an individual to possess a gun in a school zone."[5] Unlike the activity regulated in *Lopez*, the ACA was part of a comprehensive economic and regulatory framework, like the New Deal statute involved in *Wickard v. Filburn* (1942),[6] where the Court upheld Agricultural Adjustment Act of 1938, which regulated all farming, including growing wheat for one's own consumption.[7]

Concurring in the result, Scalia presented a rationale that he described as "more nuanced." While he cited cases dating back to Marshall's opinion in *McCulloch*

v. *Maryland* (1819),[8] he did not tap typical originalist sources like *The Federalist*.[9] He agreed that ACA, unlike the statute in *Lopez*, was a comprehensive effort to deal with narcotics control. There was a difference in kind, however, between channels of interstate commerce, instrumentalities of interstate commerce, and persons and things in interstate commerce, on the one hand, and activities that "substantially affect" interstate commerce, on the other hand. The recitation of the last category, he said, "without explanation is misleading and incomplete. It is *misleading* because, unlike the channels, instruments, and agents of interstate commerce, activities that substantially affect interstate commerce are not themselves part of interstate commerce, and thus the power to regulate them cannot come from the Commerce Clause alone."[10] Power is derived from the Necessary and Proper Clause, on which *Wickard v. Filburn* relied.

> The regulation of an intrastate activity may be essential to a comprehensive regulation of interstate commerce even though the intrastate activity does not itself "substantially affect" interstate commerce.... Congress may regulate even noneconomic local activity if that regulation is a necessary part of a more general regulation of interstate commerce.... Congress may regulate noneconomic intrastate activities only where the failure to do so "could ... undercut" its regulation of interstate commerce.... Congress's authority to enact all of these prohibitions of intrastate controlled-substance activities depends only upon whether they are appropriate means of achieving the legitimate end of eradicating Schedule I substances from interstate commerce.[11]

Thomas dissented in *Raich* in a more pronounced originalist opinion, which argued that the meaning of the Necessary and Proper Clause in the late eighteenth century was too narrow to permit its use to support the result in *Raich*.[12]

In the *Affordable Care Act Case* Ginsburg, writing for four Justices, relied heavily on *Raich* along with *Wickard v. Filburn*. She argued that individuals were stopped from growing wheat "because of a prophesied future transaction (the eventual sale of that wheat in the interstate market). Congress' actions were even more rational in this case, where the future activity (the consumption of medical care) is certain to occur, the sole uncertainty being the time the activity will take place."[13] Scalia disagreed in dissent:

> The case upon which the Government principally relies to sustain the Individual Mandate under the Necessary and Proper Clause is *Gonzales v. Raich*. That case held that Congress could, in an effort to restrain the interstate market in marijuana, ban the local cultivation of that drug. *Raich* is no precedent for what Congress has done here. That case's prohibition of growing and of possession did not represent the expansion of the federal power to direct into a broad new field.... Moreover, *Raich* is far different from the Individual Mandate in another respect. The Court's opinion in *Raich* pointed out that the growing and possession prohibitions were the only practicable way of enabling the promotion of interstate traffic in marijuana to

be effectively enforced. Intrastate marijuana could no more be distinguished from interstate marijuana than, for example, endangered-species trophies obtained before the specie was federally protected can be distinguished from trophies obtained afterwards – which made it necessary and proper to prohibit the sale of all such trophies.[14]

Not only was regulation of marijuana part of a comprehensive scheme, Scalia argued, marijuana is fungible. Guns are not fungible. Medical care is not fungible. While the fungible nature of the regulated product was irrelevant to the Commerce Clause, no "intelligible scheme of regulation of the interstate market in guns could have as an appropriate means of effectuation the prohibition of guns within 1,000 feet of schools (and nowhere else)."[15] The regulation of guns in the vicinity of schools was not needed in order to serve a broader purpose. Scalia's position in *Raich* foretold his conservative position in evaluating the ACA.[16]

Although a vote for federal power usually is liberal in the sphere of federal regulation, the opposite is ordinarily true in criminal law. In *United States v. Kebodeaux* (2013)[17] the Court upheld the application of the Sex Offender Registration and Notification Act (SORNA) to a discharged soldier who had served his sentence, but who had failed to register as a sex offender under SORNA, enacted after he had moved. Seven Justices found sufficient federal interest and continuity, mostly because Kebodeaux was still required to register under the superseded Wetterling Act and therefore had not been unconditionally released from his obligation to the federal government.[18] While SORNA was tougher than the Wetterling Act, for example, it required registration within three days of a move rather than seven and set the maximum prison sentence for violation as ten years rather than one year, the majority said the two acts were similar enough to provide continuity. It was a gossamer connection to the Constitution that may have been easier to accept because of the nature of the offense.

Thomas's prodefendant dissent rejected various grounds for federal power, including regulation of the militia and the Commerce Clause. "SORNA is a valid exercise of congressional authority only if it is 'necessary and proper for carrying into execution' one or more of those federal powers enumerated in the Constitution.... The Government has failed to identify any enumerated power that [SORNA's registration requirement] 'carries into Execution' in this case.... [T]he enumerated power that justified Kebodeaux's conviction does not justify requiring him to register as a sex offender now that he is a civilian."[19] Scalia joined and complemented Thomas with uncharacteristically dense language for a constitutional opinion:

> If I thought that SORNA's registration requirement were "reasonably adapted," *Raich, supra,* at 37, to carrying into execution some other, valid enactment, I would sustain it. But it is not. The lynchpin of the Court's reasoning is that Kebodeaux

was "subject to a federal registration requirement" – the Wetterling Act – at the time of the offense, and so the Necessary and Proper Clause "authorized Congress to modify the requirement as in SORNA and to apply the modified requirement to Kebodeaux.".... That does not establish, however, that the Wetterling Act's registration requirement was itself a valid exercise of any federal power, or that SORNA is designed to carry the Wetterling Act into execution. The former proposition is dubious, the latter obviously untrue.[20]

Standing was the unexpected context for Scalia's liberal dissent after Rafael Peretz had consented to having the *voir dire* in his federal prosecution heard by a Magistrate Judge appointed under Title I of the Constitution (without lifetime appointment) rather than an Article III district judge.[21] The Court had earlier held that a district judge could not delegate the *voir dire* to a Magistrate Judge over the objection of the defendant, but did not consider whether the district judge could do so when the defendant consented.[22] The majority in *Peretz* said that his consent forfeited his right to argue that the Constitution prohibited delegation. Scalia argued the Court should hear Peretz's constitutional argument; it would never decide the issue if it routinely rejected on the ground of forfeiture or waiver all cases where the defendant did not preserve his objection.[23] No federal prosecutor will ever consent to having a magistrate hear the *voir dire* when the defendant agrees, because the Supreme Court might grant *certiorari* and reverse the conviction. Allowing a defendant to argue an issue he may have forfeited was probably nonoriginalist and certainly liberal.[24]

Scalia also joined an opinion that denied standing to private individuals who sought to defend a California constitutional initiative that barred same-sex marriage, a position he otherwise endorsed in his opinions and votes. When a same-sex couple challenged the initiative, California officials declined to appeal an order that declared that the provision violated the U.S. Constitution. The official proponents of the initiative, however, sought to defend it on appeal. In an opinion by Roberts joined by Scalia, Ginsburg, Breyer, and Kagan, the Supreme Court concluded in *Hollingsworth v. Perry* (2013)[25] that they lacked Article III standing and dismissed the case. "We have never before upheld the standing of a private party to defend the constitutionality of a state statute when state officials have chosen not to. We decline to do so for the first time here."[26] Kennedy, joined by Thomas, Alito, and Sotomayor, dissented.

Finally, Scalia distanced himself from the Court's summary denial of *certiorari* in a criminal case where the question presented was: "Does a court owe deference to an executive agency's interpretation of a law that contemplates both criminal and administrative enforcement?"[27] For his negative answer Scalia relied on "the norm that legislatures, not executive officers, define crimes" and that a contrary answer would "upend ordinary principles of interpretation." He expressed his displeasure at a court of appeals' giving an executive agency a direct role in interpreting a federal criminal statute, which prejudices defendants as well as upsetting the balance created by separation of powers.[28] Nevertheless, having chastised the majority for its cramped view of separation of powers, Scalia concluded that the defendant had not sought review on the issue of deference, so denial of *certiorari* was correct. Scalia's dictum was not the exercise of judicial restraint.

PART IV

Scalia's Conflicted Constitutional Opinions *Speech*

Political Speech

Political Speech

Cases allow each side of the controversy to rely on important provisions of the Constitution, usually the Bill of Rights, and those are the ones discussed in this section. The first example, political speech, pits those who want to limit the power of wealthy individuals and entities to dominate elections against those who see restrictions on speech as unconstitutional. While most liberals may favor the former side of the dispute, it is not unanimous; constitutional arguments can be made on both sides.

That the cases discussed in this Part are among the most contentious of the past few decades should come as no surprise. They involve the "spinal column" of American democracy in cases involving limiting individual and corporate campaign speech, the life and death confrontation between antiabortion picketers and women trying to enter clinics for abortions or information on reproductive rights, an ultimate issue of the Free Exercise Clause of the First Amendment. Two other issues conclude the discussion. The first is the sensitive issue of peremptory challenges to jurors based on race, religion, and other characteristics. The other is liability for virtually unlimited punitive damages. What is conspicuous is the selective application of originalism in these distinct areas.

17

Political Speech

Since Scalia joined the Court, the most contentious issues on freedom of speech have been the constitutionality of limits on persons seeking to spend money on election campaigns and on entities, especially corporations, seeking to participate in the electoral process. Both sides of the debate claimed the mantle of freedom and liberty. For those who sought regulation of campaign finance, reasonable limitation on contributions and spending leveled the playing field and furthered democratic values. For others, including Scalia, they were unconstitutional and destructive attacks on the fundamental right of free speech. For Scalia, there was no such thing as too much speech, however lopsided it was. Another issue that occupied the Court was the constitutionality of laws restricting anonymous speech. Some saw disclosure as an antidote to the power of the wealthy to dominate the debate. This group included Scalia. To others, forced disclosure was an infringement on the constitutional right of free speech. That group included Thomas.

CONTRIBUTIONS AND EXPENDITURES

Buckley v. Valeo (1976),[1] which considered the Federal Election Campaign Act of 1971 (FECA), recognized election-campaign activities "operate in an area of the most fundamental First Amendment activities." The Court also recognized, however, that the Government has a compelling interest in the "prevention of corruption and the appearance of corruption," which the Court regarded as the *"quid pro quo"* variety, akin to bribery.[2] The Court held that FECA's contribution limitations passed constitutional muster because they represented a "marginal restriction upon the contributor's ability to engage in free communication," but that FECA's limitation on *independent* expenditures made to express one's own positions and not in coordination with a campaign restricted speech that was "at the core of our electoral process and of the First Amendment freedoms" and unconstitutional.[3]

Scalia's dissented in *Austin v. Michigan Chamber of Commerce* (1990),[4] where the Chamber, a corporation that received most of its funds from for-profit corporations, challenged a Michigan statute that criminalized a corporation's making independent expenditures supporting or opposing candidates in state elections. Marshall, joined by Rehnquist, Brennan, White, Blackmun, and Stevens upheld the statute. "We emphasize that the mere fact that corporations may accumulate large amounts of wealth is not the justification for [the statute]; rather, the unique state-conferred corporate structure that facilitates the amassing of large treasuries warrants the limit on independent expenditures. Corporate wealth can unfairly influence elections when it is deployed in the form of independent expenditures, just as it can when it assumes the guise of political contributions."[5] The media exemption was appropriate because of "the unique role that the press plays in 'informing and educating the public, offering criticism, and providing a forum for discussion and debate.'"[6]

Scalia (along with O'Connor) joined Kennedy's dissent and dissented separately. Kennedy wrote that "the Court upholds a direct restriction on the independent expenditure of funds for political speech for the first time in its history. . . . There is no reason that the free speech rights of an individual or an association of individuals should turn on the circumstance that funds used to engage in the speech came from a corporation."[7] Kennedy also objected to the blanket exemption for media corporations: "The web of corporate ownership that links media and nonmedia corporations is difficult to untangle for the purpose of any meaningful distinction." Kennedy noted that among the *amici curia* supporting the dissent were the American Civil Liberties Union, the Center for Public Interest Law, the National Organization for Women, and the Planned Parenthood Federation of America.[8]

Scalia was uncompromising: "It is rudimentary that the State cannot exact as the price of those special advantages the forfeit of First Amendment rights. . . . The categorical suspension of the right of any person, or of any association of persons, to speak out on political matters must be justified by a compelling state need. . . . Which is why the Court puts forward its second bad argument, the fact that corporations 'amas[s] large treasuries.'" Prohibiting independent contributions and singling out corporations while leaving individuals and unincorporated associations free rein was "irrational."[9] The reach of the Court's opinion disturbed Scalia: "Under this mode of analysis, virtually anything the Court deems politically undesirable can be turned into political corruption – by simply describing its effects as politically 'corrosive,' which is close enough to 'corruptive' to qualify. It is sad to think that the First Amendment will ultimately be brought down not by brute force but by poetic metaphor."[10]

Relying on Alexis de Tocqueville, who toured the United States in 1831 and who had recognized the importance of private associations, Scalia elevated libertarianism: "Governments, therefore, should not be the only active powers; associations ought, in democratic nations, to stand in lieu of those powerful private individuals whom the equality of conditions has swept away." "[T]he Court today endorses the principle that too much speech is an evil that the democratic majority can proscribe," adding that this view is "incompatible with the absolutely central truth of the First Amendment: that government cannot be trusted to assure, through censorship, the 'fairness' of political debate."[11] He concluded: "it is entirely obvious that the object of the law we have approved today is not to prevent wrongdoing, but to prevent speech."[12]

Title I of Bipartisan Campaign Reform Act of 2000 (BCRA) prohibited national party committees and their agents from soliciting, receiving, directing, or spending any "soft money" (contributions to political parties and committees and not to candidates) and limited amounts that state and local committees could expend on federal elections. It also prohibited individuals from pooling their money above limits set by Congress. Title II made it a crime for any corporation or labor union to use its general treasury funds to pay for any "electioneering communications" to large audiences, defined as a communication that referred to "a clearly identified candidate for Federal office" within thirty days of a primary and sixty days of an election. *McConnell v. FEC* (2003)[13] sought to have its provisions declared unconstitutional on their face.

Stevens and O'Connor[14] wrote (in 112 pages) to uphold Title I of the Act, which restricted contributions of "soft money" to political parties, although they struck down other provisions. With exceptions, Titles I and II were not overbroad or otherwise constitutionally wanting on the basis of an elaborate balancing of the interests promoted by the First Amendment and the need to reduce corruption or the appearance of corruption in electoral politics. Crucial to their analysis was that restrictions on campaign contributions were subject to a lesser degree of scrutiny than restrictions on campaign expenditures. Limits on individual contributions do not prevent candidates from amassing substantial sums of money to publicize their positions; "neither provision in any way limits the total amount of money parties can spend."[15]

Five Justices dissented in whole or in part – Scalia, Thomas, Kennedy, Rehnquist, and Stevens. Kennedy's dissent, joined by Scalia, argued that *Buckley v. Valeo* held that only one interest justified restrictions on campaign activity: eliminating or preventing "actual corruption or the appearance of corruption stemming from contributions to candidates . . . [and] that the corruption interest only justifies regulating candidates' and officeholders' receipt of what we can call the '*quids*' in the *quid pro quo* formulation."[16] Restrictions imposed on advocacy are unconstitutional because they perpetuate and expand the false dichotomy between issue advocacy and candidate advocacy, which have become totally intertwined.[17]

Scalia's dissent was passionate: "This is a sad day for the freedom of speech. Who could have imagined that the same Court which, within the past four years, has sternly disapproved of restrictions on such inconsequential forms of expression as virtual child pornography, tobacco advertising, dissemination of illegally intercepted communications, and sexually explicit cable programming would smile with favor upon a law that cuts to the heart of what the First Amendment is meant to protect: the right to criticize the government."[18] BCRA is an incumbent's dream, Scalia argued. "[A]*ny* restriction upon a type of campaign speech that is equally applicable to challengers and incumbents tends to favor incumbents."[19]

The rest of Scalia's dissent addressed "three fallacious propositions" on which the Court relied. First, "Money Is Not Speech," where he stated: "The right to speak would be largely ineffective if it did not include the right to engage in financial transactions that are the incidents of its exercise."[20] Second, "Pooling Money Is Not Speech," where he quoted cases to the effect that "'implicit in the right to engage in activities protected by the First Amendment' is 'a corresponding right to associate with others in pursuit of a wide variety of political, social, economic, educational, religious, and cultural ends.'"[21] Third, "Speech by Corporations Can Be Abridged." Ironically, Scalia cited legislative history to show that "[t]here is good reason to believe that the ending of negative campaign ads was the principal attraction of the legislation. . . . Another theme prominent in the legislative debates was the notion that there is too much money spent on election. . . . If our democracy is drowning from this much spending, it cannot swim. . . . Which brings me back to where I began: This litigation is about preventing criticism of the government." It was also about getting Senators and Congressmen reelected.[22]

Provisions of BCRA that restricted radio advertisements that named specific members of Congress whom listeners should contact with respect to pending legislation fell in *FEC v. Wisconsin Right to Life, Inc.* (2007).[23] Scalia concurred in the 5–4 decision and argued separately that the Court should overrule *McConnell* even though it was only four years old rather than participate in an unsatisfactory attempt to distinguish it. "This faux judicial restraint is judicial obfuscation."[24] The four liberal dissenters argued that the statute should be upheld as a valid curtailment of the pernicious effect of large sums of money on federal elections, which had been the subject of federal legislation since Congress first placed special limitations on campaign spending by corporations in the Tillman Act in 1907.

Citizen's United, a corporation, produced a film entitled *Hillary: The Movie*, a critical portrait of Senator Hillary Clinton, a candidate for the Democratic Party's presidential nomination in 2008. Uncertain of the application of BCRA to the film, Citizens United filed suit for declarative and injunctive relief. Kennedy's opinion for the five-Justice conservative majority in *Citizens United v. FEC* (2010)[25] overruled large portions of *Austin* and *McConnell*: "Speech restrictions based on the identity of the speaker are too often simply a means to control content," unless tied to important government functions. The "Court has recognized that First Amendment protection extends to corporations," including political speech, and there was a straight road to broad corporate speech, interrupted only by *Austin*, which "identified a new governmental interest in limiting political speech: an antidistortion interest." Bans on conduct that leads to *quid pro quo* arrangements have been accepted, and those are sufficient.[26]

Scalia's concurring opinion relied primarily on the text of the First Amendment. The "dissent never shows why 'the freedom of speech' that was the right of Englishmen did not include the freedom to speak in association with other individuals, including association in the corporate form." After disputing Stevens's claim that corporations were despised, Scalia pointed out that "[m]ost of the Founders' resentment toward corporations was directed at the state-granted monopoly privileges and individually chartered corporations enjoyed." Moreover, "the Framers' personal affection or disaffection for corporations is relevant only insofar as it can be thought to be reflected in the understood meaning of the text they enacted – not, as the dissent suggests, as a freestanding substitute for that text." Scalia closed his concurrence with his "principal point" – "The Amendment is written in terms of 'speech,' not speakers. Its text offers no foothold for excluding any category of speaker. . . . We are therefore simply left with the question whether the speech at issue in this case is 'speech' covered by the First Amendment. No one says otherwise."[27] Another bright line.[28]

Writing for the dissenters, Stevens emphasized the Court's break from past decisions. Special restrictions applied to students, foreigners, and government employees that were not supported by the First Amendment's text. The Court sustained statutes that prohibited the distribution or display of campaign literature near a polling place. Not only has the distinctive potential of corporations to corrupt the legislative process long been recognized, Stevens said, but within the area of campaign finance, corporate spending is also "furthest from the core of political expression, since corporations' First Amendment speech and association interests are derived largely from those of their members and of the public receiving information." Campaign-financing distinctions based on corporate identity tend to be less worrisome because the "speakers" are not natural persons, much less members of our political community, and the governmental interests are of the highest order.[29] "The final principle of judicial process that the majority violates is the most transparent: *stare decisis*. . . . In the end, the Court's rejection of *Austin* and *McConnell* comes down to nothing more than its disagreement with their results."[30]

While most people consider *Citizens United* a conservative opinion, that view is far from universal. Among the *amici curiae* who filed briefs that supported the majority was the ACLU, the primary organization in the United States supporting civil liberties. Nevertheless, the decision favored those with money.[31]

OTHER SPEECH ISSUES

McIntyre v. Ohio Elections Commission (1995)[32] invalidated a ban on distribution of anonymous campaign literature. "When a law burdens core political speech, we apply 'exacting scrutiny,' and we uphold the restriction only if it is narrowly tailored to serve an overriding state interest," Stevens wrote for the Court.[33] Unlike laws requiring candidates to disclose financial contributions, this law applied to independent activity on a much broader scale and to referendums as well as candidates. "Under our Constitution, anonymous pamphleteering is not a pernicious, fraudulent practice, but an honorable tradition of advocacy and of dissent. Anonymity is a shield from the tyranny of the majority."[34] Stevens cited a long history of anonymous (or pseudononymous) speech, including many publications during the ratification process. Thomas wrote an originalist concurrence that relied on attempts to uncover the identity of the authors of anonymous publications, mostly by the British during the colonial era.[35]

Dissenting, Scalia acknowledged that anonymous electioneering was common at the end of the eighteenth century, although less common in 1868, when the Fourteenth Amendment was adopted.[36] "But to prove that anonymous electioneering was used frequently is not to establish that it is a constitutional right.... Evidence that anonymous electioneering was regarded as a constitutional right is sparse, and as far as I am aware evidence that it was *generally* regarded as such is nonexistent.... The issue of governmental prohibition upon anonymous electioneering in particular (as opposed to a government prohibition upon anonymous publication in general) simply never arose."[37] Since the early history is sparse and inconclusive, Scalia continued, the Court should focus on a different approach – "A governmental practice that has become general throughout the United States, and particularly one that has the validation of long, accepted usage, bears a strong presumption of constitutionality." Prohibitions against anonymous campaign literature were first passed in 1890 and now exist in every state and the District of Columbia, save California. "Such a universal and long-established American legislative practice must be given precedence, I think, over historical and academic speculation regarding a restriction that assuredly does not go to the heart of free speech."[38] He added:

> [T]he usefulness of a signing requirement lies not only in promoting observance of the law against campaign falsehood (though that alone is enough to sustain it). It lies also in promoting a civil and dignified level of campaign debate – which the state has no power to command, but ample power to encourage by such undemanding measures as a signature requirement. I can imagine no reason why an anonymous leaflet is any more honorable, as a general matter, than an anonymous phone call or an anonymous letter. It facilitates wrong by eliminating accountability, which is ordinarily the very purpose of anonymity.[39]

The status of anonymous speech next arose when private parties sought to obtain copies of referendum petitions that were filed to challenge a state law extending benefits to same-sex couples. Signatories sought an injunction against the release of the petitions on the ground that they and other signers would face harassment. Writing for the Court in *Doe v. Reed* (2010),[40] Roberts stated that the signing of petitions was expressive and was therefore entitled to First Amendment protection under what has been termed "exacting scrutiny," which "requires a 'substantial relation' between the disclosure requirement and a 'sufficiently important governmental interest.'"[41]

However, states have a strong interest in preserving the integrity of the electoral process and are entitled to take steps to uncover fraud and mistakes, so the Court denied the injunction and allowed release of the petitions.

Concurring in the judgment, Scalia first expressed doubt that signing the petition came within the First Amendment, since the act of signing a petition, like the act of voting, has a component beyond the expression of one's views. "Our Nation's longstanding traditions of legislating and voting in public refute the claim that the First Amendment accords a right to anonymity in the performance of an act with governmental effect." In colonial times, voting, like legislating were public acts, with both usually accomplished by a show of hands, Scalia explained.[42] "There are laws against threats and intimidation; and harsh criticism, short of unlawful action, is a price our people have traditionally been willing to pay for self-governance," he said. "Requiring people to stand up in public for their political acts fosters civic courage, without which democracy is doomed. For my part, I do not look forward to a society which, thanks to the Supreme Court, campaigns anonymously (*McIntyre*) and even exercises the direct democracy of initiative referendum are hidden from public scrutiny and protected from the accountability of criticism. This does not resemble the Home of the Brave."[43]

The validity of restrictions on campaign speech as applied to judges produced a line-up similar to other campaign-finance cases. Minnesota's constitution provided for the popular election of all state judges, which have been nonpartisan since the early 1900s. Its election law stated that a "candidate for a judicial office, including an incumbent judge," shall not "announce his or her views on disputed legal or political issues," with sanctions ranging up to removal for incumbent judges and disbarment. Writing for the five most conservative Justices in *Republican Party of Minnesota v. White* (2002),[44] Scalia held that the law violated the First Amendment. The analysis was straightforward: the law restricted speech; the law had to pass the strict-scrutiny test, namely, the law was narrowly tailored to serve a compelling state interest; and "preserving the impartiality of the state judiciary and preserving the appearance of the impartiality of the state judiciary" did not suffice, because it did not establish that campaign statements "are uniquely destructive of open-mindedness."[45] The law was seriously underinclusive because it allowed many other ways of presenting views. Finally, there was no tradition of restricting any candidates for elective office and judges could not be singled out.

Dissents by Stevens and Ginsburg attracted four Justices. "Elected judges, no less than appointed judges, occupy an office of trust that is fundamentally different from that occupied by elected officials.... The legitimacy of the Judicial Branch ultimately depends on its reputation for impartiality and nonpartisanship."[46] Because judicial candidates do not cater to a specific constituency and are supposed to decide cases and controversies on individual records, this requires a different approach and balancing, which Minnesota achieved, or at least did not do unconstitutionally. In fact, the underinclusiveness of the law was one of its redeeming features, they argued.

Judicial candidates had other avenues to express their views. Also, the Constitution permits certain restrictions on judicial speech, such as prohibiting judicial candidate from promising to rule a certain way on a specific issue.[47]

Scalia confirmed his unequivocal stance against any restrictions on campaign contributions in 2015, when he dissented from a 5–4 decision that upheld a ban on elected judges' and judicial candidates' personally soliciting campaign contributions.[48] Scalia's dissent equated fund-raising with speech.

18

Antiabortion Picketing

Courts have restricted antiabortion demonstrators who interfered with people and cars trying to access clinics and who congregated in various numbers and chanted both with and without bullhorns; "sidewalk counselors," who approached and attempted to give passengers in cars or pedestrians antiabortion literature; and demonstrators who picketed in front of the residences of clinic physicians while shouting at passersby and handing out literature identifying the physician as a "baby killer." Some patients turned away from clinics, and the conduct took an emotional toll on clinic employees and patients alike. The Court considered whether the First Amendment gives demonstrators virtually untrammeled access to persons entering clinics. None of the Court's opinions, including those by Scalia and Thomas, addressed originalism.

From 1994 to 2014 the Court upheld restrictions on demonstrators, uniformly rejecting arguments that the injunctions were content based and therefore subject to strict scrutiny. *Madsen v. Women's Health Center, Inc.* (1994)[1] and *Schenck v. Pro-Choice Network of Western New York* (1997)[2] held that the injunctions were content neutral, even though they were entered only against antiabortionists, because they were the only ones picketing, just like labor picketing. The Court said that, "To accept [the demonstrators'] claim would be to classify virtually every injunction as content or viewpoint based."[3] *Madsen* also stated that the "inquiry in determining neutrality is whether the government has adopted a regulation of speech 'without reference to the content of the regulated speech.'" The standard would be "whether the time, place, and manner [of] regulation were 'narrowly tailored to serve a significant interest.'"

Hill v. Colorado (2000)[4] upheld a statute making it unlawful for any person to "knowingly approach" within eight feet of another person, without that person's consent, "for the purpose of passing a leaflet or handbill to, displaying a sign to, or engaging in oral protest, education or counseling with such other person." The government did not restrict speech "because of disagreement with the message it conveyed." Rather, the statute was content neutral and "simply establishes a minor place of restriction on an extremely broad category of communications with unwilling listeners. . . . [T]he contention that a statute is 'viewpoint based' simply because its enactment was motivated by the conduct of the partisans on one side of the debate is without support." The statute was narrowly tailored in time, place, and manner, and was not overbroad. "[T]he unwilling listener's interest in avoiding unwanted communications has been repeatedly identified in our cases. It is an aspect of the broader 'right to be let alone' that one of our wisest Justices characterized as 'the most comprehensive of rights and the most valued by civilized men.' *Olmstead v. United States*, 277 U.S. 438, 478 (1928) (Brandeis, J.)."[5]

McCullen v. Coakly (2014)[6] involved a Massachusetts statute that set a thirty-five-foot fixed buffer zone from which individuals were categorically excluded. The Court found a violation of the First Amendment by failing to "seriously address[] the problem through alternatives that leave the forum open for time-honored purposes."[7]

Scalia dissented in *Madsen, Schenck,* and *Hill* and wrote an angry concurrence in *McCullen.* He complained that those challenging the picketers failed to prove that the demonstrators committed acts of violence or physically tried to prevent prospective patients from obtaining medical treatment. Scalia also criticized the Court's newly created intermediate standard of review and analysis as nebulous and unnecessary,[8] calling them "made-up tests."[9] Scalia's opinion in *Madsen* began, "The judgment in today's case has an appearance of moderation and Solomonic wisdom, upholding as it does some portions of the injunction while disallowing others. This appearance is deceptive. The entire injunction departs so far from the established course of our jurisprudence that in another context it would have been regarded as a candidate for summary reversal,"[10] contrasting civil-rights cases.[11] Scalia scoffed at the claim that a buffer zone in *McCullen* was not content based when it applied only to abortion clinics, and that it explicitly allowed abortion-clinic employees to escort women into the facility. "Is there any serious doubt that *abortion-clinic employees or agents* 'acting within the scope of their employment' near clinic entrances may – indeed, often will – speak in favor of abortion ('You are doing the right thing')? Or speak in opposition to the message of abortion opponents – saying, for example, 'this is a safe facility' to rebut the statement that it is not?"[12]

For Scalia "[t]he vice of content-based legislation – what renders it *deserving* of the high standard of strict scrutiny – is not that it is *always* used for invidious, thought-control purposes, but that it *lends itself* to use for those purposes."[13] "[A]n injunction against speech is the very prototype of the greatest threat to First Amendment values, the prior restraint." "To sum up: The interest assertedly protected by the supplementary injunction did not include any interest whose impairment was a violation of Florida law or of a Florida court injunction. Unless the Court intends today to overturn long-settled jurisprudence, that means that the interests [of the State] cannot possibly qualify as 'significant interests' under the Court's new standard."[14]

In *Hill* Scalia bridled at the Court's elevating an abortion clinic to the status of the home and chided it for wrenching out of context the right to be let alone, which Brandeis had identified as "a right the Constitution 'conferred *as against the government*,'" not individuals. "To the extent that there can be gleaned from our cases a 'right to be let alone' in the sense that Justice Brandeis intended, it is the right of the *speaker* in the public forum to be free from governmental interference of the sort Colorado has imposed here."[15] Scalia also argued that the restrictions were content based: "Whether a speaker must obtain permission before approaching within eight feet – and whether he will be sent to prison for failing to do so – depends on *what he intends to say* when he gets there. I have no doubt that this regulation would be deemed content based *in an instant* if the case before us involved antiwar protestors, or union members seeking to 'educate' the public about the reasons for their strike."[16] "Suffice it to say that if protecting people from unwelcome communications (the governing interest the Court posits) is a compelling state interest, the First Amendment is a dead letter.... We have consistently held that the Constitution does not *permit* government to decide which types of otherwise protected speech are sufficiently offensive to require protection *for the unwilling listener or viewer*."[17]

19

Free Exercise of Religion

While Scalia's conservatism extended to the Establishment of Religion Clause, where he believed that religious organizations were entitled to the same rights as nonreligious organizations, it arguably did not extend to the Free Exercise of Religion Clause, where he rejected efforts to provide religious organizations with greater rights than other organizations. A scholar noted that Scalia was for weak enforcement of the Establishment Clause but for strong enforcement of the Free Exercise Clause.[1] Complicating matters is that the cases arose in the context of the Fourteenth Amendment (1868), which includes the Equal Protection Clause.

Until recently, the exercise of sincere religious beliefs prevailed unless the state imposed the least restrictive means of attaining a particularly important secular objective, sometimes referred to as a "compelling state objective" or "compelling state interest."[2] *Board of Education of Kiryas Joel Village School Distr. v. Grumet* (1999)[3] described a tradition of respecting religious practices: "Government policies of accommodation, acknowledgment, and support for religion are an accepted part of our political and cultural heritage.... Before the Revolution, colonial governments made a frequent practice of exempting religious objectors from general laws. *See* McConnell, 'The Origins and Historical Understanding of Free Exercise of Religion,' 103 *Harvard L. Rev.* 1409, 1466–1473 (1990) (recounting colonial exemptions from oath requirements, compulsory military service, religious assessments, and other general legislation)."[4] Thus, a state violated the First Amendment when it denied unemployment benefits to persons who had refused employment that required them to work on their Sabbath.[5]

Relying on a state statute of general applicability, Oregon denied members of the Native American Church unemployment benefits when they lost their jobs because they had used peyote for sacramental purposes. Scalia's opinion for the Court in *Employment Division, Dept. of Human Resources of Oregon v. Smith* (1990)[6] held that "an individual's religious beliefs [do not] excuse [an individual] from complying with an otherwise valid law prohibiting conduct that the State is free to regulate."[7] Neutral laws must be obeyed. Abandoning the narrow "compelling state interest test,"[8] Scalia readily accepted the consequences of his decision. "It may fairly be said that leaving accommodation to the political process will place at a relative disadvantage those religious practice that are not widely engaged in; but that unavoidable consequence of democratic government must be preferred to a system in which each conscience is a law unto itself or in which judges weigh the social importance of laws against the centrality of religious beliefs."[9]

Despite the enormous literature on the subject, Scalia's opinion contained almost no reference to originalism. There was a nod to textualism, but only to establish that his reading was a permissible one. Little attempt was made to present the history of excusing selected religions from laws of general applicability from the Religion Clauses; no evidence was presented regarding the application of the Free Exercise Clause to protect conduct as well as beliefs.[10] Scalia observed that companies printing newspapers must comply with generally applicable laws.[11] Just as death was not different, religion was not different. O'Connor's concurrence in the result acknowledged that, "today's holding dramatically departs from well-settled First Amendment jurisprudence . . . and is incompatible with our Nation's fundamental commitment to individual religious liberty."[12]

Four of the most liberal members of the Court dissented on the ground that the law, which placed a substantial burden on the Native American Church members, could be upheld only if it served a compelling state interest and was narrowly tailored to achieve that end.[13] They argued that some favoritism to religions was constitutional under the Free Exercise Clause and that laws of general applicability must occasionally give way. "Oregon's interest in enforcing its drug laws against religious use of peyote is not sufficiently compelling to outweigh respondents' right to the free exercise of their religion."[14] The liberal-conservative division may not have been the expected one.

When Hialeah passed a law making animal sacrifice or ritual a crime, a church of the highly controversial and frequently ostracized Santeria religion, which required sacrificing live animals, sued. Unanimously holding the law unconstitutional in *Church of the Lucumi Babalu Aye, Inc. v. City of Hialeah* (1993),[15] the Court said laws cannot discriminate against or among religions. Kennedy's opinion observed that the statute (barely) passed the test of facial neutrality, but that was not enough. The statute clearly targeted Santeria sacrifice by failing to include hunting, which also killed live animals. Scalia and Rehnquist joined Kennedy's opinion for the Court, except for its discussion of the Equal Protection Clause, which, Scalia said, focused on "the subjective motivation of the lawmakers," *i.e.*, whether the Hialeah City Counsel actually intended to disfavor the religion of Santeria. "The First Amendment does not refer to the purposes for which legislators enacted laws, but to the effects of the law enacted."[16]

In response to *Smith* Congress passed the Religious Freedom Restoration Act of 1993 (RFRA), which barred the application against religions of rules of general applicability, unless the government demonstrated "a compelling government interest" and the rule is "the least restrictive means of furthering that compelling interest."[17] An Archbishop of the Catholic Church sued when the City of Boerne, Texas, relied on its neutral historic landmark-preservation law to deny a permit to enlarge his church.[18] Holding the provision of the RFRA unconstitutional in *City of Boerne v. Flores* (1997),[19] Kennedy, joined by Rehnquist, Stevens, Scalia (except for a section on the history of the Fourteenth Amendment), Thomas, and Ginsburg argued that the "RFRA is so out of proportion to a supposed remedial or preventive object that it cannot be understood as responsive to, or designed to prevent, unconstitutional behavior. It appears, instead, to attempt a substantive change in constitutional protections.... Simply put, RFRA is not designed to identify and counteract state laws likely to be unconstitutional because of their treatment of religion."[20] In short, RFRA did more than "enforce" the First Amendment; it was more than remedial.[21] Stevens's concurrence read in full:

> If the historic landmark on the hill in *Boerne* happened to be a museum or an art gallery owned by an atheist, it would not be eligible for an exemption from city ordinances that forbid an enlargement of the structure. Because the landmark is owned by the Catholic Church, it is claimed that RFRA gives its owner a federal statutory entitlement to an exemption from a generally applicable, neutral civil law. Whether the Church could actually prevail under the statute or not, the statute has provided the Church with a legal weapon that no atheist or agnostic can obtain. This governmental preference for religion, as opposed to irreligion, is forbidden by the First Amendment.[22]

Scalia's concurrence relied on colonial charters and early state constitutions and other framing-era sources for his conclusion that, "the most plausible reading of the 'free exercise' enactments (if their affirmative provisions are read broadly, as the dissent's view requires) is a virtual restatement of *Smith*: Religious exercise shall be permitted so long as it does not violate general laws governing conduct." No case had been found "refusing to enforce a generally applicable statute because of its failure to make accommodations.... [T]o the knowledge of the academic defenders of the dissent's position ... none exists.... The issue presented by *Smith* is, quite simply, whether the people, through their elected representatives, or rather this Court, shall control the outcome of those concrete cases. For example, shall it be the determination of this Court, or rather of the people, whether ... church construction will be exempt from zoning laws? The historical evidence put forward by the dissent does nothing to undermine the conclusion we reached in *Smith*: It shall be the people."[23] Stevens concurred because law should not favor religion; Scalia concurred because the majority should prevail.

Burwell v. Hobby Lobby Stores, Inc. (2014), which voided regulations requiring small businesses to provide certain types of contraception to employees, is discussed in Chapter 27.

20

Punitive Damages

Juries have historically awarded damages above the loss suffered by the plaintiff for such intentional torts as assault, battery, and trespass, which pitted one individual against another. Starting about five decades ago, punitive or exemplary damages (the terms are used interchangeably) became much more common, were awarded in cases where large numbers of individuals sued huge corporations, and often dwarfed the amount of compensatory damages. It was not until 1991 that the Supreme Court considered the constitutionality of punitive damages under the Due Process Clauses of the Fifth and Fourteenth Amendments.[1] Political and judicial liberal-conservative issues arise in the award of punitive damages, such as attempting to balance the rights of individuals to obtain redress against an errant corporation (or its insurer) with the concept of ordered liberty that controls absolute discretion, in this case, the award of damages not tied to the injury suffered by the plaintiff. A large award certainly leans in a liberal direction. Scalia's opinions upholding jury awards of punitive damage eschewed any reliance on considerations of policy. For him the issue was resolved by an originalist reading of the Constitution; striking down a jury award of punitive damages required unteathered and unsupported substantive due process.[2] Procedural due process, however, was required.

The Supreme Court's opinion in *Pacific Mutual Life Insurance Co. v. Haslip* (1991)[3] announced that due process limited punitive damages, but was otherwise vague. "One must concede that unlimited jury discretion – or unlimited judicial discretion for that matter – in the fixing of punitive damages may invite extreme results that jar one's constitutional sensibilities. We need not, and indeed cannot, draw a mathematical bright line between the constitutionally acceptable and the constitutionally unacceptable that would fit every case. We can say, however, that general concerns of reasonableness and adequate guidelines from the court when the case is tried to a jury properly enter into the constitutional calculus." The instruction "enlightened the jury as to the punitive damages' nature and purpose, identified the damages as punishment for civil wrongdoing of the kind involved, and explained that their imposition was not compulsory."[4]

Scalia's concurring opinion bore little resemblance to the Court's.

> The fact that the common-law system for awarding punitive damages is firmly rooted in our history . . . is dispositive for due process purposes. . . . [I]t is not for the Members of this Court to decide from time to time whether a process approved by the legal traditions of our people is "due" process, nor do I believe such a rootless analysis to be dictated by our precedents. . . . [O]ur due process opinions in recent decades have indiscriminately applied balancing analysis to determine "fundamental fairness," without regard to whether the procedure under challenge was (1) a traditional one and, if so, (2) prohibited by the Bill of Rights. [Precedent] has no valid *stare decisis* claim on [me]. Our holdings remain in conflict, no matter which course I take. I choose, then, to take the course that accords with the language of the Constitution and with our interpretation of it through the first half of this century.[5]

Dissenting, O'Connor voted to declare the Alabama award unconstitutional under the Due Process Clause. While she was almost 180 degrees away from Scalia in terms of result, she was quite close in the negative perception of the process, which she knew first-hand as a state-court trial judge. "Alabama's common law scheme is so lacking in fundamental fairness that the propriety of any specific award is irrelevant. *Any* award of punitive damages rendered under these procedures, no matter how small the amount, is constitutionally infirm, . . . Due process requires that a State provide meaningful standards to guide the application of its laws."[6] The jury was told essentially, "do what you think best. . . . Not only that, the State *tells* the jury that it has complete discretion."[7] Scalia "argues that a practice with a long historical pedigree is immune to reexamination. . . . Due process is not a fixed notion. Procedural rules, 'even ancient ones, must satisfy contemporary notions of due process.'" "The Due Process Clause demands that we possess some degree of confidence that the procedures employed to deprive persons of life, liberty, and property are capable of producing fair and reasonable results."[8]

Scalia wrote opinions in five other punitive-damages cases over the next decade, three of which were from the same mold as *Haslip*. The jury in *TXO Productions Corp. v. Alliance Resources Corp.* (1993)[9] awarded Alliance $19,000 in compensatory damages and $10 million in punitive damages for common-law slander of title.[10] The plurality opinion by Stevens upheld the award largely on the ground that the procedures were similar to the ones sustained in *Haslip*. Concurring, Scalia argued that all substantive tests for punitive damages should be abolished. "I am willing to accept the proposition that the Due Process Clause of the Fourteenth Amendment, despite its textual limitation to procedure, incorporates certain substantive guarantees specified in the Bill of Rights; but I do not accept the proposition that it is the secret repository of all sorts of other, unenumerated, substantive rights – however fashionable that proposition may have been (even as to economic rights of the sort involved here) at the time of the *Lochner*-era cases the plurality relies upon."[11] Dissenting, O'Connor labeled the award "monstrous."[12]

Dr. Ira Gore, Jr., bought a new black BMW sports sedan from an authorized BMW dealer for over $40,000. When he learned nine months later that the car had been repainted by BMW at a cost of approximately $600, he sued. Under procedures identical to those in *Haslip*, the jury awarded Gore $4,000 in compensatory damages and $4 million in punitive damages, based on a determination that the nondisclosure constituted "gross, oppressive or malicious" fraud. The Supreme Court reversed. *BMW of North America, Inc. v. Gore* (1996)[13] became the first case to declare an award of punitive damages unconstitutional under the Due Process Clause. Scalia dissented: "The Court, I am convinced, unnecessarily and unwisely ventures into territory traditionally within the States' domain, and does so in the face of reform measures recently adopted or currently under consideration in legislative arenas."[14]

Scalia was receptive to challenges in a pair of cases that dealt with the required level of appellate review of awards of punitive damages. One reviewed an amendment to the Oregon Constitution that barred appellate review of the jury's award of punitive damages. The amendment also provided that the verdict would stand "unless the [trial] court can affirmatively say there is no evidence to support the verdict." Reversing the award, Stevens stated that practice, both old and modern, uniformly provided for judicial review of at least the amount of an award of punitive damages.[15] "Oregon's abrogation of a well-established common-law protection against arbitrary deprivations of property raises a presumption that its procedures violate the Due Process Clause. . . . Punitive damages pose an acute danger of arbitrary deprivation of property." Other protections do not substitute for judicial review.[16] Scalia joined the opinion of the Court, and also concurred in an originalist opinion: "The Oregon courts appear to believe that a state-law 'reasonableness' limit upon the amount of punitive damages subsists, but cannot be enforced through the process of judicial review." Judicial review "was a procedure traditionally accorded at common law. The deprivation of property without observing (or providing a reasonable substitute for) an important traditional procedure for enforcing state-prescribed limits upon such deprivation violates the Due Process Clause."[17]

The other case vacated an award of $4.5 million for punitive damages based on a $50,000 award of compensatory damages on the ground that appellate courts must reconsider the award without giving any deference to the trial judge's decision.[18] Accepting the force of *stare decisis* to the extent that the Due Process Clause imposed both substantive and procedural limitations on the award of punitive damages, Scalia reluctantly concurred in the judgment in a short opinion; his adherence to *stare decisis* was stronger than Ginsburg's, who was the sole dissenter.[19]

Peremptory Challenges

An issue that spans the Fifth, Sixth, Seventh, and Fourteenth Amendments is the right of a party to exercise peremptory challenges based on the race or gender of prospective jurors, in contrast to the exclusion of members of a race or gender from the *pool* of prospective jurors. The easy case had been decided by the time Scalia joined the Court. It was unconstitutional for a prosecutor to strike an African-American juror for his race in a criminal case when it was the same as the defendant's. So said *Batson v. Kentucky* (1986).[1]

When a *white* defendant claimed that the state prosecutor's striking both *black* venire members violated his Sixth Amendment right to "be tried by a representative cross section of the community," the Court rejected his claim in *Holland v. Illinois* (1990).[2] Scalia's majority opinion stated: "We reject [Daniel Holland's] fundamental thesis that a prosecutor's use of peremptory challenges to eliminate a distinctive group in the community deprives the defendant of a Sixth Amendment right to the 'fair possibility' of a representative jury." The constitutional goal is not a representative jury in any particular case, but an impartial one. "All we hold is that he does not have a valid constitutional challenge based on the Sixth Amendment – which no more forbids the prosecutor to strike jurors on the basis of race than it forbids him to strike them on the basis of innumerable other generalized characteristics."[3]

The Court, however, provided relief under the Fourteenth Amendment's Equal Protection Clause just one year later. Citing the central importance of the role of the jury in criminal cases both for the defendant and for the jurors themselves, the Court expanded *Batson* to jurors of any race in *Powers v. Ohio* (1991).[4] The reason was that "racial discrimination in the selection of jurors 'casts doubt on the integrity of the judicial process . . . and places the fairness of a criminal proceeding in doubt.'"[5] Defendants were entitled to assert their Equal Protection Clause claims because it was extremely difficult for jurors to assert their claims.

Dissenting, Scalia argued that the decision contradicted well-established law that had uniformly provided a right and a remedy to defendants only when jurors of the same race were excluded. Scalia had narrowed his arguments against race-conscious challenges as a result of *stare decisis*. Moreover, Scalia argued formalistically, an individual juror who is peremptorily challenged has no equal protection claim, since he has been treated the same as all other jurors. Finally, a defendant cannot assert any claim possessed by the juror because of the requirement of "injury in fact." "'Injury in perception' would seem to be the very *antithesis* of 'injury in fact,'" and is nothing more than speculation and contrary to many situations in which defendants cannot assert rights of third parties. "Today's supposed blow against racism, while enormously self-satisfying, is unmeasured and misdirected."[6]

The Court went further in *Georgia v. McCollum* (1992),[7] where a majority held that a black *defendant's* striking white jurors was unconstitutional state action, reasoning that there was enough government involvement and that the interests of the defendant were insufficient in a pluralistic society to overcome the interests of the jury and society. The opinion was of the same genre as many issued by the Warren Court, a satisfying, and perhaps politically and socially necessary, outcome based on doubtful precedent and tenuous constitutional principles.[8] Rehnquist and Thomas had reservations about the Court's conclusion but concurred on the ground of *stare decisis*.

Calling the result "perverse," O'Connor dissented; defense counsel are the antithesis of the state and were in fact fighting the state. She relied on *Polk County v. Dodson* (1981),[9] where the Court held that the actions of a public defender paid by the state were not state action, because in performing traditional defense functions, he occupied the same position as other defense attorneys in all relevant respects.[10] Scalia joined O'Connor's dissent and wrote his own short dissent, which called the decision "terminally absurd."

> A criminal defendant, in the process of defending against the state, is held to be acting on behalf of the state. Justice O'Connor demonstrates the sheer inanity of this proposition (in case the mere statement of it does not suffice), and the contrived nature of the Court's justifications.... Today's decision gives the lie once again to the belief that an activist, "evolutionary" constitutional jurisprudence always evolves in the direction of greater individual rights. In the interest of promoting the supposedly greater good of race relations in the society as a whole (make no mistake that that is what underlies all of this) we use the Constitution to destroy the ages-old right of criminal defendants to exercise peremptory challenges as they wish, to secure a jury they consider fair.[11]

PART V

Originalism Reconsidered

The previous discussion of originalism dealt almost entirely with the Court's opinions. But this is a cramped view, which often failed to take into account the complexities and uncertainties of English, colonial, and founding-era history, law, and practice. Historians provide the major impetus for criticizing the legal community,[1] but social scientists, language scholars, legal historians, and others add their objections. Before the Revolution, people did not have a dynamic view of society. Professor William E. Nelson stated that "the eighteenth century was a time when few people imagined social change was possible and nearly everyone assumed that life would go on essentially as it had for decades." The Enlightenment and the Revolution permitted people to contemplate the possibility of changes in the constitutional order, although society and technology remained essentially static until well into the 1790s and later. James Watt obtained his first patent for a steam engine in 1781.

Originalists fail to confront a basic problem, namely, that people thought differently in the late eighteenth century than they do now. Thinking then was traditional and far more concerned with collective or community interests than the modern individualist society.[2] John Adams wrote to Mercy Otis Warren on April 16, 1776: "Public Virtue cannot exist in a Nation without private, and public Virtue is the only Foundation of Republics. There must be a positive Passion for the public good, and public Interest, Honor, Power and Glory, established in the Minds of the People, or there can be no Republican Government, nor any real Liberty: and this public Passion must be Superior to all private Passions."[3] Madison asked the Virginia ratifying convention: "Is there no virtue among us? If there not be, we are in a wretched situation. No theoretical checks – no form of government can render us secure."[4] The spirit of civic virtue was pervasive. Historian David T. Konig stated that "citizens believed in an identifiable and obtainable public good different from the aggregated interests of individuals.... Rights were thus to be guaranteed by the people, constituted in republican institutions or acting through republican mechanisms."[5] There was a different frame of reference. The Salem Witch Trials of 1692 were closer in time to the Philadelphia Convention than the end of World War I is to today.

If civic virtue was antithetical to individualism, so was the concept of duty, exemplified in the communal right and requirement of a jury trial.[6] Professor Gordon S. Wood noted that the revolutionary and founding generations believed that sacrificing private desires for public good was a virtue.[7] Men of leisure and independence would run the country. Thus, Washington took no salary as commander in chief of the military and wanted none as President. Benjamin Franklin believed that members of the Executive Branch should serve without salary.[8] This was an elitist conception of government that the Anti-Federalists rejected. Farmers and tradesmen could not afford to serve without pay, although virtue was associated with farming.

The concept of security was constitutional security, which included political and financial security. Professor John Phillip Reid wrote: "In the twentieth century equality may be the most significant element in the definition of liberty. In eighteenth-century constitutional theory, the right to security was more important to liberty than was equality.... It may be that we can no longer understand what security meant to eighteenth-century liberty."[9] Elsewhere Reid wrote: "It was from custom – from receiving its authority from custom – that the eighteenth century concept of civil rights obtained much of the theoretical base making it so different from today's idea of personal rights.... Rights in the eighteenth century were thought of as restraining arbitrary government rather than as liberating the individual."[10] "Legal theorists of the eighteenth century, unlike their counterparts in the twentieth century, did not make the existence of a long list of rights a test of liberty. People were free if not subject to arbitrary government. There were, however, at least three rights essential to nonarbitrary government. To be free, people had to possess the rights of trial by jury, due process of law, and some form of representation through which 'consent' could be expressed."[11] This worldview was very different from that of originalists.

"The twentieth century may no longer understand what was going on in the 1770s," Reid added. "American Whigs were pushing against the republican grain. They wanted the certainty of the restrained, balanced constitution, not experiment with civic virtue. We see this by considering not what we think they should have wanted, but what they said they sought: a revived monarchy with a king who, in imperial government at least, would exercise the balance of a balanced constitution."[12] Parliament had been the villain, not the monarch. Many believed that there was more to fear from democracy than a monarch.[13] Elbridge Gerry of Massachusetts, who refused to sign the Constitution, considered the people the "dupes of pretended patriots" who could not be trusted, "The evils we experience flow from the excess of democracy."[14] Many believed that it was better to be ruled by a single individual than by a legislature possessing absolute power.[15] By 1787, state legislatures had demonstrated that they were indefatigably corrupt. Many of the founders distrusted the people. "Hamilton was frightened of democracy." "Jefferson no less than Disraeli feared with an ardent fear . . . the very 'mobs of great cities.'"[16] Madison had a low opinion of state legislatures and believed a national government would attract better people.[17] Prominent individuals like John Rutledge and Edmund Randolph saw a strong play for a monarchy. Jefferson, among others, expected that Washington might be President for life, that he would be a kind of elective monarch. Wood concluded that "we will never understand events of the 1790s until we take seriously, as contemporaries did, the possibility of some sort of monarchy developing in America," albeit an elected monarch. "From our vantage point," Wood explained, "the idea of America being a monarchy may seem absurd, but in 1789 it did not seem so at all."[18] Simultaneously, fear of a tyrannical national government pervaded ratification debates and contemporary writings.[19]

Many fail to appreciate the disagreements and rapid changes that occurred in the first decade or two of the Republic. Sentiment changed from a communal and somewhat aristocratic society to a more individualistic and populist one, while the nation grew and became more secure.[20] The ratification of the Constitution and Bill of Rights also marked a watershed. Before the First Congress adjourned, the victorious Federalists (supporters of ratification) had split irreversibly into two political alliances bitterly divided over constitutional issues. Beginning with the 1791 bank debate, federal constitutional discussion operated within a framework of systemic disagreement.[21] Then, major international events, such as the progress of the French Revolution in the 1790s, accelerated the pace of social change while the 1794 cotton gin marked the beginning of industrial change. Professor H. Jefferson Powell summed up the founding: "Viewed from the perspective of specific political issues, the founding era appears to have been a time of remarkably widespread constitutional dissention." People's thinking also changed, but hardly in lockstep.[22]

Lawyers approach the Constitution as generally static in another sense.[23] There is little or no recognition that historical knowledge is growing, which can change the way we see the past.[24] The expansion of knowledge is fine, even exhilarating, for historians, but it presents a difficult problem for judges who have to decide cases. To reach results, lawyers engage in oversimplification and ignore or minimize the largely indeterminate nature of the whole endeavor.[25] Historians say the Supreme Court and others are engaged in what they disparagingly label "law office history."[26] History is messy.

Most originalists do not proclaim that their theory has a historical imperative, but rather should be accepted because originalism leads to unique and generally desirable results. So it is critical for originalists that the answer to the following question be affirmative: "Is there historical evidence on which conscientious practitioners of originalism can rely that lead to clear (or reasonably clear) results?" Put simply, if originalism is no more than a competing theory without providing markedly more ascertainable results, and those results are not palatable to someone, why should someone choose originalism? Originalism may suffer from the same problems it condemns – phony objectivism.[27]

Fundamentals Reconsidered: Textualism and Originalism

TEXTUALISM

Textualism was always a component of constitutional law and often a dispositive one, as discussed in Chapter 2. Thus, Justice Joseph Story stated: "Nothing but the text was adopted by the people."[28] But there was an ebb and flow to the importance of the constitutional text, so categorical statements are difficult to defend. For Jefferson and Hamilton, H. Jefferson Powell wrote, "the Constitution's specific language is to be read in the light of its overall purpose, a purpose that cannot be stated in purely intratextual terms, and interpretive cruxes are to be resolved by reference to that purpose."[29] But in the decade after the formation of the Republic, Powell said that the "great 1790s debate over the locus of sovereignty had as its most immediate result the reinforcement of textual argument as the primary vehicle of constitutional discourse."[30] In connection with the battle over a national (or central) bank in 1791 Alexander Hamilton stated that "whatever may have been the intention of the framers of a constitution, or of a law, that intention is to be sought for in the instrument itself, according to the usual & established rules of construction."[31]

Philosophers of language and others recognize that laws may be hopelessly vague. One reason is failure to perceive ambiguities and vagueness, another is the enactors may have accepted vagueness as the only possible method of enacting the law by people who cannot agree.[32] Laws can be written that would send different messages to different audiences.[33] The words used by the Framers were often not intended to communicate a particular interpretation or to mask their true import,[34] although each faction may have pressed to engage language that favored its policies. The very purpose of the language was to absolve the enactors of any responsibility for the outcome. Moreover, different eras take different approaches to text. "When tied to the vastly different narrative demands placed upon judges in the early nineteenth century, the Founders' Textualism – if it is Textualism – is so profoundly different that it is unclear whether modern and early Textualists would agree in the mine run of difficult statutory interpretation cases."[35]

A comment noted: "Modern textualists acknowledge that words have no inherent meaning outside of context. They have no problem with relying on interpretive techniques such as semantic canons and structural analysis to resolve textual ambiguities and arrive at meanings that may not be obvious from a plain reading of the text. Textualism 'does not admit of a simple definition,' but is a sophisticated, context-sensitive approach to statutory interpretation."[36] Purposivist Richard Posner took this one step further: "We have seen Justice Scalia, the arch textualist, endorsing sundry 'canons of construction' that empower judges to resolve interpretive issues on nontextualist grounds." In a blunter evaluation Posner called the canons "a joke."[37] Posner discussed cases in which Scalia, usually with his coauthor Bryan Garner of *Reading Law*, made dubious choices in evaluating text, including inapposite dictionary definitions.[38] "Dictionaries are mazes in which judges are soon lost. A dictionary-centered textualism is hopeless."[39] Posner also challenged other aspects of Scalia's textualism, including illogical and inconsistent constructions of statutes and judicial "inventions," such as the rule of lenity.[40]

In a review of *Reading Law*, coauthored by Scalia, William N. Eskridge, Jr., concluded that an approach to reading statutes based on canons was doomed to fail. The reasons were many: the Supreme Court has identified at least 187 canons; canons are inconsistent and selection one over another is a normative decision; canons are biased, such as canons in favor of state immunity and against federal preemption are pro-state; canons are undemocratic because, for example, Congress and its staff think legislative history is second only to legislative text in importance, while unelected judges reject it; and textualism produces no more "objective" results than alternatives. "[T]he data suggest the hypothesis that a methodology that focuses on statutory text and committee reports generated by the legislative process that produced the opinion (Breyer and Ginsburg's purposivism) is one that is more constraining than a methodology that focuses on statutory text and considers 'valid canons' created by judges (Scalia and Thomas's new textualism)."[41]

Leading historians reject textualism/originalism's assumption that a close reading of the words and placement of clauses is the right way to find original meaning for the simple reason that it was not the way the founding generation operated. While the modern doctrine assumes that text and context were critically important, law school Dean Michael W. Treanor pointed out that the 1787 Constitution was created piecemeal and synthesized mostly by Gouverneur Morris without further extensive input from the attendees. Thus, assumptions that words, such as "inferior," used in one context meant the same in other contexts is without basis.[42] Aside from the uncertain reliability of sources, a judge cannot put himself in the place of the Framers, so he has to be engaged in reinterpretation.[43]

The elusiveness of any original understanding, assuming one ever existed, is aggravated by the fact that historical research continues, with new evidence and new

interpretations sprouting regularly, as exemplified by originalist Randy Barnett's article entitled, "New Evidence of the Original Meaning of the Commerce Clause."[44]
Allowing the nation's foundation document to change based on musty discoveries
makes the Constitution uncomfortably unstable. How are the people and the courts
to function if the law depends on the findings of historians along with debates over
what counts as relevant history?[45] This problem blends into the more serious problem of whether there even are historical answers to constitutional questions courts
must answer.[46]

Philosophers of language have a different perspective on absolute language than
most legally trained individuals. Professor Scott Soames reasoned that the Framers
could not have intended the "no law" language to be taken literally, since libel and
incitement laws were accepted at the time. No qualifying language to the absolute
was feasible as part of the First Amendment. Soames created a reasonable hypothetical scenario. "What was wanted, we may imagine, was a strong, but rebuttable,
legal presumption against the passage of laws by Congress regulating the freedom of
speech, or of the press. The sweeping, open-ended content of the amendment, we
may suppose, reasonably intended to put present and future members of Congress on
notice that any law restricting freedom of speech, or of the press, risked being judged
unconstitutional (and so invalid)." Soames added, "Often, constitutional provisions
are stated in language the broad purpose of which is quite plain, even though the
semantic or assertive content of that language is, by design, overly general."[47]

Scalia occasionally departed from the text of the Constitution. An example is
the Eleventh Amendment, where Scalia and others reconfigured the amendment
to grant far greater immunity to states than the amendment mandated, including
immunity for suits by its own citizens and for suits brought by foreign states. Another
is his disregard of Article III's express grant of jurisdiction over suits "between a
State . . . and foreign States." A political scientist wrote: "A textualist reading of Article
III, § 2 would have led Scalia to conclude that all state sovereign immunity had been
surrendered in the plan of the convention."[48]

Finally, Scalia relied on constitutional and institutional reasons for rejecting the
use of legislative history. "The greatest defect of legislative history is its illegitimacy."[49]
But, aside from a few stray comments, no one elevates legislative history to the
level of binding law. It is a device used to understand and clarify statutes and the
Constitution, not to replace them. Judges rely on law review articles all the time,
and they have less status than legislative history. There seems to be no persuasive
institutional objection to the use of legislative history to seek a better understanding
of laws.

ORIGINALISM

A major problem was that the founding generation was essentially starting from
scratch. There was nothing in the way of written constitutions except for the states of

the new United States[50] and little written regarding interpretation of a constitution for a federal system, although, of course, the concept did not materialize out of thin air. While the states had plenary powers, the Constitution created a new government of enumerated powers. Indeed, the concept of divided sovereignty was an unfamiliar one, although the practical division of power between England and the colonies was somewhat instructive. The Constitution papered over some big issues with vague and general language, for example, both the slave states and the nonslave states were fighting for "liberty." Big issues were the treatment of slaves for purposes of representation in the House of Representatives and the composition of the Senate (the "Great Compromise"),[51] neither of which is an issue today.

Agreement on constitutional text did not mean agreement on constitutional meaning, including many important clauses.[52] "[N]o one who had a hand in creating this nation was so foolish as to think that all interesting decisions are encoded in the original text." The meaning of words and concepts was far less developed in the late eighteenth century than it was even a generation or two later. Disparate principles of construction applied to legislation and contracts (which arguably included charters with colonies[53]) and there was no agreement that principles of construing state constitutions applied to the national Constitution.[54] Law school dean Larry Kramer concluded: "The problem is that there was *not* an agreed upon set of conventions for interpreting the Constitution at the time of the Founding."[55] "Although there was no shortage of efforts to reform legal and constitutional language, no consensus existed on how to allay concerns about the capacity of language to convey meaning."[56] "This was something the Founding generation learned to its dismay early in the 1790s. . . . [I]nsofar as there were, at the time, two or more plausible positions on the correct original public meaning of a provision of the Constitution, all one does in embracing one of them today is to take sides in a historical dispute that was not resolved at the time of the Founding, and so is not resolvable on such terms today."[57] Indeed, the concept of a constitution was different then; it was more fluid and far less tied to litigation.[58]

"The decision was to create a federal republic and let the people work out, through their representatives, the problems of time still to come. We do so pragmatically. How else does democracy work?"[59] The Framers were empirical and wanted to test their ideas against experience.[60] That implies looking at the consequences of constitutional interpretations, something which originalists reject. Leaders including Madison and Jefferson referred to the new national government as a journey that contained new concepts.

Competing historical traditions underlay constitutional or fundamental law, such as the role of natural law in construing the Constitution.[61] For many, searching for an answer in a higher law was an integral part of understanding individual rights.[62] Competing approaches included Blackstonian theory, which used a series of explicit rules of legal construction to discern the meaning, in particular, the "will of the legislator."[63] "The reigning theory of legislative interpretation in the eighteenth century was loose (or flexible, or nonliteral) construction. . . . Originalism without the interpretive theory that the Framers and the ratifiers of the Constitution expected the courts to use in construing constitutional provisions is *faux originalism*."[64] "[T]he proper methods of constitutional interpretation were not only under-resolved at the time of the Funding, they were the subject of heated and on-going debate."[65]

Reid added another dimension. "Eighteenth-century constitutional theory could not contemplate the use of government to work for equality in the form of social or economic justice, because it could not trust government. Government was necessary, there could be no liberty without the state, but government was power, and power had to be restrained or it was not constitutional. That was the role of liberty, to be a barrier against government, but the liberty that could perform the task was the liberty that came from security, the liberty encased in law and manifested by equal treatment before the law."[66] Also, "the important issue [for the 1780s] was not whether the legislative, executive, or judicial branches should ensure conformity of law to fundamental standards of right, but whether any institution should."[67]

Federalist thinking was more diverse than early studies suggested.[68] Also, Anti-Federalists were a diverse group that cut across class lines, mainly from the interior and not the elite, but included Eldridge Gerry and George Mason. People from the backwoods of Pennsylvania, usually Anti-Federalists, heard and accepted different arguments than those from Philadelphia.[69] Also, the South and the North differed greatly. The former had a plantation economy that exported tobacco while the latter featured subsidence farming and handicraft factories; the former was more aristocratic while the latter was more democratic; the former was Anglican Church while the latter had a variety of mostly radical Protestant denominations; and, of course, the former was a slave economy, while the latter was primarily a free-market economy. The idea that northerners and southerners had the same understanding of the meaning of the Fourteen Amendment is fanciful.

According to Saul Cornell, "[m]ost originalists have simply assumed the existence of a broad consensus on questions of constitutional meaning and interpretation during the Founding era. Historical scholarship over the last fifty years, by contrast, has demonstrated that conflict, not consensus, was the norm of this period. The historical divisions within the Founding generation also encompassed profound disagreements over the most basic questions about how to read constitutional texts."[70] Not only was there enormous diversity among former colonies, there was enormous diversity within them, including attitudes toward England and the Revolution and between agriculture and mercantile ventures.[71] Powell said that "[c]onstitutional interpretation wasn't a strictly historical inquiry into what someone thought at some past point in time. . . . [T]he constitutionalists of the early Republic shared, universally to my knowledge, the conviction that at times the meaning of a provision required deliberation. . . . There would have been nothing illogical, indeed, in someone noting in 1798 that he would originally have thought that the amendment meant X, and only on considering the Sedition Act had realized that X could not be correct."[72] Another historian emphasized the critical role of history in a different way: "F.W. Maitland, the greatest of all legal historians, understood that legal history is, at bottom, history rather than law, just as religious history is not theology and the history of science is not science."[73] Gordon Wood said succinctly, "There was not in 1787–1788 one 'correct' or 'true' meaning of the Constitution. The Constitution meant whatever the Federalists or Anti-Federalists could convince the country to accept."[74] Reviewing a book by a nonhistorian, Wood noted that the author

> is not really a historian, he does not have a historian's feel for the complexity, the nuances, the contexts, and the differentness of the past. . . . [H]e is so eager to counter what he sees as the moral relativity and skepticism of the present that he cannot accept the historian's instinctive assumption that all human thought and action are the products of particular historical circumstances. Instead, like many conservative political theorists, he dismisses the radical contextualism of most historians. He wants to telescope time and lump things together and reduce complexities to simple absolutisms. Above all, he seeks to hold on to some transhistorical truths, some eternal or universal judgments, that defy time and place.[75]

In 1790 Hamilton proposed the creation of a national or central bank. Among the arguments made in favor of the bank was: "If Congress may not make laws conformably to the power plainly implied, though not express in the frame of Government, it is rather late in the day to adopt it as a principle of conduct. . . . Congress may do what is necessary to the end for which the Constitution was adopted, provided it is not repugnant to the natural rights of man or to those which they have expressly reserved to themselves or to the powers which are assigned to the states."[76] Hamilton relied on the principle that Congress has power if it "relates to the general order of the finances, to the general interests of trade & being general objects . . . for *the application of money*" and on "an aggregate view of the constitution."[77] Jefferson Powell stated that Hamilton and his allies "were united by a vision of national government as a vehicle of public safety and prosperity."[78] But that was not the only vision among the participants, many of whom had attended the Philadelphia Convention or state ratifying conventions.[79]

Many scholars have concluded that Framers were not originalists. Harvard Law Professor Charles Fried, who was Reagan's Solicitor General, wrote: "Originalism was not the original interpretive doctrine of the Framers, nor of the framing generation. It was taken for granted that the Constitution, like other legal texts, would be interpreted by men who were learned in the law, arguing cases and writing judgments in the way lawyers and judges had done for centuries in England and its colonies."[80] "[T]he constitutional text does not stress any reference to the original intent of the framers," announced a nonoriginalist.[81] A lengthy study agrees, observing that James Madison did not publish his notes of the Constitutional Convention until 1840 (and never used them), the First Congress did not refer to the Convention, and important contemporaries including Thomas Jefferson and John Adams did not attend the Convention, and leaders such as Alexander Hamilton and John Marshall did not rely on the Convention.[82] Madison stated in 1796 in the House of Representatives that the Convention's debates should "never be regarded as the oracular guide" for understanding the Constitution and also that, "Let experience, the least fallible, guide of human opinions, be appealed to for an answer to these constitutional questions."[83] Original meaning, moreover, did not play a significant role in early court decisions. A 1795 case that forced a state to pay monetary compensation relied not on any original understanding, but on "principles of reason, justice and moral rectitude" and "the principles of social alliance in every free government."[84]

A problem for originalists is that the ratifying state conventions could vote only to accept or reject the entire document. Historian Jack N. Rakove noted that "the binary, up-or-down quality of the decision of 1787–88 makes it impossible to disaggregate the decision 'to form a more perfect union' into understandings of the merits and meanings of all the individual clauses that are the true objects of constitutional adjudication." The process stands in the way of reliable constitutional interpretation.[85] Harvard law professor John F. Manning elaborated: "[B]ecause the proposers presented the document to the ratifiers on a take-it-or-leave-it basis, the proposal itself constituted an essential part of the enactment process, and ignoring the compromises reflected in that proposal would negate the terms on which the several states agreed to participate in the process."[86] Many provisions of greatest importance during the ratification process, such as the composition of the Legislative Branch, overwhelmed issues of primary importance today.[87] The ratification debates are a poor guide for another reason. There were thirteen separate stories.[88] In fact, Rakove called the ratification process a "cacophonous debate in which squibs, parodies, wildly fantastic predictions, and demagogic rhetoric alternated with the more serious analysis."[89] Convention delegate Elbridge Gerry noted how the urgency of the ratification proceedings led both "parties to depart from candor."[90]

Evaluating the reliability of sources is a problem, since most were local campaign documents, or propaganda, on one side or another of the ratification debate, which is not to say that they were not learned and respected for what they were.[91] Language and positions were distorted. A scholar referred to "the slipperiness of the terms used by commentators in the founding periods, and the rapidity with which meanings could change."[92] Anti-Federalists were more concerned with inroads on separation of powers than were the Federalists. As a result, *The Federalist* and likeminded tracts sought to convince opponents of the Constitution that the national government would not be tyrannical.[93] It seems that *The Federalist*'s advantages as a substantial document were also its disadvantages as a means of creating a public understanding. A law professor noted, "*The Federalist*'s length and depth were not universally appreciated."[94] The assumption that any specific portion of *The Federalist* reflected a broad consensus of the population may or may not be accurate, more likely the latter. Rarely acknowledged are influential Anti-Federalist pamphlets, also written under pseudonyms, such as Brutus, a Federal Farmer, John de Witt, Cato, or Agrippa.

The Bill of Rights had a different history, with the states submitting proposals and James Madison collecting and rewriting them, which the House of Representatives and then the Senate edited, followed by a conference-committee edit and state ratification. The impetus for the Bill of Rights was mostly those who opposed the Constitution because it created both a too-powerful national government and one lacking a bill of rights.[95] Ordinary people had seen how Parliament had infringed traditional constitutional rights and they wanted written protection immune from legislative repeal.[96] Madison and his allies decided that the creation of a narrow bill of rights would split the opposition and secure ratification without weakening the national government and preventing a second Constitutional Convention.[97] The proposals were not abstract principles of philosophers, but were designed by ordinary citizens to prevent specific abuses that the colonists had experienced as colonialists, mostly denial to them of the rights of the English, including trial by jury and trials locally. As a result, they were piecemeal, not comprehensive, and linguistically diverse. The records of the discussions in Congress and of the ratification debates proved a limited and uneven supplement to the language itself.[98]

The Bill of Rights defused the Anti-Federalists' efforts, but did not satisfy many of them. "Amendments" to Madison meant a bill of rights.[99] To New York Governor George Clinton and Virginian Patrick Henry, the word "amendments" also connoted a weakening of the national government in favor of the states on such important questions as direct taxation, total state control of elections, a standing army in peace time (which was considered tyrannical), and the treaty-making power.[100] None of those proposals made the final cut (or even the first cut, which was Madison's). Madison and the Federalist Congress saw to that, but they satisfied enough Anti-Federalists to prevent fracturing the government. Anti-Federalists, joined by disillusioned Federalists, turned to the implementation of the Constitution, including seeking office.[101]

Another problem, particularly with interpreting the Bill of Rights, is whether the Constitution was intended to incorporate or to revise the common law. That choice can govern the scope of the rights and the disposition of cases. The words of the Bill of Rights do not provide the answer, for example, whether the Confrontation Clause was intended to mirror the common law and, if so, whose. The fact that the Framers and ratifiers of the Constitution understood that there were different approaches in England than in America and within America only complicates the problem.

Wood stated: "History is much too complicated to be used effectively by judges and the courts."[102] Princeton President Christopher L. Eisgruber agreed: "There is simply too much legitimate disagreement within originalism for it to constrain judges effectively."[103] Cornell wrote: "Although originalism focuses on the meaning of historical texts, originalist practices are largely antithetical to accepted historical methodology. The fact that originalists have used and abused history in a variety of academic debates has been well documented. . . . The historical divisions within the Founding generation . . . encompassed profound disagreements over the most basic questions about how to read constitutional text."[104] Jack Rakove emphasized the ahistorical mindset of originalist judges who focus on linguistic meaning although the key words are "fraught with political content." "What would seem strange to a historian is not the idea of recovering the original meaning of a document, which we try to do all the time, but the greater ambition of originalism, which is to equate that original meaning, however ascertained, with a document's permanent meaning. . . . Public meaning originalism . . . abandons the idea that the Constitution is to be understood or approached primarily as the outcome of a set of political deliberations."[105]

One historian wrote that "the legal community notoriously ignores the principle that the individual historical questions that its members commonly seek to answer cannot be understood except as 'part[] of a larger historical . . . whole.'"[106] "[A]ppreciating the inherent differentness of the past is *most* important when it seems otherwise familiar. . . . Not only, then, have originalists been prone to impose modern language games on eighteenth-century utterances, but they have been prone to impose modern beliefs on them as well."[107] Bernard Bailyn observed that "[t]he past is a different world."[108] Posner called the past "foreign countries so far as providing guidance to solving today's problems is concerned."[109] Historians disparage short cuts, such as relying on dictionaries rather than using all available sources, including newspapers and letters. Judges cherry-pick dictionaries and definitions. Moreover, dictionaries were idiosyncratic two centuries ago, providing how the author thought words should be used.[110] Another scholar said: "The most important of these [false] assumptions is the belief that historical research is bound to yield a definitive result. The lawyer accepts this as true because he works backwards from the answer."[111]

The legal community, including judges, lacks the skills, time, and inclination to do the work necessary to uncover whatever original understanding there was. Most practicing lawyers are not historians themselves. Historians and law professors tend to specialize by subject matter while most federal and state judges are by nature generalists, since they sit on a broad spectrum of cases. Disdain for the legal history appearing in court opinions, including those of the Supreme Court, permeates recent historian literature. While history journals are peer reviewed, historians point out that law journals are not.[112] Historians have criticized the historical scholarship of prominent law professors.[113]

Historians scoff at "law office" history, which suffers from insufficient resources and, perhaps more important, lack of training and objectivity on the part of the advocates urging their positions on the courts or in law journals. According to Cass Sunstein, constitutional lawyers who appear before Justices and judges are there to contribute "to the legal culture's repertoire of arguments and political/legal narratives that place a (stylized) past and present into a trajectory leading to a desired future."[114] More bluntly, they are there to win cases, not discover a truth (if there is one). Addressing law office history, Wood said, "we should not ever get this law history mixed up with read history that historians write."[115] Proper historians do not have a horse in the race.[116] Historical issues may not be resolvable. Recognition of uncertainty, raw meat for historians, is anathema to lawyers.[117] "Flux, not fixation, was the defining feature of post-Revolutionary era legal and political discourse."[118] For example, "[t]he court records [of Middlesex County, Massachusetts] indicate that most of the developments which transform Puritan criminal law into the criminal law of today occurred during the three decades following the American Revolution."[119]

One blatant violation of historical practice is the selection of a fictive recipient of the Constitution, such as a reasonably well-informed citizen or lawyer. It is foolish, however, to try to insert oneself into the minds of farmers and artisans, or even the assorted judiciary, in 1791, much less a "typical" one.[120] Just how can someone decide what the "typical" citizen or lawyer believed was a search and seizure in the thirteen states and England in 1791.[121] Saul Cornell wrote: "The notion of constitutional idiocy is central to virtually every brand of Originalism, new and old. The idiocy theory also enables some New Originalists to side step dealing with the actual beliefs of Americans and substitute beliefs of a fictive reader, effectively turning constitutional interpretation into an act of historical ventriloquism."[122] Rakove created a fictive character in "Joe the Ploughman Reads the Constitution, or, the Poverty of Public Meaning Originalism," a take-off on Joe the Plumber, a/k/a Samuel Joseph Wurzelbacher, who challenged Barack Obama's liberal statements during the 2008 presidential campaign.[123] "[M]ost historians have abandoned the search for a single monolithic meaning of the Constitution. Most scholars now focus on what the Constitution meant to specific groups."[124]

Scalia accepted one major problem with originalism – its "greatest defect, in my view, is the difficulty of applying it correctly," although he did not integrate that insight into his judicial philosophy.[125] Like virtually all judges, he was not a trained historian, and acknowledged that the judicial system provided neither the best environment nor the best personnel to plumb original understanding.[126] When he considered the problem of the original meaning of the language "[t]he executive Power" in Article II, § 1, he found the task daunting.[127]

> [I]t is often exceedingly difficult to plumb the original understanding of an ancient text. Properly done, the task requires the consideration of an enormous amount of material – in the case of the Constitution and its Amendments, for example, to mention only one element, the records of the ratifying debates in all of the states. Even beyond that, it requires an evaluation of the reliability of the material – many of the reports of the ratifying debates, for example, are thought to be quite unreliable. And further still, it requires immersing oneself in the political and intellectual atmosphere of the time – somehow placing out of mind knowledge that we have which an earlier age did not, and putting on beliefs, attitudes, philosophies, prejudices, and loyalties that are not those of our day. It is, in short, a task sometimes better suited to the historian than the lawyer.[128]

But elsewhere he minimized the problem almost to the point it disappeared: "Sometimes (though not very often) there will be some disagreement regarding the original meaning. And sometimes there will be disagreement as to how that original meaning applies to new and unseen phenomena."[129] He failed to acknowledge the enormity of the problem. Indeed, dueling originalist opinions appeared in case after case, including *District of Columbia v. Heller* (2008) (gun control),[130] *Planned Parenthood of Southeastern Pa. v. Casey* (1992) (right to abortion),[131] and many others.[132]

Finally, it must be emphasized that criticisms of historical methodology are not directed solely at originalists. For example, the Warren Court sought to bolster its radically new doctrines with history, much of it bad history. Criticizing the Warren Court's decisions on *habeas corpus* in the 1962 Term, Professor Dallin H. Oaks, a conservative, said that legal rules "should be cloaked in reason, not garbed in a royal patchwork of history that, on close examination, proves as embarrassingly illusory as the Emperor's new clothes."[133] Other instances abound. "Even more than in the case of Justice Scalia, Justice Kennedy's history is a matter of faith rather than study or fact."[134] "Justice Breyer's commitment to serious originalist analysis obviously evaporated when history got in the way of the desired result."[135] Souter engaged in "rhetorical ploys and distortions of the historical sources."[136] Conservative Alito has not escaped criticism.[137] Nor is criticism confined to any single version of originalism. Thomas's "social philosophy . . . leads to strained and implausible uses of history to implement his conservative vision."[138] Leonard Levy wrote: "Two centuries of Court history should bring us to understand what really is a notorious fact: the Court has flunked history."[139] Jefferson Powell agreed: "The United States Supreme Court's misuse of history is, of course, notorious."[140]

"[O]riginalism generally *does not and cannot* solve answer-specific, twenty-first century problems arising under ambiguous eighteenth-century texts."[141] The founders could not have imagined today's issues. Powell wrote that "once it is conceded that the Constitution speaks to questions that those who adopted it did not answer, it becomes obvious that in such cases the interpreter must use some process of generalization or analogy to go beyond what history can say. The inevitable disputes over whether a given interpretation over-generalizes or is based on a faulty analogy are not resolvable by historical means; at this point history, and originalism as a program of obedience to history, have no more to add to constitutional discourse."[142] Professor Thomas Y. Davies added that "originalism does not (and cannot) offer a valid method for deciding contemporary issues of constitutional criminal procedure."[143]

23

Fundamentals Reconsidered: Other Doctrines

Scalia does not address directly what role the Framers believed tradition should play in the interpretation of their Constitution, and there is scant evidence that the Framers considered, much less addressed, that problem in the raw form adopted by Scalia.[1] One historian explained: "[I]f any one theme should emerge clearly from the historical writings of the past generation, it is that the break with Britain posed questions and presented opportunities for which tested wisdom and proven precedent seemed inadequate. The narration of this 'experiment in republicanism' is replete with a sense of movement, innovation, creativity, and the uncertainties and gaps of comprehension this progress necessarily carried in its wake."[2] The Revolution was both an embracement of English values and a repudiation of them.

The United States has been a diverse country whose inhabitants do not always agree on the present, much less the past. Choosing the most specific tradition, which is Scalia's approach, is fraught with difficulty and subjective judgments.[3] The specificity of the constitutional provision affects the choice of the tradition.[4] Both what is a tradition and what is the most specific tradition are difficult questions.[5] Legal scholars have argued, "[t]here is no such thing as 'the most specific level' of a relevant tradition which may be mechanically invoked to decide a case" and that the same kinds of judgments are involved in this exercise as judges employ in their judicial duties.[6] "Legally cognizable 'traditions' instead tend to mirror majoritarian, middle-class conventions.... [H]istorical traditions are susceptible to even *greater* manipulations than are legal precedents.... [T]he method of common law can constrain a Justice interpreting the living Constitution."[7] Scalia relied on tradition, but then did other Justices, including Brennan, who used it to support a right to access to criminal trials,[8] a liberal use as opposed to opposed to Scalia's mostly conservative use, which shows the normative dimension of the exercise.[9] What emerges is a lack of clarity that originalism claims.

Uncompromising and unrelenting originalism, devoid of *stare decisis*, was not Scalia's brand. Far closer to the Platonic ideal of originalism is Clarence Thomas.[10] The pure form would not only reverse *Roe v. Wade* and *Casey*, special restrictions on capital punishment, affirmative action, the *Miranda* warning, and the exclusionary rule applied to state courts, but it could eviscerate Social Security, Medicare, Medicaid, federal securities laws, child labor laws, environmental laws, the federal minimum wage, laws regulating the manufacture and sale of food and drugs, the nationwide right to counsel in state felony cases, affirmative action, laws against discrimination of women and gays, federal limits on unequal state and congressional election districts, and the virtual incorporation of the Bill of Rights to the states.[11] That is judicial activism of an extreme sort. Scalia's flexible approach to *stare decisis* contrasts with sturdier branches of his judicial philosophy.[12] In fact, Scalia measured about average in a study on judicial activism.[13]

Professor Tribe criticized Scalia's approach to *stare decisis*: "Justice Scalia asserts that his assumption of the power to invoke *stare decisis* or not to do so does not leave him open to the charge of importing his own views and values into his method of interpretation, because he follows 'rules' as to when the disregard of *stare decisis* is appropriate. But even if we assume that Justice Scalia had such 'rules' for the selective invocation of *stare decisis*, and for whether to uphold some but not all of erroneous decisions of the Supreme Court, what is the origin of those rules? They certainly are not derived from the 'original meaning' of the text of the Constitution, as Justice Scalia's interpretative methodology would require."[14] In fact, there can be no originalist constitutional conception of *stare decisis* because there were no, and could have been no, constitutional decisions in 1789.[15] There was, however, a common-law tradition in which *stare decisis* played a prominent role.

"Moderated" or "qualified" originalists may let stand some progressive or liberal precedents. Scalia said his approach to originalism essentially left the past as it was and focused on the future. "Where originalism will make a difference is not in the rolling back of accepted old principles of constitutional law, but in the rejection of usurpatious new ones."[16] But while Scalia may have accepted *Brown v. Board of Education* as a precedent, with a majority of Scalias on the Court, however, there would be no more *Browns*, whether for gays, lesbians, transgenders, or anyone else. There would be no more "usurpatious" liberal decisions. The Constitution would depend not on its language or meaning when adopted, but when five originalists inhabit the Court.

But that formulation overstates the importance of *stare decisis* for Scalia. His individualized formula, quoted in Chapter 3, permitted him to reject the call of precedent, based in part on the importance of the issue, which he did in connection with abortion, gay rights, right to die, affirmative action, presumably gun rights, and some other important rights questions. He respected *stare decisis* more for the 1789 Constitution than for the Bill of Rights and the Civil War Amendments.

In contrast to separation of powers, discussed next, the division of authority between multiple sovereigns within the same territory was new and undertheorized. Traditional thinking held that sovereignty was unitary and indivisible. Before the debates between Massachusetts Royal Governor Thomas Hutchison and the Massachusetts legislature (the General Court) in 1773 the concept of divisible sovereignty was undeveloped, as explained by Alison L. LaCroix in *The Ideological Origins of American Federalism.*[17] A few colonists in the 1760s asserted an *ad hoc* arrangement based on a division between concerns of the empire and local matters, the emerging concept of federalism. Federalism did not play a significant role, however, in the Articles of Confederation; the national government, really just a Congress, had little authority.

No overarching theory governed the implementation of federalism at the Constitutional Convention, although Madison had spent the preceding year studying issues involving federalism. The original Constitution was a "bundle of compromises."[18] Judge Frank Easterbrook stated: "As Madison would put it after the convention ended, the delegates were working now to frame a government that would be neither national nor federal, but a novelty compounded of elements of both. And none of them could fully understand what this unprecedented compound would look like."[19] Without experience it was difficult to comprehend federalism, much less use the concept to decide difficult questions.[20] Jefferson observed that "what is practical must often govern what is pure theory."[21]

Scalia coupled strong separation of powers with elevation of the popular branches over the judiciary. However, the historical basis for Scalia's uncompromising stance on separation of powers is debatable. Separation of powers in the colonies and early state constitutions was far from complete.[22] The executive in most colonies had the power to dissolve the lower house of the legislature and to fire judges.[23] In Massachusetts the legislature made Executive Branch appointments. In most states the legislature elected the governor; in only three states was the governor popularly elected.[24] Courts through the 1780s were still generally considered an undifferentiated segment of the Executive Branch. A key concern was balance and accountability, not absolute separation. Professor Bernard Bailyn wrote: "Constitutional thought, concentrating on the pressing need to create republican governments that would survive, tended to draw away from the effort to refine further the ancient, traditional systems, and to move toward a fresh, direct comprehension of political reality."[25] What appeared to be efforts at separation of powers "derive[d] from an earlier intellectual context dominated not by the ideal of the balance of functioning branches of government but by the concept of mixed government and by a sense of the dangers it faced from 'influence' and 'corruption.'"[26]

Professor Martin Flaherty noted the uncertain status of the Executive Branch. "Once set back in its original context, perhaps all that can be asserted with assuredness is that the provision furthers at least two of the general purposes that underpinned separation of powers thinking at the time. The Clause clearly furthers the ideal of balance through an enhanced executive, whether it merely signals the location of executive power or grants them. Likewise, the provision advances the goal of governmental energy by declaring that the apex of the executive department shall be a single individual. Anything much beyond these general points quickly becomes guesswork."[27]

Although the Constitutional Convention focused considerable attention on separation of powers as an antidote to tyranny,[28] the Constitution does not provide for a complete separation of powers. The President's power to enter treaties is tempered by the requirement for Senate confirmation. War powers overlap. The Vice President presides over the Senate and can vote to break ties. The Senate passes on the appointment of high Executive Branch officials. Article III judges, including the Chief Justice, are nominated by the President and confirmed by the Senate. The House of Representatives impeaches the President and his trial by the Senate is presided over by the Chief Justice of the United States. The House may impeach and the Senate try other members of the Executive and Judicial Branches. Action by Congress is subject to presidential veto.[29] The Judicial Branch maintains some control over the size and race-discriminatory configurations of congressional districts.[30]

The history of the Constitutional Convention reflects an *ad hoc* and even somewhat casual approach to what is now called separation of powers, a term that was not used until much later.[31] The divisions of power were generally pragmatic solutions to perceived overconcentration of power and not the product of a grand plan. Hamilton said in *The Federalist* No. 66 that separation of powers "has been shown to be entirely compatible with a partial intermixture of those departments for special purposes, preserving them, in the main, distinct and unconnected." Defending the Constitution at the New York ratifying convention, he said that executive authority "was divided between two branches, supposedly the president and the Senate; legislative authority rested in 'three distinct branches properly balanced,' no doubt the president and the two houses of Congress, and the judicial was 'reserved for an independent body' whose members held office on good behavior."[32] Nevertheless, blending powers was the exception "in order more effectually to guard against an entire consolidation."[33] Unprovable is whether these exceptions should be viewed as the outer limit of interbranch involvement or representative of the kinds of branch interaction that should be accepted.

Political scientist Ralph A. Rossum stated that the Framers came to realize that preservation of liberty required coordinate and equal branches, with each performing a blend of functions, thereby balancing as opposed to strictly separating powers." The Constitution "does not inhibit, and even invites, the legislature, the executive, and the judiciary to share power in creative ways, [s]o long as the arrangements that emerge do not upset the specified design at the top of the structure."[34] John Manning rejected any overarching principle: "the Constitution reflects countless context-specific choices about how to assign, structure, divide, blend, and balance federal power. . . . [W]here no specific clause speaks directly to the question at issue, interpreters must respect the document's indeterminacy."[35] In fact, Washington approved a national bank run by a board of directors of whom only a minority was to be selected by the President.[36]

Scalia's majoritarianism was something of a stretch given limitations on popular rule in the Constitution. The people elected only one-half of one of the three branches of the national government – the House of Representatives, but it alone could do almost nothing.[37] The Framers were of two minds on giving power to the people. Experience under the Articles of Confederation led to fear of legislatures and unbridled democratic majority rule. Most Framers, an elite group, distrusted democracy.[38] Even the creation of a bicameral legislature impeded majoritarian rule.[39] Yet they believed popular sovereignty was the only valid basic constitutional principle. A scholar stressed that the early baseline was antistatist and antidemocratic.[40]

Distrust of state legislatures and the threat of rebellions led to higher willingness for the courts and juries to accept power, especially given the comparatively benign role of the judiciary in the 1760s and 1770s.[41] Despite its description as "the least dangerous branch" in *The Federalist* No. 78, it is not obvious that the framing generation expected the judiciary to be subservient to the remainder of the government.[42] Dean William Treanor found thirty-one cases in which judges voided statutes or actions of Congress on constitutional grounds and another seven where at least one judge so voted between 1787 and *Marbury v. Madison* (1803).[43] Thus, Treanor and others have demonstrated that judicial review was "relatively common"[44] pre-*Marbury*, which has supplanted the view that judicial review effectively began with *Marbury*. Judicial review was accepted both in the 1787 Constitutional Convention[45] and in the debates over ratification. Anti-Federalist George Mason of Virginia stated on July 21, 1787: "[Judges] could declare an unconstitutional law void."[46] *The Federalist* No. 78 stated that the Constitution "can be preserved in practice in no other way than through the medium of the court of justice, whose duty it must be to declare all acts contrary to the manifest tenor of the constitution void. . . . [Otherwise] all the reservations of particular rights or privileges would amount to nothing."[47] Moreover, Marshall and Story saw the federal courts, and especially the lower federal courts, as the chief bulwark against the wayward and insular states.[48]

James Wilson of Pennsylvania considered the judiciary, the President, and Congress all representatives of the people and equally important.[49] Wood stated that "in the decade following the Revolution was begun the remarkable transformation of judges from much-feared appendages of Crown power into one of 'the three capital powers of Government' – from minor magistrates tied to the colonial royal executives into an equal and independent entity in a modern tripartite republican government. . . . [T]he judges, although not elected, resembled legislators and executives in being agents or servants of the people with a responsibility equal to that of the other two branches of government to carry out the people's will, even to the point of sharing in the making of law."[50]

In *Obergefell v. Hodges* (2015),[51] Scalia dissented: "A system of government that makes the People subordinate to a committee of nine unelected lawyers does not deserve to be called a democracy." For Rakove, Scalia's position on judicial restraint demonstrated "the sheer implausibility of particularly egregious misreadings of the text."[52] "Independence of the judiciary from the political branches," a commentary pointed out, "assures a counter majoritarian constitutional check on majoritarian institutions."[53] Stephen Macedo wrote: "Direct democracy and majoritarianism were decisively rejected by the Framers, and the system of government established by the Constitution embodies that rejection."[54] The Constitution did not create a democracy, but rather a carefully constructed republic with checks and balances that gave great power to state legislatures, presidential electors, and the courts.

Scalia was not consistent in his deference to the popular branches. He seemed too ready to discard legislative enactments in favor of his often dogmatic and often unnuanced view of the Constitution, for example, striking down all gun control and all exceptions to confrontation, and sustaining all limitations on abortions. He seemed to have violated his principles in joining Roberts's activist opinion in *Shelby County, Alabama v. Holder* (2013).[55] Roberts's majority opinion identified what he called a "fundamental problem" with the preclearance provision of the Voting Rights Act:

> Congress did not use a record it compiled to shape a coverage formula grounded in current conditions. It instead reenacted a formula based on 40-year-old facts having no logical relation to the present day. The dissent relies on "second-generation barriers," which are not impediments to the casting of ballots, but rather electoral arrangements that affect the weight of minority votes.... Viewing the preclearance requires as targeting such efforts simply highlights the irrationality of continued reliance on the § 4 coverage formula, which is based on voting tests and access to the ballot, not vote dilution. We cannot pretend that we are reviewing an updated statute, or try our hand at updating the statutes ourselves, based on the new record compiled by Congress.... [W]e are not ignoring the record; we are simply recognizing that it played no role in shaping the statutory formula before us today.[56]

That was a remarkable statement for Scalia to endorse. Roberts reviewed the legislative record to decide that there was insufficient evidence for Congress to have passed a statute, decided there wasn't, and held the statute unconstitutional. The opinion also second-guessed Congress's judgment that continuation of the statute's preclearance provisions was necessary to maintain African-American voting rights. It was a blatant interference with the internal operating procedure of another branch of the government.[57] Separation of powers, federalism, and judicial restraint collided. Scalia's vote contradicted his concurrence in *United States v. Munoz-Flores* (1990),[58] which refused to consider a challenge to a revenue law that had allegedly originated in the Senate rather than the House, on the ground that a combination of separation of powers and precedent

> leads me to conclude that federal courts should not undertake an independent investigation into the origination of the statute at issue here.... We should no more gainsay Congress' official assertion of the origin of a bill than we would gainsay its official assertion that the bill was passed by the requisite quorum; or any more than Congress or the President would gainsay the official assertion of this Court that a judgment was duly considered and approved by our majority vote. Mutual regard between the coordinate Branches, and the interest of certainty, both demand that official representations regarding such matters of internal process be accepted at face value.[59]

The chapter ends with historical support for Scalia which he did not rely on and may not have known about. As mentioned above, he rejected the popular approach of balancing interests for a number of reasons, including that it enhances judicial power and that it often makes no sense, as exemplified by his example: "It is ... like judging whether a particular line is longer than a particular rock is heavy."[60] Professor Stephen B. Presser has called balancing contrary to originalism, a "license for judicial legislation and legerdemain."[61] Presser argued balancing is a relatively recent phenomenon, first explicitly appearing in the late 1930s and early 1940s; in earlier periods, constitutional decisions were decided categorically. Scholar T. Alexander Aleinikoff noted: "No Justice explained why such a methodology was a proper form of constitutional construction, nor did any purport to be doing anything novel or controversial. Yet balancing was a major break with the past, responding to the collapse of nineteenth century conceptualism and formalism as well as to half a century of intellectual and social change."[62]

24

Conservative Opinions Reconsidered: Individual Rights

The Constitution sought to guarantee rights "by creating avenues for the expression and exercise of popular will.... Rights were thus to be guaranteed by the people, constituted in republican institutions or through republican mechanisms," said David T. Konig.[1] Barry A. Shain wrote, "Most strikingly, though, is the agreement reached by the contributors in finding that culturally accepted seventeenth- and eighteenth-century rights claims, with the exception of religious conscience, were not primarily individualistic. They often were corporate in focus."[2] Saul Cornell went further, "for the Americans of the 1780s and 1790s, free exercise of religion meant the freedom of religious communities to regulate family and social life, not the freedom of the individual to do as he or she pleased."[3]

RELIGION CLAUSES

Pointing out that Jefferson went to a church located in the House of Representatives, Gordon Wood summed it up: "The Founders were confused about separation of church and state," and the circumstances were "just too complicated, too confusing, and too biased toward Protestant Christianity to be used in the courts today."[4] Thomas Drakeman observed that commentators "have poured out thousands of heavily footnoted pages divining the original meaning [of the Establishment Clause, and] [i]t is not for lack of intention, then, that there are such enduring controversies over the meaning of fairly simple words such as 'an' and 'respecting,' a situation that hardly bodes well for our ability to resolve disputes over genuinely challenging concepts, such as 'establishment' and 'religion.'"[5] A serious disagreement existed even over whether aid to all religions was consistent with the First Amendment.[6] There was disagreement over whether Sunday observance laws were consistent with separation of church and state.[7] The colonies differed radically in their attitude toward religion, with Puritan New England the most rigorous enforcer of religious orthodoxy.[8]

In general the founding generation accepted more government involvement in religion than was acceptable to the Warren and Burger Courts. Religion played a major role throughout most of the colonies just prior to the creation of the United States of America and morality was tied to religion.[9] One nonoriginalist scholar acknowledged that the founders would have accepted various measures that had a religious purpose and a main effect of supporting religion.[10] According to another, the Religion Clauses may have been intended for the narrow purpose of preventing a federally sanctioned national church or the federal funding of ministers, churches, or church property.[11] Justice Joseph Story (who was born in 1779) stated that the purpose of the Religion Clauses was to protect minority Christian, at least Protestant, denominations, and he was not the only one to say so.[12] The Framers were less religious than most of their contemporaries, and were worried about factional disputes that were alive in their memory, but they were not antireligious and were imbued with Protestantism; but mostly, they did not want religion to interfere with the new country and new Constitution through factionalism and preferential treatment. "[M]any could continue to view a vague kind of Protestantism as a useful mechanism for inculcating civic virtue."[13]

There were substantial differences among and sometimes within the colonies, so no single description suffices.[14] Depending on the definition, somewhere between three and eight states had an established church in 1786 and it took fifty years to complete disestablishment. Taxes supported churches in some states while Virginia and Maryland considered worship a duty.[15] Many post–Revolutionary War state constitutions required a belief in Christ and Christianity to hold office and engage in other activities.[16] Presbyterians opposed the adoption of the Constitution almost unanimously because they feared the possibility of established churches in some states.[17] Baptists took a similar position because the Constitution did not afford sufficient safeguards for religious freedom.

Analyses of the Establishment Clause have concluded that only a statement withdrawing federal government involvement in religion and not one that purported to set standards could have passed quickly – unlike most of the Bill of Rights, including the Freedom of Speech Clause.[18] History of Religion Professor William R. Hutchison stated that, "The founders, instead of attempting to agree, had left most of the church-state issues to the states and the courts."[19] Religious historian A. Gregg Roeber stated that the founders "intended to deny the federal government any competence in the entire area of 'religion.'"[20] Scalia agreed with this analysis; the Establishment Clause served to "prohibit an establishment of religion at the federal level," but also "to protect state establishments of religion from federal interference."[21] Thomas adopted the approach in *Elk Grove Unified School District v. Newdow* (2004),[22] the Pledge of Allegiance case from which Scalia recused himself. Scalia joined Thomas's concurrence in *Town of Greece v. Galloway* (2014),[23] which stated that "the Establishment Clause is 'best understood as a federalism provision,'" citing *Elk Grove*. Under this view incorporation of the First Amendment's

Establishment Clause into the Fourteenth Amendment provided no answers because the Establishment Clause had no substantive content. Nevertheless, Scalia found guidance in the Constitution on the subject of religion and the states.

Some of Scalia's views on religion were idiosyncratic. Relying on *McCreary County, Kentucky v. ACLU* (2005),[24] he distinguished between monotheistic religions and polytheistic religions. The frequent references to God and the Lord in founding-era speech by Presidents and others demonstrated that the government may favor and engage in monotheistic speech, such as prayers in schools and in legislative sessions. The government, however, cannot provide material support to monotheistic religions, which would be unconstitutional. Scalia's solution was creative but appears to have little historical or, for that matter, current, support.[25]

No colonial or early state constitution made a distinction between believing in a single God as opposed to no God or multiple gods.[26] There was, moreover, considerable anti-Catholic sentiment in the colonies and the early Republic.[27] One delegate to the Massachusetts ratifying convention railed against a plague of "Papists" and Mahommedans" if there were no strict religious qualification for holding federal office.[28] A North Carolina delegate said it was a mistake to invite "Jews and pagans of every kind to come among us."[29] The coupling of Islam with Christianity is certainly counterintuitive. What Framer, if he thought about it, would imagine that Islam would be in the same category as Christianity, but that Hinduism would be treated differently?

Newer approaches to the Establishment Clause by the Court's conservatives have put religions in competition with one another, with the more popular religions tending to prevail over fringe religions. Thus, conservatives will affix the Ten Commandments on some walls, but not symbols desired by Hindus, Moslems, and other mostly non-Western religions – unless, perhaps, they achieve a majority in a particular jurisdiction. As O'Connor noted, government involvement in religion may aggravate, if not create, divisions and social conflict within the United States.[30] What to make of Scalia's Establishment Clause jurisprudence? His originalist position on the substance of the Establishment Clause seemed selective and majoritarian, since the majority is the only ones that can pass laws. Since almost without exception no one has standing to challenge violations of the clause, the popular branches can do their will.[31]

SECOND AMENDMENT

Scalia's opinion in *Heller* was the subject of broad criticism by both the legal and historical communities. It was attacked by purposivists and pragmatists. Judge Posner also emphasized the importance of consequences: "I don't agree with Justice Scalia that indifference to hundreds of deaths that might result from the Supreme Court's embracing a broad interpretation of the Second Amendment is a sign of a good judge. If deaths are a consequence of deciding a case one way rather than another, that's something for the judge to consider along with other consequences."[32] Moreover, Scalia sometimes did rely on consequences, such as in his conservative opinion in *Arizona v. United States* (2012),[33] where, voting to uphold Arizona's laws adversely affecting illegal immigrants, he wrote, "Arizona bears the brunt of the country's illegal immigration problem. Its citizens feel themselves under siege by large numbers of illegal immigrants who invade their property, strain their social services, and even place their lives in jeopardy."[34]

Scalia's opinion in *Heller* was vulnerable on textualist grounds, in particular, his reliance on postenactment "legislative history" and other authority that permeated his opinion. In *Heller* Scalia cited debates and reports of the Thirty-Ninth Congress four times. He repeated the authority in *McDonald*: "In debating the Fourteenth Amendment, the 39th Congress referred to the right to keep and bear arms as a fundamental right deserving of protection."[35] No less an authority than Scalia himself condemned the use of postenactment legislative history. "The legislative history of a statute is the history of its consideration and enactment. 'Subsequent legislative history' – which presumably means the post-enactment history of a statute's consideration and enactment – is a contradiction in terms. The phrase is used to smuggle into judicial consideration legislators' expression *not* of what a bill currently under consideration means (which, the theory goes, reflects what their colleagues understood they were voting for), but of what a law *previously enacted* means. . . . In my opinion, the views of a legislator concerning a statute already enacted are entitled to no more weight than the views of a judge concerning a statute not yet passed."[36]

Stevens's dissent in *Heller* challenged Scalia on his home turf – originalism. The opinions disagreed broadly on the proper way to read the Amendment, especially the preamble. Stevens conceded that the Amendment created individual rights, but also concluded that "the Amendment is most likely read to secure to the people a right to use and possess arms in conjunction with service in a well-regulated militia."[37] The dissenters not only endorsed Stevens's originalist analysis, but supported a nonoriginalist analysis provided by Breyer in his separate dissent. For example, since state militias today are far less important than they were in the founding era, the rationale for the amendment provided in the first clause is far less persuasive and the amendment should be construed to permit strong regulation. Breyer, a pragmatic liberal,[38] described his approach as "similar to the standard the Court already employs in certain election-law speech, and due process cases."[39]

Conservative appeals judge J. Harvie Wilkinson III criticized Scalia's originalism, comparing Scalia's *Heller* opinion to Blackmun's Living Constitution opinion in *Roe v. Wade*. "Both decisions share four major shortcomings: an absence of a commitment to textualism; a willingness to embark on a complex endeavor that will require fine-tuning over many years of litigation; a failure to respect legislative judgments; and a rejection of the principles of federalism."[40] Wilkinson was pointing out that originalists were grasping at tenuous constitutional straws to defeat the popular will. Posner wrote: "The range of historical references in the majority opinion is breathtaking, but it is not evidence of disinterested historical inquiry. It is evidence of the ability of well-staffed courts to produce snow jobs."[41] Scalia's pro-gun-rights position was derided by Chief Justice Warren Burger, who in 1991 said that the Second Amendment "has been the subject of one of the greatest pieces of fraud, I repeat the word 'fraud,' on the American public by special interest groups that I have ever seen in my lifetime."[42] Treanor concluded his attack on *Heller*: "An honestly originalist court... would not take a crabbed view of the powers of Congress; it would not be hostile to gun control legislation; it would not embrace the regulatory takings doctrine."[43]

It has been among the historians that Scalia has fared worst on both textualism and originalism grounds, which demonstrates the tension between them and legal scholars. Historian David Konig stated: "It is simply not possible to understand what the Second Amendment meant to citizens of the Founding generation when they wrote, ratified, or read the amendment without taking into account the best historical methods available."[44] Jack Rakove rejected Scalia's analysis in *Heller*: "Scalia's version of originalism-textualism, as applied in this opinion, seems oblivious to the most important findings that historians from Edmund Morgan (writing on the Stamp Act) on through [Bernard] Bailyn, [Gordon S.] Wood, myself, and others have argued over the last half-century: that this was a deeply creative era in constitutionalism and political thought, and the idea that static definitions will capture the dynamism of what was going on cannot possibly be true."[45] Paul Finkelman excoriated Scalia for distorting and lifting out of context the provisions in state constitutions at the founding and for relying on claims of the defeated Anti-Federalists, rather than those of the prevailing Federalists as to the meaning of the Second Amendment.[46] Saul Cornell accused Scalia of relying on minor and discredited Anti-Federalist sources.[47] Wood had a more basic take: "At the framing people didn't draw distinctions at the heart of the Second Amendment debate.... [T]hey couldn't conceive of that debate."[48] Charles A. Miller wrote; "The framers considered a bill of rights valuable largely as a touchstone of political philosophy, rather than as a text of legal enforceable rights, and they thought history the best mode of inculcating civic virtue."[49] Scholars called Scalia opinion "sloppy and misleading"[50] and an "embarrassing performance."[51] Many of the sources for those fighting gun control were or had been on National Rifle Association's payroll.[52]

Scalia's borrowing methodology from the mid nineteenth century, which he transposed onto the late eighteenth century, "violate[d] one of the most established rules of construction from the Founding era."[53] Enormous changes in the first half of the nineteenth century, including a shift from a communal culture to individualism, affected Second Amendment analysis.[54] For historians of the eighteenth century the right to bear arms was not an individual, but a collective or corporate right at the founding. Rakove noted, "[I]f one wishes to find a perfect example of why Locke and Madison were right to worry about the slippery nature of political language, Justice Scalia's verbal sleight of hand in *Heller*, nominally waged in behalf of public meaning originalism, is a great place to begin."[55] Cornell rejected gun-rights advocates' conception of the framing era.

> Recreating the world of the eighteen century militia is not impossible, but it would require a reawakening of civic-mindedness and self-sacrifice that seems difficult to imagine in modern America.... [David] Konig's formulation of the amendment as an individual right exercised collectively seems closer to faithfully translating the dominant understanding of the amendment in the Founding era than does either the modern collective or individual rights paradigms.... [T]he subject of a private right to own firearms outside the militia was rarely discussed during the ratification debates, while the need to protect the militia from the threat posed by the Federal government received extensive commentary.... [R]ecent individual rights scholarship on the right to bear arms has been an exercise in law office history of a particularly bizarre kind.[56]

Cornell added: "Justice Scalia's use of dictionaries rests on a set of false assumptions about the relationship between early dictionaries and the history of the English language. These early dictionaries were not compiled according to modern scholarship rules, but were idiosyncratic reflections of their authors who generally sought to prescribe, not describe, contemporary patterns of usage."[57] Dictionaries are also less reliable when the issue is the meaning of more than a single word, whether it is the meaning of "bear arms" or a double negative. The terms "bear arms" and "bear guns" had different meanings in the late eighteenth century. Bearing arms had a clear military connotation.[58] William G. Merkel stated that "the original public meaning of the Second Amendment did not extend to arms possession outside the context of militia service at all, and according to the careful quantitative research of historian Nathan Kozuskanich, well over 95% of uses of the phrase 'bear arms' and its cognates surviving in pamphlets, journals, books, and recorded legislative debates in late colonial North American and the early Republic unambiguously refer to militia service or military duty."[59] Cornell disputed Scalia's discussion of the Quakers. "Quakers (Members of the Religious Society of Friends) did not oppose bearing guns, but they did oppose bearing arms, a vital distinction blurred by Justice Scalia's ahistorical approach. Rather than cite Quaker sources to support his warped view of history, Justice Scalia substitutes his own interpretation of what Quakers believed for the actual beliefs of eighteenth century Friends."[60] An important piece of evidence is that "[l]ocal communities and colonial assemblies passed regulatory legislation throughout the colonial period."[61]

Cornell and Konig attacked Scalia for his unwarranted demotion of the preamble, which in the founding era was often decisive in judging between two interpretations.[62] Konig, who analyzed preambles in state constitutions, wrote: "In the grammar of American constitutionalism, preambles were an essential feature of the syntax of rights," quoting the First Chief Justice, John Jay: "A preamble cannot annul enacting clauses; but when it evinces the intention of the legislature and the design

of the act, it enables us, in cases of two constructions, to adopt the one most consonant to their intention and design."[63] Konig concluded: "Justice Scalia's ahistorical
reliance on present-day settled rules of construction disqualif[ies] his dismissal of
the controlling force of the preamble." One cannot ignore the significance of the
well-regulated militia.[64]

However, a few liberal law professors – along with many conservatives and gun-
rights advocates – agreed with Scalia's interpretation. Harvard's Mark Tushnet said
that the evidence supports gun rights, but only narrowly.[65] Yale's Akhil Reed Amar
agreed on originalist and textualist ground rules that the Constitution should be read
to protect an individual's right to have a gun at home for self-defense.[66] Michael
Waldman, a lawyer and student of public policy who relied on historians, got it right:
"'Anti-Federalists' opposed the Constitution. They worried that the new government
would try to disarm the thirteen state militias. Critically, those militias were a product
of a world of civic duty and government compulsion utterly alien to us today. Every
white man age sixteen to sixty was enrolled. He was required to own – and bring –
a musket or other military weapon.... [The Amendment] protected the individual
right to a gun ... to fulfill the duty to serve in a militia. To the Framers, even our
question would make little sense. To us, their *answer* makes little sense."[67]

Scalia's approach contrasts with his concurrence in *City of Bourne v. Flores*
(1997)[68]: "The issue presented by *Smith* is, quite simply, whether the people, through
their elected representatives, or rather this Court, shall control the outcome of those
concrete cases. For example, shall it be the determination of this Court, or rather
of the people, whether ... church construction will be exempt from zoning laws?
The historical evidence put forward by the dissent does nothing to undermine the
conclusion we reached in *Smith*: It shall be the people."[69]

McDonald v. Chicago (2010) (5–4)[70] applied *Heller* to the states on the basis of
the Fourteenth Amendment in an opinion written by Alito and joined by Scalia,
who also wrote separately. Neither Scalia nor any other Justice in the majority
explained why the states could limit Seventh Amendment rights but not Second
Amendment rights, both of which they regarded as "fundamental."[71] Moreover,
Scalia had silently changed his position in *McDonald* from what he had said thirteen
years earlier, in *A Matter of Interpretation*. While he defended the meaning of the
Second Amendment he endorsed in *Heller*, he stated, without elaboration, "Of
course, properly understood, it is no limitation upon arms control by the states."[72]
Scalia did not explain what changed his mind, although his statement suggests he
considered the Second Amendment as largely a federalism amendment, designed
to protect states against encroachment by the new national government.

The Court's assertion in *McDonald* that the right to keep and bear arms was
considered "fundamental" to those who drafted and ratified the Bill of Rights
required accepting the narrow construction of the Amendment urged by the dissent.
Guns for hunting or for defense against criminals were hardly fundamental to the
new Republic any more than pornography was fundamental to the newly formed

system of government. Incorporation of an amendment to the Bill of Rights that was overwhelmingly related to nongovernmental uses of weapons should have created a difficult issue for the Court majority.[73]

CONSTITUTIONAL CRIMINAL PROCEDURE

Scalia considered the death penalty sacrosanct because it was widely administered in the framing era and because the Fifth Amendment seemed to accept its imposition. Tribe argued that the Fifth Amendment was merely accepting a reality and not ensconcing the death penalty; since there was a death penalty at the time, the Constitution dealt with it.[74] Another argument is that the framing generation had seen a relaxation of punishments and was aware of progress from the era when witchcraft brought the death penalty and torture was accepted. They had no reason to reject future progress that would permit their Constitution to be more humane. Simply because a constitution was written did not prevent the kinds of changes that the framing generation applauded. Originalism does not provide an incontrovertible answer.

Moreover, some death-is-different jurisprudence existed in the framing era. An in-depth study by Professor Nelson addressed early Massachusetts criminal practice in capital crimes. "When, for instance, a defendant charged with a capital offense sought to plead guilty, his plea would not have been accepted and he would be informed that he did not have to plead but could 'put the government to proof' its charges. A renewed plea of guilty would then be accepted only after the accused had been 'allow[ed] ... a reasonable time to consider what had been said to him" and after an examination had been conducted 'under oath ... as to the *sanity* of the prisoner; and whether there had not been tampering with him.'"[75] Also, the courts in a least a portion of the colonies appointed counsel for every defendant subject to the death penalty.[76] Death was different in other respects. While death sentences were almost routinely ordered for felony convictions, the rate of commutation for those sentences was high. "The common law generally allowed all convicted felons to be hanged, but first time offenders convicted of manslaughter were frequently branded with the letter 'M' for manslayer' in the 'brawn of the thumb' and released without further punishment – after having been granted benefit of clergy.... The procedure was widely sued in the colonies until after the Revolution."[77]

Scalia objected to locating a proportionality principle in the Eighth Amendment largely because the Bill of Rights has a provision against excessive fines but not against excessive other punishments. But that seems a too facile and overly textual reading of the language of the Bill of Rights in 1791, especially when there was no textualist culture. The Eighth Amendment prohibits cruel and unusual punishments, not cruel and unusual *methods of* punishment, a textualist argument that should have appealed to Scalia. A sentence of one day of solitary confinement may not be cruel and unusual, but that does not mean that a sentence of ten years of solitary confinement could not be. Linguists have so argued. "The phrase 'excessive fines' has the same structure as 'cruel punishments.' 'Excessive' picks out a subset of fines. 'Cruel' picks out a subset of punishments. . . . [I]t seems that the meaning of the text of the punishment clause of the Eighth Amendment – as it would have been understood by semantically competent ratifiers in 1789, and by semantically competent readers of the Bill of Rights in 2009 – prohibits punishments that are cruel relative to the offense."[78] Ronald Dworkin wrote that the Framers "would have expressed themselves more clearly if they had used the phrase 'punishments widely regarded as cruel and unusual on the date of this enactment' in place of the misleading language they actually used."[79] Perhaps ambiguous is a better word than misleading.

Historical evidence supports the view that "cruel and unusual punishment" encompassed proportionality. Magna Carta stated that "a freeman shall be amerced for a small offence only according to the degree of the offense; and for a grave offence he shall be amerced according to the gravity of the offense," a concept repeated over the centuries.[80] While imprisonment was just becoming common in the states, Europe was using confinement along with sentences of service in galleys (mostly in south Europe) and transportation to the colonies (mostly in England) in lieu of execution.[81] Considerable literature existed on proportionality of sentences in the Revolutionary and founding eras.[82] A number of colonial constitutions included provisions barring excessive punishment. In 1777 Jefferson drafted a Bill for Proportioning Crimes and Punishments, but Virginia never enacted it. Murder, including dueling, and treason were punished by death, counterfeiting brought six years of hard labor, while robbery brought four. Some crimes included reparation and whipping. In Pennsylvania, the state leader in punishment reform as well as the site of the 1987 Constitutional Convention, imprisonment for hard labor was the predominate punishment in the 1780s.[83] Massachusetts instituted hard labor in 1785.[84] It is also unlikely that the number of lashes imposed on a felon was unrelated to the seriousness of the crime. Speaking of the framing era, Professor Leonard Levy broadly stated that "punishment must also be proportioned to the offense."[85]

Scalia also seems wrong when he wrote in *Walton v. Arizona* (1990)[86] that the "mandatory imposition of death – without sentencing discretion – for a crime which States have traditionally punished with death cannot possibly violate the Eighth Amendment." The exercise of discretion was an integral part of the operation of the death penalty at common law and was presumably incorporated into the Eighth Amendment. Just because a crime is punishable by death does not mean that every convicted defendant must be executed. Just because judges almost always exercise their discretion in a certain direction does not mean that discretion can be taken away from them.

DUE PROCESS

From the days of Magna Carta due process was equivalent to "the law of the land." Levy declared that under many state constitutions "citizens were additionally protected by the standard 'law of the land' clause, the equivalent of a due process clause."[87] At the time of the framing, eight states had "law of the land" clauses in their constitutions.[88] While no state had a Due Process Clause in its own constitution, New York had recommended such a clause in place of the more familiar "law of the land" clause. Levy said, "[e]ither phrasing carried the majesty and prestige of the Magna Carta. Sir Edward Coke taught, and Americans believed, that due process of law meant accordance with regularized common-law procedures, especially grand jury accusation and trial by jury,"[89] but which arguably included substantive rights, which was the law of the land.[90] Due process or law of the land also seems to have had a separation of powers component. The executive acting alone would not be able to deprive persons of their rights except as provided by common law or statute, and legislatures would not be able to act beyond their proper legislative roles of enacting general rules governing future conduct.[91] Ronald Dworkin said: "Those who say that 'substantive due process' is an oxymoron, because substance and procedure are opposites, overlook the crucial fact that a demand for coherence in principle, which has evident substantive consequences, is part of what makes a process of decision making a legal process."[92]

Commentators have argued that "[t]he term 'due process of law' in the Fifth and Fourteenth Amendments is a term of art; it has a specialized legal meaning over and above the concatenation of the words in the phrase."[93] The idea that laws had to serve the public interest rather than special interests, and that exclusive privileges could not be granted to one group at the expense of another, was seen as a basic requirement of due process.[94] Words and terms had different meanings 230 years ago and some developed nonliteral meanings, such as *habeas corpus* (literally, "you have the body").

Recent scholarship by conservatives has located *Lochner*-type substantive due process dating from the Declaration of Independence,[95] although the analysis has had its detractors, including Scalia. *Lochner* involved economic rights, including an unenumerated "right" to contract. It was part of "liberty" derived in large part from England's radical Whigs and included economic liberty and property rights, contrary to more modern thinking.[96] A conservative scholar stated: "[T]he pre-New Deal Supreme Court's approach to interpreting the Due Process Clause did not recognize the modern categories of 'substantive' and 'procedural' due process."[97] Simple and facile answers are unwarranted.

SELF-INCRIMINATION AND OTHER CRIMINAL PROCEDURE

Levy stated: "Read literally and in context, the right seemed to apply only to a criminal defendant at trial": "nor should any person . . . be compelled in any criminal case to be a witness against himself." The eight states that had similar protection from compelled testimony were all over the lot in coverage. As originally drafted by Madison, the clause applied to civil as well as criminal proceedings, to any stage of a legal inquiry, and encompassed witnesses as well as parties. It applied not just to criminal liability, but to compelled evidence, for example, that placed one in public disgrace.[98] The House held no debate on the clause. The Senate changed the language without explanation and the House accepted the change, again without discussion. The practice at the time the Fifth Amendment was ratified had little to do with the language, and tended to follow Madison's broad articulation, even in those states that did not have a declaration or bill of rights. Thomas's position in *Chavez v. Martinez* (2003)[99] that the Self-Incrimination Clause was a trial right has been challenged on historical grounds; rather, the right included the pretrial right to refuse to answer questions during a Marian postarrest examination taken by justices of the peace, which conformed to mid-sixteenth-century legislation enacted during the reign of Mary Tudor and called the Marian Statutes.[100]

Scalia dissented from the Court's decision in *Mitchell v. United States* (1995)[101] that a defendant does not waive her self-incrimination plea at her sentencing by having pleaded guilty to the crime, stating: "Our hardy forebears, who thought of compulsion in terms of the rack and oaths forced by the power of law, would not have viewed the drawing of a commonsensical inference as equivalent pressure. And it is implausible that the Americans of 1791, who were subject to adverse inferences for failing to give unsworn testimony, would have viewed an adverse inference for failing to give sworn testimony as a violation of the Fifth Amendment." Viewed in the light of the history of self-incrimination, Scalia's analysis fails to convince. Levy wrote that, "torture was never sanctioned by the common law, although it was employed as an instrument of royal prerogative until 1641." The right against compelled self-incriminations was well established in the colonies by the middle of the eighteenth century.[102] Thus, it appears that the rack and other tortures were not the background for the Constitution's Self-Incrimination Clause. The history of the clause has been less bloody and more nuanced.[103]

Aside from granting *habeas corpus* to an American citizen caught up in terrorism in *Hamdi v. Rumsfeld* (2004),[104] Scalia was consistently against granting relief to aliens held at Guantanamo or elsewhere outside the United States on the ground that historically the writ did not reach foreign territory. But this originalist view in the noncitizen habeas cases has been challenged on the basis that the writ was available where the sovereign *controlled* the territory. Some historians have argued that the preconstitutional British reach of *habeas corpus* "was not contingent on total sovereignty over the land in question. Rather, an 'English court's determination of whether it could issue the writ beyond the realm turned primarily on the crown's control over the territory in question and the ability of English judges to enforce the writ, not the particular label ascribed to the territory.'"[105] Once again, history casts a flickering light.

AFFIRMATIVE ACTION

History may be against Scalia's (and Thomas's) originalist approach to affirmative action. While Scalia relied on serious legal scholarship, it appears affirmative action was accepted at the time the Fourteenth Amendment was adopted,[106] and the amendment covered characteristics other than race. Contemporaneous legislation included the Freedman's Bureau Bill of 1864, the Freedman's Bureau Act of 1865, and the Freedman's Bureau Act of 1866, all of which provided special protection and privileges for blacks. Professor Eric Schnapper wrote: "The race-conscious Reconstruction programs were enacted concurrently with the fourteenth amendment and were supported by the same legislators who favored the same constitutional guarantee of equal protection. This history strongly suggests that the framers could not have intended it generally to prohibit affirmative action for blacks or other disadvantaged groups. . . . It is inconceivable that the majority of Congress, by approving the amendment, intended to condemn their most important domestic program or to embody in the Constitution the social theory of their opponents."[107] Context is key.[108]

In fact, Congress rejected language that would have covered "race, color, or descent" and debated whether the amendment protected Chinese and American Indians.[109] "[W]hile the concerns of freed slaves were quite present in the minds of those debating the Amendment, [contemporaneous] debates concerned themselves with other groups and problems as well – most particularly immigrants, Southern Unionists, and Northern migrants to the South, all of whom were facing discrimination and social proscription."[110] Jefferson Powell placed equal protection in a broader context. "A legitimate interpretation of the scope of the equal protection clause must make sense of the clause's words and of its context, and not simply disregard them because of the interpreter's reconstruction of intentions not incorporated in the text and context. History's proper role in the clause's interpretation is to render the interpretation of the *clause* fuller and more convincing, not to supplant it. . . . It is a Constitution the interpreter is expounding, not a question of intellectual history."[111]

Powell noted that there was little communal understanding. "Few people cared in 1866 about the very narrow issues of Fourteenth Amendment jurisprudence that the Supreme Court would face over the course of the next century or about how particular cases would be decided under the new amendment." Basically, there was relief that the Fourteenth Amendment passed at all. Among other problems was answering objections to the questionable process by which the amendment was adopted.[112] William Nelson noted that "the people who framed the section, who voted for it in Congress, and who later ratified it in the states were acting primarily as statesmen and political leaders, not as legal draftsmen."[113] Confusion reigned, even over such fundamental issues as whether the Fourteenth Amendment granted former slaves the right to vote.[114] After tracing the various versions of the Fourteenth

Amendment debated in 1865 and 1866, Nelson concluded that the issue of the precise rights enumerated in the amendment was not critical at the time:

> What was politically essential was that the North's victory in the Civil War be rendered permanent and the principles for which the war had been fought rendered secure, so that the South, upon readmission to full participation in the Union could not undo them.... Once the purpose of the amendment is so understood, there will be nothing odd in the failure of its proponents to resolve specific legal issues.... The debates themselves did not reduce the vague, open-ended, and sometimes clashing principles used by the debaters to precise, carefully bounded legal doctrine. That would be the task of the courts once the Fourteenth Amendment, having been enacted into law, was given over to them to reconcile its ambiguities and its conflicting meanings.[115]

Michael W. McConnell and others have challenged the position that school segregation was universally accepted in 1868: "the belief that school segregation does in fact violate the Fourteenth Amendment was held during the years immediately following the ratification by a substantial majority of political leaders who had supported the Amendment."[116] "[S]chool segregation was understood during Reconstruction to violate the principles of equality of the Fourteenth Amendment.... Between 1870 and 1875 both houses of Congress voted repeatedly, by large margins, that *de jure* segregation of the public schools is unconstitutional."[117] Nelson observed: "When the Fourteenth Amendment itself was under consideration, segregation was not an important issue. Indeed, there was no direct discussion during the ratification debates of any of the issues subsequently raised by *Plessy v. Ferguson* or *Brown v. Board of Education*."[118] No state constitutions in 1868 required segregation, although fifteen did by 2014. The situation started deteriorating almost immediately with the occupation of the South by federal troops.[119] Finally, finding a consensus on the meaning of the Fourteenth Amendment in 1868 is unattainable in view of the chasm that existed on racial attitudes in the North and in the South.

To originalists who relied on Harlan's dissent in *Plessy v. Ferguson* (1896)[120] that the Constitution is "color-blind," Professor Mitchell N. Berman replied:

> While Justice Scalia proclaimed that "the Constitution proscribes government discrimination on the basis of race," Justice Thomas quoted and requoted the first Justice Harlan's famous declaration that "[o]ur Constitution is color-blind." Yet the basis for these assertions was and is mysterious – at least for an announced (and proselytizing) Originalist. Not only does the constitutional text say no such thing, making it radically implausible to suppose that "no racial classifications at all" was the original public meaning, but the best evidence of the original intentions is that the framers did not intend to constitutionalize a principle of strict colorblindness. To be sure, this needn't stop *living constitutionalists* from embracing colorblindness as a constitutional principle. But it should be a massive impediment – indeed an insurmountable one – for Thomas and Scalia.[121]

While Scalia rejected applying the Fourteenth Amendment to protect women's and gays' rights on originalism and textualism grounds that they are not mentioned in the Constitution and they were not protected groups in the founding era or in 1868, when the Fourteenth Amendment was ratified, blanket rejection of unenumerated rights seems counterhistorical. Many of the leading founders and Framers, especially the Federalist majority, opposed a bill of rights because they feared that the inclusion of some rights would lead to the rejection of other valuable rights.[122] Arguably, the Ninth Amendment "explicitly den[ied] the legitimacy of inferring the nonexistence of unenumerated rights from the existence of those explicitly stipulated." A battle emerged at New York's ratifying convention over the language of the Tenth Amendment, which reads: "The powers not delegated to the United States by the Constitution, nor prohibited by it to the States are reserved to the States respectively, or to the people." Anti-Federalist Thomas Tudor Tucker moved to insert the word "expressly" between "not" and "delegated." Madison responded that the same motion was made in Virginia and it did not pass. Saul Cornell wrote: "Without the insertion of the word 'expressly,' many Anti-Federalists believed that amendments were of little consequence: the new government would eventually absorb all power within its orbit."[123]

Moreover, the Fourteenth Amendment text does not distinguish between blacks, on the one hand, and women and gays, on the other hand: "nor shall any State deprive any person of life, liberty, or property without due process of law; nor deny to any person within its jurisdiction the equal protection of the laws."[124] Since for Scalia text trumped originalism in *Lucas* on the Takings Clause and permitted compensation for regulatory takings, the question arises why the text should not prevail in nonrace discrimination cases.[125] Another point may be made. The framing generation did not reject unenumerated *powers*, and the First Congress assumed the burden of state Revolutionary War debt and supported the creation of a national bank over objections that they were beyond the national government's constitutional powers.[126] A scholar concluded: "On balance, the historical evidence shows that one widespread understanding of the Due Process Clause of the Fifth Amendment in 1791 included judicial recognition and enforcement of unenumerated natural and customary rights against congressional action."[127]

PRIVACY AND RELATED DOCTRINES

Scalia argued that Colorado's constitutional amendment in *Romer v. Evans* (1996)[128] did not discriminate against the gay community. "The people of Colorado have adopted an entirely reasonable provision which does not even disfavor homosexuals *in any substantive sense*, but merely denies them preferential treatment."[129] However, the Colorado law stigmatized a minority just like the laws upheld in *Plessy v. Ferguson*. Moreover, nothing stops obese people from seeking legislation to prevent discrimination against them. Unlike gays they can get protection without having to secure a constitutional amendment. Scalia's disparagement of procedural due process was indefensible, especially in view of his strong tendency to respect procedural rights. It was one of his weakest opinions.

Scalia's reliance on precedent was misplaced. The law upheld in *Bowers* was not directed at homosexuals, as opposed to all forms of sodomy.[130] Defendants prosecuted for engaging in homosexual conduct (or committing bigamy) were guaranteed the rights accorded to all criminal defendants, while Amendment 2 provided none of those rights.[131] Finally, there was little in the way of originalist analysis of the Equal Protection Clause.[132] Seven years later the Court overruled *Bowers* in *Lawrence v. Texas* (2003),[133] where historians filed a brief that opposed the prevailing originalist views of laws against homosexual sex as historically criminal activity. Yale historian George Chauncy argued that laws against homosexuals were "a historical aberration.... [S]ame-sex sodomy, in contrast to sodomy more broadly, was not a consistent target throughout history.... [G]overnmental discrimination against homosexuals only became widespread in the twentieth century."[134]

Bowers and the polygamy statutes targeted particular conduct, while Colorado Amendment 2 targeted orientation.[135] Scalia's statement that "where criminal sanctions are not involved, homosexual 'orientation' is an acceptable stand-in for homosexual conduct" was a remarkable statement for a textualist, and he went to great pains to defend it.[136] However, the distinction between orientation and conduct is too fundamental to be eliminated in that fashion, largely because a law denying people important rights based their orientation is abhorrent. Textualist Scalia also contradicted his opinion in *Zuni Public School District No. 89 v. Department of Education* (2007),[137] which did not seem to leave room for "stand-ins": "The only sure indication of what Congress intended is what Congress enacted; and even if there is a difference between the two, the rule of law demands that the latter prevail."

For Scalia, *Obergefell v. Hodges* (2015)[138] was the Living Constitution with a vengeance. Not only were gay rights unmentioned in the Constitution, but gays and lesbians did not exist as an identifiable minority in America until the late twentieth century. No colorable historical argument based on post-Classical western experience could fashion a constitutional right for two people of the same gender to marry. Whether it was a welcomed decision depends on one's point of view, but it was a constitutional stretch or worse for those who rejected the Living Constitution. Nevertheless, like *Brown*, the Court raised a discriminated-against minority one step closer to equality under the law. Like *Brown*, many people correctly believed that the vision and promise of the United States would be compromised if the Court did not strike down discrimination against the gay and lesbian community, whatever it took.[139]

Law review comment generally disfavored Scalia's originalist right-to-die decision in *Cruzan v. Director, Missouri Department of Health* (1990).[140] A harsh article said: "Justice Scalia distorts history, legal precedent, and clinical experience in his effort to identify the Cruzan family decision to terminate Nancy's medical treatment as the equivalent of assisted suicide. . . . American courts have long held that a person has a right to refuse medical treatment even when this means acquiescing in imminent and inevitable death."[141] In equating Cruzan's case with suicide, moreover, Scalia seemed to have violated his principle that individual rights should be articulated and judged on the most specific level available. A more specific articulation was available, namely, whether a person in a vegetative state has a right to withdraw medical attention with the certain result of death.[142] Here there *was* precedent that contradicted Scalia that the literature identifies. In *Colony v. More*, a 1702 Connecticut decision, "a court dismissed a prosecution for infanticide based on evidence that a mother refused to accept help needed to keep her baby alive; the law, according to the court, prohibited the murder of infants, not merely suspicion that a mother wanted her baby dead and therefore declined medical help to keep it alive."[143] The originalist position is nonlibertarian, as is its position against a right to abortion.

A Washington State statute authorized courts to grant visitation rights if a judge found that they benefited the child. In the face of a claim of visitation rights by grandparents, parents claimed that it infringed upon the fundamental rights of parents to raise their own children. The Court declared the statute unconstitutional under the Due Process Clause in *Troxel v. Granville* (2000).[144] Dissenting, Scalia refused to enforce a claimed constitutional right by parents that predated the Revolution. "I do not believe that the power which the Constitution confers upon me as a judge entitles me to deny legal effect to laws that (in my view) infringe upon what is (in my view) that unenumerated right." While parental rights were among the "unalienable Rights" of the Declaration of Independence, that did not make the statute unconstitutional. Parental rights were unenumerated rights that state legislatures could change.[145]

25

Conservative Opinions Reconsidered: Other

The powers granted the new government reflected in part American experience under the British Empire and the Articles of Confederation. The emphasis in this chapter is primarily on rights and issues that involve the exercise of government power, particularly in the commercial or civil-litigation context.

COMMERCE CLAUSE AND REGULATION

Early manufacturing and commerce were tightly controlled in England, at least if government-sanctioned guilds are included. Often neglected is that during the late colonial period England largely controlled colonial commerce through the Privy Council. "In ordinary commercial appeals, the Privy Council encouraged predictability in commercial transactions across the trading empire," a supervision that effectively ended in 1774 after the Boston Tea Party.[1] Colonial resistance to England had been mostly on other issues, especially taxation.[2] To a significant extent the important distinction was between commercial regulation of trade, broadly defined, and taxation, rather than between manufacturing and commerce before events made that distinction peripheral.[3] The founders had a history of generally benign relations with a strong central power overseeing commerce,[4] occasioned largely to secure loyalty against France.[5]

Some framing-generation judges gave the Commerce Clause broad scope in court decisions,[6] especially when combined with the Necessary and Proper Clause. These included disputes involving the First and Second National Bank (the former in 1791), since the Constitution does not specifically allow creation of a national bank. Then, like now, there was sharp disagreement over the scope of the Commerce Clause.[7] "[E]ach of the key terms in the Clause – 'commerce,' 'among the several States,' and 'to regulate' – had both a limited and an expansive meaning in the everyday parlance of 1787. . . . Congress has always been able to regulate (including by prohibition) any market-based activity that affects more than one state."[8] The

Framers in Philadelphia sought at least to reduce commercial conflicts between states. What else they contemplated is unclear. To the extent that delegates to the Philadelphia Convention or state ratifying conventions thought about commerce, they undoubtedly focused on transportation, the most conspicuous and immediate issue, but there was more on their minds.[9] Those claiming a broad reading of the Commerce Clause rely not only on precedent but on the argument that it is impossible to interpolate forward from the insular and agricultural society of the late eighteenth century to the present highly industrialized, centralized, and mobile society.[10]

Many students of the Constitution have taken a broad view of the Commerce Clause on the ground that the whole enterprise of writing the Constitution and creating a new nation was based on the conviction that a confederation of sovereign states was untenable.[11] Justice Holmes wrote in *Swift & Co. v. United States* (1905): "commerce among the States is not a technical legal concept, but a practical one, drawn from the course of business."[12] The absence of a clearer historical answer is in part due to the focus in the late eighteenth century on foreign commerce, because conventional thinking attributed no economic value to domestic trade; it was "a mere passing of wealth around the community from hand to hand," in other words, a zero-sum enterprise. That thinking changed in the early years of the Republic.[13]

A functional approach to the scope of the Commerce Clause suggests that "commerce meant all gainful employment intended for the marketplace, as distinguished from those undertaken for personal or home use,"[14] which is similar to Rehnquist's position that a statute enacted pursuant to the Commerce Clause had to regulate *economic activity* and have to do with *economic enterprise*. Defenders of the ACA correctly pointed out that unlike *Lopez* and *Morrison*, health-care management was a national commercial problem that fit within the scope of the Commerce Clause.[15] Under that reasonable reading of the Commerce Clause, Scalia voted conservatively but historically in *United States v. Lopez* and *United States v. Morrison*, liberally but historically in *Gonzales v. Raich* (2005),[16] while conservatively and ahistorically in the *Affordable Care Act Case*.[17] Scalia argued in ACA. "*Raich* is no precedent for what Congress has done here. That case's prohibition of growing and possession did not represent the expansion of the federal power into a broad new field."[18] But when the Constitution was ratified, everything and every field was new. Congress could not and did not refrain from acting on the ground that the regulation was into a new field. Depending on when (if ever) Scalia's views prevail, there will be a bastardized and irrational division between state and federal regulation.[19]

Also, where does it say that laissez-faire is the constitutional default position on the role of governments in their relationships with business? That questionable premise seems to be both the source and product of conservative opposition to government regulation. Yet it seems counterhistorical. Even Hamilton rejected laissez-faire, as Gordon Wood observed. "He was very much the mercantilist who believed deeply in the 'need' in government for 'a common directing power.' He had only contempt for those who believed in the laissez-faire and thought that trade and interests could regulate themselves."[20] William Nelson agreed. "[T]he lack of a centrally appointed bureaucracy did not produce a laissez-faire economy. Common law institutions regulated local economies tightly. Entrepreneurs could not use land for nonagricultural purposes, such as building a mill dame or constructing an urban dwelling, without conforming to local rules and often without obtaining prior judicial consent. Courts directed the construction and superintended the maintenance of the transportation infrastructure, they oversaw the lodging and liquor industries, they administered the poor laws, they supervised the collection of taxes, and they watched over education of the young."[21]

GOVERNMENT TAKINGS

Conceding that historically the Takings Clause did not apply to regulatory takings, Scalia defended compensation for those takings on textualist grounds in *Lucas v. South Carolina Coastal Counsel* (1992): "The text of the Clause can be read to encompass regulatory as well as physical deprivations."[22] Dissenting, Blackmun argued that Scalia's Takings Clause position was inconsistent with his textualism, since one does not ordinarily say that someone takes a toy from a child when he limits the child's use of it to one hour a day, borrowing from Scalia's technique. Blackmun, who examined late-eighteenth- and early-nineteenth-century state cases and other authority far more extensively than Scalia, also found Scalia's position was inconsistent with history, stating, "the Court seems to treat history as a grab bag of principles, to be adopted where they support the Court's theory, and ignored when they do not."[23]

The obligation to compensate owners of property for taking by the state is disputed. Conservative Judge John T. Noonan, Jr., and others challenged the Court's favoring property owners,[24] including on state sovereign immunity.[25] Many of the Framers believed the government could – and in the interests of society often should and did – limit individuals' free use of property; balancing societal needs against individuals' property right was left in large part to the political process. Only Massachusetts and Vermont had explicit compensation provisions in their constitutions.[26] Anti-Federalists feared that the new, remote, and ambitious federal government would confiscate personal property, such as livestock for use in wars, as it did during Revolutionary War.[27] Dean Treanor concluded: "Eighteenth-century colonial legislatures regularly took private property without compensating the owner. . . . The just compensation clause of the Fifth Amendment reflected the liberalism of its author, James Madison, who intended the clause to have narrow legal consequences: It was to apply only to the federal government and only to physical takings."[28] James W. Ely, Jr., disagreed and argued that compensation by the states was "the usual practice," even if it not required by statute, although he acknowledged and cited exceptions.[29] Most eminent domain was to build roads and waterways, but also buildings. Ely also viewed Madison's views and role differently. Moreover, "lawmakers sometimes delegated the power of eminent domain to private individuals whose activities were seen as benefiting the community."[30] A third scholar wrote that the practice varied from colony to colony and depended largely on nonlegal factors, such as land price and how most of the landed population acquired their property.[31] The history seems unclear.

Compensating nonphysical takings is affected by concepts of property that were different in the late eighteenth century. John Reid wrote in *The Concept of Liberty in the Age of the American Revolution*: "The fact that liberty, as well as other civil rights, was property helps to explain why eighteenth-century British constitutional law accorded such high priority to the right to property. The defense of property meant the defense of liberty and rights, not merely the preservation of material possessions." Property included the intangible, like the right to vote.[32] "Liberty and security of property had always been linked in the thoughts and programs of the opponents to arbitrary power, and was an especially gravid proposition during times of constitutional crisis.... Property was liberty because property secured independence."[33]

FEDERALISM

Federal power was the issue in *Printz v. United States* (1997),[34] where Scalia's originalist opinion held unconstitutional an interim provision requiring state officials to perform background checks under the Brady Act.[35] Four Justices vigorously dissented on both historical and pragmatic grounds. Stevens argued that no constitutional provision imperiled the act's interim provision and that the presumption of constitutionality should prevail, a majoritarian position.[36] At the founding, both Federalists and Anti-Federalists welcomed commandeering. Souter argued that *The Federalist* Nos. 27 and 36 actually supported the dissent and that Nos. 36 and 45 were consistent with it. Hamilton wrote in *The Federalist* No. 27 that "the legislatures, courts, and magistrates, of the respective members, will be incorporated into the operation of the national government *as far as it is just and constitutional authority extends*; and will be rendered auxiliary to the enforcement of the laws." Jefferson used state militias to conduct first Federal Militia Census in 1802.[37] Anti-Federalists' antipathy to a standing national army was consistent with the national government's using state resources on an *ad hoc* basis rather than permanently strengthening the national government. Anti-Federalists modified their position on commandeering when their fears turned out to be unfounded. "Oscillating views toward commandeering are not surprising. The constitutional text has little to say about the issue, and present issues are far removed from the mostly forgotten concerns that motivated the Founders."[38] Similarly, Anti-Federalists opposed the creation of lower federal courts in 1789 and preferred for state courts to handle all trials and intermediate appellate review.[39] Scholars favored the dissent's more modulated arguments.[40] With the concept of federalism so vague in 1789, the originalists' search for an answer may be doomed. "The ongoing constitutional debates of the 1790s demonstrated the fragile nature of the definitions of political and legal authority that many Americans believed they had worked out in the course of the conflict with Britain."[41]

History favored Scalia, however, in *Arizona State Legislature v. Arizona Independent Redistricting Comm'n* (2015),[42] which he viewed as matter of textualism. The distinction between a republic and a democracy was on everyone's mind during the framing period, as evidenced by the care with which the national government power was allocated to different bodies – the people, the state legislatures, and the presidential electors.[43] Even though Scalia did not make the argument, equating the people with state legislatures was not good history.

ARTICLE III – STANDING AND ADVERSE PARTIES

Commentators have disputed Scalia's restrictive position on standing, starting with his requirement that each plaintiff must demonstrate standing, including particularized injury, even when there is otherwise an Article III case or controversy. Raoul Berger argued that there was no such requirement at the time of the founding, when the distinction between public and private actions was less developed. For example, private citizens prosecuted crimes.[44] Scalia seems to have based his position on the principle of separation of powers.[45] But that creates serious problems for a textualist/originalist. Separation of powers is not mentioned in the Constitution. To derive a rigorous requirement for standing based on the structure of the Constitution is not that different from Douglas's penumbras and emanations in *Griswold v. Connecticut*, which Scalia abhorred.[46]

While the framing era supports Scalia's broader point that courts are not supposed to resolve every issue,[47] it does not seem to support his position that Congress cannot create standing by statute less rigorous than Article III standing. The First Congress enacted statutes that empowered informants to enforce the law and defended the concept of citizen suits. Criminal law was enforced by ordinary citizens. Scalia himself alluded to these early indications of receptivity in his opinion in *Vermont Agency of Natural Resources v. United States ex rel. Stephens* (2000).[48] Cass Sunstein argued, "[t]here is absolutely no affirmative evidence that Article III was intended to limit congressional power to create standing."[49]

Scalia's narrow view of standing has had systemic consequences beyond the obvious one that fewer corporate actions will be challenged on the ground that they violated administrative regulations. By allowing just those regulated to obtain court review, and not complaints by consumers, for example, about an agency's failure to promulgate regulations, courts hear only claims that agencies over-regulated and none that they under-regulated. To escape judicial review and perhaps reversal and criticism, agencies are motivated to do as little as possible, with regulated corporations the beneficiaries.[50] Nevertheless, limiting standing does support the political branches and arguably reduces misallocation of resources caused by private products-liability and environmental lawsuits.[51]

For Scalia, the requirement of adverse parties in a law suit was a fundamental component of separation of powers that went to the essence of the Constitution. At issue in *United States v. Windsor* (2013)[52] was the right of Article III federal courts to decide cases that lacked adverse parties after the United States refused to support the DOMA. Kennedy's majority opinion cast the adverse-parties requirement as prudential, rather than jurisdictional. Scalia strongly disagreed and argued that *Windsor* should not have been allowed to proceed. A law review article noted, "judicial opinions conflating cases with controversy are of relatively recent vintage," and concluded that many early proceedings, going back to Chief Justice Marshall, involved claims for individual relief such as applications for pensions and licenses.[53]

A debate in 1800 in the House of Representatives involving John Marshall, not cited in any opinion, provided a mixed picture. A district judge, advised by President John Adams, turned Jonathan Robbins over to British authorities pursuant to a treaty, on the ground that Robbins was in fact a British seaman named Thomas Nash. Once the judge did, the British executed Robbins. Jeffersonian Edward Livingston introduced a resolution in the House condemning Adams for interfering in a judicial proceeding. Marshall, who served in the House between December 1799 and May 1800, argued against Livingston in a floor debate. Marshall observed that Article III vested the judiciary with power over "all cases in law and equity arising under the constitution, laws and treaties of the United States." To be a case, a question must assume a legal form, for forensic litigation, and judicial decision. "If the judicial power extended to every question under the constitution, it would involve almost every subject proper for legislative discussion and decision; if to every question under the laws and treaties of the United States it would involve almost every subject on which the executive could act. The division of power . . . could exist no longer, and the other departments would be swallowed up by the judiciary." Moreover, the constitutional system gave the political branches exclusive, *de jure* authority to answer some questions of law. For Marshall, ordinary questions of law were for the courts, while questions of "political law" or political judgment, like the Robbins matter, were for the Executive Branch. Thus, Adams's involvement was not improper. The leading constitutionalist among House Jeffersonians, Albert Gallatin, called Marshall's argument "unanswerable." The House defeated Livingston's motion by a wide margin.[54]

Marshall's general position was similar to Scalia's in *Windsor* that the power to decide constitutional issues was tied to cases or controversies. The Robbins debate rejected advisory opinions, but did not require rigorous application of standing and adverse parties. *Windsor* was in a "forensic form, for forensic litigation," unlike the

Robbins matter in the House of Representatives. Moreover, it bore some resemblance a claim for individual relief, such as a pension or a license, which Marshall accepted. While the *Windsor* majority was wrong, it is not clear whether Scalia was right. Moreover, the debate and history suggests a lack of crystallization of the difficult issues facing the Court in *Windsor*.[55]

26

Liberal Opinions Reconsidered

FREE SPEECH

The founding generation believed that the government had substantial power to punish speech after it occurred, as opposed to prior restraints.[1] States with freedom-of-the-press clauses in their constitutions allowed stamp taxes on newspapers. Truth was not assured as a defense for seditious libel. The much and justly maligned Sedition Act of 1798 included truth as a defense to libel, which changed the terms of the debate.[2] In fact, the dispute over the act was primarily a question of federalism rather than of civil liberties.[3] Reid pointed out that because issues involving liberty were not subject to judicial review in the eighteenth century, the concept was not precise, especially in Britain. He referred to the "famous paradox apparent in Blackstone's insistence that, when speech is punished according to law, '*the liberty of the Press*, properly understood, is by no means infringed or violated.'" Reid explained: "The remarkable fact is not how far we have departed from Blackstone's jurisprudence, but rather the certainty that we no longer understand his legal theory because the vocabulary of liberty has been so changed that we read his words – 'liberty,' 'freedom,' 'licentiousness' – and attach to those words our meanings, not his meanings."[4] The Court was way ahead of the Framers. Originalism has not been a factor.

No textual or historical evidence supports the contention that the society that adopted the First Amendment understood it to cover communicative activity like flag-burning.[5] Symbolic expression, such as pictures and signs, were largely included, but that was it.[6] The distinction between content-based and content-neutral speech,[7] the concepts of conduct as speech and fighting words,[8] and the idea of conduct as protected speech are mid- to late-twentieth-century creations. Does anyone think that the participants in the Boston Tea Party or a similar event a generation later would have believed that a statute that enhanced the punishment for the crime of

destroying property as part of an effort to demonstrate disaffection with the government was improper or unconstitutional?

Texas v. Johnson (1989) (flag-burning)[9] and Scalia's opinion in *R.A.V. v. City of
St. Paul* (1992) (cross burning)[10] were important step in expanding First Amendment
protection to speech (or conduct) that previously was unprotected. While all Justices
recognized that laws that restricted speech must be scrutinized to eliminate illegitimate motivation, Scalia produced a more comprehensive rationale. Professor Akhil
Reed Amar described Scalia's opinion as "an ambitious reconceptualization and
synthesis of First Amendment doctrine."[11] Then-Professor Elena Kagan observed
that "the principle of viewpoint neutrality, which now stands as the primary barrier
to certain modes of regulating pornography and hate speech, has as its core much
good sense and reason."[12] Viewpoint neutrality, Kagan noted, was consistent with
judicial restraint since it limits courts' ability to favor their point of view.[13]

SEARCH, SEIZURE, AND ARREST

While the Fourth Amendment has been long criticized for its opaqueness,[14] recent
scholarship has challenged the role of the Fourth Amendment as the exclusive
protection of searches and seizures, thereby casting doubt on originalism's search-
and-seizure jurisprudence. According to historian Thomas Y. Davies, Congress proposed and the states adopted the Fourth Amendment because of concern with
searches conducted with judicial search warrants, not warrantless searches, which
were less common and which were reviewed by a jury.[15] The specific evil was the
general search warrant, usually connected with revenue, which imposed virtually
no restraints on its holder, but allowed him comprehensive authority and discretion.
"[T]he Framers saw the Fourth Amendment as a specific constitutional barricade
against the unique threat which legislative approval of general warrants posed for
the structure of common-law authority. . . . "[16] "[T]he evidence indicates that the
Framers understood 'unreasonable searches and seizures' simply as a pejorative
label for the inherent illegality of any searches or seizures that might be made under
general warrants."[17] Davies has argued that common-law arrest standards were constitutionalized in the "due process of law" protection of the Fifth Amendment, not
in the Fourth Amendment.

Davies observed that "the authority of the peace officer was still meager in 1789"
and the community did not "perceive the warrantless officer as being capable of
posing a significant threat to the security of the person or house." Constables, the
primary peace officers of the period, had limited authority to arrest, and acted with
full authority and protection only when they proceeded pursuant to a warrant. Without a warrant neither constables nor anyone else could ordinarily arrest someone
based on hearsay.[18] No one could search a house without a warrant.[19] Moreover,
"the Framers did not address warrantless intrusions at all in the Fourth Amendment
or in earlier state provisions . . . [because] they did not anticipate that a wrongful act

by an officer might constitute a form of government illegality – rather they viewed such misconduct as only a *personal* trespass by the person who held the office."[20] The exclusionary rule converted the constable's wrongful action into state action and made it part of the prosecution process rather than a private tort.

The incorrect view that the Fourth Amendment did not condemn all warrant-less searches, but only those the Justices did not find "reasonable," dates from *Carroll v. United States* (1925),[21] and was largely the outgrowth of Prohibition and searches of automobiles.[22] Scalia followed *Carroll*: The Fourth Amendment "merely prohibits searches and seizures that are 'unreasonable.'"[23] There is, however, no sig-nificant historical basis for the conclusion that the Fourth Amendment merely prohibits searches and seizures that are unreasonable.[24] Not "a single framing-era source . . . endorsed a warrantless arrest or search on the ground that it was reasonable in the circumstances,"[25] Davies argued. There was no general reasonableness stan-dard that governed warrantless searches and seizures, even though such a standard has been generally assumed to exist by judges and Justices.

"[T]he long-standing and genuinely historical rule that warrantless arrests for less-than-felony offenses are limited to ongoing offenses witnessed by the arresting officer."[26] Warrantless arrests were limited to breaches of the peace or specific misdemeanors that required immediate detention.[27] "[I]n framing-era common law, probable cause never sufficed by itself, to justify even a warrantless felony arrest, let alone a warrantless misdemeanor arrest. . . . The historical sources show beyond any question that the Framers meant to prohibit conferral of discretionary arrests search authority on peace officers."[28] The standard for arrests for felonies, which ordinarily carried the death penalty, was stricter than for misdemeanors, and required that a felony had actually been committed and a sworn accusation, usually by the victim, and thus a potentially accountable complainant, which constituted the salient legal protection against malicious arrests.[29]

The term "seizure" was not the equivalent of arrest in the framing era, but rather was connected with searches made pursuant to warrants. The first time the Fourth Amendment standard was applied to arrests appears to have been done inadvertently in *Draper v. United States* (1959)[30] by Justice Charles Evans Whittaker, perhaps the weakest Justice appointed post–World War II, who simply cited, without discussion, Fourth Amendment decisions to decide the validity of an arrest. The dissent by Justice Douglas expanded the transformation: "With all due deference, the arrest made here on the mere word of an informer violated the spirit of the Fourth Amendment. . . . [The arresting officer] must have 'reasonable grounds to believe that the person to be arrested had committed or is committing' a violation of the narcotics law."[31] Thus, a major change in constitutional law was accomplished in passing.[32]

Davies's analysis relied largely on Sir Edward Coke's seventeenth-century four-volume treatise, titled *The Institutes and Laws of England*, and framing-era man-uals. "Taken together, Coke's statements actually constituted a fairly complete, if sometimes cryptic, summary of the common-law justifications for felony and less-than-felony warrantless arrests." Coke's writings were respected and followed in manuals used in framing-era America. "[T]he common-law standards for warrantless criminal arrests as well as for search warrants remained virtually unchanged during the century and half between Coke's writing and the framing era."[33] Thus, at the time the Framers drafted the Constitution and Congress drafted the Bill of Rights, there appears to have been a known set of precedents that governed warrantless arrests.[34]

Davies's conclusions, as normally the case with new approaches, are not universally accepted and there are other views of the colonial and founding eras – although they, too, disagree with Scalia.[35] The major point for *originalism*, however, is not whether Davies or someone else correctly described seventeenth- and eighteenth-century history and best discerned the understandings of those who wrote and ratified the Bill of Rights and their contemporaries. Rather, historians demonstrate how difficult, if not impossible, is the attempt to find a single, unchallenged understanding of an important constitutional right, at least with the present state of historical knowledge. Moreover, the discussion by historians has been on a different plane than the ahistorical and single dimension of originalists, who claim a uniform and static earlier law. Finally, sensitivity of historians to the cultures of the eighteenth century confirms how impossible it is to employ that knowledge to decide today's constitutional issues.[36]

Scalia's history was suspect in his liberal opinion in *United States v. Jones* (2012),[37] where law-enforcement officers attached a GPS monitoring device to an automobile without a warrant. He discussed the status of real property, not personal property, which was treated differently. Blackstone's First American Edition, published in 1772, seemed to require some injury for a trespass to chattels.[38] The original *Restatement of Torts* (1935) considered the strict liability for trespasses to land, then, following Blackstone, stated: "In order that an actor who interferes with another's chattel may be liable, his conduct must affect some other and more important interest of the possessor. Therefore, one who intentionally intermeddles with another's chattel is subject to liability only if his intermeddling is harmful to the possessor's materially valuable interest in the physical condition, quality, or value of the chattel, or if the possessor is deprived of the use of the chattel for a substantial time, or some other legally protected interest of the possessor is affected."[39] The original understanding does not support *Jones* or *Hicks* (movement of stereo equipment). In fact, Scalia did not explain why the concept of trespass was a component of the Fourth Amendment, which does not mention the term.[40]

Scalia's originalist opinion in *Minnesota v. Dickerson* (1993),[41] which supported the *Terry* stop, also seems unsustainable on historical grounds.[42] "It appears that there were so few legitimate reasons to be out and about at night that nightwalking was viewed almost an offense in its own right," which supports Scalia. But while a constable may have been empowered to detain a nightwalker for examination by a justice of the peace the next morning, there appears to have been no generalized authority for temporary detentions in framing-era law as suggested by Scalia, despite the special fear of nighttime crime.[43] An historian commented on instructions prepared for the Boston watch in 1662: "When the watch encountered persons 'not of known fidellitie,' they were to 'modestly demand the cause of their being abroad, and if it apeard that they are uupon ille minded imployment then to watch them narrowlye.'"[44]

While acknowledging that advances in technology affected analysis,[45] Scalia tied his test to the degree of privacy accepted when the Fourth Amendment was adopted, but that left plenty of wiggle room. The test was subjective and not dictated by originalism, as evidenced by Scalia's statement that when there was "no clear practice, either approving or disapproving the type of search at issue, at the time the constitutional provision was enacted," what is reasonable "depends largely upon the social necessity that prompts the search."[46] That led to historically uncertain applications of the Fourth Amendment, such Scalia's conclusion in *National Treasury Employees Union v. Von Raab* (1989)[47] that the government could not make an example of its Customs Service employees by subjecting them to drug testing.[48]

The problem is pervasive, Reid emphasized. "In seeking to reconstruct the foundations of American government as they were laid by the Founding Fathers, the greatest risk we run is that we no longer understand the purpose and scope of eighteenth-century rights as they were understood in the eighteenth century.... The concept of property and security were civil rights that encompassed a view of the world that... [included] the right to government of a particular type, to a limited government of constitutionalism such as was believed to exist only in Great Britain."[49] Davies observed: "The salient historical fact is that state and federal judges have been deviating from earlier understandings, and announcing novel standards, for more than two centuries since the framing era.... The bottom line is that there is no way that we can now 'return' to the original understanding of the constitutional limits on governmental arrest and search power."[50]

JURY TRIAL

Before discussing issues raised by Scalia's opinions it is worth noting that the constitutionally assumed requirement of guilt beyond a reasonable doubt was not firmly established at the time of the framing. "The beyond reasonable doubt standard... was not uniformly applied well into the next [nineteenth] century," concluded Berkeley Professor Barbara J. Shapiro.[51] Through the preceding centuries philosophy, logic, and canon law vied and interacted to produce competing standards, such as "satisfied conscience," "moral certainty," and "highest degree of probability."[52] Even concepts that are today the foundation of criminal law were uncertain at the founding.

The relationship of the judge and jury was different from now in a variety of ways. Historian Aaron T. Knapp stated: "The historical record suggests that juries in most of British North America wielded enormous discretionary authority to determine questions of both law and fact – a practice that eighteenth-century English law strictly prohibited."[53] American juries usually received little guidance.[54] The system had virtually no restrictions on the power of the jury to render verdicts without judicial modification or interference,[55] although judges would freely comment on the evidence, going so far as to tell the jury that there was only one way to read the evidence. In criminal cases juries announced sentences to the extent they were flexible,[56] and in some places imposed judgments without appellate review.[57] Starting in the late seventeenth century, "situating law-finding power in local juries" was a "powerful force" in resisting the Crown's efforts.[58] Indeed, in New England jurors were generally elected during the colonial era.[59] Professor John H. Langbein observed that what is known, at least about England, was that "[j]ury trial was crude, fast, and cheap" and that the "[j]udge and jury virtually never disagreed about anything."[60] Significantly, the tide moved toward greater judicial control and role within a decade or two of the founding.[61]

Langbein explained that "[o]nly a small fraction of eighteenth-century criminal trials constituted genuinely contested inquiries into guilt or innocence. In many cases, the accused had been caught in the act, or with the stolen goods, or otherwise had no credible defense."[62] Jury trial in late-eighteenth century England "was primarily a sentencing proceeding in which juries played a major role."[63] Since most crimes were sanction-specific, juries would exercise discretion, when they exercised it, by convicting of lesser offenses, usually ones that did not carry a death sentence, and could substitute transportation to the Americas for hanging. In the United States, unless the sentence for a crime was fixed by statute, about half the states left sentencing of convicted criminals to the jury, and frequently did so without instructions.[64]

While Scalia's attachment to the role of the jury in sentencing criminal defendants had strong common-law roots,[65] his Seventh Amendment opinions acted as though differences in the role of juries in civil cases in 1791 and the present could be ignored.[66] Some commentators have advised caution on the reach of the Seventh Amendment, including Professor Renée Lettow Lerner in an article entitled, "The Failure of Originalism in Preserving Constitutional Rights to Civil Jury Trial."[67] Lerner concluded, "The dramatic evolution of jury practice . . . suggests difficulties in maintaining a consistent jury trial right by constitutional requirement."[68] An originalist approach to the Seventh Amendment surrenders the fundamental tenet of originalism, which is to implement the practice of the founding era. "[I]t is difficult to imagine a scenario of a revived civil jury remotely similar to that of the founding era."[69] There may be a more fundamental problem. There was nothing approaching a consistent practice respecting civil juries in 1791. When the time came to apply the Seventh Amendment, it was the law of England and not the law of any of the states that became the standard, which was not what the founders were practicing.[70]

CONFRONTATION CLAUSE

Scalia's opinion for a unanimous Court in *Crawford v. Washington* (2004)[71] restricted the use of out-of-court statements, both sworn and unsworn, at criminal trials, a textualist/originalist opinion that enhanced rights of defendants. *Crawford* essentially mandated the right of criminal defendants to confront and cross-examine witnesses. While a more accurate reflection of the Sixth Amendment than the nebulous standard in *Ohio v. Roberts* (1980),[72] which it replaced, it was still largely ahistorical, both by what it included and what it excluded. The idea that "nontestimonial" statements could be admitted is not historical. Moreover, felony trials and misdemeanor trials had different rules, with broader rules of admissibility in the latter. Scalia relied on misdemeanor procedures without explanation.[73]

Davies examined the right to confront witnesses and the admissibility of hearsay at the time of the drafting of the Bill of Rights.[74] Relying on contemporary decisions, treatises, and handbooks for magistrates both in England and in British North America, he rejected the conclusions of all Justices.[75] Although he agreed that history supported Scalia's statement of the right to confront and cross-examine trial witnesses in the late eighteenth century and, in fact, two centuries earlier, Davies accused him of "using evidence law and the 'modern view' of interpretation of evidence law to support his historical interpretation of the Confrontation Clause."[76]

Significantly, framing-era evidence doctrine imposed a virtually total ban against using unsworn hearsay and out-of-court statements to prove a criminal defendant's guilt.[77] "[A]s of 1789, a dying declaration of a murder victim was the only kind of unsworn out-of-court statement that could be admitted in a criminal trial to prove the guilt of the defendant."[78] Other than unsworn dying declarations, "only one kind of out-of-court statement that could be admitted as evidence of a defendant's guilt [which was] the written record of a sworn witness examination by a person who subsequently became genuinely unavailable to testify at trial.[79] These "Marian statements" taken by justices of the peace pursuant to legislation enacted during the reign of Mary Tudor. They "provided for the taking of *ex parte* sworn statements of witnesses at the time of a felony arrest, when the justice of the peace was required to decide whether the arrestee should be released, bailed, or committed to jail to await trial."[80] The statements were usually taken in close proximity to the events and the usual practice "was for the accused to be present when this accusatory statement was taken."[81] However, "it does not appear that a prior opportunity for cross-examination had any effect on the admissibility or inadmissibility of the deposition of an unavailable witness in a framing-era trial."[82] Marian statements were not referred to as "hearsay" because of their perceived trustworthiness.[83] *Crawford* and its progeny were not historical.

Specific provisions of law cannot be understood except within the particular historical context. Nelson explained: "The colonial approach to evidentiary questions rested in large part, then, on a conception of truth that we do not share. The conception – that truth would emerge not from a weighing of credibilities and probabilities but from the sanctity of an oath – looked backward to earlier times, in which God-fearing men had attached enormous importance to a solemn oath." There was an assumption that witnesses under oath would tell the truth, and impeachment was correspondingly curtailed.[84] Davies stated that "during the Framing era an oath was still the essential requisite of legal evidence because 'hearsay is not evidence.'"[85]

The distinction between testimonial and nontestimonial statements is ahistoric. It "does not appear that framing-era sources even used 'testimonial' as an adjective, let alone as a designation for a category of hearsay, and there is no reason to think that the Framers conceived of the category of 'testimonial hearsay.' Indeed, the restrictive concept of a 'testimonial' statement that Justice Thomas introduced in *White*, and that Justice Scalia employed in *Crawford*, appears to have been unprecedented." When the term "testimonial" came to be used as an adjective in evidence discourse, it simply referred to any statement in which the words of the speaker communicated information.[86] "[T]he modern exceptions under which 'nontestimonial' hearsay can now be admitted against a criminal defendant *did not exist* when the Confrontation Clause was framed in 1789."[87] Just because what witness say on the witness stand is denominated "testimony" does not mean that that certain out-of-court statements of nontrial witnesses should be admissible. Moreover, as noted above, unsworn statements were generally inadmissible, while sworn Marian statements were admitted.

Much of the lore has been based on the unprincipled early-eighteenth-century prosecution for treason of Sir Walter Raleigh, which had none of the subtleties raised by recent cases. The prosecution simply introduced in evidence an affidavit that reiterated what a third party had said, double hearsay in today's parlance. "Confrontation" may have been a short-hand for what probably was a confused pattern of decisions that were not widely published.[88] In sum, it is virtually certain that the testimonial approach taken by the current Supreme Court has little to do with the practice in the late eighteenth century. Professor Stephanos Bibas stated, "It is not clear that there was a preexisting concept of what 'confrontation' means in a criminal trial."[89]

Commentary faults the opinions of both Scalia and Breyer in *Giles v. California* (2008)[90] on forfeiture of the right to confrontation by killing a witness. Davies observed that "both endorsed a much broader forfeiture exception than any that had existed in framing era law," adding that a "a genuine originalist analysis would not have accepted the recent expansion of the forfeiture exception."[91] "The originalist aspects of *Giles* are so highly selective that they do not amount to honest originalism at all."[92] A law professor wrote: "Justice Scalia selectively gathered historic sources to tip the balance. . . . [His] interpretation of the forfeiture doctrine is simply not clearly supported by the historical sources, as the only critical cases he references are silent rather than determinative on the issue of forfeiture."[93] "The point of the forfeiture doctrine is that the accused has acted wrongfully in a way that is incompatible with maintenance of the right," another commentator wrote.[94] But this analysis unexpectedly placed Scalia once again in the posture of relying on apparently poor history to protect the rights of a criminal defendant. A broad forfeiture doctrine should accompany broad protection under the Confrontation Clause; a broad forfeiture doctrine makes the law both more equitable and simpler.[95]

DOUBLE JEOPARDY

Double jeopardy has taken a tortuous route to its present incarnation. While the concept reaches back to Greek and Roman times, Great Britain did not consider it a fundamental right, and its nature and scope were uncertain there well into the nineteenth century. Uncertain was the significance of a possible death sentence to its application, whether it applied to misdemeanors at all, and the extent to which it depended on the nature of the earlier disposition, *e.g.*, whether it applied to prior convictions as well as acquittals. Neither Coke, who is credited with improvising the doctrine, nor Blackstone considered the doctrine absolute.[96] From the time of the framing "[i]ts contemporary lineaments have been obscured by the multiplicity of alternative meanings . . . [and] many state legislators were not certain of the meaning of the clause." While the doctrine varied from colony to colony and then state to state, no state constitution protected against a second prosecution until New Hampshire's in 1784.[97] It is not true, as many asserted, that the Constitution's Double Jeopardy Clause was a statement of the current law.[98] Attempts to limn the original understanding to decide difficult current issues seem doomed to fail.

27

Conflicted Opinions Reconsidered

CAMPAIGN FINANCING

Challenges to campaign-finance originalism can be made on two interrelated grounds. First, the Framers did not regard the First Amendment to be absolute and would not have recoiled at limited restrictions on campaign spending. Second, the distinction made between *quid pro quo* corruption (bribery) and other types of corruption had no basis in founding-era thought, so that restrictions on campaign financing and spending allowed under *Buckley v. Valeo* (1976)[1] could properly be extended to other forms of corruption. Together these points suggest that greater regulation of campaign financing is in accord with the framing-era's and, perhaps more strongly, the Revolutionary War era's balance between the First Amendment and political corruption.

The grievances that led to the Revolutionary War were many, and included corruption. Gordon S. Wood's landmark study, *The Creation of the American Republic, 1776–1787*, charged some to England, some to internal situations, but virtually all to the acceptance and expansion of vices and degeneration. Attacked were "luxury, profaneness, impiety, and a disesteem of things sacred." Planters feared "social corrosion, apparently caused by the fantastic grown of pride, ostentation and debts among the would-be aristocrats." All classes perceived the "Crown's conspiracy to numb and enervate the spirit of the American people." "[T]he pervasive fear that [Americans] were not predestined to be a virtuous and egalitarian people that in the last analysis drove them into revolution in 1776." "On the eve of the Revolution the belief that England was 'sunk in corruption' and 'tottering on the brink of destruction' had become entrenched in the minds of disaffected Englishmen on both sides of the Atlantic." It was a gnawing, internal, and fundamental corruption in which government institutions and human morality were undermined.[2]

"By corruption," Zephyr Teachout wrote in her study, *Corruption in America*, "the early generations meant excessive private interests influencing the exercise of public power. . . . Corruption was a rotting of positive ideals of civic virtue and public integrity."[3] "Though the word *corruption* was used hundreds of times in the convention and the ratification debates, only a handful of uses referred to what we might now think of as quid pro quo bribes."[4] Professor Lawrence Lessig explained that the founders were far more concerned with other forms of corruption than *quid pro quo*. His analysis of contemporary documents, including accounts of the Constitutional Convention, showed that the concern of the founders was institutional more than individual, and the great evil was dependence, especially conflicting dependencies, on the part of government officials, such as existed in Parliament's relationship with the Crown. *The Federalist* Nos. 22 and 39 emphasized the importance of the body politic as the source of power, not narrowly focused interest groups.[5]

Teachout wrote that "the framers of the Constitution . . . saw that corruption and quid pro quo bribery were different things and played different legal roles." "*Buckley* quasi-constitutionalized corruption, making it as contested as the right to bear arms or any other constitutional concept, but it did so in an entirely ahistorical way,"[6] divorcing itself from the earlier concept of undue influence and broader concepts of corruption. *Citizens United* "took that which had been named corrupt for over two hundred years and renamed it legitimate and the essence of responsiveness. . . . [T]he replacement of corruption with quid pro quo is simply untenable as a matter of legal history. *Citizens United* was a revolution in political theory, disguised as a definitional disagreement."[7] An originalist definition of corruption requires the survival of reasonable restraints on campaign contributions.[8]

On a broader view, if the Framers would have rebelled at the thought that the government could restrict how much they could speak and how wide an audience they could command, they also would have rebelled at a small minority of wealthy or aristocratic citizens being able to dominate access to the public. Decentralization of power was an essential part of the Constitution.[9] Madison's Bill of Rights was not a blueprint for plutocracy. The Framers were emphatically practical people, whose values were mostly republican. The consequences of unequal distribution of wealth were a serious concern. They were sensitive to outsized power and influence.[10] Gordon Wood concluded that denying the right to vote to those who owned no property "was based not on the fear that these people without property might confiscate the wealth of the aristocratic few, but on the opposite fear: that the aristocratic few might manipulate the corrupt and poor for their own ends."[11]

"Jefferson may have been especially dedicated to equal rights, but he did not believe that a corporate charter was one of those rights. To his dying day he never accepted the idea that corporations were private property that could not be touched or modified by the legislative body that chartered them,"[12] Wood explained. The founders would have considered seriously arguments that leveling the playing field would reduce the kind of corruption that concerned them. Laurence Tribe wrote: "In a republican system of government – a system that Article IV commands the United States to guarantee – it is a legitimate and indeed compelling goal of legislation, both state and federal, to ensure that officeholders and their staff[s] have no greater incentive to meet with, to respond favorably to the approaches of, or to be susceptible to influence by, those who either have supported their candidates financially or can be expected to do so in the future."[13]

The permissive present law on campaign financing threatens the structure contemplated by Madison. In *The Federalist* No. 10 Madison defined a faction as "a number of citizens, whether amounting to a majority or minority of the whole, who are united and actuated by some common impulse of passion, or of interest, adverse to the rights of other citizens, or to the permanent and aggregate interests of the community." Madison saw representative democracy as a counterweight to competing factions. "Publius's first concern . . . was the politics of faction."[14] While Madison may have envisaged factions as consisting of a narrower self-interest, such as fishermen or growers of tobacco, a faction consisting of campaign-spending power-brokers trumps other interests and also lacks countervailing power to militate against its parochial goals.[15] *The Federalist* No. 10 emphasized that "the most common and durable source of factions has been the various and unequal distribution of property. . . . The regulation of these various and interfering interests forms the principal task of modern legislation. . . . The inference to which we are brought is that the *causes* of faction cannot be removed and that relief is only to be sought in the means of controlling its *effects*." George Washington's Farewell Address condemned "all combinations and associations, under whatever possible character, with the real design to direct, control, counteract, or awe the regular deliberation and action of the constituted authorities."

Writing in the context of increasing government regulation, Judge Easterbrook described Madison's reasoning: "Mediating among many factions, the representative answers to none. . . . Elections from different states with different factions dilute the power of faction."[16] Huge financial resources, however, trump the premise of the Constitution's complex structure, designed to prevent "society under the forms of which the stronger faction can readily unite and oppress the weaker."[17] Unrestrained campaign spending can create a virtually permanent faction (in power and influence), which subverts "[t]he constant aim [which] is to divide and arrange the several offices in such a manner as that each may be a check on the other,"[18] namely, the separation of powers that Scalia valued so highly. Large financers of campaigns share self-interest in erasing government regulation of their money-making activities, and their power is enormous.[19] Richard A. Brisbin, Jr., commented: "In effect, [Scalia] took the strict scrutiny test and converted it from a protection of the disadvantaged into an instrument for the exploitation and expropriation of political discussion and the policy agenda of the powerful."[20]

Scalia made no scholarly effort to demonstrate that anyone living in 1791 would have protected *corporate* political speech over legislative efforts to combat corruption, broadly defined.[21] Corporations were disfavored at that time. "[C]orporate power . . . was perceived as being opposed to the ideal of individual liberty."[22] There is no evidence that the founding generation gave those corporations the fundamental rights of American citizens, much less business corporations whose goal was profit, not virtue. For-profit corporations were also rare. In fact, states issued only thirty-three charters between 1781 and 1790.[23] Jefferson opposed the national bank because "[t]he bank's stockholders, like those of the Bank of England, would forever be able to manufacture a legislative majority to suit them and corrupt the Constitution."[24] Scalia's point that most corporations were state-granted monopolies that operated bridges or ferries for a public purpose did little for his position. A pair of economic historians and a political scientist wrote that "by the middle of the nineteenth century, the very same parties and corporations that were feared in 1790 came to be seen as important elements in maintaining stability.... [P]eople initially believed that political parties and corporations were dangerous, even evil." The transition "occurred in the nineteenth, not the eighteenth century."[25] It seems futile to try to figure out how a framing-era citizen would have viewed an entity that had perpetual life, limited liability,[26] and other characteristics with which the Framers had little familiarity asserting the same rights as the citizens who fought England.[27]

Stevens captured the tenor of the founding era in his dissent in *Citizens' United*: "The truth is we cannot be certain how a law such as BCRA § 203 meshes with the original meaning of the First Amendment . . . [but] there is not a scintilla of evidence to support the notion that anyone believed it would preclude regulatory distinctions based on the corporate form. . . . The individualized charter mode of incorporation reflected the 'cloud of disfavor under which corporations labored' in the early years of this Nation. . . . As a matter of original expectations, then, it seems absurd to think that the First Amendment prohibits legislatures from taking into account the corporate identity of a sponsor of electoral advocacy."[28] Responding to Scalia's argument that an individual's right to speak entails a right to speak with others for a common cause, Stevens said that "he does not explain why those two rights must be precisely identical, or why that principle applies to electioneering by corporations that serves no 'common cause.'"[29]

Scalia was not originalist or textualist in much of his free-speech jurisprudence, including in flag-burning and cross-burning cases. But he transformed himself into an ardent textualist when he insisted that certain entities must receive protection by the First Amendment's broadly worded Free Speech Clause.[30] But then he became nonoriginalist when he insisted on a modern conception of corruption. While Scalia passionately supported the disparate parts of his free-speech position, his originalism seemed both selective and poor history.[31] Scalia to the contrary notwithstanding, campaign-financing laws are consistent with the original public understanding.[32]

ANONYMOUS (OR PSEUDONONYMOUS) SPEECH

Thomas's concurring opinion in *McIntyre v. Ohio Elections Commission* (1995),[33] which Scalia did not join, cited documents from the second half of the eighteenth century that suggested that fear of prosecution or similar concerns motivated anonymous publication – although far less so after the adoption of the First Amendment, the operative document.[34] In fact, Thomas overstated the evidence. Many historians, including Jefferson Powell, have disagreed with Thomas's assumptions and analysis. "Political prosecutions under the British were not of serious consequences for two reasons. The first was British leniency.... The second was the jury system," Nelson explained.[35] "It is now widely recognized that the American press during the colonial era and the Revolution generally exercised a very broad freedom to criticize government measures and officials without a significant interference from prosecutions for seditious libel,"[36] Powell stated.

Scalia's originalist arguments for bars on anonymous speech, discussed in Chapter 17, were not overwhelming and seemed inconsistent with arguments he made elsewhere.[37] Nevertheless, acceptance of a legislative ban on anonymous campaigning was more historically valid than he presented. Printing pamphlets and pamphlets anonymously or pseudonymously in the ratification debate apparently had little or nothing to do with modern considerations of protecting (concealing) the identity of wealthy companies and individuals who wish to co-opt elections. Nor did it have anything to do with the fear of the Crown, which was gone, or a vindictive national government, which was powerless. In any event, how could authors of pamphlets hide behind anonymity if courageous newspaper publishers were totally vulnerable, as they were during the Revolution.[38]

In fact, the practice was a product of an entirely different culture, which historian Saul Cornell has shown to include a democratic, communitarian, and even populist conceit. It was mostly, but not exclusively, the generally less prominent and less wealthy Anti-Federalists who favored anonymity. They used pseudonyms so that writings would not be intertwined with the prestige of the individual writer, in large part because they believed that the writings should be judged on an argument's intrinsic merit and not the social standing of the writer. "Only anonymous publication was compatible with republican ideals," Cornell wrote.[39] The tradition was strong enough that elite individuals such as Federalists Madison, Hamilton, and Jay published under the name Publius to avoid appearing to trade on their reputations. The practice continued after the Constitution, for example, in debates between Pacificus (Hamilton) and Helvidius (Madison) over Washington's 1793 declaration of neutrality. Scalia permitted regulating anonymous speech, albeit on different and nonoriginalist grounds. As he said, an anonymous television ad is no more worthy than an anonymous telephone call. But Scalia never challenged Thomas on originalist grounds.[40]

ANTIABORTION PICKETING

Scalia's elevation of free speech to preferred status over many other rights and interests supported antiabortion picketers. He was for robust speech, even confrontational speech. But was the protection he gave to antiabortion picketing consistent with the historical record? Conspicuously absent from his and Thomas's analysis of antiabortion picketing were references to the framing era. To the argument that antiabortion picketing did not exist at the time of the framing, one seemingly sound response is that neither did heat-sensitive searches and GPS devices that could be attached to vehicles. But while originalists reasoned from analogies there, they did not with antiabortion picketing. There seems to be no principled theory that applies originalist analysis to affixing a GPS device on a car without permission, but not to antiabortion picketing. After all, it is *a single* Constitution of the United States we are construing.

Probably the closest analogy to contemporary antiabortion picketing is labor picketing, although labor picketing as we know it did not exist in the framing era, but only after industry changed from handicrafts to assembly-line production. The earliest English law directed at picketing was enacted in 1825.[41] The first reported case in the United States appeared in 1888.[42] *Truax v. Corrigan* (1921)[43] involved an exemption for labor picketing enacted in 1913 by Arizona's first legislature. Chief Justice William Taft's opinion for the Supreme Court observed that prior to that law, "picketing was unlawful in Arizona, because it was presumed to induce breaches of the peace."[44] Justice Pitney's dissent went further. "I have no doubt that, without infringing the 'due process' clause, a state might by statute establish protection against picketing or boycotting however conducted, just as many states have done by holding them to be contrary to the common law recognizing a property value in a going business, and applying equitable principles in safeguarding it from irreparable injury through interference four unwarranted."[45]

One commentator noted in 1931 that some states banned labor picketing while the courts of most other states "have tended without analysis to conclude that everything beyond the stationing of a few pickets who carry banners or in calm terms speak to customers or employees is beyond the lawful ambit permitted the worker."[46] A contemporary student law review note stated that the "doctrine that picketing is necessarily illegal in the absence of a strike has received sporadic articulation in some states and recently been appearing as a hardened dogma at *nisi prius* in New York."[47] It was not until well into the twentieth century that the Supreme Court confirmed the right of workers to picket peacefully to press their objectives in *Thornhill v. Alabama* (1940).[48] The evidence is far from conclusive, but suggests that originalists would have a hard time finding support in early American history for broad free-speech rights for aggressive picketers of a lawful business.[49]

RELIGION

Scalia's opinion in *Employment Div., Dept. of Human Resources of Oregon v. Smith* (1990),[50] which disfavored a religious sect that smoked peyote, disturbed many. It was hostile to a minority religion, which lacked the power of popular religions to mold the law to help it, such as Catholics and Jews, who wrote provisions into Prohibition laws permitting sacramental use of wine. Scalia's argument seemed to reject the evident reasons for the Free Exercise Clause, including denominational equality and removing religion from the political process, as least insofar as the national government was concerned.[51] Gordon Wood stated the objective more generally, "by protecting the rights of minorities of all sorts against popular majorities," the Court would "become a major instrument for both curbing [American] democracy and maintaining it."[52]

Most academic comments were unsympathetic to Scalia: The Court's decision was "perhaps the most controversial free exercise opinion of the past half century," arousing the ire of the public, academia, and Congress.[53] Scalia's opinion was a "radical departure" from prior law that "sharply restricts the scope of the Free Exercise Clause" and made small religious groups vulnerable.[54] He "has used the ambiguous idea of equality to create a remarkable shift – one that is not even remotely tied to the text or history of the Religion Clauses."[55] After *Smith*, "people who have religious convictions that lead them to engage in forbidden acts have no constitutional claim to an exemption – none. An individual's religious beliefs [do not] excuse him from compliance with an otherwise valid law that the State is free to legislate."[56] Judge John T. Noonan, a widely respected, conservative Roman Catholic, penned a particularly biting indictment of *Smith* in an insightful book that accused Scalia's opinion of ignoring and distorting the unique history of religious freedom in the United States.[57] Substantial evidence, including colonial charters and state constitutions, supported a broad reading of the Free Exercise Clause.[58]

Scalia discarded precedent that required a compelling state interest to restrict a religious practice, affirmed in *West Va. State Bd. of Education v. Barnette* (1943) (exempting Jehovah's Witnesses from saluting the flag)[59] and *Wisconsin v. Yoder* (1972) (Old Order Amish excused from compulsory school attendance laws).[60] When the First Amendment was proposed, twelve of the thirteen states (Connecticut was the exception) had guarantees of religious liberty in their state constitutions, many of them using the term "free exercise," which contemplated religiously based exemptions from facially neutral legislation, provided they would not disrupt the peace and safety of the state.[61] Noonan noted the numerous exemptions from general laws, including allowing the sale of wine for sacramental purposes during Prohibition[62] and Jews in the military to wear yarmulkes.[63] "All the exemptions Congress had made, now unmentioned by the Court, stood as mute testimony to the long standing belief of the legislative and executive branches as to the respect to be accorded free exercise." Instead, the Court simply announced unprecedented tests for legislation "variously phrased as 'congruence and proportionality' or as 'congruence or proportionality,'" Noonan wrote.[64]

Relying on both precedent and history, O'Connor's dissent argued that religion should be accommodated and *Smith* should be overruled in *City of Boerne v. Flores* (1997)[65]:

[T]he Free Exercise Clause is not simply an antidiscrimination principle that protects against those laws that single out religious practices for unfavorable treatment. . . . Rather, the Clause is best understood as an affirmative guarantee of the right to participate in religious practices and conduct without impermissible governmental interference, even when such conduct conflicts with a neutral, generally applicable law. . . . Oliver Ellsworth, a Framer of the First Amendment and later Chief Justice of the United States, expressed the similar view that government could interfere in religious matters only when necessary "to prohibit and punish gross immoralities and impieties; because the open practice of these is of evil example and detriment." . . . The idea that civil obligations are subordinate to religious duty is consonant with the notion that government must accommodate, where possible, those religious practices that conflict with civil law.[66]

Many historians were also unsympathetic to the Court's decision in *Boerne*, which denied a zoning exception to a Catholic Church. One study concluded that "[t]he Court's narrow construction of Congress's authority under Section Five [of the Fourteenth Amendment] in *Boerne* cannot be justified by the history of the constitutional amendment. . . . [T]he *Boerne* Court is correct to try to learn some lessons from the post-ratification debate [on the Klu Klux Klan Act] but it gets those lessons backwards. A Congress that wanted to have the authority to enact the Klu Klux Klan Act would not have wanted Section Five to be interpreted narrowly."[67]

Burwell v. Hobby Lobby Stores, Inc. (2014)[68] impacted the Free Exercise Clause along with First Amendment rights of corporations. Alito's majority opinion, which Scalia joined, voided regulations of the Affordable Care Act that required small businesses to provide certain types of contraception to employees. The opinion said that while corporations were "persons," the rights protected were those of the shareholders, officers, and employees associated with the corporation, but principally the owners.[69] Nevertheless, under the majority's view corporations (and their shareholders) surrender nothing to obtain perpetual life and limited liability (or partial immunity) for their activities, which individuals lack. To quote Scalia, this does not resemble the Home of the Brave.[70]

Hobby Lobby changed the law from pre-*Smith*. Ginsburg's dissent demonstrated that it ignored precedent by persuasively quoting the unanimous decision in *United States v. Lee* (1982) (Burger, C.J.): "When followers of a particular sect enter into commercial activity as a matter of choice, the limits they accept on their own conduct as a matter of conscience and faith are not to be superimposed on statutory schemes which are binding on others in that activity."[71] Ginsburg continued: "The regime that RFRA aimed to restore was one in which courts are instructed by legislatures to balance on a case-by-case basis, but the results that courts reach can be revisited and overridden by legislatures – and so it answers the concern about unaccountable judicial power that played such a prominent role in *Smith*. . . . The Court has now abruptly lurched into an entirely different regime, one Congress never intended, in which religion will almost always be accommodated, even if the consequence is serious injury to non-adherents, so long as there is some *imaginable* less restrictive means for protecting those adherents – and regardless of whether that means is likely to materialize or not."[72] The Court impinged on the Establishment Clause by giving business owners the power to dictate the consequences of their religious beliefs to nonbelievers and to impose severe harm on third parties.[73] In doing so, the Court elevated religious practice to an extra-constitutional status that has no basis in the First Amendment ("Congress shall make no law respecting an establishment of religion"), precedent, or history.

Historically, nothing suggests that free-exercise rights were anything other than human rights. Theologian Donald A. Giannella wrote in the *Harvard Law Review*: "The original constitutional consensus concerning religious liberty was an outgrowth of Protestant dissent and humanistic rationalism, the viewpoints that dominated the thinking of the authors of the Constitution. These two perspectives conjoined to place the individual conscience beyond the coercive power of the states."[74] Caroline Mala Corbin stated that religious liberty "is meant to protect uniquely human attributes: a person's relationship with God, or a person's conscience, dignity, and autonomy."[75] Corporations are not voluntary associations and employees are not voluntary members of a principled group. Religious liberties were never intended to benefit for-profit corporate entities, which were disfavored at the founding if they even existed as such, and whose primary goal was making money, not proselytizing the faith.[76] Nor are corporations among the minorities that have been subject to invidious discrimination. Instead of helping workers at corporations, which the laws intended, the Court construed them to place burdens on the workers, especially women.[77] Significantly, it was Ginsburg in dissent, rather than the majority that included Scalia and Thomas, who stressed framing-era history.[78]

PART VI

Scalia's Nonconstitutional Opinions

Scalia wrote in *Green v. Bock Laundry Machine Co.* (1989): "The meaning of terms on the statute books ought to be determined, not on the basis of which meaning can be shown to have been understood by a larger handful of the Members of Congress, but on the basis of which meaning is (1) most in accord with context and ordinary usage, and thus most likely to have been understood by the *whole* Congress which voted on the words of the statute (not to mention citizens subject to it), and (2) most compatible with the surrounding body of law into which the provision must be integrated – a compatibility which, by benign fiction, we assume Congress always had in mind."[1]

More than with his constitutional opinions, Scalia altered the judicial landscape with his opinions and writings on the interpretation of statutes. His constitutional originalism is very much a minority view and has a variety of antecedents, and the Court's complement of originalists substantially overstated the philosophy's popularity and influence. Scalia's textualism and fealty to grammar, however, along with other elements of his approach to statutes, changed the way judges and lawyers regard statutes. When Scalia joined the Supreme Court in 1986, there was little written on the subject and no law school gave a course specifically on statutory methodology. The first casebook on statutes was published in 1988 by Professors William N. Eskridge, Jr., and Philip P. Frickey.[2] A decade later Eskridge stated Scalia not only filled supplements and the second edition with important cases, but stimulated much greater academic as well as public interest in the field.[3] "The Court's practice changed after Justice Scalia's appointment. After 1986, the Court's statutory opinions have more often found a 'plain meaning,' less often examined legislative history to confirm the existence of a plain meaning, and relied less often legislative history to interpret a statute against what the Court felt was its plain meaning."[4] Nevertheless, as Eskridge and his colleagues have noted, Scalia's strong claims have substantially been rejected by the Court.

Before Scalia, there was *The Legal Process*, an unpublished (until 1994), but widely used, mimeographed casebook initiated in the mid 1950s by Harvard Professors Henry M. Hart, Jr., and Albert M. Sacks. They described their thesis: *"The first task in the interpretation of any statute . . . is to determine what purpose ought to be attributed to it . . .* (a) The statute ought always to be presumed to be the work of reasonable men pursuing reasonable purposes reasonably . . . (b) The general words of a statute ought never to be read as directing an irrational pattern of particular applications. (c) What constitutes an irrational pattern of particular applications ought always to be judged in the light of the overriding and organizing purpose."[5] Breyer explained: "To determine a provision's purpose, the judge looks for the problem that Congress enacted the statute to resolve and asks how Congress expected the particular statutory words in question to help resolve that problem. The judge also examines the likely consequences of a proposed interpretation, asking whether they are more like to further than to hinder achievement of the provision's purpose."[6] "[J]udges [should] look to purpose and consequences when they interpret statutes . . . [b]ecause they will help insure democratic accountability."[7] John Manning agreed: "Since the lawmaker selected the words 'primarily to let us know the statutory purpose,' interpreters show respect for legislative supremacy by implementing the purpose rather than the letter of the law when the two diverge."[8] Judge Posner stated: "One always begins not with the words but with the name of the statute, and with some idea . . . of what the statute is about."[9]

Although many see benefits from an increased emphasis on statutory text, scholars, especially Eskridge, have challenged Scalia's textualism in its undiluted form on a number of grounds.[10] First, available evidence suggested that practice at the framing took a broad view of legislative interpretation. Blackstone's *Commentaries*, popular in America at the founding despite his Tory leanings, said that "the most universal and effective way of discovering the true meaning of a law, when the words are dubious, is by considering the spirit of it . . . for when this reason ceases, the law ought likewise to cease with it. . . . For, since laws in all cases cannot be foreseen and expressed, it is necessary that when the general decrees of the law come to be applied to particular cases, there should be somewhere a power vested of defining those circumstances (had they been foreseen) the legislature would have expressed."[11] *The Federalist* No. 78 spoke in terms of mitigating the effect of harsh statutes. Eskridge's survey of state-court judges' opinions in the founding era and of other contemporary sources supported Blackstone's description of the judicial practice at the time as closer to purposivism than textualism. While the issues in those cases tended to be constitutional rather than statutory, both the briefs and opinions focused on policy or structural grounds, such as the importance of an independent jury; "[j]udges in the founding era were not textualists when they engaged in constitutional interpretation."[12]

Second, the supposed benefits from textualism, such as greater precision and objectivity, are unproven. Just as willful purposivist judges can distort legislative history, so can willful textualist judges manipulate dictionaries, canons of construction, and other sources. The idea that textualism will make Congress act more responsibly is a chimera for many reasons, including that ambiguous texts are often intentionally so and that Congress will resist change. Indeed, Congress probably doesn't think about canons of construction, which are more tuned to the reader of legislation than the writer.[13] Abner J. Mikva, a Congressman before he served with Scalia on the D.C. Circuit, said, "when I was in Congress, the only 'canons' we talked about were the ones the Pentagon bought that could not shoot straight."[14]

Third, legislative history, when used carefully and appropriately, can supply valuable information about the meaning of a statute.[15] As Judge Robert Katzmann and others have argued, legislative history generally precedes legislative enactment and is supervised by members of Congress, who maintain it is more reliable than its critics contend.[16] Commentators cite to the fact that legislators and others, including lawyers and their clients, believe that legislative history is important.[17] Scholars argue that legislative history is at least as reliable and valuable as sources relied upon for the meaning of the Constitution, including *The Federalist*.[18]

Fourth, Scalia's constitutional imperative is without basis. Nowhere is it required that nothing other than the laws passed by both houses of Congress and signed by the President can be considered. Courts are free to use other sources to interpret the law, whether dictionaries, law review articles, or legislative history. The Constitution does not require textualism any more than it requires a purposivist method of analyzing statutes. The real issue is what is meant by the term "judicial power" in Article III of the Constitution. Separation of powers admits of cooperation between the respective branches and not absolute separation. For example, executive agencies pass rules and regulations interpreting statutes.[19]

Important is whether textualism circumscribes judicial activism; does textualism, including rejection of the use of legislative history, give judges less freedom than otherwise. Law professors Andrew Koppelman and Frederick Gedicks said no. "If – it is a big if – the purpose of the new textualism is to limit judicial discretion, then it is a failure. In practice, when freed from the need to pay any attention to what Congress was actually trying to do, the Court has been empowered to manipulate a law's language to reach politically congenial results. The fewer the sources of law, the more ambiguity and therefore the more discretion. . . . Legislative history in practice *constrains* judges."[20] Scalia strongly disagreed.

One arguable anomaly appears in Scalia's rejection of legislative history. He is a strong advocate of deference to administrative rulings under *Chevron, U.S.A. v.*

National Resource Defense Council, Inc. (1984),[21] the landmark case that held a reasonable interpretation of a statute by the agency charged with implementing it controls, even though it may not be what the court would have arrived at independently. Parties appearing before administrative agencies cite, and administrative agencies rely on, legislative history.[22] That most nonconstitutional federal-question cases involve regulatory statutes suggests that in civil cases the appropriate solution is to allow a restrained and circumscribed use of legislative history. But that approach has the disadvantage of failing to curb the time-consuming and expensive efforts by litigants to mine the expansive caverns of legislative history for support.

Nevertheless, Scalia maintains the superiority of textualism in its strong form, and it is that approach that this section of the book will consider. My thesis is not that Scalia's textualism creates a bias in favor of liberal opinions, but rather that his approach does not ordinarily stand in the way of liberal opinions and that he seems to go where his approach leads him. By and large, his liberal and conservative statutory opinions are cut from the same cloth and, more than many Justices and judges, he seems to avoid a bias in statutory construction.[23] But as critics have argued, conspicuous attention to semantic meaning sometimes prevails at the expense of what many would consider more reasonable results, including what Congress intended.

The statutory cases are organized by subject matter. After a few "special cases," there are chapters on liberal criminal opinions, liberal civil opinions, and conservative opinions. The chapter on liberal criminal opinions is subdivided under blue-collar crimes, white-collar crimes, and sentencing. Other chapters are likewise subdivided by subject matter. The alternative would have been to divide them by the legal principle involved, along the lines of the different canons of construction that Scalia espoused. That seemed less effective and ignored other important dimensions, such as whether Scalia was aiding ordinary citizens against businesses. It would also have left in limbo concepts like judicial deference to administrative agencies. Although Scalia wrote a comprehensive book (along with Bryan A. Garner) that focused on canons of construction,[24] the canons show up rather rarely in his opinions, with the exception of the rule of lenity in criminal cases. The fact that canons are rarely cited as such prevents them from becoming the language of textualism.

28

Four Liberal Special Cases

Most cases can easily be divided into criminal or civil, but some proceedings and issues are not neatly classifiable. Although they are civil cases, the process and potential sanctions for aliens have much in common with criminal prosecutions. From the perspective of the alien denied the right to live in the United States, especially when the individual has lived a long time in the United States and created a family, can exceed that of imprisonment. Another special case is the immunity of prosecutors from civil suit based on misfeasance or nonfeasance of their prosecutorial and related activities in criminal cases. The third situation involves the rules of evidence (here the creation of a psychotherapist-patient privilege) which are applied in both civil and criminal trials. The final category includes certain procedural issues, especially *habeas corpus*, which is a civil proceeding, although one that concerns the criminal-justice system.

IMMIGRATION AND NATURALIZATION

Alien-rights cases can have powerful political overtones. Joseph Patrick Doherty, a prominent member of the Provisional Irish Republican Army, was convicted in Britain of killing a British army officer. The Immigration and Naturalization Service, which interrupted Doherty's surreptitious entry into the United States in 1982, commenced deportation proceedings. Doherty asked for asylum under the Immigration and Nationality Act and moved to stay deportation. The Extradition Magistrate denied extradition because his crimes fell into the political exception to the extradition treaty. With that favorable decision in hand, Doherty withdrew his application for asylum and to stay deportation, and conceded deportability. He designated Ireland as the country to which he would be deported, to which both INS and Ireland acquiesced. When a new extradition treaty permitted extradition to the United Kingdom, he filed a motion to reopen his withdrawn asylum application, claiming the treaty was a new development. Attorney General Edwin Meese, however, denied his motion, reversed the immigration authorities, and ordered him deported to the United Kingdom, on the ground that his deportation to Ireland would harm the interests of the United States.[25]

A Supreme Court majority upheld the deportation order in *INS v. Doherty* (1992).[26] Relying principally on the analogy of motions to reopen court judgments, it held that Doherty had waived his claims to asylum and to bar deportation. Furthermore, Doherty should have known that granting a motion to reopen was discretionary and that the Attorney General could redirect the deportation. Scalia attacked the Court's opinion. First, the majority wrongly equated reopening administrative proceedings with reopening court judgments, which is far narrower.[27] Second, statutory language severely limited the Attorney General's discretion, so his rejection of Doherty's designation of Ireland, which that country had accepted, was an unexpected development.[28] Moreover, Doherty was denied the opportunity to reopen even though INS itself engaged in a number of procedural defaults: "The term 'arbitrary' does not have a very precise content, but it is precise enough to cover this," Scalia concluded.[29] His dissent was less technical and less formalistic than the majority's, and granted aliens greater rights.

Aliens who entered illegally or who were stopped at the country's border, called "inadmissible aliens," generally have fewer protections than those who entered the country legally. Nevertheless, the same statutory language applied to both categories. The question in *Clark v. Martinez* (2005)[30] was whether a different meaning should be given to the language when applied to an alien who had criminal convictions in the United States than to a legal alien who had no record. Scalia's opinion for the Court concluded that the statute applied identically to all categories of aliens: "To give these same words a different meaning for each category would be to invent a statute rather than interpret one. [T]he statute can be construed 'literally' to authorize indefinite detention or . . . it can be read to 'suggest [less than] unlimited discretion' to detain. It cannot, however, be interpreted to do both at the same time." Scalia observed that despite the rule of lenity that applied to statutes creating criminal but not civil liability, language in statutes that provided both criminal and civil penalties has been construed identically, resulting in a construction stripped down to its "lowest common denominator."[31] Here, Scalia took the more formalistic and textual approach, but assisted inadmissible aliens. "The Government fears that the security of our borders will be compromised if it must release into the country inadmissible aliens who cannot be removed. If that is so, Congress can attend to it."[32]

INS claimed that Juozas Kungys had participated in executing Lithuanian citizens for the Nazis in 1941 and had misrepresented facts to secure U.S. citizenship in 1954. The issues in his denaturalization proceeding included whether a showing of materiality was required to sustain denaturalization under one statute and what the appropriate definition of materiality should be under another. Writing for the plurality, Scalia remanded the case for further factual findings, an intermediate result.[33]

Finally, the Court confronted the meaning of "well-founded fear" in an asylum statute's requirement for obtaining asylum. The conservative dissent said it meant "clear probability" of danger while the liberal majority held it meant something less. Scalia joined the liberals, but wrote separately. "I agree with the Court that the plain meaning of 'well-founded fear' and the structure of the Immigration and Naturalization Act (Act) clearly demonstrate that the 'well-founded fear' standard and the 'clear probability' standard are not equivalent."[34]

PROSECUTORIAL IMMUNITY

Immunity is an exemption from a generally applicable law and usually refers to protection from prosecution, arrest, or suit. The United States enjoys immunity from suit in tort except to the extent it has waived that protection and consented to be sued, as it did in the Federal Torts Claims Act. A sitting President cannot be arrested or prosecuted while serving as President, but, as Bill Clinton learned to his everlasting sorrow, he can be sued, although only for conduct outside the scope of his duties as the head of the Executive Branch of the Government.[35]

Immunity can be of one of two types, either absolute or qualified (partial). The former is self-explanatory; the latter applies generally to actions taken in good faith or, as it is alternatively framed, immunity can be defeated by a showing of malice on the part of a prosecutor. Absolute immunity exists for all claims relating to a judge's decisions and a prosecutor's filing charges and engaging in trials. When an individual sues a prosecutor for violating his rights under the Civil Rights Act of 1871, a conservative judge would be inclined to support the prosecutor and grant broad immunity, since limited immunity would tend to interfere with vigorous performance of the law-enforcement function. Those who endorse broader immunity argue that prosecutors are involved as a matter of practice in investigations and that it is a good thing that they are, because they are a professional and moderating force.[36] In two cases where he wrote an opinion, Scalia supported limited rather than absolute immunity for prosecutors.

Cathy Burns informed the Muncie, Indiana, police that an unknown assailant had entered her house, knocked her unconscious, and shot and wounded her two sons while they slept. The police were skeptical. Even though she denied committing the crime and passed a polygraph examination, they regarded her as their prime suspect and speculated that she had multiple personalities. The police decided to interview her under hypnosis, and obtained permission from the chief deputy prosecutor, Richard Reed. While under hypnosis, Burns referred to the assailant as "Katie" and also referred to herself by that name. Reed authorized her arrest, telling the police they "probably had probable cause" to arrest Burns.[37] Under questioning by Reed at a hearing before a county judge to obtain a search warrant, the testifying police officer told the judge that Burns had confessed to shooting her children. No one told the judge that she had been under hypnosis when questioned and had otherwise consistently denied the shooting. After her arrest Burns was placed in the psychiatric ward of a state hospital for four months, during which she lost her employment and the state obtained temporary custody of her sons. The medical experts at the hospital eventually concluded that she did not have multiple personalities.[38] An Indiana grand jury indicted Burns for attempted murder of her sons, but when the trial judge granted Burns's motion to suppress the statement given under hypnosis, the prosecution dismissed all charges against her.[39]

Burns's gratitude went only so far. She filed suit in a U.S. District Court against Reed, the police, and others for violating her constitutional rights under 42 U.S.C. § 1983, the Civil Rights Act of 1871. She settled with other defendants and went to trial against Reed. The trial judge granted Reed's motion for a directed verdict on the ground that he was absolutely immune from liability. The Eighth Circuit affirmed. Like the circuit courts, the Justices were divided.

Expressing concern that granting only qualified immunity to prosecutors would result in unfounded litigation that would divert prosecutorial resources, the Court (per White) held in *Burns v. Reed* (1991)[40] that prosecutors were absolutely immune for their conduct in initiating a prosecution and in presenting the State's case insofar as that conduct is "intimately associated with the judicial phase of the criminal process." That included actions in any hearing before a tribunal that performed a judicial function, such as a prosecutor's appearing before a judge to seek a search warrant. White concluded, however, that providing advice to the police was different and had little to do with the judicial phase of the criminal process. Also, it would be incongruous to grant total immunity to the person who made the decision to conduct a search or seek a search warrant, but give police officers only partial immunity for following his advice.

Writing for Blackmun and in part for Marshall, Scalia embraced a more liberal approach. "'We do not have a license to establish immunities from § 1983 actions in the interests of what we judge to be sound policy.' . . . [O]ur role is to interpret the intent [*sic*] of Congress in enacting § 1983, not to make a freewheeling public policy choice." In the present case, therefore, "the first and crucial question [is] whether the common law recognized [the absolute immunity asserted]."[41] Scalia rejected the majority's methodology and historical analysis, and decided that Reed should have only limited immunity for initiating the search-warrant proceeding.[42]

A similar case came before the Court two years later in *Buckley v. Fitzsimmons* (1993).[43] Stephen Buckley accused the State's Attorney of fabricating evidence, misrepresenting a boot print found near the crime scene, and making defamatory statements at a press conference announcing the return of the indictment, which just happened to coincide with his reelection campaign. The Court found limited immunity applied to both investigative work and the press conference.[44] In another liberal-originalist alliance Scalia joined Stevens's opinion for the Court and also wrote a concurring opinion that was the most liberal in the case. "I have some reservation about the historical authenticity of the 'principle that acts undertaken by a prosecutor in preparing for the initiation of judicial proceedings or for trial, and which occur in the course of his role as an advocate for the State, are entitled to the protections of absolute immunity.'"[45] Four Justices gave limited immunity to statements made during the press conference, but argued that the prosecutors were entitled to absolute immunity on Buckley's claim that law-enforcement personnel conspired to manufacture false evidence.[46] The Court's decision, they said, provided prosecutors with little protection, since almost all in-court conduct is preceded by out-of-court conduct; what the majority called investigation, the dissent called preparation for trial. While this argument has surface appeal, it is difficult to see how preparation for trial can be said to proceed before settling on a defendant.[47]

RULES OF EVIDENCE

The Federal Rules of Evidence apply in both federal civil and criminal trials. Rule 501, which governs privileges, authorizes federal courts to define new privileges by interpreting "the principles of the common law ... in the light of reason and experience." The Court created a psychotherapist privilege in *Jaffee v. Redmond* (1996),[48] when it denied giving the plaintiff in a suit for damages the notes of a social worker's treatment of a police officer who had shot and killed a suspect. The seven-Justice majority (per Stevens) cited the public interest both regarding the patient and the public "by facilitating the provision of appropriate treatment for individuals suffering the effects of a mental or emotional problem."[49] Moreover, all fifty states recognized such a privilege in some form. The Court created an absolute privilege for all forms of psychotherapy, including by all licensed social workers.

Not everyone would agree that Scalia's dissent was liberal, primarily because he challenged a modern therapy and rejected applying the privilege to social workers rather than limiting it to physicians and licensed psychologists, although that was the case with many of the states and has been the practice with the medical and legal privileges. His principal point was that a privilege interferes with ascertaining the truth and, unlike such rules as *Miranda*, which harm the state, "[f]or the rule proposed here, the victim is more likely to be some individual who is prevented from proving a valid claim – or (worse still) prevented from establishing a valid defense."[50] Moreover, Scalia asked, "[w]hen is it, one wonders, that the psychotherapist came to play such an indispensable role in the maintenance of the citizenry's mental health?"[51] Congress should decide the scope of any privilege; "our federal courts will be the tools of injustice rather than unearth the truth where it is available to be found."[52]

A troublesome question under the Federal Rules of Evidence involved the exception to the hearsay rule for statements against penal interest, Rule 804(b)(3). The prosecution introduced against defendant Williamson the confession of his accomplice on the theory that it was a statement against the accomplice' penal interest. Objecting, Williamson claimed that only those specific statements that incriminated the accomplice were admissible against him, and that collateral statements were wrongfully admitted. Scalia joined the liberal opinion of O'Connor and wrote a concurrence, reversing the conviction.[53] Three Justices dissented.[54]

PROCEDURAL ISSUES

Procedural protections and rights are as important as those provided by substantive law. The following cases occurred in the context of criminal prosecutions but did not involve the interpretation of substantive criminal law. A state court convicted Robert Mitchell Jennings of capital murder. On federal *habeas corpus* he alleged that his attorney provided inadequate representation at a sentencing hearing that resulted in the death penalty, both by failing to investigate evidence of his mental impairment (*Wiggins* theory) and by expressing resignation to the death penalty during his closing argument, when he said that he could not "quarrel with" a death sentence (*Spisak* theory). Jennings prevailed in the federal district court on *Wiggins*, but lost on *Spisak*.[55] On appeal, the Fifth Circuit reversed on the *Wiggins* theory and determined that it lacked jurisdiction over the *Spisak* claim because Jennings had not filed a notice of appeal to challenge the district court's rejection of that claim. The technical issue in *Jennings v. Stephens* (2015)[56] was whether Jennings, who won in the district court, was required to file a notice of appeal in order to prevail in the court of appeals on a theory that the district judge had rejected.

Scalia's opinion holding for Jennings relied on the principle that a prevailing party in the district court is not required to file a notice of appeal if all he seeks is the same result as the district court ordered. A win under either theory would give Jennings, at the State's option, release, resentencing, or commutation of his sentence. Thomas, joined by Kennedy and Alito, dissented on the ground that Jennings had received a "conditional-release order," which entitled Jennings to a new sentencing proceeding free of the specific constitutional violation identified by the district court. "Because a conditional-release order embodies this specific right, an appellee's attempt to add additional errors is an attempt to modify or expand his rights under the judgment."[57] The Court's decision, the dissenters said, allowed a prisoner to circumvent demanding preconditions for obtaining an appeal required by the Antiterrorism and Effective Death Penalty Act of 1996 (AFDPA), including "a substantial showing of the denial of a constitutional right," Thomas argued.[58] Further, the majority's decision will burden courts of appeals with countless frivolous appeals.

The dissent's claims were greatly exaggerated. *Jennings* involved the rare case where a prisoner wins in the district court on a habeas petition and, moreover, wins on fewer than all of his claims, the state decides to appeal what *it* lost, and the prisoner decides to reargue the ones *he* lost. Otherwise, it is undisputed that a losing prisoner must file a notice of appeal to reverse a denial of *habeas corpus* and also satisfy the AFDPA. In fact, only one of the cases cited by the dissenters as part of their parade of horrors of inmates raising a huge number of frivolous arguments was like *Jennings*. The arcane arguments of Thomas, Kennedy, and Alito would have denied Jennings a chance to save his life.

Two cases can be dealt with summarily. After his state conviction became final, Patrick Day filed a petition for *habeas corpus* in the federal district court. The state's answer conceded the petition was filed within one year as required, but a Magistrate Judge recalculated the time, found the petition late, and dismissed it. Ginsburg concluded that even though a party's failure to allege a statutory time limitation in its answer waives the defense under Rule 4 of the Federal Rules of Civil Procedure, the Magistrate Judge did not abuse his discretion in raising the defense *sua sponte*.[59] Scalia dissented. Historically, there was no time limitation to *habeas corpus*, and the courts have no basis for creating a nonstatutory one.[60]

William Dotson brought a § 1983 action to challenge new parole procedures under which he was denied parole. He claimed that use of more stringent guidelines adopted after he began serving his sentence violated the *Ex Post Facto* Clause and denied him due process. Dotson's procedural problem was that a prisoner cannot use a § 1983 action to challenge his confinement, but must proceed by *habeas corpus*. The latter is more burdensome, for example, by requiring exhaustion of state remedies. Scalia joined Breyer's majority opinion, which decided that Dotson could proceed under § 1983 because he did not seek immediate release and did not challenge the legality of his sentence. Scalia's concurrence observed that requiring a prisoner to rely on *habeas corpus* "would utterly sever the writ from its common-law roots."[61]

29

Liberal Criminal Statutory Opinions

Scalia rejection of the use of legislative history applied especially to criminal statutes, primarily because legislative history fails to provide fair notice of what conduct was criminal. That principle blends into another precept, embraced in the rule of lenity, namely, "when a criminal statute is ambiguous[,] [t]he more lenient interpretation must prevail."[1] He explained: "This venerable rule not only vindicates the fundamental principle that no citizen should be held accountable for a violation of a statute whose commands are uncertain, or subjected to punishment that is not clearly prescribed. . . . We interpret ambiguous criminal statues in favor of defendants, not prosecutors."[2] While the principal reasons for the rule of lenity is fair notice, other reasons such as separation of powers, the nondelegation doctrine, and humanitarian concerns have supported the rule.[3] Scalia also gave a pragmatic reason for the liberal rule: "It also places the weight of inertia upon the party that can best induce Congress to speak more clearly and keeps courts from making criminal law in Congress's stead."[4] Often, the culprit was the poorly drafted statute. There was no shortage of culprits.

Perhaps the best approach to understanding Scalia's opinions is to group them by the attributes of the defendant, in particular, whether the defendant was a blue-collar criminal, such as a bank robber, or a white-collar criminal, such as a forger, although categorizing a case may occasionally be difficult, such as possession of a small amount of marijuana.[5] Blue-collar criminals famously use guns or crowbars, while white-collar criminals use financial statements and computers. Scalia's evenhandedness with the two categories of criminal defendants should not be taken for granted. His colleagues on the Court frequently treated the two classes differently, with conservative Justices more sympathetic to white-collar defendants than to blue-collar defendants and vice versa.[6] This discussion implicates the question of whether pro-government votes in prosecutions of businessmen are more liberal than pro-defendant votes, which has validity but is not the approach taken here. The chapter concludes with cases on sentencing.

One case cannot be readily categorized; sex offenders are both white collar and blue collar. Sex offender Thomas Carr, who had traveled in interstate commerce before the statute's effective date without having registered under SORNA (discussed in Chapter 16), did not register after its effective date. The Court construed the registration provisions not to apply.[7] Scalia concurred in part and concurred in the judgment, largely on the ground that the "text, context, and structure demonstrate that the meaning of 18 U.S.C. § 2255(a) is plain."[8]

BLUE-COLLAR CRIMES

Blue-collar crimes tend to be committed without particular regard for the words of the criminal statute. Likewise, they usually entail conduct that was a crime at common law, which ordinarily required *mens rea*, or a guilty mind. While notice to the perpetrator is arguably less significant, individuals must be relieved of liability for conduct that did not violate any criminal law. Three cases raised the question of whether the defendant committed the crime charged, which means that even if the prosecutor proved everything he alleged in the indictment, the jury could not properly convict the defendant for the crime, or so at least Scalia argued, for he was always in dissent.

A pair of cases that implicated mangled statutes concerned the specific culpable state of mind needed to convict the defendant. Criminal statutes often specify that a criminal act must be "willful." Stevens's opinion for the Court in *Holloway v. United States* (1999)[9] began: "Carjacking 'with the intent to cause death or serious bodily harm' is a federal crime. The question presented in this case is whether that phrase requires the Government to prove that the defendant had unconditional intent to kill or harm in all events, or whether it merely requires proof of intent to kill or harm if necessary to effect a carjacking."[10] The Court chose the latter, because that was the "commonsense reading of the carjacking statute," enacted to stop a form of criminal activity that was a matter of national concern. It was a purposivist opinion.

Scalia's dissent probed the meaning of the statutory language: "in customary English usage the unqualified word 'intent' does not usually connote a purpose that is subject to any conditions precedent except those so remote in the speaker's estimation as to be effectively nonexistent – and it *never* connotes a purpose that is subject to a condition which the speaker hopes will not occur."[11] Thus, "it is *not* common usage – indeed, it is an unheard-of usage – to speak of my having an 'intent' to do something, when my plans are contingent upon an event that is not virtually certain, and that I hope will not occur. When a friend is seriously ill, for example, I would not say that 'I intend to go to his funeral next week.' I would have to make it clear that the intent is a conditional one: 'I intend to go to his funeral next week if he dies.'"[12] The rule of lenity would require any ambiguity to be resolved in the defendant's favor.[13] Congress almost certainly intended something closer to the majority, even though it did not say so. Reasonable questions are whether judges should refuse to give a statute its obvious meaning and which approach more respects the elected branches of the government.

Fowler v. United States (2011)[14] involved a statute with at least three plausible interpretations. The federal witness-tampering statute makes it a crime "to kill another person, with intent . . . to prevent the communication by any person to a law enforcement officer . . . of the United States" of "information relating to the . . . possible commission of a federal offense."[15] When local police officer Todd Horner came upon a group of men under suspicious circumstances, he pulled his gun and identified one of them by name. Charles Fowler said, "Now we can't walk away from this thing," and shot Horner dead. The men had been meeting to prepare to rob a (federally insured) bank. The issue was the statute's applicability when "a defendant killed a person with the intent to prevent that person from communicating with law enforcement officers in general but where the defendant did not have federal law enforcement officers (or any specific individuals) in mind."[16] Writing for a six-Justice majority, Breyer rejected the argument that the government must

> show *beyond a reasonable doubt* (or even that it is *more likely than not*) that the hypothetical communication would have been to a federal officer. No Circuit has adopted this interpretation, and no party argues for it here. . . . And for good reason: The relevant question concerns the defendant's intent. The Government will already have shown beyond a reasonable doubt that the defendant possessed broad indefinite intent, namely, the intent to prevent the victim from communicating with (unspecified) law enforcement officers. . . . [A] defendant can kill a victim with *an intent* to prevent the victim from communicating with federal enforcement officers even if there is some considerable doubt that such communication would otherwise take place.[17]

Breyer concluded that "the Government must show *a reasonable likelihood* that, had, *e.g.*, the victim communicated with law enforcement officers, at least one relevant communication would have been made to a federal law enforcement officer."[18] In other words, the undifferentiated intent encompassed the specific intent.

Alito (joined by Ginsburg) dissented on the ground that all that was necessary was that "a rational jury could infer that Fowler's intent was to prevent information about what Officer Horner had seen from reaching any person who could bring about his arrest and conviction. . . . And since the information that Officer Horner possessed related to, among other things, the possible commission of a federal crime, a rational jury could infer that this group included law enforcement officers who were employed by the United States."[19] This was more conservative.

Scalia alone argued that "the Government must prove that the defendant intended to prevent a communication which, had it been made, would beyond a reasonable doubt have been made *to a federal law enforcement officer*."[20] The specific intent was an element of the crime and one of the facts the Government must prove to secure a conviction. For Scalia the words "to prevent the communication to a law enforcement officer . . . of the United States" could not be ignored or tempered, regardless of its devastating impact on prosecutions under the statute and the unlikelihood that Congress would have wanted that result. Under his standard, there was insufficient evidence to convict Fowler and Scalia would dismiss the case. His opinion was uncompromisingly textual; it was also the most liberal.

The final blue-collar case involved the materiality of a misrepresentation, an element of the crime. The defendant was the purchaser of a hand gun who represented to the seller that he was the actual buyer, when, in fact, he was purchasing the hand gun for someone else who could legally have purchased the hand gun himself. Kagan's majority opinion for the ordinarily liberal Justices held the misrepresentation was material and upheld the conviction.[21] The anti-gun liberal position trumped the pro-defense liberal position. Scalia's dissent for the ordinarily conservative Justices incorporated the law of agency into the statute and found for the defendant.[22]

WHITE-COLLAR CRIMES

As noted above, the importance of language in statutes involving white-collar crimes is greater than in blue-collar crimes because many of the acts were not criminal at common law and because virtually all white-collar crimes are premeditated, and some even committed after receiving legal advice. In the initial group of cases discussed Scalia concluded that the statute did not cover (or may not have covered) the crime charged.

Use of the mails to facilitate a crime is a time-honored federal crime and "[t]he relevant question at all times is whether the mailing is part of the execution of the scheme as conceived by the perpetrator at the time, regardless of whether the mailing later, through hindsight, may prove to have been counterproductive and return to haunt the perpetrator of the fraud."[23] In an early case corporate officers set up dummy corporations to divert profits into their own pockets. As part of this fraudulent scheme, the defendants caused one corporation to issue checks payable to them, which they then cashed personally at a local bank. The Court held that the local bank's mailing the checks to the drawee bank for collection could not supply the mailing element of the mail-fraud charge, because the defendants' fraudulent scheme had previously reached its fruition.[24] Similarly, when the defendant stole his roommate's credit card and used it to charge food and lodging, the Court held that mailings by the proprietors of the establishments to the bank that issued the credit card could not support mail-fraud charges.[25]

Wayne T. Schmuck purchased used cars, rolled back their odometers, and then sold the cars to retail dealers for prices artificially inflated because of low mileage readings. The dealers resold cars to customers at prices enhanced by Schmuck's fraud. Blackmun held the mailings sufficient in *Schmuck v. United States* (1989)[26]:

> To complete the resale of each automobile, the dealer who purchased it from Schmuck would submit a title application form to the Wisconsin Department of Transportation on behalf of his retail customer. The receipt of a Wisconsin title

was a prerequisite for completing the resale; without it, the dealer could not obtain Wisconsin tags. The submission of the title-application form supplied the mailing element of each of the alleged mail frauds.... [27]

A rational jury could have concluded that the success of Schmuck's venture depended upon his continued harmonious relations with, and good reputation among, retail dealers, which in turn required the smooth flow of cars from the dealers to their Wisconsin customers.... Schmuck's scheme would have come to an abrupt halt if the dealers either had lost faith in Schmuck or had not been able to resell the cars obtained from him. Thus, although the registration form mailings may not have contributed directly to the duping of either the retail dealers or the customers, they were necessary to the passage of title, which in turn was essential to the perpetration of Schmuck's scheme. [28]

Dissenting, Scalia argued that the relationship between the fraud and the mailings was not sufficiently close. "[I]t is obvious that, regardless of who the ultimate victim of the fraud may have been, the fraud was complete with respect to each car when the defendant pocketed the dealer's money." [29] But the indictment alleged in the language of the statute that Schmuck had engaged in a "scheme" to defraud multiple people. Scalia was too generous to Schmuck.

Another federal statute criminalized, "Whoever, with unlawful or fraudulent intent, transports in interstate or foreign commerce any falsely made, forged, altered, or counterfeited securities . . . knowing the same to have been falsely made, forged, altered, or counterfeited.... " [30] The issue in *Moskal v. United States* (1990)[31] was whether a person who knowingly procures genuine vehicle titles that incorporate fraudulent odometer readings receives those titles "knowing [them] to have been falsely made." Raymond J. Moskal, Sr., mailed the title documents that contained the false odometer readings from Pennsylvania to an accomplice in Virginia, who submitted them to the Virginia authorities, who mailed them back to him in Pennsylvania. Marshall's opinion for the Court concluded that the words of § 2314, "falsely made," were broad enough to encompass washed titles containing fraudulent odometer readings.

Scalia's dissent distinguished between something that was "falsely made" and something that was "false." The meaning the majority gave to "falsely made" is "quite *extra*ordinary." The established specialized meaning for "falsely made," regularly used since Blackstone, Scalia argued, has been that the document is false, not genuine, without regard to the truth or falsity of the statements in contains. [32] The argument that Congress had a broad purpose in passing the statute "is simply question-begging. The whole issue here is how 'broad' Congress' purpose was in enacting § 2314." "I feel constrained to mention, though it is surely superfluous for decision of the present case, the so-called Rule of Lenity." [33] In distinguishing "false" from "falsely made," however, Scalia proceeded differently from his approach in the Second Amendment cases, where he looked at the definition of the individual words "bear" and "arms," and did not search for a specialized historical meaning of the term "bear arms."

Lawyer John Bruce Hubbard filed on behalf of his client a bankruptcy petition under Chapter 7 of the Bankruptcy Code, which falsely denied that machine parts belonging to the bankrupt were stored at a warehouse. An indictment charged Hubbard with making a false statement knowingly and willfully "in any matter within the jurisdiction of any department or agency of the United States" in violation of 18 U.S.C. § 1001. Earlier, *United States v. Bramblett* (1955)[34] held that Congress and the courts were departments or agencies of the United States, so the trial judge instructed the jury that a bankruptcy court was a department of the United States. The jury convicted Hubbard, and the Court of Appeals affirmed. Stevens wrote the opinion in *Hubbard v. United States* (1995)[35] that overruled *Bramblett* and held that denominating a court as an agency or department of the Government could not be justified linguistically or otherwise.

Scalia concurred. The fact that "so many Courts of Appeals have strained so mightily to discern an exception that the statute does not contain . . . demonstrates how great a potential for mischief federal judges have discovered in the mistaken reading of 18 U.S.C. § 1001. . . . [The statute creates] a serious concern that the threat of criminal prosecution under the capacious provisions of § 1001 will deter vigorous representation of opposing interests in adversarial litigation, particularly representation of criminal defendants, whose adversaries control the machinery of § 1001 prosecutions."[36] Unusual was that Scalia alone relied on the *consequences* of keeping or discarding the forty-year-old precedent on which the case turned.[37]

The Court reversed the conviction of a state legislator under the Hobbs Act for extorting a bribe from physicians who sought favorable legislation. Robert McCormick claimed the payments were legitimate campaign contributions. White's majority opinion in *McCormick v. United States* (1991)[38] agreed: "Whatever ethical considerations and appearances may indicate, to hold that legislators commit the federal crime of extortion when they act for the benefit of constituents or support legislation furthering the interests of some of their constituents, shortly before or after campaign contributions are solicited and received from those beneficiaries, is an unrealistic assessment of what Congress could have meant by making it a crime to obtain property from another, with his consent, 'under color of official right.' . . . We thus disagree with the Court of Appeals' holding in this case that a *quid pro quo* is not necessary for conviction under the Hobbs Act when an official receives a campaign contribution."[39]

Scalia concurred in reversing the conviction but went further, suggesting but not concluding that the courts had been misconstruing the Hobbs Act for decades, and that hundreds of convictions had been wrongly obtained.

It is acceptance of the assumption that "under color of official right" means "on account of one's office" that brings bribery cases within the statute's reach, and that creates the necessity for the reasonable but textually inexplicable distinction the Court makes today. That assumption is questionable. "The obtaining of property... under color of official *right*" more naturally connotes some false assertion of official *entitlement* to the property. This interpretation might have the effect of making the § 1951 definition of extortion comport with the definition of "extortion" at common law.... I mean only to raise this argument, not to decide it, for it has not been advanced and there may be persuasive responses.[40]

Stevens, Blackmun, and O'Connor voted to affirm the conviction: "It is perfectly clear that the indictment charged a violation of the Hobbs Act, 18 U.S.C. § 1951, and that the evidence presented to the jury was adequate to prove beyond a reasonable doubt that [McCormick] knowingly used his public office to make or imply promises or threats to his constituents for purposes of pressuring them to make payments that were not lawfully due him."[41]

In two cases the Court majority upheld statues after construing them in order to sustain their constitutionality, which Scalia thought reprehensible. He would have construed the statutes more broadly, that is, to apply to more defendants' conduct, and then held them unconstitutional. In *United States v. X-Citement Video, Inc.* (1994)[42] a statute subjected to criminal penalty

(a) Any person who –
    (1) *knowingly* transports or ships . . . [in] interstate or foreign commerce . . . any visual depiction, if –
        (A) the producing of such visual depiction involves the use of a minor engaging in sexually explicit conduct; and
        (B) such visual depiction is of such conduct.[43]

To preserve the constitutionality of this provision against First Amendment attack, the Court applied the *knowingly* requirement to (a)(1)A) and (a)(1)(B), which Scalia argued was grammatically indefensible; there was no grammatical connection between the adverb "knowingly" in the relative *who*-clause and the two conditional *if*-clauses. The unprecedented result was a completely different statute from what Congress passed. "The equivalent, in expressing a simpler thought, would be the following: 'Anyone who knowingly double parks will be subject to a $200 fine if that conduct occurs during the 4:30-to-6:30 rush hour.' It could not be clearer that the scienter requirement applies only to the double-parking, and not to the time of day." "I would find the statute, as so interpreted, to be unconstitutional, by imposing criminal liability upon those not knowingly dealing in pornography."[44]

The other case involved fraud. Earlier, *McNally v. United States* (1987)[45] reversed Charles McNally's conviction under a statute that made criminal "any scheme or artifice to defraud, or for obtaining money or property by means of false or fraudulent pretenses, representations, or promises." A state officer who selected Kentucky's insurance agent arranged to procure a share of the agent's commissions via kickbacks. The prosecutor did not charge that the conduct caused the Commonwealth to overpay, but rather alleged that the kickback scheme "defraud[ed] the citizens and government of Kentucky of their right to have the Commonwealth's affairs conducted honestly." The Supreme Court found that there was no violation of the statute. In response to *McNally*, Congress passed 18 U.S.C. § 1346, which prohibited "a scheme or artifice to deprive another of the intangible right of honest services."

Skilling v. United States (2010)[46] was an aggravated case of securities fraud by an executive of Enron Corporation, the seventh highest-revenue-grossing company in America when it crashed into bankruptcy in 2001. Charging a violation of § 1346, the government alleged that Skilling had artificially inflated stock prices by making false statements. Skilling argued that the statutory provision was unconstitutionally vague. Writing for the Court, Ginsburg stated that a strong presumption of validity attaches to an act of Congress. "We agree that § 1346 should be construed rather than invalidated."[47] The majority explored whether the statute was amenable to a limiting construction under the doctrine (or canon) of constitutional avoidance. "Congress' reversal of *McNally* and reinstatement of the honest-services doctrine, we conclude, can and should be salvaged by confining its scope to the core pre-*McNally* applications," namely, "offenders who, in violation of a fiduciary duty, participated in bribery or kickback schemes." Thus narrowed, the statute was constitutional. However, the statute as construed did not apply to Skilling and the Court reversed.[48]

Scalia accused the Court of flagrant activism by rewriting a criminal statute to create one that Congress did not pass. "[I]n transforming the prohibition of 'honest-services fraud' into a prohibition of 'bribery and kick-backs' [the Court] is wielding a power we long ago abjured: the power to define new federal crimes." Scalia did not dispute that Congress passed § 1346 to restore pre-*McNally* law, but there was no evidence that § 1346 was the same as pre-*McNally* law. The earlier cases did not mention bribery or kickbacks and not one was limited to bribery and kickbacks.[49] How can the majority decide that Congress meant to equate honest services with bribery and kickbacks, rather than more – or less, Scalia reasonably asked.

> The Court replaces a vague criminal standard that Congress adopted with a more narrow one (included within the vague one) that can pass constitutional muster. I know of no precedent for such "paring down," and it seems to me clearly beyond judicial power.... As we have seen (and the Court does not contest), no court before *McNally* concluded that the 'deprivation of honest services' meant *only* the acceptance of bribes or kickbacks.... The canon of constitutional avoidance, on which the Court so heavily relies,... states that "when the constitutionality of a statute is assailed, if the statute be reasonably susceptible of two interpretations, by one of which it would be unconstitutional and by the other valid, it is our plain duty to adopt the construction which will save the statute from constitutional infirmity."... Here there is no choice to be made between two "fair alternatives."[50]

The first two of the four remaining cases reprised the meaning of the word "willfully," which Scalia construed demandingly. Because of their complexity, a special rule was developed for tax cases that "willfully" meant "a voluntary, intentional

violation of a known legal duty," as opposed to ignorance or a good-faith misunderstanding of the duty. But that was not John L. Cheek, who claimed that some of the
provisions of the tax code were unconstitutional. "They do not arise from innocent
mistakes caused by the complexity of the Internal Revenue Code. Rather, they reveal
full knowledge of the provisions at issue and a studied conclusion, however wrong,
that those provisions are invalid and unenforceable."[51] John Cheek's defense was
that he believed the federal income-tax laws were unconstitutional and that wages
were not income, so his failure to file a return lacked the willfulness required for
conviction. The Supreme Court reversed Cheek's conviction. While Cheek was not
entitled to a jury instruction that he could not be convicted if he believed that the
Code was unconstitutional, he was entitled to an instruction that he could not be
convicted if he believed the Code imposed no duties on him to file or pay taxes
because he had no income.

Scalia concurred in the reversal, but went further. The laws, including the criminal tax laws, have long required proof of "bad purpose" or "evil motive" to establish
intentionally violating a known legal duty. "It seems to me that today's opinion
squarely reverses that long-established statutory construction when it says that a
good-faith erroneous belief in the unconstitutionality of a law is no defense. It is
quite impossible to say that a statute which one believes unconstitutional represents
a 'known legal duty.'"[52]

Blackmun and Marshall dissented. "[I]t is incomprehensible to me how, in this
day, more than 70 years after the institution of our federal income tax system . . . any
taxpayer of competent mentality can assert as his defense to charges of statutory
willfulness the proposition that the wage he receives for his labor is not income, irre-
spective of a cult that says otherwise and advises the gullible to resist income tax collections."[53] Two liberal Justices were the only votes against a white-collar defendant.

The issue in *Bryan v. United States* (1998),[54] a prosecution for conspiring to
engage in the business of selling firearms without a license as well as the substantive
crime, was the meaning of the word "willfully" in a statute that prohibited willfully
dealing in firearms without a federal license.[55] Sillasse Bryan engaged in prohibited
acts and knew his conduct was unlawful, both of which the jury found based on
evidence that he employed straw intermediaries and filed serial numbers off the
firearms. The Court's majority opinion held that while willful has many meanings,
it ordinarily meant "undertaken with a bad purpose," and rejected a number of
defenses, including that the statute required knowledge that the precise conduct
was unlawful.

Scalia's dissent argued that the Court's definition of *mens rea* was so broad as to
be meaningless and must have intended something more than knowledge that a
defendant was doing something wrong.

Everyone agrees that § 924(a)(1)(D) requires some knowledge of the law; the only
real question is *which* law? The Court's answer is that knowledge of *any* law is

enough – or, put another way, that the defendant must be ignorant of *every* law violated by his course of conduct to be innocent of willfully violating the licensing requirement. The Court points to no textual basis for that conclusion other than the notoriously malleable word "willfully" itself. Instead, it seem to fall back on a presumption (apparently derived from the rule that ignorance of the law is no excuse) that even when ignorance of the law *is* an excuse, that excuse should be construed as narrowly as the statutory language permits.[56]

Ultimately, rather than try to figure out what Congress meant, Scalia declared that he would apply "the rule that 'ambiguity concerning the ambit of criminal statutes should be resolved in favor of lenity.'"[57] Scalia was wrong. The Court stated in a 1933 tax case: "The word ['willfully'] often denotes an action which is intentional, or knowing, or voluntary, as distinguished from accidental. But, when used in a criminal statute, it generally means an act done with a bad purpose, without justifiable excuse, stubbornly, obstinately, perversely."[58] While Scalia had let off a gun dealer, he seems to have taken the same approach in *Cheek*, a tax prosecution.

Scalia relied on the rule of lenity in the two last white-collar cases. James O'Hagan, an attorney who represented the bidder in a tender offer, was convicted of violating federal securities laws in connection with insider information on which he relied to purchase the common stock of the subject company. Normally, the government premises liability on a fiduciary relationship between an insider and a purchaser or seller of the company's stock. But the government argued the "misappropriation theory" of securities fraud, which premised liability on a fiduciary-turned-trader's deception of those who entrusted him with access to confidential information.[59] The Supreme Court affirmed the conviction in *United States v. O'Hagan* (1997).[60] Scalia concurred in part and dissented in part in a short opinion that emphasized an ambiguity in the statute: "While the Court's explanation of the scope of § 10(b) and Rule 10b-5 would be entirely reasonable in some other context, it does not seem to accord with the principle of lenity that we apply to criminal statutes. . . . In light of that principle, it seems to me that the unelaborated statutory language: '[t]o use or employ, in connection with the purchase or sale of any security . . . any manipulative or deceptive device or contrivance,' § 10(b), must be construed to require the manipulation or deception of a party to a securities transaction."[61]

The final case in this group involved "whether the term 'proceeds' in the federal money-laundering statute, 18 U.S.C. § 1956(a)(1), meant 'receipts' or 'profits.'" Scalia concluded that in ordinary meaning, under criminal law statutes, including money-laundering statutes, the term could mean either one. Interpreting "proceeds" to mean "receipts" would make many disparate crimes subject to the money-laundering statute. Arguments based on the purpose and role of the statute were insufficient to decide the case. So the rule of lenity required giving the term "proceeds" its narrower meaning, namely "profits," and Scalia's opinion reversed Efrain Santos's conviction for running an illegal lottery.[62] Congress, however, apparently had something else in mind, and amended the statute the following year to define proceeds as gross receipts.[63]

SENTENCING AND SENTENCING ENHANCEMENTS

Scalia's liberal opinions included sentencing. The first two cases involved original sentencing while the final two concerned resentencing.[64] Instead of paying money for drugs, John Angus Smith exchanged an automatic MAC-10 and silencer for two ounces of cocaine. In *Smith v. United States* (1993)[65] the Court stated the issue as "whether the exchange of a gun for narcotics constitutes 'use' of a firearm 'during and in relation to . . . [a] drug trafficking crime' within the meaning of 18 U.S.C. § 924(c)(1). We hold that it does."[66] O'Connor's opinion for six Justices surveyed dictionary definitions and concluded that definitions of "use" were easily broad enough to cover Smith's activities.

Scalia argued that the elastic verb "use" was at least ambiguous, so that employing dictionary definitions was not appropriate. Giving the word its ordinary meaning supported his view, such as when someone asks, "Do you use a cane?" The question would not cover the display of a grandfather's cane, Scalia informed, but whether someone employed a cane to walk.[67] "Given our rule that ordinary meaning governs, and given the ordinary meaning of 'uses a firearm,' it seems to me inconsequential that 'the words "as a weapon" appear nowhere in the statute,'" as the majority argues; "they are reasonably implicit," a statement that reflects a more nuanced textualism. Moreover, other statutory provisions confirm a restricted definition; context was informative. "At the very least, it may be said that the issue is subject to some doubt. Under these circumstances, we adhere to the familiar rule that, where there is ambiguity in a criminal statute, doubts are resolved in favor of the defendant."[68]

As noted, originalists rely, sometimes heavily, on dictionaries published 200 years ago. The question can legitimately be asked why, if dictionary definitions should be treated with skepticism in *Smith* in 1993, they should be given substantial weight in interpreting language over 200 years old. Dictionary definitions are blunt instruments often wrenched from context.

The Juvenile Delinquency Act[69] limited the length of detention to "the maximum term of imprisonment that would be authorized if the juvenile had been tried and convicted as an adult." The issue in *United States v. R.L.C.* (1992)[70] was whether "maximum sentence" referred to the maximum in the statute that defined the crime or the maximum after application of the Sentencing Guidelines, which at the time were mandatory and which provided for generally shorter maximum sentences. The Court held it was the latter. A plurality, not including Scalia, considered the textual evolution and statutory history, and concluded they unambiguously supported the

Guidelines approach.[71] Concurring in the judgment, Scalia found the provision ambiguous: "In my view it is not consistent with the rule of lenity to construe a textually ambiguous penal statute against a criminal defendant on the basis of legislative history."[72]

The final two cases reviewed the resentencing of defendants following additional violations of law. In the first case Ralph Granderson, a letter carrier, pleaded guilty to one count of destruction of mail. Applying the Sentencing Guidelines, which provided for zero to six months in prison, the district judge sentenced him to five years' probation and a $2,000 fine. When Granderson tested positive for cocaine, the judge sent him to prison for one-third of his probation, *i.e.*, twenty months, under a statute providing that if a person serving a sentence of probation possesses illegal drugs, "the court shall revoke the sentence of probation and sentence the defendant to not less than one-third of the original sentence." The circuit court, applying the rule of lenity, held that the "original sentence" referred to the term of imprisonment provided by the Guidelines. Since Granderson had served eleven months, more than the six months under then-mandatory Guidelines, it ordered him released from custody.

In *United States v. Granderson* (1994)[73] five liberal Justices essentially accepted the circuit court's analysis. Rehnquist and Thomas followed the district court and dissented. Scalia's concurring opinion concluded that Granderson was subject to an additional fine, so he owed money as well as being owed the extra five months he served in jail, which placed Scalia in the middle of the Court, although closer to the liberal end. He declared it a wash: "I can neither pronounce the results reached by a straightforward reading of the statute utterly absurd nor discern any other self-evident disposition for which they are an obviously mistaken replacement. . . . It seems to me that the other interpretations proposed today suffer, in varying degrees, the double curse of producing *neither* textually faithful results *nor* plausibly intended ones. It is best, as usual, to apply the statute as written, and to let Congress make the needed repairs. That repairs are needed is perhaps the only thing about this wretchedly drafted statute that we can all agree upon."[74]

In the remaining criminal case a statute authorized a district judge to "revoke a term of supervised release, and require the person to serve in prison all or part of the term of supervised release without credit for the time previously served on postrelease supervision" if he commits another crime while on supervised release. When Cornell Johnson did just that, the judge revoked his supervised release and sent him to prison, to be followed by a term of supervised release. In *Johnson v. United States* (2000)[75] eight Justices held that "the district court may require service of a further term of supervised release following the further incarceration" for the commission of another crime. Scalia disagreed in another homey opinion. "Finding in this statute an authorization for imposition of *additional* supervised release is an act of willpower rather than of judgment." Under the ordinary meaning of "revoke," which is "to annul by recalling or taking back," . . . the "revoked" term of supervised release is simply canceled; and since there is no authorization for a new term of supervised release to replace the one that has been revoked, additional supervised release is unavailable. . . . Of course the acid test of whether a word can reasonably bear a particular meaning is whether you could use the word in that sense at a cocktail party without having people look at you funny. The Court's assigned meaning would surely fail that test, even late in the evening. Try telling someone, "Though I do not cancel or annul my earlier action, I revoke it." The notion that Congress, by the phrase "revoke a term of supervised release," meant "recall but not cancel a term of supervised release" is both linguistically and conceptually absurd.[76]

Scalia concluded: "Today's decision invites [courts of appeals] to return to headier days of not-too-yore, when laws meant what judges knew they ought to mean. I dissent."[77]

Below is a chart that shows agreement and disagreement with all Scalia's liberal criminal opinions – constitutional and statutory, substantive and procedural, merits and sentencing, direct appeal and *habeas corpus*.

AGREEMENT WITH ALL SCALIA'S LIBERAL CRIMINAL OPINIONS

Stevens	44–28	61%
Ginsburg	34–25	58%
Thomas	34–31	51%
Roberts	13–19	41%
Rehnquist	7–44	14%
Alito	4–29	12%

30

Liberal Civil Statutory Opinions

This chapter considers statutory construction in civil cases in which Scalia's positions were on balance not only liberal in outcome, but sometimes expanded the scope of federal government regulation, anathema to conservatives. Scalia's principal tool of construction was a rigorous textualism, the same approach that manifested itself in *King v. Burwell* (2015)[1] and *Arizona State Legislature v. Arizona Independent Redistricting Comm'n* (2015).[2] Discussed is a diverse assortment of twenty-two cases.

Arguably, Scalia's most important liberal civil statutory opinion was his dissent in *National Cable & Telecommunications Ass'n v. Brand X Internet Services* (2005).[3] The issue was the scope of an "offer" of "telecommunications service" in amendments to the Communications Act of 1934, which subjected some providers of internet services to mandatory Federal Communications Commission regulations, but exempted others. While Thomas construed the term narrowly and limited the scope of federal regulation, Scalia's dissent, joined by liberals Souter and Ginsburg, favored an expanded federal role as a result of a more pragmatic interpretation of the statute:

> The Federal Communications Commission . . . has once again attempted to correct "a whole new regime of regulation (or of free-market competition) under the guise of statutory construction." . . . Actually, in these cases it might be more accurate to say the Commission has attempted to establish a whole new regime of *non-*regulation, which will make for more or less free-market competition, depending on whose experts are believed. The important fact, however, is that the Commission has chosen to achieve this through an implausible reading of the statute, and has thus exceeded the authority given it by Congress.[4]

Scalia sided with plaintiffs in three employment-discrimination cases. In *International Union, United Automobile Workers of America v. Johnson Controls, Inc.* (1991)[5] the union sued when Johnson Controls, which manufactured batteries that contained lead, announced "that women who are pregnant or who are capable of bearing children will not be placed into jobs involving lead exposure or which could expose them to lead through the exercise of job bidding, bumping, transfer or promotion rights." Blackmun's opinion held that the policy explicitly discriminated-against women because "fertile men and not fertile women are given a choice as to whether they wish to risk their reproductive health for a particular job." Scalia agreed with the Court's result, but not its reasoning. It was irrelevant whether Johnson Controls had or did not have a factual basis for believing that all or most women would be harmed by lead. Under the law that is for the women involved to decide, not the employer.[6] It was a woman-empowering opinion.

The Age Discrimination in Employment Act (ADEA) exempted employer actions "otherwise prohibited" by the ADEA if "based on reasonable factors other than age." *Meacham v. Knolls Atomic Power Laboratory* (2008)[7] considered who had the burden of persuasion on that issue. Souter, writing for six Justices, reviewed the language and structure of the statute, the legislative history, and precedent before placing the burden of proof on the employer. Concurring separately, Scalia concluded that Congress left the issue to the sound judgment of the Equal Employment Opportunity Commission, a generally liberal federal agency that had taken a pro-worker position. "Because administration of the ADEA has been placed in the hands of the Commission, and because the agency's position on the questions before us are unquestionably reasonable (as the Court's opinion ably shows), I defer to the agency's views."[8]

Writing for the Court in *EEOC v. Abercrombie & Fitch Stores, Inc.* (2015),[9] Scalia held that a rejected job applicant did not have to show that a prospective employer had "actual knowledge" of her need for religious accommodation to sustain a claim for disparate impact, but need show only that her need was a motivating factor in the employer's decision. Thomas alone dissented on the ground that "[m]ere application of a neutral policy cannot constitute intentional discrimination"; for him proof of a discriminatory motive or purpose was required.[10]

Although unsympathetic to environmental laws, Scalia also supported plaintiffs in four environmental cases. The Department of Labor rejected Harriet Pauley's claim for compensation under the Black Lung Benefits Reform Act. Giving *Chevron* deference to the Department of Labor's (DOL) interpretation of its regulations and finding its interpretation reasonable, Blackmun, writing for the Court, held for the defendant company.[11] Even though he strongly supported deference to administrative agencies' rulings,[12] Scalia alone dissented in favor of Pauley. "The disputed regulatory language is complex, but it is not ambiguous, and I do not think *Chevron* deference . . . requires us to accept the strained and implausible construction advanced by the Department of Labor (DOL)."[13] In another case Scalia wrote for the Court reversing DOL regulations on the black-lung act as unduly restrictive to claimants in violation of the statute.[14] In both opinions Scalia enhanced the Court's role at the expense of the Executive Branch, while supporting victims of industrial polluters.[15]

Scalia supported the Environmental Defense Fund when it sued Chicago for dumping hazardous ash in a nonhazardous site. Rejecting Chicago's claim (endorsed by the Solicitor General) that ash was exempt from the Environmental Protection Act, Scalia's opinion for seven Justices relied on the language of the statute, the history of amendments to the original act, other environmental legislation, and regulations promulgated by the Environmental Protection Agency (EPA).[16] The fourth case[17] involved the EPA's interpretation of its powers under the Clean Air Act[18] with respect to its regulation of greenhouse-gas emissions. Roberts and Kennedy joined Scalia's intermediate opinion in full; Ginsburg, Breyer, Sotomayor, and Kagan dissented from a conservative section of the opinion; Thomas and Alito dissented from a liberal section.

The Federal Tort Claims Act renders the Government liable "for money damages . . . for injury or loss of property, or personal injury or death caused by the negligent or wrongful act or omission of any employee of the Government while acting within the scope of his office or employment, under circumstances where the United States, if a private person, would be liable to the claimant in accordance with the law of the place where the act or omission occurred." After Horton Johnson, a Coast Guard helicopter pilot, died in a crash while on duty performing a rescue mission on the high seas, his personal representative sued the government, claiming that Federal Aviation Administration civilian flight controllers negligently caused his death.

In *United States v. Johnson* (1987)[19] five Justices concluded that suit was barred under the rationale of *Feres v. United States* (1950),[20] which rejected liability created by another member of the military. "Although all of the cases decided by this Court under *Feres* have involved allegations of negligence on the part of members of the military, this Court has never suggested that the military status of the alleged tortfeasor is crucial to the application of the doctrine." First, "[t]he relationship between the Government and members of its armed forces is 'distinctively federal in character.'" Second, the victim received generous disability and death benefits. Third, "the '*type*[s] of claims, . . . if generally permitted, would involve the judiciary in sensitive military affairs at the expense of military discipline and effectiveness.'"[21]

Scalia's dissent, joined by three liberals, first argued that *Feres* was wrongly decided. While Johnson did not ask the Court to overrule *Feres*, the decision certainly should not be extended. Not only was there no general exception for the military, Scalia argued, but one provision excepted claims "arising out of the combatant activities of the military or naval forces, or the Coast Guard during time of war," which demonstrated that Congress specifically provided what it thought needful for the special requirements of the military. To the argument that servicemen should not be subject to nonuniform recovery, Scalia responded that nonuniform recovery was better than uniform nonrecovery, uncharacteristically choosing a dimmer line instead of a brighter one. While suits by servicemen might sometimes adversely affect discipline, the same possibility would occur if Johnson's helicopter crashed into a private home and killed a civilian. The argument that Congress would not have wanted double recovery is answered by the fact that there was already double recovery for nonservice-related injuries suffered by servicemen.[22] It was a textual analysis supported by consideration of consequences.

Conservatives oppose the Freedom of Information Act. Scalia said, "I'm not a great fan of FOIA."[23] Exempt from discovery under FOIA are "records or information compiled for law enforcement purposes" that could reasonably be expected to interfere with enforcement proceedings. *John Doe Agency v. John Doe Corp.* (1990)[24] decided whether the pseudononymous John Doe Corporation could gain access to its own records, which it had given the government years earlier during a routine examination. In the meantime the records had been incorporated into a criminal investigation, and the prosecutor claimed that the records had been compiled for law-enforcement purposes. Agreeing, the Court ruled that the exemption covered the company's documents. "This Court itself has used the word 'compile' naturally to refer even to the process of gathering at one time records and information that were generated on an earlier occasion and for a different purpose."[25]

Scalia, joined only by Marshall, found the word "compiled" ambiguous not because it arguably meant "originally compiled," but "because 'compiled' could connote a more creative activity. It may be "compose" or "construct," as in "a states-man has 'compiled an enviable record of achievement.'... If used in this more generative sense, the phrase 'records or information compiled for law enforcement purposes' would mean material that the Government has acquired or produced for those purposes – and not material acquired or produced for other reasons, which it later shuffles into a law enforcement file.... [T]he regime that the Court's interpretation establishes lends itself to abuse so readily that it is unlikely to have been intended [*sic*]." Even if the two interpretations of "compiled" are both reasonable, the ambiguity should be resolved in favor of narrow exemptions, a point usually made by supporters of FOIA.[26]

Seven more Scalia opinions supported consumers over businesses, while an eighth, decided and discussed first, favored small businesses over a conglomerate. Independent Texaco retailers battled the oil conglomerate in the context of Section 2(a) of the Robinson-Patman Act,[27] which prohibited price discrimination by a seller not warranted by its cost savings. Texaco charged lower prices to two large gasoline distributors that picked up gasoline at Texaco's bulk plant than to smaller independent retailers. The distributors sold gasoline both to drivers of cars retail and to gas stations, which the stations resold at lower prices than the independents. Writing for the Court in *Texaco, Inc. v. Hasbrouck* (1990),[28] Stevens announced that "we have already decided that a price discrimination within the meaning of § 2(a) 'is merely a price difference.'"[29] Texaco's argument "would create a blanket exemption for all functional discounts. Indeed, carried to its logical conclusion, it would exempt all price differentials except those given to competing purchasers," and there was an "an extraordinary absence of evidence to connect the discount to any savings enjoyed by Texaco."[30] Concurring in the result, Scalia was blunter. Texaco argued that "the 'functional discount' is an efficient and legitimate commercial practice that is ordinarily cost based, though it is all but impossible to establish cost justification in a particular case. The short answer to this argument is that it should be addressed to Congress. . . . There is no exception for 'reasonable' functional discounts that do not meet this requirement. Indeed, I am at a loss to understand what *makes* a functional discount 'reasonable' *unless* it meets this requirement."[31]

Three Scalia opinions construed laws to assist consumers, two more favored bankrupts against creditors, while the final pair allowed consumers to proceed in the court of their choice. The FTC charged title-insurance companies with horizontal price fixing in setting fees for title searches. Defendants relied on an exemption from federal antitrust laws when a state announced a policy that encouraged price fixing and actively supervised the policy. Rejecting the defense in *FTC v. Ticor Title Ins. Co.* (1992),[32] the liberal majority held that "[i]mmunity is conferred out of respect for ongoing regulation by the State, not out of respect for the economics of price restraint" and "[t]he mere potential for state supervision is not an adequate substitute for a decision by the State."[33] Although Scalia's concurring opinion agreed with dissenters that the decision "will be a fertile source of uncertainty and (hence) litigation, and will produce total abandonment of some state programs because private individuals will not take the chance of participating in them," that was not dispositive. "I am willing to accept these consequence because I see no alternative within the constraints of our 'active supervision' doctrine, which has not been challenged here; and because I am skeptical about the *Parker v. Brown*, 317 U.S. 341 (1943), exemption for state-programmed private collusion in the first place."[34] Scalia opposed corporate defendants and federalism.

Bradley Nigh sued an automobile dealer under the Truth in Lending Act (TILA),[35] for falsely charging him $965 for an extra he did not order. As originally enacted in 1968, TILA provided for minimum/maximum awards of $100/$1,000. Successfully arguing that Congress's 1995 amendments removed the limitation, Nigh received a judgment of $24,192.80, a sum equal to twice the finance charge. Eight Justices reversed.[36] Changes in cross-referencing and otherwise made a mess of the statute, leaving "under this subparagraph" relentlessly obscure. In page after page the Court parsed the statute before concluding that the amendments provided for a cap of $200/$2,000. Scalia dissented: "It is beyond our province to rescue Congress from its drafting error, and to provide for what we might think is the preferred result." "The Court should not fight the current structure of the statute merely to vindicate the suspicion that Congress actually made – but neglected to explain clearly – a different policy decision."[37]

Karen L. Jerman brought suit against a law firm that had instituted a foreclosure action against her even though she had paid her debt in full. Writing for the Court, Sotomayor stated that Congress enacted the Fair Debt Collection Practices Act "to eliminate abusive debt collection practices, to ensure that debt collectors who abstain from such practices are not competitively disadvantaged, and to promote consistent state action to protect consumers."[38] Fearing that the majority was unnecessarily expanding the exception to liability for clerical mistakes to include mistakes of fact, Scalia read the statute more broadly to provide relief against businesses that were exploiting vulnerable debtors.

Two cases involved the Bankruptcy Code; Scalia alone dissented in both. Scalia dissented in favor of requiring the bankrupt to make smaller payments. Bankrupts were required to pay creditors a portion of their "projected disposable income" and the issue was whether that amount was limited by actual past wages or whether it could be increased by improvements in the debtor's income that were virtually certain to occur. The Court allowed an increase in debtor payments over Scalia's dissent that the statutory language limited payments to projections that were exclusively based on past earnings.[39] The other case involved the Bankruptcy Abuse Prevention and Consumer Protection Act of 2005, which provided a schedule of expenses that a bankruptcy barred creditors from reaching.[40] Eight Justices took the seemingly reasonable position that a bankrupt could not include car-loan payments when he owned his car outright and made no such payments.[41] Scalia based his dissent on an interpretation of the statutory language that mandated uniform amounts for all bankrupts in the schedule of expenses, and precluded examination of expense items based on the circumstances of individual bankrupts.

In two cases Scalia sided with plaintiffs against claims that they had no right even to be in court, exceptions to his normally unsympathetic position. In one case the defendant argued the statute of limitations barred plaintiffs' securities-law claim. Statutes of limitations were enacted to prevent suit on old or "stale" claims. At first it was a set number of years. Then, legislatures or judges allowed relief when the plaintiff did not discover that he had a claim until much later, for example, in a case of fraud or medical malpractice. Almost always, the discovery rule was qualified by requiring a plaintiff to show he could not have discovered the claim with the exercise of reasonable diligence. Plaintiffs alleged that Merck had concealed defects in its product, and the issue was whether the language "2 years after the discovery of the facts constituting the violation" allowed Merck to defend on the ground that the plaintiffs should have discovered that they had a claim. The Court said yes, while Scalia's textualist opinion said that the language required actual knowledge, a pro-plaintiff interpretation.[42]

Class plaintiffs sued Allstate in New York federal court for a statutory penalty because it was not paying insurance benefits promptly. New York law barred class actions when plaintiffs sought a statutory penalty, so the defendants wanted the federal court to apply New York law. Writing for a plurality, Scalia said that the issue did not affect the substantive rights of the parties, so it was "covered by one of the Federal Rules [of Civil Procedure],"[43] a textual approach that favored national standards, class actions, and plaintiffs. The dissenters said the issue was governed by state law under *Erie R.R. v. Tompkins* (1938),[44] which required applying the more restrictive state law under a more purposivist analysis that favored federalism, ordinarily the province of conservatives.[45]

A final quartet of cases, two of which were in Scalia's first Term on the Court, dealt with federal preemption, which precludes states from legislating on a subject, which in turn depends on what Congress said and meant in the related federal statute. Preemption itself is generally neutral in outcome. Whether it is liberal or conservative in a particular case depends on the context, although a finding of preemption supports national power over state power. Scalia proclaimed a presumption against federal preemption, but found preemption in a number of cases.[46]

When employees sued for gender discrimination under federal law, the Court rejected the bank's defense of preemption. Marshall's opinion relied both on a clause in the act that disclaimed any intent to preempt and the absence of inconsistency between the federal and state statutes on rights to pregnant women.[47] Employers were free to grant all their employees the same rights as pregnant women; there was no required preference for the latter. Scalia succinct concurrence read: "[W]hether or not the PDA prohibits discriminatorily favorable disability treatment for pregnant women, § 12945(b)(2) of the California Code cannot be pre-empted, since it does not remotely purport to require or permit any refusal to accord federally mandated equal treatment to others similarly situated. No more is required to decide this case."[48]

When a woman sought court-ordered child support from a father whose sole means of satisfying his obligation was Veterans Affairs benefits, Marshall rejected the defense of preemption; none of the statutes or regulations precluded the order.[49] Concurring separately, Scalia agreed with the result but disagreed with Marshall's *dicta*.[50] White's dissent rejected the power of state courts over veterans' benefits, which enhanced federal power, but at the expense of needy women.

In an important voters-rights case, the National Voter Registration Act of 1993 (NVRA)[51] required an applicant to aver that he was a citizen under penalty of perjury. NVRA also required states to "accept and use" a uniform federal form to register voters for federal elections. Plaintiffs challenged an Arizona statute that required voters also to present concrete evidence of citizenship. Writing for the Court, Scalia held that Arizona's law was preempted by the federal law. "Accept and use" in the NVRA was susceptible to two interpretations: either that Arizona accept the form as a complete and sufficient application or that it employ it somehow in the registration process. Scalia concluded that the former definition must prevail. Maintaining a simple system not susceptible to abuse was a primary purpose of the NVRA. "[T]he Federal Form guarantees that a simple means of registering to vote in federal elections will be available."[52] The decision favored voters' rights and federal control. Once again, Scalia's analysis of "use" was pragmatic and liberal, as it was in *Smith v. United States* (2003),[53] the sentence-enhancement case where cocaine was traded for a gun. Thomas and Alito dissented largely on the ground that states traditionally controlled elections.[54]

The final case raised the question of which court should decide whether there was preemption, and here Scalia sided with the state, which was the more liberal outcome. Individual taxpayers who pledged their anticipated tax refunds to secure short-term loans sued the lending bank in state court solely on the theory that the bank's interest rate was usurious under state law. Debtors and borrowers prefer local state courts to federal courts. When the bank removed the state-court action to the federal courts, the taxpayers moved to remand to the state courts, a motion the bank opposed. Seven Justices led by Stevens held for the bank on the ground the National Bank Act preempted all state claims against national banks.[55] Scalia accused the majority of distorting removal jurisdiction, arguing that plaintiffs should not be denied the opportunity to litigate the preemption issue in the court of their choosing. The state court would be free to dismiss the state-law claim if it was preempted.[56]

AGREEMENT WITH SCALIA'S LIBERAL OPINIONS

	Total		Constitutional		Nonconstitutional	
Stevens	68–45	60%	41–22	65 %	27–23	54%
Ginsburg	53–36	60%	34–19	64%	19–17	53%
Thomas	49–48	51%	32–25	56%	17–23	43%
Roberts	18–28	39%	7–18	28%	11–10	52%
Rehnquist	15–72	16%	7–43	14%	8–29	22%
Alito	5–43	10%	3–23	12%	2–19	9%

31

Conservative Statutory Opinions

One unsympathetic commentator observed, "In virtually every case involving government benefits, Justice Scalia votes to defeat the claims of public assistance recipients."[1] This chapter considers a sampling of Scalia's conservative statutory opinions. A full recitation would require a much longer book. The cases seem to mirror in approach his liberal statutory opinions.

The Voting Rights Act of 1965, as amended, applies when covered minorities "have less opportunity than other members of the electorate to participate in the political process and to elect representatives of their choice."[2] Before Congress's 1982 amendments, the statute covered judges. After the amendments, which *expanded* the coverage of the act, however, it covered only "representatives." *Chisom v. Roemer* (1991)[3] involved the method of electing judges of the Louisiana Supreme Court from the New Orleans area. The complaint alleged that a multijudge district concentrated in one of the four parishes comprising the district diluted the black vote. The Court (per Stevens) said that Congress clearly did not intend to contract the coverage of the act in any respect. The use of the word "representative" without more, the majority said, was insufficient to *remove* elected judges from its coverage. "[T]he better reading of the word 'representatives' describes the winners of representative, popular elections."[4]

Scalia dissented: "Section 2 of the Voting Rights Act of 1965 is not some all-purpose weapon for well-intentioned judges to wield as they please in the battle against discrimination. It is a statute. I thought we had adopted a regular method for interpreting the meaning of language in a statute: first, find the ordinary meaning of the language in its textual context; and second, using established canons of construction, ask whether there is any clear indication that some permissible meaning other than the ordinary one applies. If not – and especially if a good reason for the ordinary meaning appears plain – we apply that ordinary meaning. It is precisely because we do not *ordinarily* conceive of judges as representatives that we held judges not within the Fourteenth Amendment's requirement of 'one person, one vote.'"[5]

The rules of the Professional Golfers Association (PGA) prohibited the use of a golf cart, and the PGA barred Casey Martin, whose disease prevented him from walking the course, from using one. The majority in *PGA Tour, Inc. v. Martin* (2001),[6] held Title III of the Americans with Disabilities Act (ADA)[7] covered professional golf tours (a "place of public accommodation"); Martin was an "individual" who was discriminated against in the "full and equal enjoyment of the . . . facilities"; the PGA had failed to make a reasonable accommodation for Martin; and the requested accommodation did not "fundamentally alter the nature" of the sport. Scalia (with Thomas) argued that Title III gave rights to customers, such as people seeking inn accommodations. Martin, however, was a professional participant in a sport and decidedly not a customer. Including him would make a "muddle" of the ADA as a whole and Title III in particular.[8] Nothing required a provision to be fundamental or essential, and even if there were, "it is quite impossible to say that any of a game's arbitrary rules is 'essential.'" The Court went even further afield when it equated other players' fatigue from walking with Martin's fatigue from his condition. In the end, Scalia said, sports *and* the disabled would suffer, for the reason, among others, that sports organizations will create voluminous rules that label every element essential, and will studiously refrain from permitting modifications.[9]

Before *Morrison v. National Australia Bank* (2010),[10] whether federal securities laws reached overseas activities was regarded as an issue of federal-court jurisdiction, propelled by a purposivist approach to statutory construction, *i.e.*, would the legislature have wanted the federal courts to assert jurisdiction in a case, for example, where fraud originated in the United States but was committed solely abroad and on foreign exchanges.[11] *Morrison* reconfigured the issue to a question of statutory construction, while requiring the offending securities transaction to have occurred on an American exchange on the basis of statutory language that required unlawful conduct "in connection with the purchase or sale of any security registered on a national securities exchange or any security not so registered."[12] The Court overruled a long line of circuit-court cases that applied the Act when the conduct in the United States or the effect on American securities markets or investors was significant.[13] Scalia's opinion for the Court noted that it was a "longstanding principle of American law that legislation of Congress, unless a contrary intent appears, is meant to apply only within the territorial jurisdiction of the United States."[14] The decision protected companies and brokers from suits by wronged customers.

Scalia's iconic textualist opinion, nearly a quarter of a century later, was his dissent in *King v. Burwell* (2015),[15] which rejected the majority's claim that the term "established by the State" in the Affordable Care Act was ambiguous and should be read to include exchanges established by the federal government on the basis of context and other rules of construction. The Court's inclusive opinion by Roberts, which emphasized reading the statute as a whole and giving weight to the intent of Congress, pleased liberals and outraged conservatives. Scalia's dissent challenged Roberts's opinion at every turn:

Words no longer have meaning if an Exchange that is *not* established by the State is "established by the State.".... [O]ther parts of the Act sharply distinguish between the establishment of an Exchange by a State and the establishment of an Exchange by the Federal Government.... [W]hile the rule against treating a term as a redundancy is far from categorical, the rule against treating it as a nullity is as close to absolute as interpretative principles get.... Equating establishment "by the State" with Establishment by the Federal Government makes nonsense of other parts of the Act.... The Court has not come close to presenting the compelling contextual case necessary to justify departing from the ordinary meaning of the law. [But] "even the most formidable argument concerning the statute's purposes could not overcome the clarity [of] the statute's text.".... Compounding its errors, the Court forgets that it is no more appropriate to consider one of the statute's purposes in isolation than it is to consider one of its words that way.[16]

For Scalia, the phrasing of the pertinent term was not an "inartful drafting" error and the actual phrasing was consistent with the intent "that tax credits were restricted to State Exchanges deliberately – for example to encourage States to establish their own Exchanges." Moreover, the identical alleged error appeared seven other places in the Act. In *National Federation of Independent Business v. Sibelius* (2012) and *King v. Burwell* (2015), Scalia opined the Court had so transformed the Act, "We should start calling this law SCOTUScare."[17]

The Court's decision reflects the philosophy that judges should endure whatever interpretative distortions it takes in order to correct a supposed flaw in the statutory machinery. That philosophy ignores the American people's decision to give *Congress* "[a]ll legislative Powers" enumerated in the Constitution. Art. I, § 1. They made Congress, not this Court, responsible for both making laws and mending them. This Court holds only the judicial power – the power to pronounce the law as Congress has enacted it. We lack the prerogative to repair laws that do not work out in practice, just as the people lack the ability to throw us out of office if they dislike the solutions we concoct.... [T]he Court forgets that ours is a government of laws and not of men. That means we are governed by the terms of our laws, not by the unenacted will of our lawmakers.[18]

As a matter of textualism, Scalia's opinion was far more convincing than the majority's, which should have taken a purposivist approach supported by the absurdity doctrine that Scalia disparaged. The absurdity doctrine permitted courts to rewrite statutes when the results were "absurd," an approach rejected by strong textualists.[19] The fact that an error was repeated argues against what has been called "scrivener's error." But it does not negate repeated cases of unintended and erroneous phrasing resulting from a failure to conform portions of a long and complex statute to a last-minute change. Judge Posner explained thirty years earlier: "The conditions under which legislators work are not conducive to careful, farsighted, and parsimonious drafting. Nor does great care guarantee economy of language; a statute that is the product of compromise may contain redundant language as a by-product of the strains of the negotiating process."[20] It was a closer question than Scalia acknowledged.[21]

Other areas where Scalia sided with business included requirements to file class actions[22]; denial of court costs sought by consumers or civil-rights plaintiffs,[23] and enforcement of provisions in contracts drafted by businesses to require consumers to arbitrate, thereby denying consumers the advantages of class actions otherwise authorized by state law.[24]

The discussion of statutes concludes with Scalia's berating Congress for its opaque definition of "violent felony," despite (or perhaps because of) his stated deference to the elected branches:

> We face a Congress that puts forth an ever-increasing volume of laws in general, and of criminal laws in particular. It should be no surprise that as the volume increases, so do the number of imprecise laws. And no surprise that our indulgence of imprecisions that violate the Constitution encourages imprecisions that violate the Constitution. Fuzzy, leave-the-details-to-be-sorted-out-by-the-courts legislation is attractive to the Congressman who wants credit for addressing a national problem but does not have the time (or perhaps the vote) to grapple with the nitty-gritty. In the field of criminal law, at least, it is time to call a halt. I do not think it would be a radical step – indeed, I think it would be highly responsible – to limit ACCA to the named violent crimes. Congress can quickly add what it wishes. Because the majority prefers to let vagueness reign, I respectfully dissent.[25]

PART VII

Finale

32

The Other Originalist Justice

Thomas is also an originalist, but hardly a faint-hearted or qualified one. Many scholars tend to equate the jurisprudence of Thomas and Scalia because they are both originalists and textualists. For example, "Further confirming the association of originalism with political conservatism, the originalist Justices Scalia and Thomas almost invariably cast votes that political conservatives applaud."[1] The disparity in votes between the two originalists on the Court may be Exhibit A in the argument against originalism and its claim that it leads to a result certain. One number seriously undermines one of Scalia's principal arguments for originalism – 49. That is the percentage that Thomas, the other proclaimed originalist on the Court, sat with Scalia on cases in which Scalia wrote a liberal constitutional opinion and *disagreed* with Scalia. The actual vote was 49–48, as can be seen in the chart at the end of Chapter 30. Since one of the main arguments Scalia trumpeted on behalf of originalism is that it provides certainty by removing the subjective element from decision making, that figure should unsettle textualists/originalists.

One principal area of constitutional law where originalists tend to agree is the primacy of the jury in making findings in criminal prosecutions. Scalia noted that it was the single right contained both in the 1787 Constitution and the 1791 Bill of Rights.[2] Scalia wrote liberal opinions in seven of these cases and Thomas agreed in six of them.[3] This analysis means that in cases involving such important constitutional rights as freedom of speech and petition,[4] search and seizure,[5] right to counsel,[6] double jeopardy,[7] and the right to confront witnesses,[8] freedom of religion,[9] *ex post facto* laws,[10] the right of citizenship,[11] the sufficiency of an indictment,[12] venue in criminal cases,[13] the Commerce Clause,[14] and the Eleventh Amendment[15] Thomas joined Scalia's liberal view just than half of the time. Scalia joined nonoriginalist opinions in *United States v. Lopez* (1995) (regulation of firearms near schools)[16] and *Gonzales v. Raich* (2005) (regulation of home-grown marijuana),[17] rather than Thomas's originalist opinions on the issue of the scope of the Commerce Clause, agreeing with his result in the former, but not in the latter.[18]

A 2007 study compared the reliance of Scalia and Thomas on originalist arguments, where either of them wrote an explicitly originalist opinion. They both sat
on twenty-three such cases. Thomas "won" 19–11½.[19] Thomas was more often on the
originalist side of the debate than Scalia, whose willingness to accept precedent far
outdid Thomas's. In contrast to Scalia Thomas was an "originalist" on commercial
speech[20] and "an ardent defender of commercial free-speech rights."[21] In 2006 Professor Randy E. Barnett, an originalist, identified Thomas as the only originalist on
the Court.[22] Bruce Ackerman wrote in 1997: "With the exception of that judicial revolutionary, Clarence Thomas, the modern Court is entirely unprepared to launch a
frontal assault on the ringing constitutional affirmation of the national welfare state
by the Supreme Court in [*United States v. Darby*, 312 U.S. 100 (1941), and *Wickard
v. Filburn*, 317 U.S. 111 (1942)]."[23]

Thomas alone dissented in toto in *Virginia v. Black* (2003),[24] a cross-burning case,
where Scalia wrote: "In my view, whatever expressive value cross burning has, the
legislature simply wrote it out by banning only intimidating conduct undertaken
by a particular means. A conclusion that the statute prohibiting cross burning with
intent to intimidate sweeps beyond a prohibition on certain conduct into the zone
of expression overlooks not only the words of a statute but also reality."[25] Thomas
proceeded to summarize the history of cross burning in the United States and, in particular, Virginia. "Accordingly, this statute prohibits only conduct, not expression.
And, just as one cannot burn down someone's house to make a political point and
then seek refuge in the First Amendment, those who hate cannot terrorize and intimidate to make their point. In light of my conclusion that the statute here addresses
only conduct, there is no need to analyze it under any of our First Amendment
tests."[26]

Thomas focused on the original understanding in *Brown v. Entertainment Merchants Ass'n* (2011,[27] while disagreeing with Scalia:

> The Court's decision today does not comport with the original public understanding
> of the First Amendment. The majority strikes down, as facially unconstitutional, a
> state law that prohibits the direct sale or rental of certain video games to minors
> because the law "abridg[es] the freedom of speech." U.S. Const., Amdt. 1. But I
> do not think that the First Amendment stretches that far. The practices and beliefs
> of the founding generation establish that "the freedom of speech," as originally
> understood, does not include a right to speak to minors (or a right of minors to
> access speech) without going through the minors' parents or guardians. ... [T]he
> founding generation understood parents to have a right and duty to govern their
> children's growth," including by supervising the books they read and the life they
> led.... In light of this history, the Framers could not possibly have understood 'the
> freedom of speech' to include an unqualified right to speak to minors. I would hold
> that the law at issue is not facially unconstitutional under the First Amendment,
> and reverse and remand for further proceedings.[28]

Thomas stated his creed: "When faced with a clash of constitutional principle
and a line of unreasoned cases wholly divorced from the text, history, and structure

of our founding document, we should not hesitate to resolve the tension in favor of the Constitution's original meaning."[29]

Thomas invoked natural law, including citing the Declaration of Independence, black sociologist W. E. B. DuBois, and William O. Douglas in support of natural law,[30] and relied on natural law to oppose affirmative action. Natural rights and natural law were, however, a softer concept than the one Thomas described. True, they were "universal, immutable, and inalienable," but they were broad generalities that were imprecise and usually cited as a back-up argument to sources, such as common law, that were the real basis for claims.[31]

Votes by Thomas were less in agreement with Scalia's liberal nonconstitutional opinions than with his constitutional ones. Thomas agreed with Scalia's liberal opinions in seventeen of thirty-nine of these cases, with a positive correlation in criminal cases and a negative one in civil cases. In white-collar prosecutions Thomas agreed with Scalia's liberal opinions five times and disagreed once. In blue-collar prosecutions he agreed with Scalia four times and disagreed six times. (Some cases cannot be categorized, such as sex offenders and probation violators.) In other words, Thomas was decidedly more liberal with white-collar criminals.

Two of their three agreements in civil cases involved the scope of prosecutorial immunity. The third case of agreement limited defenses when Thomas supported a defendant sued for improper debt-collection practices. Thomas's nonliberal votes were in actions for employment discrimination, voting rights, price fixing, aliens, probation revocation, and judicial misconduct. As noted above, a study analyzing votes by Justices in tax case through 2002 placed Thomas first for taxpayers among the eleven Justices, while Scalia was ninth.[32] Voting for the taxpayer is generally conservative; it favors the wealthy and denies the government money that might be used for social programs.

33

Conclusion

The above discussion suggests several conclusions about Justice Scalia's originalism.

First, it is both selective and passionate. Selective because he does not rely on originalism consistently when he interprets the Constitution, although the split is not ideologically based. One conspicuous example is his failure to look to the original understand or meaning on many First Amendment issues, including the most basic questions of free speech. The right to free speech as we know it is largely a construct of the second half of the twentieth century. The concept of free speech in the late eighteenth century was the absence of prior restraint, although there were rumblings, but only rumblings, of broader protection. There was, for example, no concept of content-based distinctions. Scalia was passionate about his originalism when he relied on it, which was most of the time. But whether he talked about gun rights or the death penalty, on the one hand, or what constituted a search and seizure or a violation of the Confrontation Clause, on the other, he took no prisoners.

Scalia tempered his originalism. An example is the Establishment Clause. Thus, he accepted that there can be no government financial aid to religion, even though some states had supplied aid to certain or even all denominations. While he rejected Madison's concept of a wall of separation between church and state, which seemed to be the practice in some states, he did not acknowledge the diversity of positions and meanings attributed to the concept of establishment of religion.[1] It is far from clear that his concept fit any particular state's practice.

Second, Scalia was not an historian, as he acknowledged. Like the great majority of originalists, although he recognized the problems with applying originalism, in practice he seemed to practice law office history. His originalist opinions were almost always one-dimensional, without acknowledgment of the complexity he identified in his nonjudicial writings. Many of his historical assumptions and applications were dogmatic. One pervasive problem is that originalism is based on the flawed conception that it is possible to extract institutions and practices from two and a quarter centuries ago and drop them into the second decade of the twenty-first century, even when there was something of a uniform practice. We simply cannot go back, for example, to juries who were neighbors who knew about the facts of the cases before them. We cannot extract legal principles from an era when women were appendages to their husbands or when interstate and, especially, international commerce, was a trivial part of the economy of much of the country.

Third, textualism/originalism tends to be conservative and Scalia's version was no exception. Most prominently, aversion to unenumerated rights prejudices minorities and underclasses, including suspects not provided with a *Miranda* warning, pregnant women, and gays. Another example was Scalia's attention to standing, which benefited the regulated at the expense of those seeking to enforce regulation. Scalia's originalism, however, was far less conservative than, for example, Thomas's, whose version has been purer and who generally rejects *stare decisis*.

Finally, more than most Justices, Scalia followed his understanding of originalism and textualism, warts and all, where it took him.[2] For Scalia, originalism was not a consistent mechanism to reach conservative results. Rather, it almost certainly was a jurisprudence that inhibited him from reaching *more* conservative results, at least in a number of significant areas. In this respect he was principled. This is not to say that he didn't reach outcomes that seemed at odds with an objective view of his flawed history. Rather, he accepted that his allegiance would often produce results that clashed with his personal views. He selected originalism because it provided him with the most reassuring structure, one that he believed constricted his freedom. Someone with Scalia's intelligence and philosophy could certainly have arrived at more conservative constitutional outcomes if that was his goal. Both Alito and Thomas, the former a nonoriginalist and the latter a stricter originalist, have done just that.

Scalia's dedication to originalism, uneven as it may have been, led directly to his liberal constitutional opinions. After all, Scalia was a dedicated conservative. True, he sometimes misread history to reach conservative results. But then he sometimes misread history to reach liberal results, such as his interpretation of some aspects of the Fourth Amendment's search and seizure and laws that distinguished speech based on its content. His First Amendment jurisprudence seemed way undertheorized for someone who is committed to a coherent concept of the Constitution.

Scalia's textualism was of a piece with his originalism in that he generally applied it consistently. There were some inconsistencies, such as his total rejection of legislative history for statutes while he relied on *The Federalist* to understand the original Constitution. His explanation that *The Federalist* helped him to understand how contemporaries construed the Constitution is only partially satisfactory. In the long run, measured for these purposes in scores of years and perhaps centuries, Scalia's textualism may be more important than his originalism. He raised important issues and reprioritized the analysis. He also raised the bar for textual analysis.[3]

Why does Scalia have a reputation as a dogmatic conservative? For one thing, he was outspoken, and the issues on which he was conservative were hot-button issues – privacy, abortion, death penalty, religion, gay rights, gun control, affirmative action, property rights, and Commerce Clause. Even though he may have been as enthusiastic and uncompromising on liberal issues, his position on trial by jury, confrontation, what constitutes a search, and free speech are less important to the public. Scalia made himself a lightening rod.

A major problem for originalists is that conscientious originalism is inherently unstable. As more evidence of the original understanding is uncovered by historians, constitutional scholars, and others, the originalist position should logically change. Originalist Lawrence B. Solum noted: "[O]riginalist interpretation of the provisions of the Constitution that some believe are especially open-ended ... can only be completed by many organist scholars over an extended period of time."[4] But even good history may conflict with the rational development in the law. "There is also a risk that the originalist judge, refusing to extend the principles reflected in old cases, will ensure incoherence in the law, and thus a form of unfairness, since similarly situated people will not be treated similarly. This might be referred to as the *Bowers v. Hardwick* problem: 'Thus far and no more!' does not produce much coherence in the law."[5] Scalia would have frozen future change because there will be no more instances of *stare decisis* paving the way to nonoriginalist solutions, at least if the Court comes to be dominated by originalists, which presumably originalists would welcome. In any event, you cannot adhere to a judicial philosophy that operates on the assumption that it will always remain a minority view.

There is a more fundamental problem that confronts originalism. The United States is not philosophically oriented. Louis Hartz's classic, *The Liberal Tradition in America*, repeatedly pointed out that the United States is an undertheorized society and that pragmatism rules. From the Federalists to Andrew Jackson to the Civil War to the Gilded Age to the New Deal, and beyond, Americans rejected the confines of philosophically based government in favor of a loosely liberal, pragmatic society. While Hartz emphasized the absence of a feudal heritage that had to be confronted, dismantled, and explained away, what matters is that Americans want workable solutions to their problems whether it be race, rights of criminal defendants, inequality of incomes, foreign policy, or whatever. Americans do not like great theories. They care about results. The party in power tends to stay in power if things are good. A rigid theory that leads to extreme and unpredictable outcomes has been alien to Americans. Gay marriage has been widely accepted, even by those who do not like it. It has the ring of justice, however much Scalia and others railed against it as contrary to the historic Constitution and therefore without constitutional validity. Creating a Bill of Rights is not to reject considerations of results; the goal of good results was why a Bill of Rights was adopted in the first place.

What would happen if originalists won and decided to adhere strictly to history and historical principles? Some positions would change. Rigid application of historically oriented originalism would change free-speech rights to allow just about anything but prior restraint. Capital punishment would be constitutional not only for homicide, but for rape and forgery, not only for sane adults, but for children and the insane. The size of congressional and state representative districts would vary widely, essentially at the whim of the party in power. Districts would be gerrymandered based on race. Not only would *Roe v. Wade* be gone, so would *Griswold v. Connecticut.* The Commerce Clause would be construed to invalidate not only the Affordable Care Act, but much if not all of the Pure Food and Drug Act, the EPA, FCC, OSHA, perhaps the SEC, NLRB, Social Security, federal securities laws, and much else.[6] In *Lopez* Thomas confined the term commerce to "selling, buying, and battering, as well as transporting for these purposes" and did not include manufacturing or agriculture.[7] The role of the courts in protecting civil liberties is a comparatively recent development. "From the founding era through the 1920s, courts were often indifferent or hostile to claims by dissenters that their free speech had been suppressed, and, through the 1950s, they continued to defer to efforts by the president and Congress to suppress unpopular speech or to circumvent ordinary criminal procedures."[8] And this would be accomplished without even the claim that the Constitution dictates originalism. Jefferson Powell wrote: "Originalism [in its pure state] is a proposal for revolutionary change, for an almost wholesale reformation of constitutional law."[9]

Looking over the past eighty years most will agree that this is a more enlightened, democratic, and equal nation than it was. Originalists argue that jurisprudence unteathered from the original Constitution can create reactionary regimes as well as liberal ones. But to a large extent, the original public meaning of the Constitution, if liberal by the standards of the late eighteenth century, is conservative if not reactionary in today's world. Nonoriginalists tend to adhere to precedent – although depart when it seems necessary, as in the New Deal, the Warren Court's changes in criminal procedure, and the civil-rights revolution, none of which would have occurred under an originalist Court. Nonoriginalists are not unprincipled, as reflected in much serious literature, including, for example, Stephen Breyer's *Active Liberty*,[10] which he wrote in part to challenge Scalia's originalism.

This is not to say that originalism and textualism have nothing constructive to say to the present and future generations, especially if they take their history seriously. It *is* important for today's and tomorrow's lawmakers and judges to understand the environment in which the Constitution was written. It likewise *is* important for today's and tomorrow's lawmakers and judges to pay attention to the language and semantic meaning of statutes. The rigorous search for new governing principles may lead to a system that combines the best of judicial philosophies. It is difficult to argue that today's jurisprudence is inferior to that of a century ago. Legal realism, for example, opened people's eyes to the subjectivism and irrationality of much of the law. Taking from a variety of approaches, including originalism and textualism, may bring us to a new plateau a century from now.

Scalia's sudden death in February 2016 changed the Supreme Court. In the short term, it meant that decisions that would otherwise have been 5–4 with Scalia in the majority were either dismissed or reargued. In the slightly longer run a new Justice joins the Court, one highly unlikely to duplicate Scalia's jurisprudence, much less his personality. Some room exists to the right of Scalia, more room exists to the left. Thomas alone sounds the trumpet for originalism far less outspoken and subtle than Scalia, Thomas will almost certainly preside over the decline of originalism as a force in the Court and perhaps in the academic community. He lacks other important qualities possessed by Scalia – a respect for the hard work of his predecessors on the Supreme Court (*stare decisis*), a brilliant and creative mind, a vivid and captivating writing style, an oft-exercised wit, and an oversized presence. A silent sphinx is a poor candidate to lead a revolution. Since law clerks play a predominant role in writing opinions, questions at oral argument provide an important measure of a Justice's mind; Thomas has chosen to opt out.[11] There are signs that without Scalia as a drag on his unmitigated originalism, Thomas is moving toward a more conservative position.[12] It is too early to evaluate the impact of Scalia's tenure on the Court. But it is safe to say that he will be remembered as one of the most conspicuous and innovative Justices in the history of the Court. Even with a decline of originalism, the future Court needs a Justice not only with impeccable legal credentials, of whom there are many, but one who also possesses a command of history and historical principles, which is rare. The threat from originalism remains.

Appendices

Justices Who Served with Scalia

Lewis F. Powell	–1987
William J. Brennan, Jr.	–1990
Thurgood Marshall	–1991
Byron R. White	–1993
Harry A. Blackmun	–1994
Sandra Day O'Connor	–2006
John Paul Stevens	–2010
William H. Rehnquist (C.J.)	**–2005**
Antonin Scalia	_1986–2016_
Anthony M. Kennedy	1988–
David H. Souter	1990–2009
Clarence Thomas	1991–
Ruth Bader Ginsburg	1993–
Stephen G. Breyer	1994–
John G. Roberts, Jr. (C.J.)	**2005–**
Samuel Alito	2006–
Sonia Sotomayor	2009–
Elena Kagan	2010–

Scalia's Nonjudicial Writings

BOOKS

books

"A Matter of Interpretation; Federal Courts and the Law" (1997)

"Reading Law: The Interpretation of Legal Texts" (2012) (with Bryan A. Garner)

ARTICLES AND BOOK CHAPTERS

"Sovereign Immunity and Nonstatutory Review of Federal Administrative Action: Some Conclusions from the Public-Lands Cases," 68 *Michigan Law Review* 867 (1970)

"Appellate Justice: A Crisis in Virginia," 57 *Virginia Law Review* 3 (1971) (with Graham C. Lilly)

"The Hearing Examiner Program," 1971 *Duke Law Journal* 319 (1971)

"Procedural Aspects of the Consumer Product Safety Act," 20 *U.C.L.A. Law Review* 899 (1973) (with Frank Goodman)

"Don't Go Near the Water," 25 *Federal Communications. Bar Journal* 111 (1972–73)

"Introductory Remarks," 28 *Food Drug Cosmetic Law Journal* 661 (1973) (with George Burditt)

"Oversight and Review of Agency Decisionmaking – the Legislative Veto," 28 *Administrative Law Review* 569, 684 (1976)

"The Judicialization of Standardless Rulemaking: Two Wrongs Make a Right," Regulation (July/August 1977)

"Guadalajara! Regulation by Munificence," Regulation (March/April 1978)

"Vermont Yankee: The APA, the D.C. Circuit, and the Supreme Court," 1978 *Supreme Court Review* 345 (1978)

"The ALJ Fiasco – A Reprise," 47 *University of Chicago Law Review* 57 (1979)

"The Disease as Cure: 'In Order to Get beyond Racism, We Must First Take Account of Race,'" 1979 *Wash. U.L.Q.* 147 (1979)

"The Legislative Veto: A False Remedy for System Overload," Regulation (November/December 1979)

"A Note on the Benzene Case," Regulation (July/August 1980)

"The Judges Are Coming," Panhandle, Spring 1980, reprinted at 126 Cong. Rec. E3456 (July 21, 1980)

"Regulatory Reform – The Game Has Changed," Regulation (January/February 1981)

"Back to Basics: Making Law without Making Rules," Regulation (July/August 1981)

"On Making It Look Easy by Doing It Wrong: A Critical View of the Justice Department," in Private Schools and the Public Good (E.M. Gaffney, ed.) (1981)

"Separation of Functions: Obscurity Preserved," 34 *Administrative Law Review* v (1982)

"The Freedom of Information Act Has No Clothes," Regulation (March/April 1982)

"The Two Faces of Federalism," 6 *Harvard Journal Law & Public Policy* 19 (1982)

"The Doctrine of Standing as an Essential Element of the Separation of Powers," 17 *Suffolk Law Review* 881 (1983)

"Historical Anomalies in Administrative Law," 1985 *Supreme Court Historical Society Year Book* 103 (1985)

"The Role of the Judiciary in Deregulation," 55 *Antitrust Law Journal* 191 (1986)

"Morality, Pragmatism and the Legal Order," 9 *Harvard Journal Law & Public Policy* 123 (1986)

"Specialized Courts: Answer to Backlog? " Pennsylvania Lawyer (April 1987)

"Economic Affairs as Human Affairs," in Economic Liberty and the Judiciary 31–32 (J.A. Dorn ed. 1987)

"Responsibilities of Regulatory Agencies under Environmental Laws," 24 *Houston Law Review* 97 (1987)

"Fulfilling the American Dream," ADL Bulletin (May 1987)

"Is There an Unwritten Constitution?" 12 *Harvard Journal Law & Public Policy* 1 (1988)

"Originalism: The Lesser Evil," 57 *University of Cincinnati Law Review* 849 (1989)

"Judicial Deference to Administrative Interpretations of Law," 1989 *Duke Law Journal* 511 (1989)

"The Rule of Law as a Law of Rules," 56 *University of Chicago Law Review* 1175 (1989)

"Assorted Canards of Contemporary Legal Analysis," 40 *Case Western Reserve Law Review* 581 (1990)

"Tribute to Emerson G. Spies," 77 *Virginia Law Review* 427 (1990)

"Foreword: Symposium Issue on Separation of Powers," 18 *Pepperdine Law Review* xvii (1990)

"The Dissenting Opinion," Journal of Supreme Court Historical Society, 1994
    Yearbook 33
"The Role of a Constitutional Court in a Democratic Society," *The Judicial
    Review, Journal of the Judicial Commission of New South Wales*, vol. 2, no. 2
    (March 1995)
"Commentary," 40 *St. Louis University Law Journal* 1119 (1996)
"Federal Constitutional Guarantees of Individual Rights in the United States of
    America," in Human Right and Judicial Review – A Comparative Perspective
    (David M. Beatty ed.)
"God's Justice and Ours," First Things, May 2002, p. 17
"Keynote Address: Foreign Legal Authority in the Federal Courts," 98 *American
    Society of International Law Procedure* 305 (2004)
"Review of Steven D. Smith's Law's Quandary," 55 *Catholic Law Review* 687
    (2006)
"Foreword: The Importance of Structure in Constitutional Interpretation," 83
    Notre Dame Law Review 1417 (2008)
Foreword, 31 *Harvard Journal Law & Public Policy* 871 (2008)
"A Dialogue with John F. Manning on Statutory and Constitutional Interpreta-
    tion," 80 *George Washington Law Review* 1610 (2012)

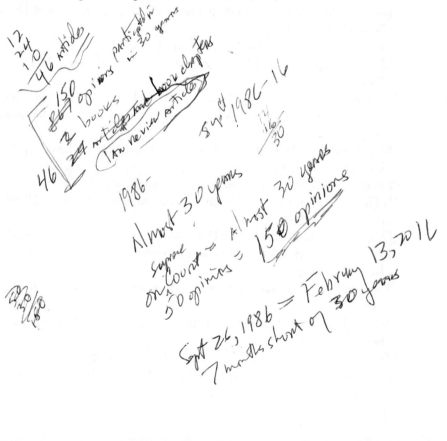

Votes of Other Justices on Scalia's Liberal Opinions[1]

While most of the cases are clear, some are not, and I exercised my judgment in accordance with the concepts provided in the introduction. All the listed cases are cited in the text or in the endnotes and appear in the case index at the end of the volume. Notes to Appendix C appear on page 355.

	C.J.[2]	Thomas	Alito	Ginsburg	Stevens
Abramski v. United States. 134 S.Ct. 2259 (2014) (D)	Y	Y	Y	N	–
Almendarez-Torres v. United States, 523 U.S. 224 (1998) (D)[3]	N	Y	–	Y	Y
Apprendi v. New Jersey, 530 U.S. 466 (2000) (C)	N	Y	–	Y	Y
Arizona v. Gant, 556 U.S. 332 (2009) (C)	N	Y	N	Y	Y
Arizona v. Hicks, 480 U.S. 321 (1987)	N	–	–	–	Y
Arizona v. Inter Tribal Council of Ariz., 133 S.Ct. 2247 (2013)	Y	N	N	Y	–
Bailey v. United States, 133 S.Ct. 1031 (2013)	Y	N	N	Y	–
Begay v. United States, 553 U.S. 137 (2008) (C)	Y	N	N	Y	Y
Beneficial Nat'l Bank v. Anderson, 539 U.S. 1 (2003)	N	Y	–	N	N
Black v. United States, 561 U.S. 465 (2010) (C)[4]	Y	Y	N	N	N
Blakely v. Washington, 542 U.S. 296 (2004)	N	Y	–	Y	Y
Borough of Duryea v. Guarnieri, 131 S.Ct. 2488 (2011) (C, D)	N	Y	N	N	–
Brown v. Ent. Merchants Ass'n, 131 S.Ct. 2729 (2011)	N	N	N	Y	–
Bryan v. United States, 524 U.S. 184 (1998) (D)	Y	N	–	Y	N
Buckley v. Fitzsimmons, 509 U.S. 259 (1993) (C)	N	Y	–	–	Y
Burns v. Reed, 500 U.S. 478 (1991) (C, D)	N	–	–	–	N

(cont.)

(cont.)

	C.J.	Thomas	Alito	Ginsburg	Stevens
Calif. Fed. Sav. & Loan Ass'n v. Guerra, 479 U.S. 272 (1986) (C)	N	–	–	–	Y
California v. Roy, 519 U.S. 2 (1997) (C)	N	N	–	Y	N
Carella v. California, 491 U.S. 263 (1989) (D)	N	–	–	–	N
Carr v. United States, 560 U.S. 438 (2010) (C)	Y	N	N	N	Y
Chambers v. Nasca, Inc., 501 U.S. 32 (1991) (D)	Y	–	–	–	
Cheek v. United States, 498 U.S. 192 (1991) (C)	N	–	–	–	N
Chicago v. Environmental Def. Fund, 511 U.S. 328 (1994)	Y	Y	Y	N	
City of Houston, Texas v. Hill, 482 U.S. 451 (1987)	N	–	–	–	N
Clark v. Martinez, 543 U.S. 371 (2005)	N	N	–	Y	Y
County of Riverside v. McLaughlin, 500 U.S. 44 (1991) (D)	N	–	–	–	Y
Coy v. Iowa, 487 U.S. 1012 (1988)	N	–	–	–	Y
Crawford v. Washington, 541 U.S. 36 (2004)	N	Y	–	Y	Y
Cruz v. New York, 481 U.S. 186 (1987)	N	–	–	–	Y
Danner v. Kentucky, 525 U.S. 1010 (1998) (D) (cert. den.)	N	Y	–	N	N
Day v. McDonough, 547 U.S. 198 (2006) (D)	N	Y	N	N	N
Derby v. United States, 131 S.Ct. 2858 (2011) (D) (*cert. den.*)	N	N	N	N	–
EEOC v. Abercrombie & Fitch Stores, Inc., 135 S.Ct. 2028 (2015)	Y	N	Y	Y	–
EEOC v. Arabian American Oil Co., 499 U.S. 244 (1991) (C)	N	–	–	–	Y
Florida v. Jardines, 133 S.Ct. 1409 (2013)	N	Y	N	Y	–
Florida Star v. B.J.F., 491 U.S. 524 (1989) (C)	N	–	–	–	Y
Fowler v. United States, 131 S.Ct. 2045 (2011) (C)	N	N	N	N	–
FTC v. Ticor Title Ins. Co., 504 U.S. 621 (1992) (C)	N	N	–	–	Y
Gall v. United States, 522 U.S. 38 (2007) (C)	Y	N	N	Y	Y
Gasperini v. Center v. Hum., Inc., 518 U.S. 415 (1996) (D)	Y	Y	–	N	Y
Giles v. California, 554 U.S. 353 (2008)	Y	Y	Y	Y	Y
Gonzales v. Raich, 545 U.S. 1 (2005)	N	N	–	Y	Y
Granfinanciera, S.A. v. Nordberg, 492 U.S. 33 (1989)	Y	–	–	–	Y
Hamdi v. Rumsfeld, 542 U.S. 507 (2004) (D)	N	Y	–	Y	Y
Hamilton v. Lanning, 560 U.S. 505 (2010) (D)	N	N	N	N	N
Healy v. Beer Institute, Inc., 491 U.S. 324 (1989) (C)	N	–	–	–	N
Holloway v. United States, 526 U.S. 1 (1999) (D)	N	Y	–	N	N
Hubbard v. United States, 514 U.S. 695 (1995) (C)	N	Y	–	Y	Y

(cont.)

	C.J.	Thomas	Alito	Ginsburg	Stevens
Indiana v. Edwards, 554 U.S. 164 (2008) (D)	N	Y	N	N	N
INS v. Cardoza-Fonseca, 480 U.S. 421 (1987) (C)	N	–	–	–	Y
INS v. Doherty, 502 U.S. 314 (1992) (C, D)	N	–	–	–	Y
Int'l Union, UAW v. Johnson Cont., Inc., 499 U.S. 187 (1991) (C)	N	–	–	–	Y
Jaffee v. Redmond, 518 U.S. 1 (1996) (D)	Y	N	–	N	N
James v. United States, 550 U.S. 192 (2007) (D)	N	Y	N	Y	Y
Jennings v. Stephens, 135 S.Ct. 793 (2015)	N	N	N	Y	–
Jerman v. Carlisle, McNellie, LLP, 559 U.S. 573 (2010) (C)	Y	Y	N	Y	Y
John Doe Agency v. John Doe Corp., 493 U.S. 146 (1989) (D)	N	–	–	–	Y
Johnson v. United States, 529 U.S. 694 (2000) (D)	N	N	–	Y	N
Johnson v. United States, 559 U.S. 133 (2010)	N	N	N	Y	Y
Johnson v. United States, 135 S.Ct. 2551 (2015)	Y	N	N	Y	N
Jones v. Thomas, 491 U.S. 376 (1989) (D)	N	–	–	–	Y
Jones v. United States, 526 U.S. 227 (1999)	N	Y	–	Y	Y
Jones v. United States, 135 S.Ct. 8 (2014) (D) (cert. den.)	N	Y	N	N	–
Kimbrough v. United States, 552 U.S. 85 (2007)	Y	N	N	Y	Y
Koons Buick Pontiac GMC, Inc. v. Nigh, 543 U.S. 50 (2004) (D)	N	N	–	N	N
Kungys v. United States, 485 U.S. 759 (1988)	Y	–	–	–	N
Kyllo v. United States, 533 U.S. 27 (2001)	N	Y	–	Y	N
Lebron v. Nat'l R.R. Passenger Corp., 513 U.S. 374 (1995)	Y	Y	–	Y	Y
Lilly v. Virginia, 527 U.S. 116 (1998) (C)	N	N	–	N	Y
Marlowe v. United States, 555 U.S. 963 (2009) (D) (cert. den.)	N	N	N	N	N
Maryland v. Craig, 497 U.S. 836 (D) (1990)	N	–	–	–	Y
Maryland v. King, 133 S.Ct. 1958 (2013)	N	N	N	Y	–
Maryland v. Shatzer, 559 U.S. 98 (2010)[5]	Y	N	Y	Y	N
Martinez v. Court App. of Cal., 528 U.S. 152 (2000) (C)	N	N	–	N	N
Massachusetts v. Oakes, 491 U.S. 576 (1989) (C, D)	N	–	–	–	Y
McCormick v. United States, 500 U.S. 257 (1991)	Y	–	–	–	N
Meacham v. Knolls Atomic Power Lab., 554 U.S. 84 (2008) (C)	?[6]	N	?	Y	Y
Melendez-Diaz v. Massachusetts, 557 U.S. 305 (2009)	N	Y	N	Y	Y
Merck & Co. v. Reynolds, 559 U.S. 633 (2010) (C)	N	Y	N	N	N

(cont.)

(cont.)

	C.J.	Thomas	Alito	Ginsburg	Stevens
Michigan v. Bryant, 131 S.Ct. 1143 (2011) (D)	N	N	N	Y	–
Minnesota v. Dickerson, 508 U.S. 366 (1993) (C)	N	N	–	–	Y
Mirles v. Waco, 502 U.S. 9 (1991) (D)	N	N	–	–	Y
Mistretta v. United States, 488 U.S. 361 (1989) (D)	N	–	–	–	N
Monge v. California, 524 U.S. 721 (1998) (D)	N	N	–	Y	N
Morrison v. Olson, 487 U.S. 654 (1988) (D)	N	–	–	–	N
Moskal v. United States, 498 U.S. 103 (1990) (D)	N	–	–	–	N
National Cable & Tel. Ass'n v. Brand X, 545 U.S.967 (2005) (D)	N	N	–	Y	N
Nat'l Treas. Employees v. Von Raab, 489 U.S. 656 (1989) (D)	N	–	–	–	Y
Neder v. United States, 527 U.S. 1 (1999) (C, D)	N	N	–	Y	N
Oregon v. Ice, 555 U.S. 160 (2009) (D)	Y	Y	N	N	N
Pacific Mut. Life Ins. Co. v. Haslip, 499 U.S. 1 (1991) (C)	Y	–	–	–	Y
Pauley v. Bethenergy Mines, Inc., 501 U.S. 680 (1991) (D)	N	–	–	–	N
Peretz v. United States, 501 U.S. 923 (1991)	N	–	–	–	N
Pittston Coal Group v. Stebben, 488 U.S. 105 (1988)	N	–	–	–	N
Ransom v. FIA Card Services, 131 S.Ct. 716 (2011) (D)	N	N	N	N	–
Riley v. Nat'l Fed. of the Blind, 487 U.S. 781 (1988) (C)	N	–	–	–	Y
Ring v. Arizona, 536 U.S. 584 (2002) (D)	N	Y	–	Y	Y
Rita v. United States, 551 U.S. 338 (2007)	N	Y	N	N	N
Rogers v. Tennessee, 532 U.S. 451 (2001) (D)	N	Y	–	N	Y
Rose v. Rose, 481 U.S. 619 (1987) (C)	Y	–	–	–	Y
Schmuck v. United States, 489 U.S. 705 (1989) (D)	N	–	–	–	N
Shady Grove Assoc. v. Allstate Ins. Co., 559 U.S.393 (2010)	Y	Y	N	N	Y
Skilling v. United States, 561 U.S. 358 (2010) (C)[7]	Y	Y	N	N	N
Smith v. Massachusetts, 543 U.S. 462 (2005)	N	Y	–	N	Y
Smith v. United States, 508 U.S. 223 (1993) (D)	N	N	–	–	Y
Sorich v. United States, 555 U.S. 1204 (2009) (D) (cert. den.)	N	N	N	N	N
Sullivan v. Louisiana, 508 U.S. 275 (1993)	N	Y	–	–	Y
Sykes v. United States, 131 S.Ct. 2267 (2011) (D)	N	N	N	Y	–
Thornton v. United States, 541 U.S. 615 (2004) (C)	N	N	–	Y	Y
Tull v. United States, 481 U.S. 412 (1987) (C, D)	N	–	–	–	Y

(cont.)

	C.J.	Thomas	Alito	Ginsburg	Stevens
United States v. Booker, 543 U.S. 220 (2005) (C, D)	N	N	–	N	Y
United States v. Dixon, 509 U.S. 688 (1993)	N	N	–	–	N
United States v. Gonzalez-Lopez, 548 U.S. 140 (2006)	N	N	N	Y	Y
United States v. Granderson, 511 U.S. 39 (1994) (C)	N	N	–	Y	Y
United States v. Johnson, 481 U.S. 681 (1987) (D)	N	–	–	–	Y
United States v. Kebodeaux, 133 Sup.Ct. 2496 (2013)	N	Y	N	N	–
United States v. O'Hagan, 521 U.S. 642 (1997) (C, D)	Y	Y	–	N	N
United States v. Resendiz-Ponce, 549 U.S. 102 (2007) (D)	N	N	N	N	N
United States v. R.L.C., 503 U.S. 291 (1992) (C)	Y	Y	–	–	N
United States v. Rodriquez-Moreno, 526 U.S. 275 (1999) (D)	N	N	–	N	Y
United States v. Santos, 553 U.S. 507 (2008)	N	Y	N	Y	Y
United States v. Stevens, 559 U.S. 460 (2010)	Y	Y	N	Y	Y
United States v. X-Citement Video, Inc., 561 U.S. 358 (1994)	N	Y	N	N	N
United States v. Williams, 514 U.S. 527 (1995) (C)	N	N	–	Y	Y
Utility Air Reg. Group v. EPA, 134 S.Ct. 2427 (2014)	Y	N	N	Y	–
Virginia v. Black, 538 U.S. 343 (2003) (C, D)	Y	N	–	Y	Y
Virginia Office for Prot. v. Stewart, 131 S.Ct. 1632 (2011)	N	Y	N	Y	–
Watchtower Bible Soc. v. Stratton, 536 U.S. 150 (2002) (C)	N	Y	–	Y	Y
West Lynn Creamery, Inc. v. Healy, 512 U.S. 186 (1994) (C)	N	Y	–	Y	Y
Whitman v. United States, 135 S.Ct. 352 (2014) (D) (cert. den.)	N	Y	N	N	–
Wilkinson v. Dotson, 544 U.S. 74 (2005)	Y	Y	Y	Y	Y
Williamson v. United States, 512 U.S. 594 (1994) (C)	N	N	–	Y	Y
Witte v. United States, 515 U.S. 389 (1995) (C)	N	Y	–	N	Y
Yates v. Evatt, 500 U.S. 391 (1991) (C)	N	–	–	–	N
Young ex rel. Vuitton, S.A. v. U.S., 481 U.S. 787 (1987) (C)	N	–	–	–	Y

Notes

1 Lee Epstein, Jeffrey A. Segal, Harold J. Spaeth & Thomas G. Walker, *The Supreme Court Compendium* 569–602 (6th ed. 2015).

2 There were 350 opinions for the Court, 270 concurrences, 203 dissents, and 44 that concurred in part and dissented in part, as calculated by me. Concurring opinions that merely rejected legislative history are not included in the totals. Opinions of Scalia that all Justices joined are included in the overall total but not in the total of liberal opinions listed in Appendix C. Liberal opinions on petitions for *certiorari* are included in Appendix C.

3 Donald L. Drakeman, "What's the Point of Originalism?," 37 *Harvard Journal of Law & Public Policy* 1123, 1134 (2014).

4 United States v. Estate of Romani, 523 U.S. 517, 535 (1998).

5 Sullivan v. Finkelstein, 496 U.S. 617, 632 (1990).

6 Webster v. Reproductive Health Services, 492 U.S. 490, 532 (1989).

7 539 U.S. 558, 588 (2003). Kennedy wrote for the Court: "at the heart of liberty is the right to define one's own concept of existence, of meaning, of the universe, and the mystery of human life." *Id.* at 574, quoting Planned Parenthood of Southeastern Pa. v. Casey, 505 U.S. 833, 843 (1992) (O'Connor, Kennedy & Souter, JJ.).

8 Obergefell v. Hodges, 135 S.Ct. 2584, 2630 n. 22 (2015) (Scalia, J., dissenting).

9 Humanism didn't qualify.

10 When I asked Scalia whether he had read Breyer's *Making Our Democracy Work; A Judge's View* (2010), Scalia replied that he hadn't, because if he read it he would feel compelled to respond to it.

11 *E.g.*, Sanford Levinson, "The Confrontation of Religious Faith and Civil Religion: Catholics Becoming Justices," 39 *DePaul Law Review* 1047, 1074–1081 (1990); George Kannar, "The Constitutional Catechism of Antonin Scalia," 99 *Yale Law Journal* 1297 (1990); *cf.* Kannar, "Strenuous Virtues, Virtuous Lives, the Social Vision of Antonin Scalia," 12 *Cardozo Law Review* 1845 (1990) (discussing Scalia's concept of virtue). Arguably, the Catholic Church has been more accommodating to change than originialists have been. *See* John T. Noonan, Jr., *A Church That Can and Cannot Change* (2005). I eagerly await articles on the catechism of William Brennan and the catechism of Sonia Sotomayor. It is noteworthy that the dogma of the Catholic

Church changes but the dogma of originalism does not. In addition to Scalia's Catholic and Italian heritage, he was the son of a professor of Romance languages, which left legacies of linguistic precision and abstract thinking.

12 I will merely note that it is always easier to explain something after it has happened than to predict something before it happens.

13 I told Scalia that my book would come down hard on originalism both in concept and in practice. He was not fazed and looked forward to debating my comments. Scalia did not care what people said about his opinions and views, but he did care about attacks on his ethics, such as his refusing to recuse himself in a case in which then–Vice President Richard Cheney, with whom he went duck shooting, was a party.

14 531 U.S. 98 (2000). Writers on the subject are divided between those who see the opinion as an unmitigated exercise in partisanship and those who believe that the Supreme Court saw itself as the only entity that could restore order to the country.

15 Others hold this view. *E.g.*, Kannar, 99 *Yale Law Journal* at 1299.

16 *E.g.*, Larry Kramer, "Judicial Asceticism," 12 *Cardozo Law Review* 1789, 1790–1791 (1991); Richard B. Saphire, "Constitutional Predispositions," 23 *University of Dayton Law Review* 277, 290 (1998).

INTRODUCTION: WHAT IS LIBERAL?

1 David A. Schultz & Christopher E. Smith, *The Jurisprudential Vision of Justice Antonin Scalia* 33, 77 (1996); *see* Stephen Macedo, *Liberal Virtues* (1990). There is similar uncertainty over what constitutes a "conservative." One study stated that "[a]t least six major schools of conservative jurisprudence can be identified in the legal community today." James B. Staab, *The Political Thought of Justice Antonin Scalia* xv–xxi (2006).

2 *See generally* Mark Tushnet, *Red, White, and Blue: A Critical Analysis of Constitutional Law* (1988).

3 John Gray, *Liberalism* x (1986); Stephen B. Smith, *Modernity and the Discontents; Making and Unmaking the Bourgeois from Machiavelli to Bellow* 268–270 (2016) ("For Josiah Berlin, liberalism is concerned not only with the protection of the rights and liberties of individuals from intrusion by other individuals or from collective agencies like the state. Rather, it is also concerned with respecting and perpetuating the fundamental diversity of human beings ... ").

4 *E.g.*, John Rawls, *Political Liberalism* xvii (1993).

5 *E.g.*, *Rawls, supra*; Judith Shklar, "The Liberalism of Fear," in *Liberalism and the Moral Life* 21 (Nancy L. Rosenblum ed. 1989).

6 *E.g.*, Shaun P. Young, *Beyond Rawls; An Analysis of the Concept of Political Liberalism* 23–46 (2002) (listing eight, including liberty, toleration, consent, and private property). *Compare* Richard A. Brisbin, Jr., *Justice Antonin Scalia and the Conservative Revival* 65 (1997), which omitted secularism, antimilitarism, and pro–gun control; James G. Wilson, "Constraints of Power: The Constitutional Opinions of Judges Scalia, Bork, Posner, Easterbrook, *and* Winter," 40 *University of Miami Law Review* 1171, 1177 (1986), which listed opinions favoring criminal defendants, media defendants, and civil plaintiffs as the test for a constitutional liberal. A more comprehensive definition by several well-known legal scholars read: "The term liberal represents the voting direction of the justices across the various issue areas. It

is most appropriate in the areas of civil liberties, criminal procedure, civil rights, First Amendment, due process, privacy, and attorneys where it signifies pro-defendant votes in criminal procedure cases, pro-women or pro-minority in civil rights cases, pro-individual against the government in First Amendment, due process, and privacy cases and pro-attorney in attorneys' fees and bar membership cases. In Takings Clause cases, however, a pro-government/anti-owner vote is considered liberal. The use of the term is perhaps less appropriate in union cases, where it represents pro-union votes against both individuals and the government, and in economic cases, where it represents pro-government votes against challenges to federal regulatory authority and pro-competition, anti-business, pro-liability, pro-injured person, and pro-bankruptcy votes. In federalism and federal taxation, liberal indicates pro-national government positions; in judicial federal power cases, the term represents pro-judiciary positions." Lee Epstein, Jeffrey A. Segal, Harold J. Spaeth & Thomas G. Walker, *The Supreme Court Compendium* 276 (6th ed. 2015); *see id.* at 572 (similar definition). The definition in this book is similar, although it also addresses the secular–religious divide, the conflict over the Second Amendment, government transparency, and prosecutorial immunity.

7 It can be argued that energetic prosecution of business defendants rather than favoring their rights is the truly liberal opinion. The issue is noted in the discussion of individual cases. One contrary argument is that voting pro-defendant in blue-collar cases and pro-prosecution in white-collar cases is unprincipled.

8 Ackerman, "Off Balance," in *Bush v. Gore; the Question of Legitimacy* 199–200 (Ackerman ed. 2002).

CHAPTER 1 THE CONFIRMATION HEARINGS

1 Joan Biskupic discusses Scalia's life in *American Original; The Life and Constitution of Supreme Court Justice Antonin Scalia* (2009).

2 Hearings, Sen. Jud. Comm., 99th Cong., 2d Sess., Aug. 5, 1986, on Nomination of Judge Antonin Scalia, to be Associate Justice of the Supreme Court of the United States (Hearings) 43–44.

3 *Id.* at 45–46, 94–96, 100–107.

4 *Id.* at 40.

5 *Id.* at 32.

6 *Id.* at 81–82.

7 *Id.* at 40.

8 *Id.* at 108.

9 *Id.* at 38.

10 *Id.* at 37–38.

11 *Id.* at 48, 101.

12 *Id.* at 48–49, 108.

13 *Id.* at 49.

14 *Id.* at 89–90.

15 703 F.2d 586, 622 (D.C. Cir. 1983) (*en banc*) (Scalia, J., dissenting), *rev'd sub nom.,* Clark v. Community for Creative Non-Violence, 468 U.S. 288 (1984).

16 Hearings at 52.

17 *Id.* at 98.

18 *Id.* at 76.

19 *Id.*
20 *See id.* at 133–135.
21 *Id.* at 12.
22 *Id.* at 14, 27.
23 *Id.* at 166.
24 *Id.* at 217.
25 *Id.* at 28.
26 *Id.* at 155–156.
27 Panels reflecting pro- and anticonfirmation alternated. No one challenged Scalia's intelligence or qualifications. A number of witnesses, liberal as well as conservative, addressed his conservative philosophy but acknowledged that he was in the mainstream and had fine personal qualities, including integrity. *E.g., id.* at 152–153, 159, 236, 274, 276–285. Panelists questioned Scalia's views on abortion, *id.* at 205–206; prayer at schools and public events, *id.* at 296–298; standing, *id.* at 196, 198–200; affirmative action, *id.* at 169–170; and the rights of criminal defendants, and argued that the substitution of Scalia for Warren Burger would create "a significant drift to the right." *Id.* at 208, 209, 212.

CHAPTER 2 SCALIA'S PRINCIPLES OF DECISION MAKING

1 Scalia, "Originalism: The Lesser Evil," 57 *University of Cincinnati Law Review* 849, 861, 866 (1989).
2 Marcia Coyle, *The Roberts Court: The Struggle for the Constitution* 165 (2013). Flogging was not eliminated from federal law until 1839, and continued in many states. John H. Langbein, Renée Lettow Lerner & Bruce P. Smith, *History of the Common Law: The Development of Anglo-American Legal Institutions* 626 (2009).
3 *E.g.,* Ralph A. Rossum, *Understanding Clarence E. Thomas: The Jurisprudence of a Constitutional Restoration* 15 (2014) ("Since his elevation to the Supreme Court, Scalia has assiduously and consistently employed an original public meaning approach to interpretation.").
4 Some nonoriginalists employ historical arguments not because they believe them but to convince readers. *See* Christopher L. Eisgruber, *Constitutional Self-Government* 126–127 (2001) ("When the judge's decision flies in the face of national electoral majorities, the task of reconciling justice and American public opinion may be especially challenging. Here historical argument may play a special role. By appealing to history, judges may attach a popular pedigree to unpopular decisions.").
5 William N. Eskridge, Jr., "The New Textualism," 37 *U.C.L.A. Law Review* 621, 626, 641–650 (1990).
6 The original materials consisted of a mimeographed edition dated 1958 and dealt with a range of statutory issues in a broad context. A Harvard professor called it "[t]he most influential and widely used text in American law schools during the 1950s." Morton J. Horwitz, *The Transformation of American Law 1870–1960*, at 254 (1992). The materials were later published without change. Henry M. Hart, Jr., & Albert M. Sacks, *The Legal Process: Basic Problems in the Making and Application of Law* 1374 (Eskridge & Philip P. Frickey eds. 1994).
7 *E.g.,* Kelly v. Robinson, 479 U.S. 36 (1986).
8 Breyer, *Active Liberty: Interpreting Our Democratic Constitution* 88, 99 (2005).

9   Henry J. Friendly, "Mr. Justice Frankfurter and the Reading of Statutes," in Friendly, *Benchmarks* 217 (1967). The internal quote is from Utah Junk Co. v. Porter, 328 U.S. 39, 42 (1946) (Frankfurter, J.).

10 Learned Hand, *The Spirit of Liberty* 108–110 (2d ed. 1954).

11 *See, e.g.,* Carl H. Esbeck, "Uses and Abuses of Textualism and Originalism in Establishment Clause Interpretation," 2011 *Utah Law Review* 489, 495 ("a jurist who is an originalist is first a textualist before she is an originalist").

12 *See* George Kannar, "The Constitutional Catechism of Antonin Scalia," 99 *Yale Law Journal* 1297, 1347 (1990).

13 Hugo L. Block, "The Bill of Rights," 35 *New York University Law Review* 865 (1960).

14 *See, e.g.,* Michael J. Gerhardt, "A Tale of Two Textualists: A Critical Comparison of Justices Black and Scalia," 74 *Boston University Law Review* 25, 28 (1994). Black eliminated judicial discretion from the free-speech inquiry. Mark Tushnet, "The Federalist and Fundamental Rights," in *Framers and Fundamental Rights* 133 (Robert A. Licht ed. 1992). So did Scalia, but in a somewhat different way.

15 Breyer, *Active Liberty* at 115–118.

16 West Virginia Univ. Hosp. v. Casey, 499 U.S. 83, 112–116 (1991).

17 Scalia, *A Matter of Interpretation; Federal Courts and the Law* 132 (1997). The book was based on the Tanner lectures Scalia gave at Princeton University in 1995, followed by comments by Gordon S. Wood, Laurence H. Tribe, Mary Ann Glendon, and Ronald Dworkin, all followed by a Scalia response.

18 Scalia, "The Rule of Law as a Law of Rules," 56 *University of Chicago Law Review* 1175, 1184 (1989). Attention to language is not new.

19 Scalia, *Interpretation* at 17.

20 *Id.* at 37.

21 *Id.* at 17, 18–19.

22 *Id.* at 23; *see* Scalia & Garner, *supra* at xxi, 24, 39–40, 192, 211–212, 244, 299–300, 355–363, 366, 427, 431.

23 Frank H. Easterbrook, "Statutes Domain," 50 *University of Chicago Law Review* 533 (1983).

24 From the founding until the Civil War, the Court invalidated only two acts of Congress, a minor jurisdictional provision in *Marbury v. Madison* and the statute in the *Dred Scott* case. Bruce Ackerman, *We the People: Foundations* 63 (1991). One definition of judicial activism is "when and to the extent that [a judge] is willing to strike down legislation or other acts and decisions by other branches of government." Cass R. Sunstein, "Beyond *Bush v. Gore,*" in *Bush v. Gore; The Question of Legitimacy* 189 (Bruce Ackerman ed. 2002).

25 Note, "Textualism as Fair Notice," 123 *Harvard Law Review* 542 (2009).

26 Scalia & Garner, *supra* at 107, 180. The authors listed 57 canons of statutory construction and rejected 13 "anti-canons."

27 Scalia has been a leader in this direction. "Justice Scalia and Judge Easterbrook have essentially founded a new school of thought about legislative history." Eskridge, 37 *U.C.L.A. Law Review* at 650.

28 Const. Art. I, § 7, cls. 2–3.

29 John F. Manning, "Justice Scalia and the Legislative Process," 62 *New York University Annual Survey of American Law* 33, 36 (2006).

30 Eskridge, "Textualism, the Unknown Ideal?," 96 *Michigan Law Review* 1509, 1511 (1998); *see* David M. Zlotnick, "Justice Scalia and His Critics: An Exploration of Scalia's Fidelity to His Constitutional Methodology," 48 *Emory Law Journal* 1377

(1999); Jeffrey Rosen, "How New Is the New Textualism?," 25 *Journal of Law & Humanities* 43, 47 (2013) ("during the past two decades, there has been an explosion of new textualist arguments in the legal academy on which advocates were able to draw").

31 Conroy v. Aniskoff, 507 U.S. 511, 519 (1993) (Scalia, J., concurring in the judgment). Scalia also criticized its use on practical grounds. Scalia quoted from an opinion of Justice Robert Jackson: "I should concur in this result more readily if the Court could reach its analysis of the statute instead of by psychoanalysis of Congress. When we decide from legislative history, including statements of witnesses at hearings, what Congress probably had in mind, we must put ourselves in the place of a majority of Congressmen and act according to the impression we think this history should have made on them. Never having been a Congressman, I am handicapped in that weird endeavor. That process seems to me not interpretation of a statute but a creation of a statute." United States v. Public Utilities Comm'n of Cal., 345 U.S. 295, 319 (1953) (Jackson, J., concurring), quoted in Scalia, *Interpretation* at 30–31. Scalia criticized the use of legislative history in Hirschey v. FERC, 777 F.2d 1, 7–8 (D.C. Cir. 1985) (Scalia, J., concurring). In Wisconsin Public Intervenor v. Mortier, 501 U.S. 597, 617 (1991), Scalia, concurring, said, "We use [committee reports] when it is convenient, and ignore them when it is not."

32 Scalia & Garner, *Reading Law* 373–374 (2012); Daniel A. Farber & Philip P. Frickey, "Legislative Intent and Public Choice," 84 *Virginia Law Review* 423 (1988); Eskridge, "The New Textualism," 37 *U.C.L.A. Law Review* 621, 624 (1990); Robert A. Katzmann, *Judging Statutes* 44–47 (2014), citing various studies. Not all textualists/originalists abhor the use of legislative history. Andrew Tutt, "Fifty Shades of Textualism," 29 *Journal of Law & Policy* 309, 324 (2014).

33 Scalia, *Interpretation* at 38.

34 Eskridge, *supra* at 666.

35 *Id.* at 624, 667.

36 E.g., Richard A. Posner, *Reflections on Judging* 4–5, 108–116, 248–252 (2013). "The formalist is someone who feels bound to interpret texts in a way that is 'indifferent or nearly so to the consequences of his interpretation in the real world.'" Jeremy Waldron, "Unfettered Judge Posner," *The New York Review of Books*, March 20, 2014.

37 The word *originalism* was coined only in 1980; before that the common term was "intentionalism." Paul Brest, "The Misconceived Quest for the Original Understanding," 60 *Boston University Law Review* 204 (1980). One scholar traced modern originalism back to the 1960s. Keith E. Whittington, "The New Originalism," 2 *Georgetown Journal Public Policy* 599, 600–603 (2004). It is at least curious that the creation of modern originalism coincided with a rejection of its premise by legal historians. Thus, "legal historians in the years immediately preceding and immediately following 1960 [lost] their collective sense that the purpose in the field was to obtain data that would help them solve pending legal problems." William E. Nelson & John Phillip Reid, *The Literature of American Legal History* 304, 310 (1985).

38 *Dred Scott* was originalist. Chief Justice Taney concluded that the Court must not "give to the words of the Constitution a more liberal construction in their favor than they were intended to bear when the instrument was framed and adopted.... [I]t must be construed now as it was understood then." Scott v. Sandford, 60 U.S. (19 How.) 393, 426 (1857). The lead dissent by Justice Benjamin Robbins Curtis, also

originalist, accused Taney of bad history. *See* Gary L. McDowell, *The Language of Law and the Foundations of American Constitutionalism* 379–384 (2010).

39 Kannar, 99 *Yale Law Journal* at 1309–1310; *see* Posner, *Reflections* at 353; Randy E. Barnett, "An Originalism for Nonoriginalists," 45 *Loyola Law Review* 611 (1998).

40 *See, e.g.*, Charles A. Miller, *The Supreme Court and the Uses of History* 26, 47, 140–141 (1969); William Anderson, "The Intention of the Framers: A Note on Constitutional Interpretation," 49 *American Political Science Review* 340 (1955); Marie Carolyn Klinkhamer, "The Use of History in the Supreme Court, 1789–1835," 36 *University of Detroit Law Journal* 553 (1959).

41 347 U.S. 483 (1954); 367 U.S. 643 (1961). In the lower courts, the name of plaintiff or the prosecuting entity comes first. In the U.S. Supreme Court the name of the party that lost below and seeks review comes first.

42 367 U.S. 643 (1961).

43 369 U.S. 186 (1962); 377 U.S. 533 (1964).

44 372 U.S. 335 (1963).

45 372 U.S. 391 (1963).

46 381 U.S. 479 (1965).

47 384 U.S. 436 (1966).

48 Dennis J. Goldford, *The American Constitution and the Debate Over Originalism* 23, 40–50 (2005); *see, e.g.*, Adamson v. California, 332 U.S. 46, 68 (1947) (Black, J., dissenting). Goldford presented Black as an originalist based on his approach to incorporation. On First Amendment free speech Black's textualism trumped his originalism.

49 Robert Bork, *The Tempting of America* 177 (1990); Goldford, *The American Constitution* at 36.

50 James E. Fleming, "Fidelity to Our Imperfect Constitution," 65 *Fordham Law Review* 1335, 1344 (1997).

51 The objections existed long before Meese. *E.g.*, Miller, *The Supreme Court and the Uses of History* at 150–161. In fact, linguistic philosophy shows the difficulty of the concept of the intent of even a single author. *See, e.g.*, Roland Barthes, "The Death of the Author" (1967); *see* Richard Ekins, *The Nature of Legislative Intent* (2012). Some scholars redefined legislative intent and purpose to avoid, or at least minimize, the problem. *Id.* at 246–247 ("The meaning of a statute is 'what one *reasonably* infers the enacting legislature intended.'"). One scholar called this a "broad-based purposivism." Donald A. Drakeman, "Charting a New Course in Statutory Interpretation: A Commentary on Richard Ekins' The Nature of Legislative Intent," 24 *Cornell Journal of Law & Public Policy* 107, 120 (2014). Another wrote: "The purposes of a law or other legal provision, sought in the adjudication of hard cases, are not the causally efficacious motivators that produced the law or provision, but the chief reasons publicly offered to justify and explain its adoption." Scott Soames, "What Vagueness and Inconsistency Tell Us about Interpretation," in *Language in the Law* 54 (Andrei Marmor & Soames eds. 2011). Soames also pointed out that it is impossible to ignore the author's intent and accuses Scalia of error in ignoring legislative intent and purpose. "Any defensible form of textualism must recognize the importance of the illocutory intentions of the law-makers." *Id.* at 42–43. But Scalia argued not that legislative intent is necessarily irrelevant but that legislative history is illegitimate and unreliable. Nevertheless, original-intent originalists persist. *See* Sunstein, "There Is Nothing That Interpretation Is," 30 *Constitutional Commentary* 192, 197 (2015);

Donald L. Drakeman, "What's the Point of Originalism?," 37 *Harvard Journal of Law & Public Policy* 1123, 1134 (2014).

52 Pauline Maier, *Ratification: The People Debate the Constitution, 1787–1788* (2010).

53 *See* H. Jefferson Powell, "Rules for Originalists," 73 *Virginia Law Review* 659, 681–683 (1987); John F. Manning, "The Role of the Philadelphia Convention in Constitutional Adjudication," 80 *George Washington Law Review* 1753, 1756–1768 (2012). More fundamental, but less conspicuous, was the argument that in the framing era the author's intent was equated with the meaning of the words he wrote. Powell, "The Original Understanding of Original Intent," 98 *Harvard Law Review* 885, 903–904 (1985) ("The framers shared the traditional common law view – so foreign to much hermeneutical thought in more recent years – that the import of the document they were framing would be determined by reference to the intrinsic meaning of its words or through the usual judicial process of case-by-case interpretation."); Powell, 7 *University of St. Thomas Law Journal* at 265–266 ("In the end, one comes away from reading [Chief Justice John] Marshall, with the sense that there was usually very little difference in his mind between talking about the intentions and purposes of the framers and ratifiers, the meaning understood by the people, and his own construction of the words through the exercise of reason and principle.").

54 Randy E. Barnett, "Scalia's Infidelity: A Critique of 'Faint-Hearted' Originalism," 75 *University of Cincinnati Law Review* 7, 9 (2006).

55 Minnesota v. Dickerson, 508 U.S. 366, 379 (1993) (Scalia, J., concurring).

56 Barnett, "An Originalism for Nonoriginalists," 45 *Loyola Law Review* 611 (1999).

57 Powell, 7 *University of St. Thomas Law Journal* at 265–266.

58 *E.g.,* Powell, 98 *Harvard Law Review* 885; Powell, 7 *University of St. Thomas Law Journal* at 268 ("In actual fact, there never was a time in our constitutional past in which originalism in the modern sense, indeed in any substantive sense, has enjoyed a generally accepted primacy among American constitutionalists. Claims to the contrary are an indulgence in the imagination."); *see* Alexander Hamilton, who wrote that "whatever may have been the intention of the framers of a constitution, or of a law, that intention is to be sought for in the instrument itself, according to the usual & established rules of construction." Hamilton, *Opinion on the Constitutionality of the Bank* (Feb. 23, 1791), reprinted in Powell, *Languages of Power* 43 (1991).

59 57 *University of Cincinnati Law Review* 849, 862 (1989). Michael McConnell stated: "All power stems from the sovereign people, and the authority of the Constitution comes from their act of sovereign will in creating it. It follows that the Constitution should be interpreted according to their understanding. This is the theoretical foundation of originalism. If the Constitution is authoritative because the people in 1787 had an original right to establish a government for themselves and their posterity, the words they wrote should be interpreted – to the best of our ability – as they meant them." McConnell, "Textualism and the Dead Hand of the Past," 66 *George Washington Law Review* 1127, 1132 (1998).

60 There is almost a deification of the Founding Fathers, which they warned against. *See* Miller, *The Supreme Court* at 175–178. The founders venerated the study of history. In part, this may have been the result of their having lived in a static society economically, technologically, and socially, so the past was like the present. Change emerged with the French Revolution and the Industrial Revolution. Yet the United States clings to a past, some real, some invented. *See id.* at 179–188 ("The Constitution, like the era from which it came, is an object of almost religious adoration.").

61 Scalia, *Interpretation* at 147–148.

62 Scalia, 57 *University of Cincinnati Law Review* at 864.
63 For a more comprehensive description of the origins of modern originalism as well as a theoretical analysis of its application, *see* Lawrence B. Solum, "The Fixation Thesis: The Role of Historical Fact in Original Meaning," 91 *Notre Dame Law Review* 1 (2015), which takes a more linguistic than historical approach. Jonathan Gienapp, "Historicism and Holism: Failures of Originalist Translation," 84 *Fordham Law Review* 935 (2015). Scalia was far less theorized. For a theoretical nonoriginalist analysis, *see, e.g.*, Richard H. Fallon, Jr., "The Meaning of Legal 'Meaning' and Its Implications for Theories of Legal Interpretation," 82 *University of Chicago Law Review* 1235 (2015).
64 Eskridge, "Textualism, the Unknown Ideal?," 96 *Michigan Law Review* 1509, 1511 (1998); Zlotnick, 48 *Emory Law Journal* at 1387 n. 41; *see* Lino A. Graglia, "The Constitution and 'Fundamental Rights," in *The Framers and Fundamental Rights* 86 (Robert A. Licht ed. 1992) ("The nightmare of the American intellectual elite (broadly speaking) is that the control of public policy will fall into the hands of the American people."). Nonoriginalists make the same argument against originalism. "Originalism substitutes historical materials that will routinely be open-ended and that will invite the interpreter to inject his own views." David A. Strauss, "Originalism, Conservatism, and Judicial Restraint," 34 *Harvard Journal of Law & Public Policy* 137, 144 (2010); *see* Thomas B. Colby & Peter J. Smith, "Living Originalism," 59 *Duke Law Journal* 239, 243 (2009). There are differences among originalists on the weight that should be given to early practice under the Constitution. Scalia and Thomas relied on early practice, in contrast to leading academic originalist Steven G. Calabresi. Calabresi & Michael W. Perl, "Originalism and *Brown v. Board of Education*," 2014 *Michigan State Law Review* 429, 511, 521–523.
65 *E.g.*, James E. Fleming, "Are We All Originalists Now? I Hope Not!" 91 *Texas Law Review* 1785, 1787 (2013); Ronald Dworkin, *Freedom's Law* 2 (1996).
66 Breyer, *Making Our Democracy Work* 79 (2010).
67 Posner, *Problems of Jurisprudence* 138 (1990).
68 A complete survey of originalist theory is obviously beyond the scope of this book. One study stated: "A review of originalists' work reveals originalism to be not a single coherent, unified theory of constitutional interpretation, but rather a smorgasbord of distinct theories that share little in common except a misleading reliance on a single label." Colby & Smith, 59 *Duke Law Journal* at 244. There is a more flexible and liberal originalism, usually called new originalism or new textualism. *See, e.g.*, Jack M. Balkin, *Living Originalism* 14, 101 (2011); James E. Fleming, *supra*; Richard H. Fallon, Jr., "Are Originalist Constitutional Theories Principled or Are They Rationalizations for Conservatism?," 34 *Harvard Journal of Law & Public Policy* 5 (2010). This book does not dwell on liberal originalism. First, its methodology suffers from the same defects as other originalism. *See, e.g.*, Saul Cornell, "The Original Meaning of Original Understanding: A Neo-Blackstonian Critique," 67 *Maryland Law Review* 150 (2007) ("In essence, the 'new' originalism is really nothing more than the old law-office history under a new guise."); Neil S. Siegel, "Jack Balkin's Rich Historicism and Diet Originalism: Health Benefits and Risks for the Constitutional System," 111 *Michigan Law Review* 931 (2013); Eric J. Segall, "Originalist Defenses of Overturning Same-Sex Marriage Ban," Feb. 9, 2015, in *Dorf on Law*, www.dorfonlaw.org/2015/02/originalist-defenses-of-overturning.html. Second, no Justice has ever subscribed to the approach and it has had limited influence outside of academia. The focus here is the originalism of Justice Scalia.

69 Tribe, *God Save This Honorable Court* 47 (1985); Tribe, *American Constitutional Law* 771 (2d ed. 1988). But Tribe also said: "I nonetheless share with Justice Scalia the belief that the Constitution's written text has primacy and must be deemed the ultimate point of departure; that nothing irreconcilable with the text can properly be considered part of the Constitution; and that some parts of the Constitution cannot plausibly be open to significantly different interpretations." Scalia, *Interpretation* at 77 (comment by Tribe).

70 *Id.*, quoting Owen Fiss, "The Supreme Court 1978 Term – Foreword: The Forms of Justice," 93 *Harvard Law Review* 1, 9, 11 (1979); *see* Trop v. Dulles, 356 U.S. 86, 101 (1958) (Warren, C.J.) (Constitution incorporates the "evolving standards of decency that mark the progress of a maturing society").

71 William G. Merkel, "Uncoupling the Constitutional Right to Self-Defense from the Second Amendment: Insights from the Law of War," 45 *Connecticut Law Review* 1809, 1823 & n. 50 (2013) (quoting Thomas Jefferson: "We might as well require a man to wear still the coat which fitted him as a boy, as civilized society to remain ever under the regimen of their barbarous ancestors.").

72 Sanford Levinson, *Our Undemocratic Constitution* (2006); *see* Woody Holton, *Unruly Americans and the Origins of the Constitution* 188 (2007) (arguing that the Constitutional Convention placed curbs on popular democracy to protect the economy).

73 Posner, *The Problems of Jurisprudence* at 137–138.

74 Michael H. v. Gerald D., 491 U.S. 110, 141 (1989) (Brennan, J., dissenting); *see* Dworkin, *Freedom's Law.*

75 Brennan, "The Constitution of the United States: Contemporary Ratification," 27 *South Texas Law Review* 433, 435, 438 (1986); Brennan, "Speech to the Text and Teaching Symposium," in *Originalism; One-Quarter Century of Debate* 59 (Calabresi ed. 2007).

76 Brennan, "The Constitution of the United States: Contemporary Ratification," in *American Constitutional Interpretations* 239 (Walter F. Murray, James E. Fleming & Sotirios A. Barber eds. 2d ed. 1995).

77 Stevens, "Originalism and History," 48 *Georgia Law Review* 691, 702 (2014).

78 Robert Post & Reva Siegel, "Originalism as a Political Practice – The Right's Living Constitution," 75 *Fordham Law Review* 545, 561 (2006).

79 Morgan Cloud, "A Conclusion in Search of a History to Support It," 43 *Texas Tech Law Review* 29 (2010); *see* Miller, *The Supreme Court* at 192.

80 Wilkinson III, *Cosmic Constitutional Theory* 45 (2012).

81 *E.g.*, Philip Bobbitt, *Constitutional Fate* 11–12 (1982); Balkin, *Living Originalism* (2011).

82 *E.g.*, Bobbitt, *Constitutional Interpretation* 11–22 (1991). Of course, some constitutional provisions demand an originalist approach, such as the Seventh Amendment: "In Suits at common law, where the value in controversy shall exceed twenty dollars, the right of trial by jury shall be preserved." The language commands a reference to the law in 1791. That the Framers of the Bill of Rights knew how to attach an originalist meaning suggests they did not necessarily intend an originalist interpretation of the balance is a nonoriginalist argument. Other provisions have an originalist meaning by common consent (although not necessarily in practice), such as the impeachment clause, which requires proof of "high crimes and misdemeanors."

83 Rebecca L. Brown, "History for the Non-Originalist," 26 *Harvard Journal of Law & Public Policy* 69, 71 (2003); *see* Powell, 7 *University of St. Thomas Law Journal* at 276–278.

84 Dworkin, "The Arduous Virtue of Fidelity: Originalism, Scalia, Tribe, and Nerve," 65 *Fordham Law Review* 1249–1250, 1253 (1997).

85 Jennifer Senior, "In Conversation: Antonin Scalia," *New York Magazine*, Oct. 6, 2013, http://nymag.com/news/features;antonin-scalia-2013-10.

86 *E.g.*, Calabresi & Andrea Matthews, "Originalism and *Loving v. Virginia*," 2012 *Brigham Young Law Review* 1393, 1396 (2013); *see generally* Keith E. Whittington, *Constitutional Interpretation: Textual Meaning, Original Intent, and Judicial Review* (1999).

87 *See* Harry H. Wellington, "Common Law Rules and Constitutional Double Standards: Some Notes on Adjudication," 83 *Yale Law Journal* 221, 311 (1973). This use of "tradition" should be distinguished from the looser use as of the word "traditional" as an equivalent of "ordinary" or "run of the mill," or "standard." Bruesewitz v. Wyeth, LLC, 131 S.Ct. 1068, 1074 (2011) (Scalia, J.) ("traditional tort suit for damages"); Staub v. Proctor Hosp., 131 S.Ct. 1186, 1193 (2011) (Scalia, J.) ("traditional tort-law concept of proximate cause"). It is also used differently in references to "the liberal tradition."

88 497 U.S. 62 (1990).

89 *Id.* at 95–96 (Scalia, J., dissenting); *see* Nevada Commission on Ethics v. Carrigan, 131 S.Ct. 2343, 2347–2348 (2011) (Scalia, J.), quoting Republican Party of Minnesota v. White, 536 U.S. 765, 785 (2002) (Scalia, J.). One Scalia critic noted that the spoils system had been under attack as early as 1935 by Senator Calhoun. L. Benjamin Young, "Justice Scalia's History and Tradition: The Chief Nightmare in Professor Tribe's Anxiety Closet," 78 *Virginia Law Review* 581, 607 n. 145 (1991)

90 County of Sacramento v. Lewis, 523 U.S. 833, 862 (1998).

91 "Symposium," 28 *Administrative Law Review* 689–690 (1976); *see, e.g.*, Allen V. Kamp, "The Counter-Revolutionary Nature of Justice Scalia's 'Traditionalism,'" 27 *Pacific Law Journal* 99, 102–103 (1995). Warranting mention is 44 Liquormart, Inc. v. Rhode Island, 517 U.S. 484 (1996), a commercial-speech case that invalidated a Rhode Island statute that prohibited off-site advertising of liquor retail prices. The vote was unanimous to reject the state's argument that its statute was designed to reduce liquor sales and was therefore constitutional under the Twenty-First Amendment. Scalia joined the Court's opinion and added a short concurrence: "I will take my guidance as to what the Constitution forbids, with regard to a text as indeterminate as the First Amendment's preservation of 'the freedom of speech,' and where the core offense of suppressing particular political ideas is not at issue, from the long accepted practices of the American people." *Id.* at 517. Thomas wrote a solo opinion to the right of the other Justices to elevate commercial speech to the same level as other speech.

92 491 U.S. 110 (1989). The case is Scalia's most detailed exposition of his favoring use of the most specific tradition.

93 *Id.* at 128 n. 6.

94 Dissenting, Brennan said, "[w]e are not an assimilative, homogenized society, but a facilitative, pluralistic one in which we must be willing to abide someone else's unfamiliar or even repellent practice because the same tolerant impulse protects our own idiosyncrasies.... In a community such as ours, 'liberty' must include the freedom not to conform.... [Justice Scalia's opinion] squashes this freedom by requiring specific approval from history before protecting anything in the name of liberty." *Id.* at 141; *see* Michelman, *Brennan and Democracy* 26–29 (1999); *see* Tribe & Michael C. Dorf, "Levels of Generality in the Definition of Rights," 57 *University of Chicago Law Review* 1057 (1990). Moreover, a more specific level could be based on the

nature of the adulterous relationship, *e.g.*, was the marriage effectively over. *Id.* at 1087, 1091, 1100–1101.

95 Scalia, "The Two Faces of Federalism," 6 *Harvard Journal of Law & Public Policy* 19, 22 (1982).

96 Payne v. Tennessee, 501 U.S. 808, 834–835 (1991) (Scalia, J., concurring). An argument can be made for *stare decisis* based on *The Federalist* No. 78. "To avoid arbitrary discretion in the courts, it is indispensable that they should be bound down by strict rules and precedents which serve to define and point out their duty in every particular case that comes before them."

97 Boys Markets, Inc. v. Retail Clerks Union, 398 U.S. 235, 241 (1970) (Brennan, J.); *see* Dworkin, "The Arduous Virtue of Fidelity: Originalism, Scalia, Tribe, and Nerve," 65 *Fordham Law Review* 1249, 1254 (1997) ("Citizens, lawyers, and judges should not try to answer [difficult constitutional questions] on a clean slate, ignoring the answers that others, particularly judges, have given to them in the past.").

98 McDonald v. City of Chicago, 561 U.S. 742, 791 (2010); *see* Tushnet, *The New Constitutional Order* 123–125 (2003). Incorporation also federalized much of state criminal law.

99 "When faced with a clash of constitutional principle and a line of unreasoned cases wholly divorced from the text, history, and structure of our founding document, we should not hesitate to resolve the tension in favor of the Constitution's original meaning." Kelo v. City of New London, 545 U.S. 469, 523 (2005) (Thomas, J., dissenting).

100 "Stare decisis has been part of our law from time immemorial, and we must bow to it." Scalia & Garner, *Reading Law* 413–414 (2012); *see, e.g.*, Nelson Lund, "Stare Decisis and Originalism: Judicial Disengagement from the Supreme Court's Errors," 19 *George Mason Law Review* 1029, 1030 (2012) (repudiating *stare decisis* in constitutional cases, advocated by some, "turns out to be inconsistent with originalism itself. *Stare decisis*, in various different versions to be sure, had long served a central function in all of the Anglo-American courts familiar to the founding generation.").

101 Scalia, "Originalism: The Lesser Evil," 57 *University of Cincinnati Law Review* 849, 861 (1989).

102 490 U.S. 805 at 825.

103 Scalia, *Interpretation* at 138–140; *see, e.g.*, South Carolina v. Gathers, 490 U.S. 805, 825 (1989) (Scalia, J., dissenting); Mitchell N. Berman, "Originalism Is," 84 *New York University Law Review* 1, 10–11 (2009); Posner, "Against Constitutional Theory," 73 *New York University Law Review* 1, 6 (1998); Jeffry Toobin, *The Oath* 247 (2012).

104 Scalia e-mail to author, Jan. 29, 2015. References were to Roe v. Wade, 410 U.S. 113 (1973), and Planned Parenthood v. Casey, 505 U.S. 833 (1992); *see* Scalia & Bryan A. Garner, *Reading Law* 411–414 (2012). Scalia gave more weight to *stare decisis* in statutory cases because Congress can change the law if it disagrees. *Id.* at 255. Scalia seemed less concerned than many about the impact of overruling a prior decision on the reputation, legitimacy, and effectiveness of the Court, which is related to a strong theory of judicial supremacy. *E.g.*, Tushnet, *The New Constitutional Order* 92–93, 124–125 (2003). Scalia did not adhere to a strong concept of judicial supremacy.

105 Solum & Robert W. Bennett, *Constitutional Originalism* 71, 155–158 (2011). Indeed, some originalists argue that it is unconstitutional for the Supreme Court to follow a precedent that deviates from the original meaning of the Constitution. Gary Lawson,

"The Constitutional Case against Precedent," 17 *Harvard Journal of Law & Public Policy* 23, 27–28 (1994); Barnett, "Scalia's Infidelity: A Critique of 'Faint-Hearted' Originalism," 75 *University of Cincinnati Law Review* 7, 18 (2006).

106 Solum & Bennett, *Constitutional Originalism* at 116. Efforts have been made to accommodate originalism and *stare decisis*, but most end up with a balancing of interests that is not very different from what most judges already do. *See, e.g.,* John O. McGinnis & Michael B. Rappaport, "Originalism and Precedent," 34 *Harvard Journal of Law & Public Policy* 121 (2010).

107 *See* Barnett, 75 *University of Cincinnati Law Review* at 13.

108 Scalia, "The Legislative Veto: A False Remedy for System Overload," *Regulation* 19 (Oct.–Nov. 1979). Scalia cofounded *Regulation* magazine with Murray Weidenbaum, a conservative economist.

109 Evan Tsen Lee, *Judicial Restraint in America* (2011); *see* Steven Goldberg, "Antonin Scalia, Baruch, Spinoza, and the Relationship between Church and State," 23 *Cardozo Law Review* 653, 659 (2002). Tushnet, *Red, White, and Blue* 10 (1988) ("the framers, as liberals, had no reason to think that judges would be any less attached to possessive individualism than were the representatives whom the judges were to restrain"); *see generally, e.g.,* Tushnet, *Taking the Constitution Away from the Courts* (1999).

110 Scalia, "The Rule of Law as a Law of Rules," 56 *University of Chicago Law Review* 1175, 1180–1181 (1989). A respected conservative nonoriginalist judge called pragmatism, which focuses on evidence and outcome, an activist approach. Wilkinson, *Cosmic Constitutional Theory* at 93–96.

111 Bendix Autolite Corp. v. Widwesco Enterprises, Inc., 486 U.S. 888, 897 (1988) (Scalia, J., concurring in judgment).

112 56 *University of Chicago Law Review* at 1180–1182. Scalia had unlikely company in Justices Black and Douglas, who argued that *ad hoc* balancing gave judges too much power, in part because the metaphor of balancing concealed the necessary elements of judgment that went into constitutional adjudication and in part because opinions justifying outcomes as the result of *ad hoc* balancing gave too little guidance to other lawmakers. Laurent B. Frantz, "The First Amendment in the Balance," 71 *Yale Law Journal* 1424 (1962); Tushnet, *Taking the Constitution* at 112 ("Formulas help the Supreme Court guide lower courts; balancing tests keep power in the Supreme Court's hands for who except the justices can tell how the balancing comes out."); Tushnet, *A Court Divided; The Rehnquist Court and the Future of Constitutional Law* 145, 147 (2005) (Scalia's concern for rules "was his major intellectual contribution to the Rehnquist Court"); *see* Douglas G. Smith, "Originalism and the Affirmative Action Decisions," 55 *Case Western Law Review* 1 (2004).

113 Friendly recognized that it would create work for judges; it would take "judges into the business of judging by requiring them to base decisions on differences of degree," quoting Holmes's statement that "[t]he whole law does so as soon as it is civilized." Henry J. Friendly, *The Dartmouth College Case and the Public-Private Penumbra* 22–23 (1971), quoting LeRoy Fibre Co. v. Chicago, Milwaukee & St. Paul Ry., 232 U.S. 340, 354 (1914) (Holmes, J., concurring).

114 *E.g.,* M. David Gelfand & Keith Werhan, "Federalism and Separation of Powers on a 'Conservative' Court: Currents and Cross-Currents from Justices O'Connor and Scalia," 64 *Tulane Law Review* 1443 (1990).

115 Scalia, "Foreword: The Importance of Structure in Constitutional Interpretation," 84 *Notre Dame Law Review* 1417, 1418 (2008); BFP v. Resolution Trust Corp., 511

U.S. 531, 546 (1994) (Scalia, J.) ("where the intent to override [state legislation] is doubtful, our federal system demands deference to long-established traditions of state regulation"). Many originalists and federalists blame Chief Justice John Marshall's opinion in McCulloch v. Maryland, 17 U.S. (4 Wheat.) 315 (1819), for creating an unduly expansive and powerful national government. *See, e.g.,* Philip B. Kurland, "Curia Regis: Some Comments on the Divine Right of Kings and Courts to Say What the Law Is," 23 *Arizona Law Review* 582, 591 (1981); Mark Graber, "Unnecessary and Unintelligible," in *Constitutional Stupidities, Constitutional Tragedies* 43 (Eskridge & Levinson eds. 1998); John Yoo, "*McCulloch v. Maryland,*" in *id.* at 241; Bradford R. Clark, "The Constitutional Structure and the Jurisprudence of Justice Scalia," 47 *St. Louis Law Journal* 753 (2003).

116 Rossum and Gary L. McDowell, "Politics, Statesmanship, and the Constitution," in *The American Founding* 6 (Rossum & McDowell eds. 1981); *see generally The Federalist.*

117 17 *Suffolk Law Review* 881 (1983).

118 *Id.* at 881.

119 Scalia, "Foreword," 18 *Pepperdine Law Review* xvii, xviii (1990).

120 Morrison v. Olson, 487 U.S. 654, 727 (Scalia, J., dissenting); *see* Plaut v. Spendthrift Farms, Inc., 514 U.S. 211, 219 (1995). Liberals also value separation of powers (and federalism) as important components of liberty. *E.g.,* Norman Dorsen, "Separation of Powers and Federalism: Two Doctrines with a Common Goal: Confining Arbitrary Power," 41 *Albany Law Review* 53 (1977).

PART II SCALIA'S CONSERVATIVE CONSTITUTIONAL OPINIONS

1 David Schultz, "Scalia, On Decision Making and Long Standing Traditions: How Rights Always Lose," 31 *Suffolk Law Review* 319, 346 (1997).

CHAPTER 3 FIRST AND SECOND AMENDMENTS

2 *See* Rodney A. Smolla, *Free Speech in an Open Society* 36 (1992); Steven J. Heyman, *Free Speech and Human Dignity* 21 (2008).

3 *E.g.,* Leonard W. Levy, *Freedom of Speech and Press in Early American History: Legacy of Suppression* ix (1963). In Lebron v. Washington Met. Area Transit Auth., 749 F.2d 893 (D.C. Cir. 1984) (Bork, J.), the court struck down a public authority's ban of a political advertisement in public transportation in Washington, D.C., because it was deceptive. Scalia said that "a scheme that empowers agencies of a political branch of government to impose prior restraint upon a political message because of its falsity is unconstitutional." *Id.* at 898.

4 Laurence Tribe & Joshua Matz, *Uncertain Justice* 124 (2014).

5 Smolla, *supra* at 32.

6 493 U.S. 215 (1990).

7 *Id.* at 258.

8 United States v. Playboy Ent. Group, Inc., 529 U.S. 803, 831 (2000) (Scalia, J., dissenting).

9 501 U.S. 560 (1991).

10 *Id.* at 575, 576; *see* Community for Creative Non-Violence v. Watt, 703 F.2d 586, 622 (D.C. Cir. 1983) (*en banc*) (Scalia, J., dissenting), *rev'd sub nom.*, Clark v. Community for Creative Non-Violence, 468 U.S. 288 (1984).

11 Miller v. Civil City of South Bend, 904 F.2d 1081, 1095 (7th Cir. 1990) (*en banc*) (Posner, J., concurring).

12 505 U.S. 577, 631, 633 (1992).

13 512 U.S. 687, 732, 748 (1994) (Scalia, J., dissenting) (citations omitted); *see* Scalia, "The Role of a Constitutional Court in a Democratic Society," 2 *Journal Judicial Commission of New South Wales* 141, 144 (1995).

14 482 U.S. 578 (1987) (Brennan, J.).

15 403 U.S. 602 (1971).

16 482 U.S. at 586–594.

17 Lamb's Chapel v. Center Moriches Union Free School District, 508 U.S. 384, 398 (Scalia, J., concurring in judgment) (citations omitted).

18 545 U.S. 844 (2005).

19 *Id.* at 887, 893; *see* Stephen B. Presser, *Recapturing the Constitution; Race, Religion, and Abortion Reconsidered* 86–97, 159–160 (1994).

20 545 U.S. at 894, 906.

21 Zelman v. Simmons-Harris, 536 U.S. 639 (2002).

22 *E.g.*, Board of Ed. of Westside Community School v. Mergens, 496 U.S. 226 (1990); Lamb's Chapel, 508 U.S. at 400; Good News Club v. Milford Central School, 533 U.S. 98, 120 (2001) Scalia, J., dissenting).

23 Lee v. Weisman, 505 U.S. 577 (1992) (Scalia, J., dissenting).

24 Santa Fe Independent School District v. Doe, 530 U.S. 290 (2000).

25 *New York Times*, Oct. 20, 2003.

26 Texas Monthly, Inc. v. Bullock, 489 U.S. 1, 30 (1989) (Scalia, J., dissenting).

27 Board of Ed. of Kiryas Joel Village School District v. Grumet, 512 U.S. 687, 732 (1994) (Scalia, J., dissenting).

28 Locke v. Davey, 540 U.S. 712, 726 (2004).

29 508 U.S. 384, 401 (1993) (Scalia, J., concurring). Scalia's view contrasted with the views of other Justices, including O'Connor, whose test was "government endorsement or disapproval of religion." Lynch v. Donnelly, 465 U.S. 668, 688 (1984). Kennedy used the rubric of psychological coercion. Lee v. Weisman, 505 U.S. at 588. For Scalia, "[t]he coercion that was a hallmark of historical establishments of religion was coercion of religious orthodoxy and of financial support *by force and threat of penalty.*" *Id.* at 641.

30 392 U.S. 83 (1968).

31 551 U.S. 587 (2007).

32 Lee v. Weisman, 505 U.S. at 641.

33 542 U.S. 1, 49–50 (2004) (Thomas, J., concurring).

34 134 S.Ct. 1811, 1835 (2014).

35 554 U.S. 570 (2008).

36 Edward L. Rubin, "Question Regarding *D.C. v. Heller*: As a Justice, Antonin Scalia Is (A) Great, (B) Acceptable, (C) Injudicious," 54 *Wayne Law Review* 1106, 1113 (2008).

37 554 U.S. at 582, 584.

38 *Id.* at 636.

39 Cass Sunstein called the opinion "exceedingly narrow" in "Second Amendment Minimalism: *Heller* as *Griswold*," 122 *Harvard Law Review* 246, 267 (2008). Some

writers considered Scalia's enumeration of legitimate gun-control provisions as nonoriginalist *dicta*. Frank B. Cross, *The Failed Promise of Originalism* 15–16, 103–106
(2013). Laurence Tribe said that "we discover a ruling so exquisitely attuned to the
living constitutionalism that Scalia so vehemently disdains." Tribe & Joshua Matz,
Uncertain Justice 172 (2014). It turned out that excepted weapons were few. Caetano
v. Massachusetts, 136 S.Ct. 1027 (2016) (*per curiam*).

40 561 U.S. 742 (2010).
41 *Id.* at 750, 767, 775.
42 Law and morality have been and are inseparable, history and law far less.
43 *Id.* at 804–805 (citation omitted).

CHAPTER 4 CONSTITUTIONAL CRIMINAL PROCEDURE

1 *E.g.*, Furman v. Georgia, 408 U.S. 238 (1972) (*per curiam*); Gregg v. Georgia, 428 U.S.
   153 (1976); Jurek v. Texas, 428 U.S. 262 (1976).
2 Leonard W. Levy construed the language differently than most. Levy, *Origins of the
   Bill of Rights* 208 (1999) ("punishment need not be unusual as well as cruel; any
   punishment that is cruel would meet the constitutional ban whether or not it is also
   unusual").
3 *E.g.*, Simmons v. South Carolina, 512 U.S. 154, 185 (1994) (Scalia, J., dissenting).
4 428 U.S. 280 (1976).
5 497 U.S. 639, 671 (1990).
6 *E.g.*, Stanford v. Kentucky, 492 U.S. 361, 379 (1989).
7 487 U.S. 815 (1988).
8 *Id.* at 864–865. Blackstone was well known to the founders and was quoted in *The
   Federalist* Nos. 69 and 84.
9 *Id.* at 870.
10 536 U.S. 304 (2002).
11 *Id.* at 347–348.
12 543 U.S. 551 (2005).
13 *Id.* at 608, 617.
14 *Id.* at 624–625.
15 *Id.* at 627.
16 482 U.S. 496 (1987).
17 *Id.* at 499–503.
18 *Id.* at 504–509.
19 482 U.S. at 519–521. Some of Scalia's views took hold in Payne v. Tennessee, 501 U.S.
   808 (1991), with the latter overruling four-year-old *Booth*. Scalia was not addressing
   the real issue, namely, whether the criminal law could value lives unequally, for
   example, by punishing the killing of an individual with children more severely than
   it could punish the killing of an individual without children.
20 501 U.S. 957, 976 (1991); *see, e.g.*, Ewing v. California, 538 U.S. 11, 31 (2003) (Scalia,
   J., concurring).
21 The historical record is more complex and more unclear. For example, New Hampshire's constitution provided for proportionality in punishment and some states, especially Pennsylvania, were imposing prison terms in lieu of other punishments in the
   1780s. Mark E. Kann, *Punishment, Prisons, and Patriarchy; Liberty and Power in the
   Early American Republic* 119, 126, 131–132 (2005).

22 Scalia voted with the majority in McCleskey v. Kemp, 481 U.S. 279 (1987), which held statistics alone were insufficient to establish a violation of the Equal Protection Clause in imposing the death penalty against blacks. *See* Christopher F. Smith & Madhavi McCall, "Justice Scalia's Influence on Criminal Justice," 34 *University of Toledo Law Review* 535, 548–550 (2003).

23 *E.g.*, California v. Hodari D., 499 U.S. 621 (1991).

24 Terry v. Ohio, 392 U.S. 1 (1968); Maryland v. Buie, 494 U.S. 325 (1990).

25 *E.g.*, Indianapolis v. Edmond, 531 U.S. 32, 48 (2000).

26 Veronia School District 47J v. Acton, 515 U.S. 646 (1995) (Scalia, J.) (sustaining random urinalysis requirement for participation in interscholastic athletics largely on basis that minors involved); Ferguson v. City of Charleston, 532 U.S. 67, 91 (2001) (Scalia, J., dissenting) (dissenting from holding unconstitutional state hospitals' warrantless performance of diagnostic tests for cocaine on pregnant women with positive results forwarded to law-enforcement authorities in some circumstances, on ground that women consented to the taking of urine samples and could not object to what the hospitals did with the test results).

27 Government employees are discussed in Chapter 8.

28 232 U.S. 383 (1914).

29 367 U.S. 643 (1961). One collateral effect of the exclusionary rule was to integrate an unlawful search with the merits of the criminal trial. Previously, the existence of an unlawful search was considered outside the criminal process, for example, in a suit for damages by the criminal defendant. Search and seizure issues suddenly became critical in federal and state prosecutions.

30 Henry J. Friendly, "The Bill of Rights," in *Benchmarks* 260, 262 (1967).

31 People v. Defore, 242 N.Y. 13, 21 (1926).

32 In Hudson v. Michigan, 547 U.S. 586 (2006), Scalia joined by four colleagues held that violation of the requirement that police officers knock and announce their presence before executing a search warrant did not require the suppression of all evidence found in the search. Exclusion of unconstitutionally seized evidence had been thoroughly marginalized by the end of the Rehnquist Court. Thomas Y. Davies, "The Supreme Court Giveth and the Supreme Court Taketh Away: The Century of Fourth Amendment Search and Seizure Doctrine," 100 *Journal of Criminal Law and Criminology* 933, 1031 (2010).

33 526 U.S. 314, 331 (1999).

34 384 U.S. 436 (1966).

35 530 U.S. 428 (2000).

36 *Id.* at 443.

37 *Id.* at 435 n. 1. Scalia was willing to look to foreign practice when it was demonstrably better than the practice employed in the United States. Chaflin v. Chaflin, 133 S.Ct. 1017, 1030 (2013) (joining concurring opinion that discussed practice of England and Wales under the Hague Convention on the Civil Aspects of International Child Abduction).

38 530 U.S. at 448–461. Thomas joined Scalia's opinion. The majority called *Miranda* "a constitutional rule." *Id.* at 431. Possibly because he rejected *Miranda* as a constitutional decision, Scalia omitted any discussion of the original understanding of the Self-Incrimination Clause. *See generally* Levy, *Original Intent and the Framers Constitution* 247–266 (1988).

39 556 U.S. 586 (2009). Souter and Breyer joined the opinion; Stevens and Ginsburg dissented.

40 *Id.* at 593–594. Stevens and Ginsburg dissented. Only Scalia and Thomas dissented in Padilla v. Kentucky, 559 U.S. 356 (2010), where the majority held that counsel engaged in a deficient performance when he failed to tell his client that his plea of guilty made him subject to automatic deportation. "The Sixth Amendment guarantees the accused a lawyer 'for his defense' against a 'criminal prosecutio[n]' – not for sound advice about the collateral consequences of conviction. . . . Adding to counsel's duties an obligation to advise about a conviction's collateral consequence has no logical stopping point." *Id.* at 388, 390.

41 489 U.S. 288 (1989).

42 *See* Butler v. McKellar, 494 U.S. 407 (1990); Lambrix v. Singletary, 520 U.S. 518 (1997); Schriro v. Summerlin, 542 U.S. 348 (2004). The Court relied, *inter alia*, on its decision in *Linkletter v. Walker*, 381 U.S. 618, 622 (1965), where Black and Douglas dissented.

43 381 U.S. 618, 629 (1965). That is a different issue than creating law only for the future. The historical justification for overruling precedent was that the prior decision had always been wrong and was never the law. The court had merely discovered the correct law. Scalia said prospective decision making "is quite incompatible with the judicial power," and courts, in contrast to legislatures, "have no authority to engage in the practice" and is the "handmaid of judicial activism and the born enemy of stare decisis." Harper v. Virginia Dept. of Taxation, 509 U.S. 86, 105–106 (1993) (Scalia, J., concurring).

44 Scalia joined an opinion for the Court that accepted retroactivity. Danforth v. Minnesota, 552 U.S. 264 (2008).

45 *See* Brown v. Plata, 131 S.Ct. 1910, 1950 (2011) (Scalia, J., dissenting).

46 487 U.S. 266, 277 (1988) (Scalia, J., dissenting in 5–4 decision).

47 501 U.S. 797 (1991) (Scalia, J.) (6–3).

48 512 U.S. 339, 355 (1994) (Scalia concurring in 5–4 decision).

49 513 U.S. 298, 342 (1995) (Scalia dissenting in 5–4 decision).

50 523 U.S. 637, 646 (1998) (Scalia dissenting in 7–2 decision).

51 529 U.S. 473, 490 (2000) (Scalia concurring in part, dissenting in part in 7–2 decision).

52 560 U.S. 631, 660 (2010) (Scalia dissenting in 7–2 decision).

53 132 S.Ct. 641, 656 (2012) (Scalia dissenting in 8–1 decision); *see* Christopher E. Smith & Madhavi McCall, "Justice Scalia's Influence on Criminal Justice," 34 *University of Toledo Law Review* 535, 540–547 (2003).

54 132 S. Ct. 912, 929 (2012) (Scalia dissenting in 7–2 decision).

55 133 S.Ct. 1911, 1924 (2013) (Scalia dissenting in 5–4 decision).

CHAPTER 5 PRIVACY AND INDIVIDUAL RIGHTS

1 Some scholars have rejected the distinctions between enumerated and unenumerated rights. Ronald Dworkin suggested that views on abortion are part of freedom of religion for both sides of the debate. Dworkin, "Unenumerated Rights," 59 *University of Chicago Law Review* 381 (1992). In Lawrence v. Texas, 539 U.S. 538, 597 (2003), Scalia rejected a claim based on the right to engage in homosexual conduct on the ground that it "is not a fundamental right 'deeply rooted in this Nation's history and tradition.'"

2 381 U.S. 479 (1965).

3 410 U.S. 113 (1973).

4 478 U.S. 186 (1986).
5 488 U.S. 469 (1989). At the same time Scalia called for overruling United Steelworkers
   of America v. Weber, 443 U.S. 193 (1979), a significant Title VII reverse-discrimination
   case, as untethered from precedent and unworthy of being saved by *stare decisis*. Scalia
   stated his rejection of affirmative action a decade earlier in "The Disease as Cure:
   'In order to get beyond racism, we must first take account of race,'" 1979 *Washington
   University Law Quarterly* 147.
6 488 U.S. at 477–480.
7 *Id.* at 534–539; *see* Regents of the University of California v. Bakke, 438 U.S. 265,
   355–366 (1978) (Marshall, J., dissenting).
8 *Id.* at 520–521.
9 *Id.* at 521–528; *see* Adarand Constructors, Inc. v. Pena, 515 U.S. 200, 239 (1995) (Scalia,
   J., concurring in part, dissenting in part).
10 Scalia, 1979 *Washington Law Review* at 156.
11 539 U.S. 306 (2003).
12 *Id.* at 332.
13 *Id.* at 346–349. Scalia also joined Rehnquist's and Thomas's longer and more traditional dissents. In Schuette v. Coalition to Defend Affirmative Action (BAMN), 134
   S.Ct. 1623 (2014), a challenge to an amendment to a state constitution that prohibited
   race-conscious admissions policies in public universities, Scalia rejected the idea
   that a facially neutral law could be held unconstitutional solely because it had a
   racially disproportionate impact. The Fourteenth Amendment was violated only if a
   discriminatory purpose existed.
14 133 S.Ct. 2612 (2013).
15 *Id.* at 2644; *see* Ruth Bader Ginsburg, *My Own Words* 292–296 (2016) (Ginsburg's
   bench announcement).
16 381 U.S. 479 (1965).
17 *E.g.*, Jaffee v. Redmond, 518 U.S. 1, 25 n. 1 (1996) (Scalia, J., dissenting).
18 505 U.S. 833 (1992).
19 *Id.* at 979–980 (citations omitted). Pro-choice advocates urged a variety of arguments
   against Scalia's position, including originalism arguments, which were not their
   strongest, but also right based due process and equal protection. Arguments included
   a constitutional right to gender equality. *See* Gonzales v. Carhart, 550 U.S. 124, 169,
   185 (2007) (partial-birth-abortion case) (Ginsburg, J., dissenting).
20 497 U.S. 261 (1990).
21 *Id.* at 280, 284, 286. The Court's opinion discussed laws against suicide and against
   assisting suicide. Rehnquist was joined by White, O'Connor, Scalia, and Kennedy.
   Brennan, Marshall, Blackmun, and Stevens dissented.
22 *Id.* at 293.
23 *Id.* at 296, 300.
24 518 U.S. 515 (1996).
25 *Id.* at 576. Scalia argued that the Court changed by bare fiat the standard of review
   from intermediate to strict scrutiny, which had been applied only to race and national
   origin. He said that intermediate scrutiny "required only a substantial relation between
   end and means, not a perfect fit.... [W]e held that a classification need not be
   accurate 'in every case' to survive intermediate scrutiny so long as, 'in the aggregate,'
   it advances the ultimate objective." *Id.* at 573–574.
26 Scalia noted that women were not a minority that needed court protection.
27 *Id.* at 576.

28 *Id.* at 600–601.
29 478 U.S. at 194.
30 135 S.Ct. 2584 (2015).
31 United States v. Salerno, 481 U.S. 739, 745 (1987).
32 517 U.S. 620 (1996).
33 *Id.* at 627, 630, 631, 634.
34 *Id.* at 635, quoting *Civil Rights Cases*, 109 U.S. 3, 24 (1883).
35 Akhil Reed Amar, "Attainder and Amendment 2: *Romer*'s Rightness," 95 *Michigan Law Review* 203, 204 (1996); *see* Chai Feldbaum, "Gay Rights," in *The Rehnquist Court* 136 (Herman Schwartz ed. 2002).
36 517 U.S. at 644.
37 *Id.* at 639.
38 *Id.* at 636.
39 *Id.* at 653. Scalia's dismissal of (procedural) due process so cavalierly was indefensible. Liberal Mark Tushnet agreed with Scalia in one respect. "The justices are members of the cultural elite, and they are likely to see the future moving in the direction the elite wants. And yet, one thing that gives a cultural elite its status is precisely the power to shape the future. The Court could do worse that follow the views of cultural elites if it wants to predict the future." Tushnet, *Taking the Constitution Away from the Courts* 150–151 (1999). Of course, predicting the future was very low on Scalia's list of priorities.
40 478 U.S. 186 (1986).
41 *Id.* at 641 & n. 2. The Equal Protection Clause forbids state action that "single[s] out" a class and accords it a lesser degree of protection by the laws. Strauder v. West Virginia, 100 U.S. 303, 308 (1879); *The Civil Rights Cases*, 109 U.S. 3, 24 (1883); *see* H. Jefferson Powell, "The Lawfulness of *Romer v. Evans*," 77 *North Carolina Law Review* 241 (1998). Powell also challenged Scalia's argument that the greater includes the lesser, by pointing out, *inter alia*, that *Bowers* required the state to prove an "individual's commission of relevant conduct through the rigors of criminal due process. . . . Simply put, *Bowers* was irrelevant to the decision in *Romer*." *Id.* at 255–256.
42 517 U.S. at 649. Scalia did not mention that the Constitution gave Congress plenary power to admit new states, which undermined the analogy. Art. IV, § 3.
43 539 U.S. 558 (2003).
44 *Id.* at 567.
45 381 U.S. 479 (1965).
46 505 U.S. 833 (1992).
47 539 U.S. at 562.
48 410 U.S. 113 (1973).
49 539 U.S. at 602–605.
50 133 S.Ct. 2675 (2013).
51 *Id.* at 2693.
52 *Id.* at 2695–2696.
53 *Id.* at 2709–2710.
54 Richard Posner described Alito's dissent in the case as "a religious argument." Posner, *Divergent Paths* 186–187 (2016).
55 135 S.Ct. 2584 (2015).
56 *Id.* at 2627.
57 *Id.* at 2628. Thomas's dissent had a spiritual quality. After noting that the Constitution had no "dignity clause," although the majority relied on dignity, he wrote: "Human

dignity has long been understood in this country to be innate. When the Framers proclaimed in the Declaration of Independence, that 'all men are created equal' and 'endowed by their Creator with certain unalienable Rights,' they referred to a vision of mankind in which all humans are created in the image of God and therefore of inherent worth. That vision is the foundation upon which this Nation was built. The corollary of that principle is that human dignity cannot be taken away by the government. Slaves did not lose their dignity (any more than they lost their humanity) because the government allowed them to be enslaved. Those held in internment camps did not lose their dignity because the government confined them. And those denied governmental benefits certainly do not lose their dignity because the government denies them these benefits. The government cannot bestow dignity, and it cannot take it away." *Id.* at 2639. Brennan voiced a more humanistic view. A punishment must not be "so severe as to be utterly and irreversibly degrading to the very essence of human dignity." Brennan, "In Defense of Dissents," 37 *Hastings Law Journal* 427, 435–436 (1986).

CHAPTER 6 GOVERNMENT POWER AND REGULATION

1 304 U.S. 144, 153 n. 4 (1938).
2 Scalia, "Economic Affairs as Human Affairs," in *Economic Liberties and the Judiciary* 31–32 (James A. Dorn & Henry G. Manne eds. 1987); *see* Dolan v. City of Tigard, 514 U.S. 374 (1994); Pennell v. San Jose, 485 U.S. 1 (1985); Nollan v. California Coastal Comm'n, 483 U.S. 825 (1987); *see generally* David A. Schultz & Christopher E. Smith, *The Jurisprudential Vision of Justice Antonin Scalia* 1–29 (1996). While Scalia was a leader of the property-rights movement in the Supreme Court, a 2013 study placed him as the least pro-business of the Court's sitting conservatives and moderate, behind Alito, Roberts, Thomas, and Kennedy, but well ahead of the remaining four Justices. Lee Epstein, William M. Landes & Richard A. Posner, "How Business Fares in the Supreme Court," 97 *Minnesota Law Review* 1431, 1451–1452 (2013).
3 545 U.S. 1 (2005).
4 514 U.S. 549 (1995) (Rehnquist, C.J.).
5 529 U.S. 598 (2000) (Rehnquist, C.J.).
6 132 S.Ct. 2566 (2012).
7 5 U.S. (1 Cranch) 1 (1803).
8 17 *Suffolk Law Review* 881–882 (1983).
9 *See* Evan Tsen Lee, *Judicial Restraint in America* 167–172 (2011).
10 *See* 17 *Suffolk Law Review* at 892.
11 504 U.S. 555 (1992).
12 *Id.* at 560–564.
13 *Id.* at 573–577. A plurality of the Court joined portions of the opinion.
14 *See* Steven L. Winter, "What If Justice Scalia Took History and the Rule of Law Seriously?," 12 *Duke Environmental Law & Policy Forum* 155, 158–160 (2001).
15 528 U.S. 167 (2000). O'Connor and Kennedy, who dissented in NWF, joined the new majority. Scalia and Thomas dissented.
16 *Id.* at 187.
17 Scalia, "Review of Steven D. Smith's *Law's Quandary*," 55 *Catholic Law Review* 687, 692 (2006). Scalia took a narrow view of redressability.
18 Scalia also construed environmental statutes narrowly when the plaintiff established standing. *E.g.*, Babbitt v. Sweet Home Chapter of Committee for a Greater Oregon,

515 U.S. 687, 714 (1995) (Scalia, J., dissenting); *see* Karin P. Sheldon, "'It's Not My Job to Care': Understanding Justice Scalia's Method of Statutory Construction through *Sweet Home* and *Chevron*," 24 *Environmental Affairs Law Review* 487 (1997); William N. Eskridge, Jr., "Nino's Nightmare: Legal Process Theory as a Jurisprudence of Toggling between Facts and Norms," 57 *St. Louis University Law Journal* 865 (2013).

19 133 S.Ct. at 2688.
20 *Id.* at 2699–2701 (joined by Roberts and Thomas). That the legislative power is vested in Congress does not mean it can pass statutes outside its constitutional powers.
21 438 U.S. 104 (1978).
22 Lucas v. South Carolina Coastal Council, 505 U.S. 1003, 1027 (1992).
23 Palozzolo v. Rhode Island, 533 U.S. 606, 637 (2001).
24 Pennell v. San Jose, 485 U.S. 1, 11 (1988) Scalia, J., concurring in part, dissenting in part); Dolan v. City of Tigard, 512 U.S. 374 (1994)(Rehnquist, C.J.); *see* David Schultz, "Scalia, Property, and *Dolan v. City of Tigard*: The Emergence of a Post-*Carolene Products* Jurisprudence," 29 *Akron Law Review* 1 (1995); Richard J. Lazarus, "The Measure of a Justice: Justice Scalia and the Faltering Property Rights Movement within the Supreme Court," 57 *Hastings Law Journal* 759 (2006).
25 *Lucas*, 505 U.S. at 1028 n. 15.
26 505 U.S. 1003 (1992).
27 *Id.* at 1028 n. 15. Scalia relied on legislative history.
28 521 U.S. 902 (1997).
29 *Id.* at 905.
30 *Id.* at 909, 928.
31 *Id.* at 926, citing New York v. United States, 505 U.S. 144, 188 (1992).
32 491 U.S. 1, 29 (1989) (Scalia, J., concurring in part, dissenting in part).
33 501 U.S. 775 (1991).
34 527 U.S. 666 (1999).
35 538 U.S. 721 (2003). Scalia cast votes in favor of states in Seminole Tribe of Florida v. Florida, 517 U.S. 44 (1996); Alden v. Maine, 527 U.S. 706 (1999); Kimel v. Florida Bd. of Regents, 528 U.S. 62 (2000); and Board of Trustees of University of Alabama v. Garrett, 531 U.S. 356 (2001). An exception from this pattern of favoring the states was Scalia's opinion in Virginia Office for Protection & Advocacy v. Stewart, 131 S.Ct. 1632 (2011), discussed in Chapter 15.
36 135 S.Ct. 2652 (2015).
37 *Id.* at 2668.
38 *Id.* at 2677–2692.
39 Scalia argued that the Constitution left "it to private interest to censure the law" and that courts do not resolve direct disputes between two political branches of the same government. Presumably, a harmed congressional candidate could object. *Cf.* Bush v. Gore, 531 U.S. 98 (2000). Scalia concluded elsewhere that "claims of unconstitutional gerrymandering do not present a justiciable case or controversy.... [N]o party or judge has put forth a judicially discernible standard by which to evaluate them." League of United Latin American Citizens v. Perry, 548 U.S. 399, 511 (2006) (Scalia, J., concurring in part, dissenting in part). Scholars are divided. The Supreme Court might, however, create a rule requiring *states* to set standards to combat gerrymandering and then judge whether the actual redistricting met those standards, similar to the resolution of punitive-damage awards. Some scholars have concluded that the "one-person, one-vote" decisions of the Court have made gerrymandering worse by cutting districts loose from established subdivisions, such as counties, and

sanctioning weirdly shaped districts to remove minor deviations from population equality. Michael W. McConnell, "The Redistricting Cases: Original Mistakes and Current Consequences," 24 *Harvard Journal of Law & Politics* 103, 112 (2000); *see* Bernard Bailyn, *The Origins of American Politics* 80–81 (apportionment "by normal eighteenth-century standards... was remarkably equitable"). While scholars dispute whether the original Constitution required one-person, one-vote, almost all agree that the decision has been salutary. *E.g.*, Jeffrey Rosen, *The Most Democratic Branch* 125–126 (2006).

40 135 S.Ct. at 2697. Thomas joined Scalia's dissent.

41 531 U.S. 98 (2000).

42 Leading to the debacle was a confusing "butterfly ballot" that led many Gore supporters to cast their votes for Patrick Buchanan, an arch conservative, and the failure of the election machinery to dislodge chads consistently from punch cards and to count properly the votes cast.

43 Laurence Tribe argued that uniformity was impossible in counting ballots. "Tribe, 'eroG v. hsuB,'" in *Bush v. Gore; the Question of Legitimacy* 45–47 (Ackerman ed. 2002). Furthermore, there were innumerable other procedural errors and anomalies. *Id.* at 47–53.

44 Richard Posner, *Breaking the Deadlock; The 2000 Election and the Court* (2001). Posner argued that the Supreme Court sacrificed its prestige for the good of the nation and prevented chaos. Some liberal scholars agreed with Posner in varying degrees. *E.g.*, Cass R. Sunstein, "Lawless Order and Hot Cases," in *A Badly Flawed Election* 75 (Ronald Dworkin ed. 2002). Others argued there was no sign of chaos or that the Constitution and statutes gave resolution of the dispute to the political branches. *E.g.*, Jeffrey Rosen, "Political Questions and Hazards of Pragmatism," in *Bush v. Gore* at 145–162; Mark Tushnet, "The Conservatism in *Bush v. Gore*," in *id.* at 173–175; Dworkin, Introduction, *A Badly Flawed Election* at 1–2.

45 Originalist Steven G. Calabresi argued that the Supreme Court "quite simply lacked jurisdiction to decide *Bush v. Gore*," Calabresi, "A Political Question," in *id.* at 129–144, and should have deferred to the political branches in any event. *See* Ackerman, "Off Balance," in *id.* at 195 ("The Court's defense – that no time remained for Florida to meet the state's own December 12 deadline – is simply preposterous.").

46 429 U.S. 252 (1977).

47 Jed Rubenfeld, "Not as Bad as *Plessy*, Worse," in *id.* at 34–36; Guido Calabresi, "In Partial (but Not Partisan) Praise of Principle," in *id.* at 75–83.

48 *See id.* at 67–75. Indeed, it disclaimed any precedential effect.

49 Scalia's response both publicly and to me was "Get Over It." It was reminiscent of Ring Lardner's line in *The Young Immigrants*: "'Shut up,' he explained." Scalia also claimed, probably correctly, that the result would have been the same without the Supreme Court's involvement, since the Republican Florida legislature almost certainly would have certified Bush as the victor. *See* Art. II, § 1, cl.2; Amend. XII. But that is certainly beside the point.

50 Post, "Sustaining the Premise of Legality: Learning to Live with *Bush v. Gore*," in *Bush vs. Gore* at 97, 100, 109; *see, e.g.*, Margaret Jane Radin, "Can the Rule of Law Survive *Bush v. Gore*?," in *id.* at 110–114 ("five Republican members of the Court decided the case in a way that is recognizably nothing more than a naked expression of these justices' preference for the republican party"). Radin singled out the Court's decision to stop the vote count and to forbid the Florida Supreme Court from addressing the constitutional problems the Supreme Court purported to find.

PART III SCALIA'S LIBERAL CONSTITUTIONAL OPINIONS

1 Frank B. Cross, *The Failed Promise of Originalism* 191 (2013).
2 David A. Strauss, "Why Conservatives Shouldn't Be Originalists," 31 *Harvard Journal of Law & Public Policy* 969 (2008). In fact, one thesis of mine is that it is easier to manipulate history than precedent.
3 542 U.S. 507 (2004).
4 Rasul v. Bush, 542 U.S. 466, 503 (2004).
5 513 U.S. 374 (1995).
6 *Id.* at 400.

CHAPTER 7 FIRST AMENDMENT: FREEDOM OF SPEECH AND MORE

7 Scalia wrote libel decisions in the Court of Appeals. *E.g.*, Ullman v. Evans, 750 F.2d 970 (D.C. Cir. 1984).
8 The divisive and controversial subject of "hate speech," as a matter both of public policy and of constitutional law, has been the subject of many scholarly inquiries, *e.g.*, Jeremy Waldron,*The Harm in Hate Speech* (2012); John Paul Stevens, "Should Hate Speech Be Outlawed?," *The New York Review of Books*, June 7, 2012.
9 491 U.S. 576 (1989).
10 *Id.* at 582, 584.
11 *Id.* at 576, 587. Brennan, Marshall, Blackmun, and Stevens joined Scalia's opinion.
12 536 U.S. 150 (2002).
13 *Id.* at 167.
14 *Id.* at 171.
15 491 U.S. 397 (1989) (joined by Thomas).
16 Section and subsection designations are omitted.
17 *Id.* at 406–407, 414. Brennan added, "If... the speaker's opinion... gives offense, that... is a reason for according it constitutional protection, because... free speech under our system of government... best serves its high purpose when it induces a condition of unrest, creates dissatisfaction with conditions as they are, or even stirs people to anger." *Id.* at 408–409.
18 Tinker v. Des Moines Independent Community School District, 393 U.S. 503, 505 (1969).
19 Brown v. Louisiana, 383 U.S. 131, 141–142 (1966).
20 *E.g.*, Food Employees v. Logan Valley Plaza, Inc., 391 U.S. 308, 313–314 (1968).
21 491 U.S. at 414.
22 *Id.* at 422. White, Stevens, and O'Connor joined Rehnquist's dissent.
23 505 U.S. 377 (1992) (joined by Rehnquist, Kennedy, Souter, and Thomas).
24 *Id.* at 380–381.
25 466 U.S. 485, 505 (1984).
26 505 U.S. at 385, 388.
27 *Id.* at 386, 391, 395–396. Scalia rejected as a ground for reversal that the ordinance was "substantially overbroad," meaning that it prohibited legitimate conduct along with illegitimate, saying simply, "We find it unnecessary to consider this issue." *Id.* at 381.
28 413 U.S. 568, 572 (1942).
29 505 U.S. at 384, 392.

30 *See* Guy-Uriel E. Charles, "Colored Speech: Cross-Burning, Epistemics, and the Triumph of the Crits," 93 *Georgetown Law Journal* 575, 588 (2004). Scalia distinguished R.A.V. and upheld the conviction in Virginia v. Black, 538 U.S. 343 (2003). The Virginia statute was content neutral; it banned public cross-burning with "intent to intimidate a person or group of persons."

31 505 U.S. at 397. White, Blackmun, O'Connor, and Stevens, a diverse group, dissented.

32 481 U.S. 497 (1987).

33 *See* Miller v. California 413 U.S. 15 (1973).

34 Cohen v. California, 403 U.S. 15, 25 (1971).

35 481 U.S. at 504–505.

36 131 S.Ct. 2729 (2011).

37 *Id.* at 2742–2746. The Act covered games "in which the range of options available to a player includes killing, maiming, dismembering, or sexually assaulting an image of a human being, if those acts are depicted" in a manner that a "reasonable person, considering the game as a whole, would find appeals to a deviant or morbid interest of minors," that is "patently offensive to prevailing standards in the community as what is suitable for minors" and that "causes the game, as a whole, to lack serious literary, artistic, political, or scientific value for minors."

38 559 U.S. 460 (2010) (Roberts, C.J.).

39 131 S.Ct. at 2376, 2738, 2739.

40 *Id.* at 2765–2771. In Riley v. National Fed. of the Blind, 487 U.S. 781, 803 (1988), Scalia joined Brennan's liberal opinion and added a short concurrence granting broad First Amendment rights to commercial speech. Scalia emphasized that except to combat fraud, "the dissemination of ideas cannot be regulated to prevent it from being unfair or unreasonable.... [The State] cannot impose a prophylactic rule requiring disclosure even where misleading statements are not made." Rehnquist and O'Connor dissented on the ground that states should be permitted to regulate paid solicitors for charities, a limited intrusion on freedom of speech. As in the case of white-collar crime, an argument can be made that the liberal view would allow regulation of commercial speech. Thomas alone advocated broad rights for commercial speech in 44 Liquormart, Inc. v. Rhode Island, 517 U.S. 484, 518 (1996).

41 491 U.S. 524 (1989).

42 *Id.* at 533.

43 *Id.* at 541–542. Scalia played a large role in the Ford Administration's opposition to creating a federal newsman's privilege to protect journalists from having to disclose their sources. Joan Biskupic, *American Original* 54–55 (2009).

44 491 U.S. at 550–552.

45 Borough of Duryea, Pennsylvania v. Guarneri, 131 S.Ct. 2488 (2011), involved the First Amendment's Petition Clause, which protects the "right . . . to petition the Government for a redress of grievances." The Court held that the Petition Clause was limited to matters of public concern. Scalia's solitary dissent was liberal on that issue, arguing that the clause also covered private grievances. Both the text and historical analysis, including that most petitions at the time of the founding related to private claims, supported Scalia: "it is ahistorical to say that petitions on matters of public concern constitute 'core petitioning activity.'" The Speech Clause, not the Petition Clause, granted heightened protection to speech of public concern. *Id.* at 2505–2506. Scalia rejected a thirty-nine-year-old precedent along with the majority's historical analysis. It was a liberal originalist position.

CHAPTER 8 FOURTH AMENDMENT: SEARCH AND SEIZURE

1 *E.g.,* Illinois v. Rodriquez, 497 U.S. 177 (1990); California v. Acevedo, 500 U.S. 565 (1991) (Scalia, J., concurring); Richard A. Brisbin, Jr., *Justice Scalia and the Conservative Revival* 224–231(1997).
2 In this respect Scalia resembled another generally conservative Justice, Felix Frankfurter.
3 Arizona v. Gant, 556 U.S. 332, 338 (2009) (Stevens, J.), quoting Katz v. United States, 389 U.S. 347, 357 (1967). Scalia narrowed the Court's broad doctrine often used before 1990 that all warrantless searches were presumptively unconstitutional to only those warrantless searches that were directed at the home and immediate vicinity. Richard H. Seamon, *"Kyllo v. United States* and the Partial Ascendance of Justice Scalia's Fourth Amendment," 79 *Washington University Law Quarterly* 1013, 1026–1029 (2001).
4 480 U.S. 321 (1987). Joining Scalia's opinion were Brennan, White, Marshall, Blackmun, and Stevens; Rehnquist, White, and O'Connor dissented.
5 *Id.* at 325.
6 *Id.* at 329. Scalia found no search and seizure of a person in California v. Hodari D., 499 U.S. 621 (1991). Writing for the Court, he rejected the argument that the seizure of a person occurs when a reasonable person would not feel free to leave, and insisted that seizure did not occur until the person was physically grasped, a conservative opinion that reduced individual rights.
7 *Id.* at 324–325, citing Illinois v. Andreas, 463 U.S. 765 (1983).
8 *Id.* at 326–327. As noted above, framing-era law did not permit searches of a home without a warrant.
9 Stanley v. Georgia, 394 U.S. 557, 571 (1969).
10 George Kannar, "The Constitutional Catechism of Antonin Scalia," 99 *Yale Law Journal* 1297, 1323–1328 (1990).
11 533 U.S. 27 (2001). Souter, Thomas, Ginsburg, and Breyer joined Scalia, while Rehnquist, O'Connor, Kennedy, and Stevens dissented.
12 389 U.S. 347 (1967).
13 Scalia, joined by Souter, Thomas, Ginsburg, and Breyer.
14 533 U.S. at 35–39.
15 *Id.* at 40; *see* Edwin J. Butterfoss, "Bright Line Breaking Point: Embracing Justice Scalia's Call for the Supreme Court to Abandon as Unreasonable Approach to Fourth Amendment Searches and Seizures Law," 82 *Tulane Law Review* 77, 88 nn. 75, 76 (2007).
16 533 U.S. at 43.
17 *See id.* at 46–51.
18 132 S.Ct. 945 (2012).
19 *Id.* at 949, quoting Boyd v. United States, 116 U.S. 616, 626 (1888).
20 Scalia did not cite any cases for the proposition that any trespass constituted a search under the Fourth Amendment. Professor Thomas Y. Davies described the position as "unprecedented." Davies e-mails to author, Dec. 3 & 5, 2014.
21 133 S.Ct. 1958 (2013).
22 *Id.* at 1980.
23 *Id.* at 1980–1982.
24 *Id.* at 1989.
25 134 S.Ct. 1683 (2014) (Thomas, J.).

26 *Id.* at 1697. Scalia's dissent is reminiscent of the solitary dissent by Justice Douglas in Draper v. United States, 358 U.S. 307, 324 (1959): "Here the officers had no evidence – apart from the mere word of an informer – that petitioner was committing a crime.... No magistrate could issue a warrant on the mere word of an officer, without more." Scalia did not cite Douglas.

27 133 S.Ct. 1409 (2013). Thomas, Ginsburg, Sotomayor, and Kagan joined the opinion.

28 There is some tension between *Jardines* and Ferguson v. Charleston, 532 U.S. 67 (2001) (Scalia, J., dissenting), where Scalia said that women's consent to having urine samples taken by a hospital precluded their objecting when the hospitals forwarded results of testing of samples that contained cocaine to law-enforcement authorities.

29 489 U.S. 656 (1989) (Kennedy, J.).

30 *Id.* at 670, 671.

31 *Id.* at 680, 683.

32 *Id.* at 686–687. *Von Raab* was the outer limit of Scalia's rejection of workplace testing for drugs. He joined the opinion for the Court in Skinner v. Railway Labor Executives' Ass'n, 489 U.S. 602 (1989), which upheld urine, blood, and breath tests of railroad employees who were involved in a major train accident and urine and breath tests following less serious accidents. While Scalia did not write an opinion in *Skinner*, he explained that vote in *Von Raab*: "I joined the Court's opinion [in *Skinner*] because the demonstrated frequency of drug and alcohol use by the targeted class of employees, and the demonstrated connection between such use and grave harm, rendered the search a reasonable means of protecting society." 489 U.S. at 680–681.

33 392 U.S. 1 (1968).

34 508 U.S. 366 (1993).

35 *Id.* at 380–381 (joined by Stevens).

36 267 U.S. 132, 153 (1925).

37 Craig M. Bradley, "Two Models of the Fourth Amendment," 83 *Michigan Law Review* 1468 (1984) (nearly twenty exceptions).

38 453 U.S. 454 (1981).

39 541 U.S. 615 (2004).

40 *Id.* at 621, 623.

41 *Id.* at 632; *see* Edwin J. Butterfoss, "Bright Line Breaking Point: Embracing Justice Scalia's Call for the Supreme Court to Abandon as Unreasonable Approach to Fourth Amendment Searches and Seizures Law," 82 *Tulane Law Review* 77, 116 (2007).

42 556 U.S. 332 (2009). After Rodney Gant left his stopped car, police arrested him for driving with a suspended license, handcuffed him, and locked him in the back of a patrol car. The arresting police officers then searched his car and found a gun and cocaine in the passenger compartment, which Gant claimed violated his Fourth Amendment rights. Stevens's opinion for the Court joined by Scalia, Souter, Thomas, and Ginsburg (three liberals and two originalists) upheld Gant's claim.

43 *Id.* at 351, 353.

44 *See* Colin Miller, "Stranger than Dictum: Why *Arizona v. Gant* Compels the Conclusion That *Buie* Searches Incident to Lawful Suspicionless Arrests Are Unconstitutional," 62 *Baylor Law Review* 1 (2010); George M. Derry III, "A Case of Doubtful Certainty: The Court Relapses into Search Incident to Arrest Confusion in *Arizona v. Gant*," 44 *Indiana Law Review* 395 (2011). Scalia joined Sotomayor's liberal opinion in Missouri v. McNeeley, 133 S.Ct. 1552 (2013), which held that the warrant requirement to take blood from an unwilling driver suspected of driving while intoxicated did

not differ from other contexts even though blood-alcohol levels dissipated rapidly. Concurring in part and dissenting in part were Roberts, Breyer, and Alito, while Thomas dissented. In Rodriquez v. United States, 135 S.Ct. 1609 (2015), Scalia joined Ginsburg's liberal opinion for the Court, which held that delaying a lawful traffic stop to secure a drug-sniffing dog violated the Fourth Amendment. Thomas, Alito, and Kennedy dissented. The third special category was the limited rights of students. *E.g.*, Morse v. Frederick, 551 U.S. 393 (Roberts, C.J.) Veronia School Distr. 47J v. Acton, 515 U.S. 646 (1995) (Scalia, J.).

45 Gerstein v. Pugh, 420 U.S. 103, 113 (1975).
46 500 U.S. 44 (1991). Rehnquist, White, Kennedy, and Souter joined O'Connor's opinion.
47 *Id.* at 52–53.
48 *Id.* at 59.
49 *Id.* at 70, 71. A case involved detention of persons during the execution of search warrants, an exception to the requirement of probable cause. Ordinarily, agents detain people who are present at the scene of the search, but just before the police executed a search warrant at Chunon Bailey's apartment, two other police saw him leave the apartment, followed him, and detained him nearly a mile from the apartment. Kennedy's opinion for the Court held the detention unconstitutional in Bailey v. United States, 133 S.Ct.1031 (2013). Detention was permitted for the safety and efficiency of executing a search warrant; detention nearly a mile away was not within the exception. Citing his opinion in *Thornton*, Scalia joined Kennedy and filed a concurring opinion that emphasized that there should be a bright-line rule based on the location of the subject. Breyer, Thomas, and Alito dissented on the ground that the detention was lawful.

CHAPTER 9 FIFTH AMENDMENT: CRIMINAL APPLICATIONS

1 549 U.S. 102 (2007).
2 *Id.* at 107–108.
3 *Id.* at 111–113.
4 378 U.S. 347 (1964).
5 532 U.S. 451 (2001). Rehnquist, Kennedy, Souter, and Ginsburg joined O'Connor's opinion.
6 *Id.* at 462.
7 *Id.* at 466–467.
8 Scalia was joined by Stevens, Thomas, and, in part, Breyer.
9 532 U.S. at 467–468.
10 *Id.* at 468–471.
11 Every one of the six student law-review commentaries supported Scalia's dissent over the opinion of the Court, a few in strong language. Note, "Supreme Court, 2001 Term," 115 *Harvard Law Review* 170, 189 (2001); Comment, 81 *North Carolina Law Review* 317 (2002); Comment, 30 *Northern Kentucky Law Review* 415 (2003); Comment, 44 *South Texas Law Review* 645 (2003); Comment, 36 *Suffolk Law Review* 289 (2002); Comment, 71 *University of Cincinnati Law Review* 1141 (2003).
12 513 U.S. 64 (1994).
13 561 U.S. 358 (2010).

14 Maryland v. Shatzer, 559 U.S. 98 (2010). While normally the break would entail release from custody, for Shatzer it was a release into the general prison population. Scalia joined a liberal Ginsburg opinion reversing a conviction for murder based on violations of *Miranda* in Thompson v. Keohane, 516 U.S. 99 (1995). Rehnquist and Thomas dissented.

15 During the first Congress, the Senate substituted the somewhat cryptic constitutional language for Madison's version, "no person shall be subject... to more than one punishment or one trial for the same offense." Unresolved is whether the change should be viewed as changing the meaning and, if so, in what way. Scalia frequently took conservative positions in cases under the Double Jeopardy Clause. E.g., Grady v. Corbin, 495 U.S. 508 (1990) (preclusive effect of prior plea of guilty to lesser offense); Yeager v. United States, 557 U.S. 110 (2009) (preclusive effect of acquittal on some counts on other counts on which the jury hung).

16 The principal exception is when the jury or judge returns a verdict of guilty and the trial or appellate court sets aside that verdict because of errors of law at the trial.

17 509 U.S. 688 (1993).

18 Citing Grady v. Corbin, 495 U.S. 508 (1990).

19 509 U.S. at 694, 699–700.

20 *Id.* at 743. Scalia seemed incorrect as a matter of textualism. Whether or not the drug offense contained no new element, the two offenses were not "the same," which means *identical.* Since the two were not "the same offense," double jeopardy should not apply. Scalia was using an approach more suitable to *res judicata*, which determines whether an earlier decision binds a later court.

21 David M. Zlotnick, "Battered Women & Justice Scalia," 41 *Arizona Law Review* 847, 849 (1999).

22 Amar, "Double Jeopardy Made Simple," 106 *Yale Law Journal* 1807, 1832–1833 (1997). Amar's alternative would erode defendants' rights.

23 Scalia dissented in Grady v. Corbin, 495 U.S. 508 (1990), from the Court's liberal holding that a plea of guilty to two traffic tickets for which the defendant received a fine and a six-month suspension of his license barred future prosecution for manslaughter and other crimes under the Double Jeopardy Clause because the same conduct was at issue. Scalia's textualist dissent was that the Double Jeopardy Clause prohibited a second prosecution for the same *offense*, not the same *conduct*.

24 491 U.S. 376 (1989).

25 *Id.* at 381–382.

26 *Ex parte* Lange, 85 U.S. 163 (1874); *In re* Bradley, 318 U.S. 50 (1943).

27 491 U.S. at 387.

28 Joined by Stevens and, except for one unrelated footnote, by Brennan and Marshall.

29 *Id.* at 391.

30 *Id.* at 392–394, 396. Scalia repeated his disagreement with other Justices on the scope of the clause in Witte v. United States, 515 U.S. 389, 406–407 (1995) (Scalia, J., concurring in the judgment) ("It is not true (as the Court claims) 'the language of the Double Jeopardy Clause protects against... the actual imposition of two punishments for the same offense.' *Ante*, at 396. What the Clause says is that no person 'shall... be subject for the same offense to be twice *put in jeopardy* of life or limb,' U.S. Const. Amdt. 5 (emphasis added), which means twice *prosecuted* for the same offense.)"; *see* Department of Revenue of Montana v. Kurth Ranch, 511 U.S. 767, 798 (1994) (Scalia, J., dissenting) (same).

31 543 U.S. 462 (2005).
32 Joining Scalia were Stevens, O'Connor, Souter, and Thomas.
33 *Id.* at 470–473.
34 Ginsburg did not cite Scalia's dissents in Jones v. Thomas, 491 U.S. 376 (1989), and Rogers v. Tennessee, 532 U.S. 451 (2001).
35 18 U.S.C. § 924(e)(1)
36 550 U.S. 192 (2007).
37 *Id.* at 205–208, 209, 211.
38 *Id.* at 227. Stevens and Ginsburg joined Scalia.
39 *Id.* at 219–225.
40 *Id.* at 225 (citation omitted).
41 Begay v. United States, 553 U.S. 137 (2008). The rule of lenity is discussed in Chapters 28 and 29.
42 Breyer's opinion limited violent felonies to those enumerated. Based on his canons, Scalia disagreed and took a more conservative position.
43 Johnson v. United States, 559 U.S. 133, 140 (2010) (citations omitted). Alito and Thomas dissented.
44 Sykes v. United States 131 S.Ct. 2267, 2287 (2011).
45 Derby v. United States, 131 S.Ct. 2858 (2011) (Scalia, J., dissenting from denial of *certiorari*).
46 135 S.Ct. 2551 (2015). Thomas concurred on the narrow ground that the statute did not cover the conviction for being a felon in possession of a firearm (a short-barreled shotgun).
47 *Id.* at 2557–2558.
48 *Id.* at 2562–2563.
49 Alito's dissent said: "in a due process vagueness case, we will hold that a law is facially invalid 'only if the enactment is impermissibly vague in *all* of its applications.'" *Id.* at 2580. Thomas's concurrence stated that the Constitution did not permit the courts "to nullify an Act of Congress that contains an unmistakable core of forbidden conduct." *Id.* at 2573. Their point was that a serial murderer would have no ground to argue that the residual clause was unconstitutionally vague as to him, so the statute had viability in some cases and therefore could not be declared unconstitutional on its face. But that allows Congress to pass vague statutes (*e.g.*, "No one shall do anything that harms society") and to force the Court, in effect, to rewrite them, which was the problem with the Court's opinion in Skilling v. United States, 561 U.S. 358 (2010). Thomas and Alito would require people to try to comply with nebulous standards of conduct at their peril, a position Scalia rejected. Scalia provided me with the example, "No one shall do anything that harms society."
50 *Id.* at 2573. One month after Scalia died, the Court held in Welch v. United States, 136 S.Ct. 1257 (2016), that *Johnson* should be applied retroactively to cases on collateral review. The vote was 7–1, with Alito joining Kennedy's opinion for the Court and only Thomas dissenting. The ground was that *Johnson* created a new substantive rule, which generally does apply retroactively, as opposed to a new procedural rule, which generally does not. The decision was formalistic and did not consider the problems created by making the ruling retroactive or why the rule made sense. *See* Benjamin Cardozo, *The Nature of the Judicial Process* 148–149 (1921) (retroactivity should be determined "by consideration s of convenience, of utility, and of the deepest sentiments of justice").

CHAPTER 10 SIXTH AMENDMENT: RIGHT TO TRIAL BY JURY

1 Neder v. United States, 527 U.S. 1, 30–31 (1999) (Scalia, J., concurring in part, dissenting in part).
2 Blakely v. Washington, 542 U.S. 296, 306 (2004).
3 *Id.* at 264.
4 Rule 52(a) of the Federal Rules of Criminal Procedure provides, "Any error, defect, irregularity or variance which does not affect substantial rights shall be disregarded."
5 491 U.S. 263 (1989).
6 *Id.* at 268–269 (joined by Brennan, Marshall, and Blackmun). In California v. Roy, 519 U.S. 2 (1996) (*per curiam*), the Court reversed for failure to apply the correct standard of review. Scalia (with Ginsburg joining in relevant part) argued to deny *habeas corpus* the jury must have found all elements of the crime beyond a reasonable doubt.
7 500 U.S. 391 (1991).
8 *Id.* at 414.
9 *Id.* at 413–414. Blackmun joined this part of Scalia's concurrence.
10 527 U.S. 1 (1999).
11 *Id.* at 9–11.
12 *Id.* at 15–20.
13 *Id.* at 30–32, 35, 38 (joined by Souter and Ginsburg), Stevens concurred in the Court's analysis of the harmless-error doctrine and did not join Scalia's opinion "because it is internally inconsistent and its passion is misdirected." Scalia made the same point in California v. Roy, 519 U.S. 2, 6 (1997) (Scalia, J., concurring). What makes the position of the majority harder to understand was its unanimous decision four years earlier in United States v. Gaudin, 515 U.S. 506, 522–523 (1995) (Scalia, J.) ("The Constitution gives a criminal defendant the right to have a jury determine, beyond a reasonable doubt, his guilt of every element of the crime with which he is charged. The trial judge's refusal to allow the jury to pass on the materiality of Gaudin's false statement infringed that right.").
14 523 U.S. 224 (1998) (Breyer, J.).
15 *Id.* at 226–227, 239, 243–244, 246.
16 *Id.* at 249, 261. Stevens, Souter, and Ginsburg joined Scalia's opinion. The relevant question, however, is not what judges "typically" do, but what the Constitution requires, as Scalia noted elsewhere.
17 524 U.S. 721 (1998).
18 The majority opinion concluded that the Double Jeopardy Clause did not apply to noncapital sentencing. *Id.* at 728–734. Dissenting, Stevens objected to the state's having "a second bite at the apple," thus treating the deficient record at the sentencing the same as a deficient record on the guilt or innocence phase. *Id.* at 735.
19 *Id.* at 734–737.
20 530 U.S. 466, 490 (2000). Stevens was joined by Scalia, Souter, Thomas, and Ginsburg.
21 Stevens relied on Hale, *Pleas of the Crown*, published posthumously in 1736, and J. Archbold, *Pleading and Evidence in Criminal Cases* (15th ed. 1862).
22 530 U.S. at 498–499. O'Connor, with Rehnquist, Kennedy, and Breyer, dissented. The dissent questioned reliance on an 1862 treatise. *Id.* at 526. The first edition was in 1822. Scalia took a similar position the previous year concurring in Jones v. United States, 526 U.S. 227, 253 (1999).

23 536 U.S. 584 (2002).

24 497 U.S. 639 (1990).

25 408 U.S. 238 (1972) (*per curiam*).

26 536 U.S. at 611–612; *cf.* Aaron T. Knapp, "Law's Revolutionary: James Wilson and the Birth of American Jurisprudence," 29 *Journal of Law & Politics* 189, 295 (2013) (*Apprendi* revived "judicial *acceptance* of juries as determiners of both law and facts and thus as potential nullifiers"). By accepting the need for aggravating factors, Scalia was bowing to *stare decisis.*

27 542 U.S. 296 (2004).

28 *Id.* at 303–306, 308. Stevens, Souter, Thomas, and Ginsburg joined Scalia's opinion.

29 *Id.* at 330–340.

30 555 U.S. 160 (2009).

31 *Id.* at 168.

32 *Id.* at 173. The Oregon statute allowed consecutive sentences when the "criminal offense . . . caused or created a risk of causing greater or qualitatively different loss, injury to harm to the victim or . . . a different victim." Roberts, Souter, and Kennedy joined Scalia.

33 The constitutionality of the Sentencing Commission itself is discussed in Chapter 15.

34 543 U.S. 220 (2005).

35 Review of sentences by courts of appeals would be for unreasonableness rather than *de novo.* The Court conceded that it was engaging in somewhat creative excision. "'Reasonableness' standards are not foreign to sentencing law and will not create untoward problems. In the light of the Court's constitutional holding this comes closest to what Congress would have wanted." *Id.* at 262. Scalia responded: "In order to rescue from nullification a statutory scheme designed to eliminate discretionary sentencing, it discards the provisions that eliminate discretionary sentencing." Because a judge need give only his reasons for deviating from the Guidelines, "logic compels the conclusion that the sentencing judge, after considering the recited factors (including the Guidelines), has full discretion, as full as what he possessed before the Act was passed, to sentence anywhere within the statutory range. . . . " With the elimination of mandatory Guidelines, there should be nothing for the courts of appeals to do. "Time may tell, but today's remedial majority will not." *Id.* at 303–313.

36 Breyer, joined by Rehnquist, O'Connor, and Kennedy.

37 *Id.* at 313.

38 Marlowe v. United States, 555 U.S. 963 (2009).

39 Jones v. United States, 135 S.Ct. 8, 9 (2014) (joined by Thomas and Ginsburg); *see* Kimbrough v. United States 552 U.S. 85 (2007) (Scalia, J., concurring); Rita v. United States, 551 U.S. 338 (2007); Gall v. United States, 552 U.S. 38, 60 (2007).

40 Because some defendants were shipped to England or Nova Scotia for trial, the location of trials was of concern in colonial America. John Phillip Reid, *Constitutional History of the American Revolution; The Authority of Rights* 177–183 (1986).

41 526 U.S. 275 (1999).

42 *Id.* at 282–284 (joined by Stevens).

CHAPTER 11 SIXTH AMENDMENT: CONFRONTATION CLAUSE

1 Bernard Schwartz, II, *The Bill of Rights: A Documentary History* 235 (Virginia), 263 (Pennsylvania), 278 (Delaware), 282 (Maryland), 287 (North Carolina), 323 (Vermont), 342 (Massachusetts), and 377 (New Hampshire). North Carolina's

Declaration of Rights read: "to confront the accusers and witnesses with other testimony," which is different and suggests that the concept and definition of "confrontation" may be more complicated than originalists contend.

2 Crawford v. Washington, 541 U.S. 36, 60 (2004).

3 448 U.S. 56, 66 (1980) (Blackmun, J.). Brennan, Marshall, Blackmun, and Stevens joined Scalia.

4 Ohio v. Roberts changed a rule with a series of exceptions to an evaluation of reliability. See Bibas, "Originalism and Formalism in Criminal Procedure: The Triumph of Justice Scalia, the Unlikely Friend of Criminal Defendants?," 94 Georgetown Law Journal 183, 192–193 (2005). Roberts presented an easy case that could have been sustained on narrow grounds. The challenged testimony had been given under oath at a preliminary hearing in the case and Roberts's counsel had questioned the witness. The dissent (Brennan with Marshall and Stevens) argued only that the prosecution's evidence of unavailability was insufficient.

5 481 U.S. 186 (1987).

6 Id. at 192–193.

7 Id. at 196–198. Scalia, in the minority, took an uncompromising view of the Confrontation Clause in cases involving the introduction of accomplice confessions as declarations against interest. Lilly v. Virginia, 527 U.S. 116, 143 (1998) (Scalia, J., concurring). However, he had no constitutional problem when in a trial of multiple defendants one defendant's name was redacted from the confession of a codefendant even though the jury might reasonably infer that the codefendant's confession implicated the defendant on trial. Gray v. Maryland, 523 U.S. 185, 194–195 (1998) (Scalia, J., dissenting). There is some tension between Scalia's opinions in Gray and Cruz on the presumption that jurors follow instructions.

8 487 U.S. 1012 (1988).

9 Joanmarie Ilaria Davoli, "Justice Scalia for the Defense?," 40 University of Baltimore Law Review 687, 721 (2011).

10 487 U.S. 1019. Richard II, Act I, Scene 1: "Then call them to our presence – face to face, and frowning bow to bow, ourselves will hear the accuser and the accused freely speak." 487 U.S. at 1016. Oath, opportunity to observe, and opportunity to cross-examination involve different concepts of truth telling.

11 Id. Scalia, joined by Thomas, dissented from the denial of certiorari in a similar case, Danner v. Kentucky, 525 U.S. 1010 (1998).

12 487 U.S. at 1022–1025.

13 497 U.S. 836 (1990).

14 Id. at 840–843.

15 Id. at 843–852.

16 Id. at 861–862 (joined by Brennan, Marshall, and Stevens).

17 Id. at 867–870. Earlier Supreme Court decisions accepted special circumstances. George Kannar, "The Constitutional Catechism of Antonin Scalia," 99 Yale Law Journal 1297, 1329–1334 (1990).

18 541 U.S. 36 (2004).

19 Id. at 40–41.

20 "This was the position of the great evidence scholar John Henry Wigmore and of Justice John Marshall Harlan the younger." Stephanos Bibas, "The Limits of Textualism in Interpreting the Confrontation Clause," 37 Harvard Journal of Law & Public Policy 737, 738–739 (2014). Scalia noted that the word "witness" has several meanings: (1) a person who actually testifies in court; (2) an eyewitness; or (3) anybody whose statements are used as evidence.

21 541 U.S. at 43, 60.

22 *Id.* at 53–54 & n. 5.

23 *Id.* at 56.

24 Brendan Beery, "When Originalism Attacks: How Justice Scalia's Resort to Original Expected Application in *Crawford v. Washington* Came Back to Haunt Him in *Michigan v. Bryant*," 59 *Drake Law Review* 1047 (2011).

25 Melendez-Dias v. Massachusetts, 557 U.S. 305, 317 (2009), quoting *Crawford*.

26 547 U.S. 813 (2006).

27 *Id.* at 822. Thomas dissented in part on the ground that the earlier statements were admissible because they were not part of "a formalized dialogue" falling within the Confrontation Clause. *Id.* at 840. It seems that the less solemn the circumstances, the more admissible the unsworn statement. While this may be true of excited utterances, the principle has little support in the context of considered statements and it seems weak as the basis for a distinction of constitutional dimensions. *Cf.* Jones v. Thomas, 491 U.S. 376, 391 (1989) (Scalia, J., dissenting) (rejecting Court's distinguishing imprisonment+imprisonment from fine+imprisonment).

28 557 U.S. 305 (2009).

29 *Id.* at 329.

30 *Id.* at 330. Two years after Melendez-Diaz, a 5–4 majority, including Scalia, reversed a conviction in Bullcoming v. New Mexico, 131 S.Ct. 2705 (2011), where the testifying blood-alcohol analyst had neither conducted nor reviewed the test. Kennedy, joined by Rehnquist, Breyer, and Alito, argued that *Melendez-Diaz* should not be extended. "Here a knowledgeable representative of the laboratory was present to testify and to explain the lab's processes and the details of the report . . ." *Id.* at 2723. They also complained that the *Crawford* "line of cases has treated the reliability of evidence as a reason to exclude it." *Id.* at 2725.

31 131 S.Ct. 1143 (2011).

32 The prosecutor neglected to argue that the statement was a dying declaration.

33 *Id.* at 1168. One commentary called the majority's reasoning "absurd" but managed to put part of the responsibility on Scalia's shoulders: "Had he not anchored the Court to an unworkable, narrow, original expected application of the Confrontation Clause, the Court would not have had to resort to such unseemly contortions to reach its preferred result." Beery, 59 *Drake Law Review* at 1084.

34 131 S.Ct. at 1169–1170, 1174. Scalia chastised the Court for relying on the apparent reliability of the victim's statement, a test that *Crawford* explicitly rejected.

35 *Id.* at 1176. Ginsburg's dissent was a shorter and milder version of Scalia's.

36 554 U.S. 353 (2008).

37 *Id.* at 358–359.

38 *Id.* at 357–373. Scalia argued that considerable protections remained for women in abusive relationships, because *Crawford* applied only to *testimonial* statements and not to statements to friends or counselors or to nontestimonial statements to police. *Id.* at 374–377.

39 *Id.* at 401–406.

CHAPTER 12 SIXTH AMENDMENT: RIGHT TO COUNSEL

1 372 U.S. 335 (1963).

2 422 U.S. 806 (1975).

3 *Id.* at 834.

4 Neder v. United States, 527 U.S. 1, 31 (1999) (Scalia, concurring in part and dissenting in part).
5 The trial judge had wrongly disqualified counsel on the mistaken ground he had communicated with a represented party in violation of the state rules of professional conduct.
6 548 U.S. 140 (2006).
7 *Id.* at 147–148.
8 554 U.S. 164 (2008).
9 *Id.* at 167.
10 *Id.* at 177.
11 *Id.* at 180, 182, 185 (only Stevens joined Scalia).
12 *Id.* at 186–187.
13 317 U.S. 269, 280 (1942).
14 554 U.S. at 189.
15 Martinez v. Court of Appeal of California, 528 U.S. 152, 159 (2000) (Stevens, J.).
16 *Id.* at 165.

CHAPTER 13 SEVENTH AMENDMENT: RIGHT TO JURY TRIAL

1 Long before the eighteenth century, English courts were divided into law and equity. The chancellor in equity operated without a jury. In general, law courts awarded money damages while equity courts gave other relief, such as an injunction or restitution.
2 The Seventh Amendment has continually occupied the courts. *E.g.*, Frank W. Hackett, "Has a Trial Judge of a United States Court the Right to Direct a Verdict?," 24 *Yale Law Journal* 127 (1914).
3 *E.g.*, Akhil Reed Amar, *The Bill of Rights* 96 (1998).
4 481 U.S. 412 (1987).
5 *Id.* at 414.
6 *Id.* at 427.
7 *Id.* at 427, 428.
8 Granfinanciera, S.A. v. Nordberg, 492 U.S. 33 (1989).
9 *Id.* at 68.
10 Gasperini v. Center for Humanities, Inc., 518 U.S. 415, 434, 436–438 (1996).
11 Stevens's dissent iterated his support for the Court's interpretation of the 7th Amendment.
12 *Id.* at 467–468.
13 *Id.* at 450–451 (Justice Joseph Story specifically made that point sitting as a Circuit Judge in 1812).
14 *Id.* at 456–458.

CHAPTER 14 HABEAS CORPUS

1 71 U.S. 2 (1866).
2 317 U.S. 1 (1942).
3 18 U.S.C. § 4001(a).
4 542 U.S. 507 (2004).

5 For understandable reasons Thomas did not cite his "best" authority, Karematsu v. United States, 323 U.S. 214 (1944), the notorious Japanese-American internment case.

6 542 U.S. at 519.

7 *Id.* at 533.

8 *Id.* at 542–545.

9 *Id.* at 548–551.

10 *Id.* at 558.

11 *Id.* at 558–559.

12 *Id.* at 570.

13 *Id.* at 575–578.

14 Rasul v. Bush, 542 U.S. 466, 488 (2004); Hamdan v. Rumsfeld, 548 U.S. 557, 655 (2006); Boumediere v. Bush, 553 U.S. 723, 826 (2008).

CHAPTER 15 SEPARATION OF POWERS AND FEDERALISM

1 481 U.S. 787 (1987).

2 *Id.* at 793, 795, 796.

3 *Id.* at 800.

4 *Id.* at 804.

5 Brennan, Marshall, Blackmun, and Stevens. There is simply no way to tell whether a defendant was prejudiced. *See, e.g.,* Brady v. Maryland, 373 U.S. 83 (1963) (prosecution has duty of disclosure); *cf.* United States v. Gonzales-Lopez, 548 U.S. 140 (2006) (wrongful disqualification of defendant's counsel required reversal without showing prejudice).

6 481 U.S. at 815–816.

7 158 U.S. 564 (1895).

8 481 U.S. at 819.

9 Relying on *Young*, Scalia dissented in Chambers v. Nasco, Inc., 501 U.S. 32, 58, 60 (1991), where a judge imposed sanctions for a party's flagrant, bad-faith breach of contract and the Supreme Court affirmed. "[A] court's inherent power [does not] reach[] 'beyond the court's confines' that does not 'interfer[e] with the conduct of the trial. . . . [T]he district court here had no power to impose any sanctions for petitioner's flagrant, bad-faith breach of contract."* Kennedy (joined by Rehnquist and Souter) dissented separately.

10 28 U.S.C. §§ 591–599.

11 *E.g.,* Bernard Schwartz, "Administrative Law Cases during 1988," 41 *Administrative Law Review* 131 (1989) ("The *Morrison* decision represents a welcome departure from the Court's overrigid separation of powers approach in recent years.").

12 487 U.S. 654 (1988).

13 U.S. Const., Art. II, § 2, cl. 2.

14 487 U.S. at 670–678.

15 *Id.* at 677–685.

16 *Id.* at 693–696.

17 *Id.* at 698–699.

18 Boumediene v. Bush, 553 U.S. 723, 833 (2008) (Scalia, J., dissenting).

19 487 U.S. at 705; *see* Symposium, "The American Constitutional Tradition of Shared and Separated Powers," 30 *William & Mary Law Review* 209–431 (1989). Laurence Tribe and Michael Dorf called the majority opinion in *Morrison v. Olson* a case in which the Court relied on prior holdings "while ignoring their rationales." Earlier

decisions focused "clearly on the nature of the powers given to an official removable by the Executive," *Morrison* simply substituted an "unthinking balancing test." Tribe & Dorf, "Levels of Generality in the Definition of Rights," 57 *University of Chicago Law Review* 1057, 1082 (1990). Curiously, Article I states, "All legislative Powers herein granted show be vested in a Congress of the United States. . . . ," while Article II states, "The executive Power shall be vested in a President of the United States of America."

20 487 U.S. at 703–704.
21 Bernard Schwartz, who applauded *Morrison*, agreed with Scalia on this point. "Unless the Court is suggesting that, despite the 'good cause' restriction, the President's removal power is not limited, this statement is contrary to both language and the law. If the 'good cause' language was not intended to limit the removal power, why was it put in the statute?" Schwartz, *supra* at 136.
22 487 U.S. at 715–723.
23 *Id.* at 704.
24 *Id.* at 702–715.
25 *See* Hadley Arkes, *The Return of George Sutherland* 175–179 (1994).
26 487 U.S. at 726–727.
27 "The Federal Prosecutor," address delivered at the Second Annual Conference of United States Attorneys, April 1, 1940. www.justice.gov/&/04-01-1940.pdf.
28 487 U.S. at 727–734.
29 Ten years after *Morrison* Sunstein attacked the statute on the ground that "it imposes harmful incentives on Members of Congress, the media, and the independent counsel himself. . . . [I]t encourages scandal mongering. . . . " Sunstein, "Bad Incentives and Bad Institutions," 86 *Georgetown Law Journal* 2267, 2268–2269 (1998).
30 *See* Norman Dorsen, "Separation of Powers and Federalism: Two Doctrines with a Common Goal: Confining Arbitrary Power," 41 *Albany Law Review* 53 (1977).
31 Scalia voted with the unanimous Court to allow Paula Jones's lawsuit to proceed against Bill Clinton. Clinton v. Jones, 681, 702 (1992) (Stevens, J.) (the case "appears to us highly unlikely to occupy any substantial amount of petitioner's [Clinton's] time").
32 488 U.S. 361 (1989).
33 *Id.* at 384–397.
34 *Id.* at 380, 386, 395; *see* Maeva Marcus, "Separation of Powers in the Early National Period," 30 *William & Mary Law Review* 269 (1989) (drawing distinction between judges acting as a court and acting in a nonjudicial capacity).
35 *Id.* at 407.
36 *Id.* at 410.
37 131 S.Ct. 1632 (2011).
38 209 U.S. 123 (1908). Edward T. Young was a state official whom a federal court enjoined from enforcing a state statute it held unconstitutional. When Young violated the injunction, the court held him in contempt. Scalia described the holding in *Young*: "[B]ecause an unconstitutional legislative enactment is 'void,' a state official who enforces that law 'comes into conflict with the superior authority of [the] Constitution,' and therefore is 'stripped of his official or representative character and is subjected in his person to the consequences of his individual conduct. The State has no power to impart to him any immunity from responsibility to the supreme authority of the United States.'" 131 S.Ct. at 1638.

CHAPTER 16 COMMERCE CLAUSE AND OTHER PROVISIONS

1 132 S.Ct. 2566 (2012).
2 545 U.S. 1 (2005).
3 *Id.* at 5, 17.
4 514 U.S. 549 (1995). The plurality also distinguished United States v. Morrison, 529 U.S. 598 (2000), which invalidated the Violence against Women Act of 1994. Members of the plurality had dissented in *Lopez* and *Morrison*. Scalia was in the majority in the two cases. In *Lopez*, however, he joined Rehnquist's majority opinion rather than Thomas's originalist opinion. *See* Randy E. Barnett, "Scalia's Infidelity: A Critique of 'Faint-Hearted' Originalism," 75 *University of Cincinnati Law Review* 7, 14 (2006).
5 545 U.S. at 23.
6 317 U.S. 111 (1942).
7 545 U.S. at 23–33.
8 17 U.S. (4 Wheat.) 315, 421–422 (1819).
9 Note, "Scalia's *Raich* Concurrence: A Significant Departure from Originalist Interpretation?," 90 *Marquette Law Review* 1043, 1064–1065 (2007).
10 545 U.S. at 34.
11 *Id.* at 37–40; *see, e.g.*, United States v. Comstock, 560 U.S. 126, 172 (2010) (Thomas, J., dissenting) (quoting Madison that "the sweeping clause . . . only extend[s] to the enumerated powers," although Thomas cited only a nonverbatim account of a statement Madison supposedly made at a state ratifying convention, a remarkably weak piece of "legislative" history); *see* Jack T. Valauri, "Originalism and the Necessary and Proper Clause," 39 *Ohio Northern University Law Review* 773, 776, 792 (2013); Steven G. Calabresi, "A Critical Introduction to the Originalism Debate," 31 *Harvard Journal of Law & Public Policy* 875 (2008).
12 *See* Randy E. Barnett, "Scalia's Infidelity: A Critique of 'Faint-Hearted' Originalism," 75 *University of Cincinnati Law Review* 7, 14–16 (2006) (criticizing Scalia for not joining Thomas's originalist opinion). Chief Justice John Marshall produced a weaker definition of "necessary" than some, relying not on originalism – he cited no historical sources for his definition – but on the fact that "absolutely necessary" appeared in Art. I, § 10, so that "necessary" must mean something less, a textualist approach. *McCulloch*, 17 U.S. at 316, 388; *cf.* Chapter 15, n. 19.
13 132 S.Ct. at 2617.
14 *Id.* at 2646–2647 (citations omitted).
15 545 U.S. at 41 n. 3.
16 Scalia wrote two other liberal Commerce Clause opinions. In West Lynn Creamery, Inc. v. Healy, 512 U.S. 186, 207 (1994), he grudgingly concurred (with Thomas) in an opinion that held unconstitutional a milk-distribution system that charged fees to all fluid-milk producers and redistributed the fees to Massachusetts milk farmers as a subsidy. Rehnquist and Blackmun dissented. In Healy v. Beer Institute, Inc., 491 U.S. 324, 344 (1989), Scalia joined an opinion declaring unconstitutional a Connecticut statute that required out-of-state shippers of beer to affirm that their posted prices were, at the moment of posting, no higher than prices in neighboring states. Scalia's ground was that the statute facially discriminated against interstate commerce; the majority's was that the statute regulated out-of-state conduct. Rehnquist, Blackmun, and O'Connor dissented.
17 133 S.Ct. 2496 (2013).

18 The Jacob Wetterling Crimes against Children and Sexually Violent Offender Registration Act, 42 U.S.C. §§ 14071 *ff.*

19 133 S.Ct. at 2512–2514, 2516 (Thomas, J., dissenting).

20 *Id.* at 2509–2510 (Scalia, J., dissenting). Arguably, *Kebodeaux* is a conservative opinion because it abrogated federal power.

21 Peretz v. United States, 501 U.S. 923 (1991) (Scalia, J, dissenting).

22 Gomez v. United States, 490 U.S. 858 (1989).

23 On the merits Scalia concluded that magistrates did not have the power to conduct the *voir dire*, which was part of the trial and required supervision by an Article III judge. Thus, Scalia found himself unnecessarily deciding a constitutional issue.

24 Wellness Int'l Network, Ltd. v. Sharif, 135 S.Ct. 1932 (2015), allowed an Article I Bankruptcy Judge to hear matters ordinarily cognizable only before an Article III judge if no objection was made. Put differently, consent can create subject-matter jurisdiction. Dissenting, the four most conservative Justices said the decision should have rested on the ground that the case was within the jurisdiction of the Bankruptcy Court.

25 133 S.Ct. 2652 (2013).

26 *Id.* at 2668.

27 Whitman v. United States, 135 S.Ct. 352 (2014) (joined by Thomas).

28 It was not entirely clear whether Scalia's position was constitutionally based or not, and if so, on what constitutional provision. The rule of lenity is a proper component of separation of powers in the federal system, where federal courts cannot create federal crimes. However, the Constitution does not prohibit state courts from creating state common-law crimes, so long as there is proper notice and no other constitutional violation. This suggests that a state court could expand the scope of a state criminal statute on the basis of construction by a state agency under the executive's control. Thus, Scalia seems to have relied on a constitutional rule applicable only to the federal system because of its constitutional separation of powers. Scalia told me he agreed with my analysis.

CHAPTER 17 POLITICAL SPEECH

1 425 U.S. 1 (1976).

2 *Id.* at 14, 25–27, 45, 47.

3 *Id.* at 20–21, 39, 71 n. 85. Two years later, the Court struck down state statutes that prohibited corporations from expending their funds to promote issues, including in referendums, unrelated to their business. First Nat'l Bank of Boston v. Bellotti, 435 U.S. 765 (1978); *see* FEC v. Massachusetts Citizens for Life, Inc., 479 U.S. 238, 252 (1986) (federal statute requiring corporations to make independent political expenditure only through special segregated funds burdens corporate freedom of expression).

4 494 U.S. 652 (1990).

5 *Id.* at 660.

6 *Id.* at 667–668.

7 *Id.* at 695, 707.

8 *Id.* at 710.

9 *Id.* at 680. Scalia also challenged the exemption for media corporations. "Amassed corporate wealth that regularly sits astride the ordinary channels of information is

much more likely to produce the New Corruption (too much of one point of view) than amassed corporate wealth that is generally busy making money elsewhere." *Id.* at 691.

10 *Id.* at 684.
11 *Id.* at 679–680.
12 *Id.* at 693–644.
13 540 U.S. 93 (2002).
14 Souter, Ginsburg, and Breyer joined the opinion.
15 *Id.* at 134–143.
16 *Id.* at 291, 292.
17 *Id.* at 334–338. Rehnquist's dissent argued primarily that Title I of BCRA was overbroad. *Id.* at 350. Thomas's dissent argued that the evidence supporting the incursions on the First Amendment was far too "sparse" and far too unfocused to sustain BCRA. *Id.* at 264.
18 *Id.* at 248 (citations omitted).
19 *Id.* at 249. Scalia did not cite any authority to bar facially neutral laws that favored incumbents.
20 *Id.* at 252.
21 *Id.* at 256, quoting Roberts v. United States Jaycees, 468 U.S. 609, 622 (1984) (Brennan, J.).
22 *Id.* at 256–262. Arguably, there is a difference in relying on legislative history to discover the key issues as opposed to the meaning of a statute. *But see* Scalia & Garner, *Reading Law* 386–389 (2012). That would, however, undermine Scalia's approach in another context. Cornell, "A New Paradigm for the Second Amendment," 22 *Law & History Review* 161, 164–167 (2004) ("the subject of a private right to own firearms outside the militia was rarely discussed during the ratification debates, while the need to protect the militia from the threat posed by the Federal government received extensive commentary").
23 551 U.S. 449 (2007).
24 *Id.* at 499 n. 7.
25 558 U.S. 310 (2010).
26 *Id.* at 340, 348.
27 *Id.* at 386, 387, 392–393.
28 Scalia criticized on policy grounds political-action committees, at least compared to patronage, to fund political campaigns. "Increased reliance on money-intensive campaign techniques tends to entrench those in power more effectively than patronage – but without the attendant benefit of strengthening the party system. A challenger can more easily obtain the support of party workers (who can expect to be rewarded even if the candidate loses – if not this year, than the next) than the financial support of political action committees (which will generally support incumbents, who are likely to prevail)." Rutan v. Republican Party of Illinois, 497 U.S. 62, 106 (1990) (Scalia, J., dissenting).
29 558 U.S. at 423–425.
30 *Id.* at 413–414. The majority defended overruling recent precedent and Roberts devoted his entire concurring opinion to rebutting the argument that the Court violated the principle of *stare decisis. Id.* at 372.
31 *See* Mark Tushnet, *Taking the Constitution Away from the Courts* 131–133 (1999).
32 514 U.S. 334 (1995).
33 *Id.* at 347.

34 *Id.* at 357. In other words, the public might react negatively to certain advertisements paid for by enormously wealthy contributors.
35 *Id.* at 360–371.
36 Scalia's references to the understanding in 1868 suggested that he might have accepted different standards for freedom of the press and religion for states than the federal government. *Id.* at 375.
37 *Id.* at 371–374.
38 514 U.S. at 375–377.
39 *Id.* at 381–382, 385 (joined by Rehnquist).
40 561 U.S. 186 (2010).
41 *Id.* at 196, quoting Buckley v. Valeo, 424 U.S. 1, 64 (1976).
42 *Id.* at 220–221.
43 *Id.* at 228.
44 536 U.S. 765 (2002).
45 *Id.* at 774–775, 781.
46 *Id.* at 797, 802 (Stevens, J., dissenting).
47 *Id.* at 819 (Ginsburg, J., dissenting).
48 Williams-Yulee v. Florida Bar, 135 S.Ct. 1656 (2015) (Roberts, C.J.). The other dissenters were Thomas, Alito, and Kennedy.

CHAPTER 18 ANTIABORTION PICKETING

1 512 U.S. 753 (1994) (Rehnquist, C.J.).
2 519 U.S. 357 (1997) (Rehnquist, C.J.).
3 512 U.S. at 762.
4 530 U.S. 703 (2000) (Stevens, J.).
5 *Id.* at 716–717.
6 134 S.Ct. 2518 (2014) (Roberts, C.J.).
7 *Id.* at 2541.
8 530 U.S. at 790–792.
9 United States v. Virginia, 518 U.S. 515, 570 (1996).
10 512 U.S. at 784–785.
11 458 U.S. 886 (1982), citing NAACP v. Clairborne Hardware Co., 458 U.S. 886 (1982); *see Hill,* 530 U.S. at 800. Thomas and Kennedy generally joined Scalia.
12 134 S.Ct. at 2546. Originalists' and conservatives' views on antiabortion picketing are libertarian, although not on antiabortion bills themselves.
13 512 U.S. at 794, 797.
14 *Id.* at 812, 813.
15 530 U.S. at 803.
16 *Id.* at 794.
17 *Id.* at 748–751. Scalia dissented from the denial of *certiorari* in Lawson v. Murray, 525 U.S. 955 (1998), where the issue was the First Amendment rights of antiabortion picketers.

CHAPTER 19 FREE EXERCISE OF RELIGION

1 Kathleen M. Sullivan, "Justice Scalia and the Religion Clauses," 22 *Hawaii Law Review* 449, 466 (2000).
2 Sherbert v. Verner, 374 U.S. 398 (1963).

3 512 U.S. 687 (1994) (Souter, J.).

4 *Id.* at 723.

5 Hobbie v. Unemployment Appeals Comm'n of Florida, 480 U.S. 136 (1987); Frazee v. Illinois Dept. of Employment Security, 489 U.S. 829 (1989).

6 494 U.S. 872 (1990).

7 *Id.* at 895.

8 *Smith* rewrote the law. After *Smith*, it appears only laws targeting religion were unconstitutional.

9 *Id.* at 890.

10 Richard A. Brisbin, Jr., "Antonin Scalia, William Brennan, and the Politics of Expression: A Study of Legal Violence and Repression," 87 *American Political Science Review* 912, 916 (1993) (Scalia "very quickly moved to read the text to protect conduct as well as belief, repudiating a distinction first established over a century ago").

11 494 U.S. at 878–879.

12 *Id.* at 891 (O'Connor, J., concurring); *see id.* at 921 (Blackmun, J., dissenting).

13 The majority consisted of Rehnquist, White, Stevens, Scalia, and Kennedy; Brennan, Marshall, and Blackmun dissented but relied on the insufficiency of evidence that peyote use caused harm, which meant there was a failure to prove a compelling state interest.

14 *Id.* at 921.

15 508 U.S. 520 (1993).

16 *Id.* at 558–559.

17 42 U.S.C. § 2000bb *et seq.*

18 508 U.S. at 532–534.

19 521 U.S. 507 (1997).

20 *Id.* at 532, 534–535; *see* John T. Noonan, Jr., *Narrowing the Nation's Power* 25–31 (2002).

21 The Fourteenth Amendment enhanced federal power. Section 5 gave Congress power to define the scope of the Amendment.

22 521 U.S. at 537.

23 *Id.* at 539–544. Scalia claimed the dissent misconstrued early documents that excepted from compliance conduct other than that which kept the peace and maintained order. To Scalia early sources equated that with obeying the law, although he did not claim that his was the only possible interpretation of the early history on exemptions from neutral laws. *Id.* at 537–541. The historical record seems mixed. The literature is considerable.

CHAPTER 20 PUNITIVE DAMAGES

1 Earlier, the Court rejected challenges to punitive damages under the provision of the Constitution barring excessive fines on the ground that the clause applied only to the government. Browning-Ferris Industries v. Kelco Disposal, Inc., 492 U.S. 257 (1989).

2 Richard A. Brisbin, Jr., *Justice Antonin Scalia and the Conservative Revival* 90 (1997).

3 499 U.S. 1 (1991) (Blackmun, J.).

4 *Id.* at 18–19.

5 *Id.* at 27, 36–38.

6 *Id.* at 42–44.

7 *Id.* at 42–44, 46.

8 *Id.* at 60, 61–63.

9 509 U.S. 443 (1993).

10 The case was unusual because the claim for punitive damages was based on the act of bringing a lawsuit. Alliance claimed that TXO had "knowingly and intentionally brought a frivolous declaratory action" when its "real intent" was to reduce royalty payments it would owe under an oil and gas lease.

11 *Id.* at 470–472 (joined by Thomas). Scalia rejected the concept of substantive due process in, *e.g.*, Chavez v. Martinez, 538 U.S. 760, 780 (2003).

12 509 U.S. at 473.

13 517 U.S. 559 (1996).

14 *Id.* at 607. Ginsburg dissented in a calmer version of Scalia's dissent. In the third case in the *Haslip* mold, Scalia dissented in State Farm Mutual Auto. Ins. Co. v. Campbell, 538 U.S. 408 (2003), which overturned a punitive-damage award as excessive. In Philip Morris USA v. Williams, 556 U.S. 178 (2007) (5–4) (Breyer, J.), Scalia joined Ginsburg's dissent when the majority reversed on the ground that the punitive damages award was erroneously based on harm to others than the plaintiff.

15 Honda Motor Co. v. Oberg, 512 U.S. 415 (1994).

16 *Id.* at 430, 432.

17 *Id.* at 435–436. Ginsburg, joined by Rehnquist, dissented on the ground that the protections afforded in Oregon were far greater than in Alabama and "are adequate to pass the Constitution's due process threshold."

18 Cooper Industries, Inc. v. Leatherman Tool Group, Inc., 532 U.S. 424 (2001).

19 *Id.* at 443–444. Thomas announced that he would overrule BMW v. Gore.

CHAPTER 21   PEREMPTORY CHALLENGES

1 476 U.S. 79 (1986) (Burger, C.J.) (noting that peremptory challenges were allowed in eighteenth-century England as well as in the colonies, probably in ancient Greece and Rome, and were part of the First Judiciary Act). In Miller-El v. Cockrell, 537 U.S. 322 (2003), seven Justices held that the petitioner had presented sufficient evidence of prosecutor bias to warrant an appeal, which had been denied. Scalia's concurrence said it was a closer case than the majority said. Thomas dissented on the ground that since "petitioner has not shown, by clear and convincing evidence, that any peremptory strikes of black veniremen were exercised because of race, he does not merit a certificate of appealability (COA)." *Id.* at 354.

2 493 U.S. 474 (1990).

3 *Id.* at 487. Kennedy's concurrence suggested that he would have sustained a claim based on the Fourteenth Amendment's Equal Protection Clause. *Id.* at 488. Marshall, Brennan, Blackmun, and Stevens dissented.

4 499 U.S. 400 (1991) (Kennedy, J.).

5 *Id.* at 412.

6 *Id.* at 423–431 (joined by Rehnquist). Edmonson v. Leesville Concrete Co., 500 U.S. 614 (1991), extended to civil cases the bar against race-based peremptory challenges. Scalia dissented, along with O'Connor and Rehnquist, partly on the ground that the practice of peremptory challenges in civil cases, especially in conjunction with extensive *voir dire* of prospective jurors, was wasteful and inefficient, an unusual argument in a constitutional setting. When the Court extended the ban in J.E.B. v. Alabama, 511 U.S. 127 (1994), to include strikes based on gender, Scalia again dissented.

7 505 U.S. 42 (1992).

8 It has been widely accepted that the Warren Court's primary goal was to curb racist tendencies of many state criminal-justice institutions.

9 454 U.S. 312 (1981).

10 505 U.S. at 62–68.

11 *Id.* at 69, 70. This was an unusual case in which Thomas felt bound by *stare decisis* and Scalia did not. It was Thomas's first Term.

PART V ORIGINALISM RECONSIDERED

1 No attempt is made in this book to deal with recent and complex developments in historicism or the philosophy of language. *See, e.g.,* Saul Cornell, "Meaning and Understanding in the History of Constitutional Ideas: The Intellectual History Alternative to Originalism," 82 *Fordham Law Review* 721 (2013).

2 Attitudes changed within a generation of the framing for reasons that included spread of commerce, religious dissent, and organized party politics. Nelson, *Dispute and Conflict Resolution in Plymouth County, Massachusetts, 1725–1825,* at 152 (1981).

3 *The Founders' Constitution,* Vol. 1, ch. 18, doc. 9 (Philip B. Kurland & Ralph Lerner eds. 1987). Sunstein agreed: "The Framers were republicans, and they were republicans in the distinctive sense that they prized civic virtue and sought to promote deliberation in government – deliberation oriented toward right answers about the collective good. We cannot understand our constitutional heritage without resort to these points." Sunstein, "The Idea of a Usable Past," 95 *Columbia Law Review* 601, 605 (1995); *see* Martin Flaherty, "History 'Lite' in Modern American Constitutionalism," 95 *Columbia Law Review* 523 (1995); Reena Raggi, "A Dialogue with Federal Judges on the Role of History in Interpretation," 80 *George Washington Law Review* 1889, 1895 (2012).

4 Powell, *The Moral Tradition of American Constitutionalism* 70 n. 85 (1993).

5 Konig, "Why the Second Amendment Has a Preamble: Original Public Meaning and the Political Culture of Written Constitutions in Revolutionary America," 56 *U.C.L.A. Law Review* 1295, 1320–1321 (2009); Bernard Bailyn, *To Begin the World Anew; The Genius and Ambiguities of the American Founding* 34–35 (2003) ("In a morally enervated world overcome with corruption, America, they believed, was unique; and their sense of moral integrity; nourished in the awareness of provincial simplicity and innocence and discussed endlessly, almost obsessively, in their political writings, fortified and justified their determination to defy tradition, to build their own, different political world, and to create a new and permanent model for the benevolent use of power."); *see* Presser, *Recapturing the Constitution; Race, Religion, and Abortion Reconsidered* 87–90 (1994); Charles A. Miller, *The Supreme Court and the Uses of History* 49 (1969).

6 Wood, *The Creation of the American Republic* (1969).

7 Statement of Franklin at Constitutional Convention on June 2, 1787, reprinted in *The Anti-Federalist Papers and the Constitutional Convention Debates* 43–47 (Ralph Ketcham ed. 1986).

8 Men like John Hancock and Robert Morris ruined themselves trying to live up to that ideal. North *et al., Violence and Social Orders* at 264. Another study blamed Morris's rampant speculations for his financial downfall. Fergus M. Bordewich, *The First Congress* 301 (2016).

9 Reid, *Constitutional History of the American Revolution; The Authority of Law* 75–76 (1993); *see* Wood, *supra* at 306–307; Douglass C. North, John J. Wallis & Barry

R. Weingast, *Violence and Social Orders; A Conceptual Framework for Interpreting Recorded Human History* 190–193, 234–238 (2009). The late eighteenth century was a period of great political change in America, which went from colonies, to the Revolution, to the Articles of Confederation, to the Constitution. The most complex American period from a theoretical standpoint was the colonial experience. *See, e.g.,* Reid, "The Authority of Rights at the American Founding," in *The Nature of Rights at the American Founding and Beyond* 67–115 (Barry A. Shain ed. 2007).

10 Reid, *Authority of Law* at 73; *see* Miller, *supra* at 49 (1969) ("The framers did not believe that the welfare of the state was essentially different from the welfare of the people.").

11 Reid, *supra* at 135. Cornell was not impressed by the quality of originalism research regarding the 1790s. Cornell, *The Other Founders* at 222–230.

12 Reid, *supra* at 154.

13 Wood, *supra* at 238–242.

14 Robert A. Rutland, *The Birth of the Bill of Rights, 1776–1791,* at 109–110 (1955), quoting III *Records of the Federal Convention* 48 (Max Farrand ed.); *see* Mark E. Kann, *The Gendering of American Politics* xiv (1999) ("Most founders were convinced that ordinary men had dangerous passions, impulses and interests that threatened to subvert public order.").

15 Reid, *supra* at 79–80. Reid also discussed how the coercive acts Parliament enacted in 1774 fed a fear of legislative tyranny in the colonies. *Id.* at 40–42. While Americans embraced the monarch, the British did not. "There was no mistaking where British constitutionalists located liberty and which institution, everyone, even members of the ministry, identified as the one serious threat to liberty. Liberty was located in Parliament and the threat was from the crown." *Id.* at 163. "Given the British constitution of 1775 and the legacy of the Glorious Revolution, the choice was not only between the supremacy of Parliament and American legislative autonomy, it was also between the supremacy of Parliament and the king's prerogative." *Id.* at 172.

16 Louis Hartz, *The Liberal Tradition in America* 89, 121 (1955).

17 Wood, *The Purpose of the Past* 24–26 (2008). Woody Holton, *Unruly Americans and the Origins of the Constitution* 99–105, 145–161 (2007), argued that in the 1780s both pro-debtor state legislatures and agrarian insurrection, *e.g.,* the Shay's Rebellion, mostly against higher taxes, undermined the economy and created strong pressures for a strong national government. Legislatures, and sometimes the courts, protected farmers and fought attempts to repay and pay interest to holders of Revolutionary War bonds, which required high taxes or the issuance of large amounts of paper currency. Contributing to the malaise was a recession that gripped the colonies in the 1780s. Holton referred to the "chasm in Americans' attitudes toward state governments that emerged from the Revolutionary War." *Id.* at 175.

18 Wood, *The Idea of America* 238–239 (2011). Before 1774, "American monarchism was the logical product of their attachment to the principle of the old English constitution, the proof of their sincerity to constitutionalism." Americans would salute the English monarch. Reid, *supra* at 152. Madison's notes of the Constitutional Convention described Hamilton's argument for the election of a President for life. Mary Sarah Bilder, *Madison's Hand; Revising the Constitutional Convention* (2015).

19 Tyranny was associated with arbitrary power, which was the antithesis of liberty. *See* John P. Reid, *The Concept of Liberty in the Age of the American Revolution* 57–59, 65–67 (1988).

20 *E.g.*, Stephen B. Presser, *The Original Misunderstanding* 21–36 (1991); Nelson, *Marbury v. Madison* at 36–37.
21 H. Jefferson Powell, "The Political Grammar of Early Constitutional Law," 71 *North Carolina Law Review* 949, 1008 (1993).
22 *E.g.*, Saul Cornell, "'To Assemble Together for Their Common Good': History, Ethnography, and the Original Meanings of the Rights of Assembly and Speech," 84 *Fordham Law Review* 915 (2015); *see* Bernard Bailyn, *Sometimes an Art; Nine Essays on History* 103–104 (2015) (noting similar changes in England).
23 Two legal historians criticized a third as appearing "to have had a lawyer's perspective on legal history, which led him to view contract law as essentially a body of rules and principles that have not changed since they were first imported into English law in the late sixteenth and seventeenth centuries" rather than "understanding that contract law, like all law, responds to social and economic change," including how "ambiguous eighteenth century materials [showed] how contract law responded to the nation's shift from a pre-capitalist, agrarian economy to a bourgeois, industrialist one." William E. Nelson & Reid, *The Literature of American Legal History* 314 (1985).
24 Virginia jurist Abel Parker Upshur observed in 1840 that "[t]he Constitution is much better understood at this day than it was at the time of its adoption." Jack N. Rakove, "Early Uses of *The Federalist*," in *Saving the Revolution* 245 (Charles R. Kesler ed. 1987).
25 Georg C. Iggers, *Historiography in the Twentieth Century: From Scientific Objectivity to the Postmodern Challenge* 8–9 (1997).
26 *See, e.g.*, Alfred H. Kelly, "Clio and the Court: An Illicit Love Affair," 1965 *Supreme Court Review* 119, 122 n. 13 ("By 'law-office history,' I mean the selection of data favorable to the position being advanced without regard to or concern for contradictory data or proper evaluation of the relevance of the data proffered."). An example might be a partner telling an associate, "Get me something from *The Federalist* that we can cite in this argument."

CHAPTER 22   FUNDAMENTALS RECONSIDERED: TEXTUALISM
AND ORIGINALISM

27 J. Harvie Wilkinson III, *Cosmic Constitutional Theory* 57 (2012).
28 1 Joseph Story, *Commentaries on the Constitution of the United States* 288 (1858).
29 H. Jefferson Powell, *A Community Built on Words* 30 (2002).
30 Powell, "The Political Grammar of Early Constitutional Law," 71 *North Carolina Law Review* 949, 996 (1993).
31 Hamilton, *Opinion on the Constitutionality of the Bank* (Feb. 23, 1791), reprinted in Powell, *Languages of Power* 43 (1991).
32 A language scholar said that "[t]he process of legislation itself is plagued with strategic behavior that tries to overcome the lack of initial cooperation between the relevant agents." Andrei Marmor, "On Some Pragmatic Aspects of Strategic Speech," in *Language in the Law* 98 (Marmor & Scott Soames eds. 2011).
33 Of course, how the courts treat language may affect the practice of drafters both in trying to be clear and trying to be unclear. *Id.* at 100–104.
34 Madison and Hamilton pressed for a vague Art. V, cl. 1, which avoided an explicit statement that the new federal government would redeem Revolutionary War bonds

at par. Woody Holton, *Unruly Americans and the Origins of the Constitution* 215 (2007).

35   Andrew Tutt, "Fifty Shades of Textualism," 29 *Journal of Law & Policy* 309, 313 (2014).

36   Note, "Textualism and the Presumption of Reasonable Drafting," 38 *Harvard Journal of Law & Policy* 711, 712 (2015), quoting John F. Manning, "Textualism and Legislative Intent," 91 *Virginia Law Review* 419, 420 (2005).

37   Posner, "What Is Obviously Wrong with the Federal Judiciary, Yet Eminent Curable, Part II," 19 *Green Bag 2d* 257, 265 (2016); Posner, *Reflections on Judging* 186–187, 205–218, 353 (2013). Posner and Scalia became embroiled in a personal dispute over Scalia's textualism, which included the correctness of citations used to substantiate judicial use of canons in *Reading Law*. Posner, "The Incoherence of Antonin Scalia," *New Republic*, Aug. 24, 2012; William Domnarski, *Richard Posner* 228–231 (2016). Breyer argued that canons are not applied consistently and therefore fail to accomplish their purpose. Breyer, *Active Liberty*; *Interpreting Our Democratic Constitution* 99 (2005); *but see* John F. Manning, "Legal Realism & the Canons' Revival," 5 *Green Bag 2d* 283 (2002).

38   Posner, *supra* at 198–205.

39   *Id.* at 200. "Judges do discuss the meanings of words and sometimes look for those meanings in dictionaries, but they don't stop there." *Id.* at 204–205. For an excellent example, see Frigaliment Importing Co. v. B.N.S. Int'l Sales Corp., 190 F. Supp. 116 (S.D.N.Y. 1960), discussed in David M. Dorsen, *Henry Friendly, Greatest Judge of His Era* 315–317 (2012).

40   Posner, *supra* at 209–219.

41   Eskridge, "The New Textualism and Normative Canons," 113 *Columbia Law Review* 531, 540 (2013); *see* Abbe Gluck & Lisa Schultz Bressman, "Statutory Interpretations from the Inside: An Empirical Study of Legislative Drafting, Delegation, and the Canons," 65 *Stanford Law Review* 901 (2013); Karl N. Llewellyn, "Remarks on the Theory of Appellate Decisions and the Rules or Canons about How Statutes Are to Be Construed," 3 *Vanderbilt Law Review* 395 (1950).

42   Treanor, "Taking Text Too Seriously: Modern Textualism, Original Meaning, and the Case of Amar's *Bill of Rights*," 106 *Michigan Law Review* 487, 523 (2007); *but see* John F. Manning, "The Role of the Philadelphia Convention in Constitutional Adjudication," 80 *George Washington Law Review* 1753, 1785–1793 (2012) (great care at Philadelphia Convention paid to specific language in Constitution).

43   Robert Post, "Theories of Constitutional Interpretation," 30 *Representations* 13 (1990); Powell, "The Original Understanding of Original Intent," 98 *Harvard Law Review* 885 (1985); Robert A. Burt, "Precedent and Authority in Antonin Scalia's Jurisprudence," 12 *Cardozo Law Review* 1685, 1688–1693 (1991); Mark Tushnet, "A Note on the Revival of Textualism in Constitutional Theory," 58 *Southern California Law Review* 682 (1985); Frederick Schauer, "Formalism," 97 *Yale Law Journal* 509 (1988); *but see* Alexander Hamilton, *Opinion on the Constitutionality of the Bank* (Feb. 23, 1791), reprinted in Powell, *Languages of Power* 43 (1991) ("whatever may have been the intention of the framers of a constitution, or of a law, that intention is to be sought for in the instrument itself, according to the usual & established rules of construction.").

44   68 *University of Chicago Law Review* 101 (2001); *see* City of Boerne v. Flores, 521 U.S. 507, 543 (1997) (Scalia, J., concurring) ("I have limited this response to the new items of 'historical evidence' brought forward by today's dissent.").

45   This approach creates incentives to misrepresent history.

46 There are also new trends in historiography, such as more attention to background and to the "interior worlds" of participants. Bernard Bailyn, *Sometimes an Art* 53–79 (2015).

47 Soames, "What Vagueness and Inconsistency Tell Us about Interpretation," in *Language in the Law* 49–51 (Marmor & Soames eds. 2011). Soames's approach is not ideologically grounded; for example, it rejects the broad right of privacy articulated in Griswold v. Connecticut, 381 U.S. 479 (1965). "Although the contents of the constitutional guarantees [Douglas] mentions may, legitimately, evolve over time to better serve their motivating purposes, and although each may correctly be said to have been aimed at securing privacy (of a certain sort), such a characterization is incomplete, and insufficiently specific. Once this defect is eliminated, and the purposes governing the constitutional provisions are fully and specifically stated, the resulting set of privacy rights – though open ended and subject to continuing change – does not encompass any general right to privacy that prohibits contraception or abortion." Soames, *supra* at 56–57.

48 Ralph A. Rossum, *Antonin Scalia's Jurisprudence; Text and Tradition* 111 (2006). Rossum also questioned Scalia's approach to § 5 of the Fourteenth Amendment (granting Congress the power to legislate), which Scalia confined to racial issues. *Id.* at 106–124; *see* Tennessee v. Lane, 541 U.S. 509, 564 (2004) (Scalia, J., dissenting).

49 Conroy v. Aniskoff, 507 U.S. 511, 519 (1993) (Scalia, J., concurring in judgment); *see* Herschey v. FERC, 777 F.2d 1, 7–8 (D.C. Cir. 1985) (Scalia, J., concurring).

50 Royal charters had some of the characteristics of constitutions. Bernard Bailyn, *The Ideological Origins of the American Revolution* 190–193 (1967).

51 Jack N. Rakove, *Original Meanings* 58 (1996).

52 Saul Cornell, "Meaning and Understanding in the History of Constitutional Ideas: The Intellectual History Alternative to Originalism," 82 *Fordham Law Review* 721, 732–733 (2013). Cornell explained that the purpose and context of a communication were essential to its understanding. This included the identity of the speaker and the person hearing it. *See* Daniel J. Boorstein, "The Real Constitution," *Commentary* (Dec. 1953), p. 604.

53 *See* Wood, *The Creation of the American Republic* 268–271 (1969).

54 The use of similar but nonidentical language in state constitutions has been used to support the argument both that the federal Constitution should be construed identically with the state constitutions, District of Columbia v. Heller, 554 U.S. 570, 600–603 (2008) (Scalia, J.), and that the Constitution should be construed to mean something different, *id.* at 646–648 (Stevens, J., dissenting).

55 Kramer, "Two (More) Problems with Originalism," 31 *Harvard Journal of Law & Public Policy* 907, 912 (2008). Blackstone and tradition offered some guiding principles.

56 Konig, "Why the Second Amendment Has a Preamble: Original Public Meaning and the Political Culture of Revolutionary America," 56 *U.C.L.A. Law Review* 1295, 1316 (2009).

57 Kramer, "Panel on Originalism and Pragmatism," in *Originalism; A Quarter-Century of Debate* 154–155 (Steven G. Calabresi ed. 2007); *see generally, e.g.*, Presser, *The Original Misunderstanding* (1991) (judicial career of Samuel Chase in context of Federalist-Republican cross-currents); Martin Flaherty, "History Right? Historical Scholarship, Original Understanding, and Treaties as Supreme Law of the Land," 99 *Columbia Law Review* 2095 (1999); Stephen M. Griffin, "Rebooting Originalism," 2008 *University of Illinois Law Review* 1185.

58 Edward A. Purcell, Jr., *Originalism, Federalism, and the American Constitutional Enterprise* 182 (2007).

59 Easterbrook, "Pragmatism's Role in Interpretation," 31 *Harvard Journal of Law & Public Policy* 901, 902 (2008).

60 Rakove, *Original Meanings* at xv.

61 Stephen B. Presser, *Recapturing the Constitution* 35–36, 115–123, 133–136, 142 (1994). Acceptance of natural law and natural rights was common and included Chief Justice John Marshall. Morton J. Frisch, "John Marshall's Philosophy of Constitutional Republicanism" in *The American Founding* 141–142 (Rossum & Gary L. McDowell eds. 1981).

62 A number of late-eighteenth-century decisions challenged statutes on the ground they violated "the laws of nature," including the *Writ of Assistance Case* in 1763, which unsuccessfully challenged a search warrant. Some state courts invalidated legislation on this ground well into the 1790s. William E. Nelson, *Marbury v. Madison* 36–37 (2000). Framing-era reliance on natural law, which is outside the Constitution, lends support to the claim for unenumerated rights.

63 Cornell, "*Heller*, New Originalism, and 'Law Office History': 'Meet the Boss, Same as the Old Boss,'" 56 *U.C.L.A. Law Review* 1095, 1106 (2009).

64 Richard A. Posner, "In Defense of Looseness," *New Republic*, Aug. 27, 2008 (nonoriginalist theorists seek rationales for deviations from original understanding).

65 Kurt T. Lash, "Originalism All the Way Down?," 30 *Constitutional Commentary* 149, 165 (2014); Aaron T. Knapp, "Law's Revolutionary: James Wilson and the Birth of American Jurisprudence," 29 *Journal of Law & Politics* 189, 224–231 (2013).

66 Reid, *The Concept of Liberty in the Age of the American Revolution* 114 (1988).

67 Nelson, *Marbury v. Madison* at 15, 34.

68 Rakove, *Saving the Revolution* at 262–263, 285.

69 Cornell, 82 *Fordham Law Review* at 739–740. For example, the hoi polloi read a radical publication called the *Centinel*. Pauline Maier, *Ratification: The People Debate the Constitution, 1787–1788*, at 75–77, 80–83 (2010).

70 Cornell, 82 *Fordham Law Review* at 752; *see id.* at 722–724; Rebecca L. Brown, "History for the Non-Originalist," 26 *Harvard Journal of Law & Public Policy* 69, 71 (2003).

71 *E.g.*, Wood, *The Creation of the American Republic* (1969); Nelson, *Marbury v. Madison* 23–24, 30–32 (2000).

72 Powell, *A Community Built on Words* 65 (2001).

73 Bruce H. Mann, "Afterword: The Death and Transfiguration of Early American History," in *The Many Legalities of Early America* 446 (Christopher L. Tomlins and Mann eds. 2001).

74 Wood, *The Idea of America* 18 (2011); *see generally* William E. Nelson, *The Common Law in Colonial America (Vol. III): The Chesapeake and New England Colonies* (2016); Rakove, *Original Meanings* (1996).

75 Wood, *The Purpose of the Past* 271 (2008) (collection of his book reviews). Wood identified flaws in nonhistorical thinking, including Whiggism, the "anachronistic foreshortening that makes the past a mere anticipation of what would later occur," and presentism, which sees the past through the assumptions and concept of the present. *Id.* at 174–175, 273–308.

76 Speech in House of Representatives, Feb. 3, 1791, in Powell, *Languages of Power* 40–41 (1991).

77 Opinion on the Constitutionality of an Act to Establish a Bank, February 23, 1791, in *id.* at 43–50.

78 *Id.* at 54. The constitutionality of a national bank was considered a close question. Ron Chernow, *Alexander Hamilton* 350–355 (2004).

79 Another fundamental issue that the First Congress confronted was whether the President had the power to remove a member of the Cabinet without the Senate's approval. There was no automatic response. Rakove, "Early Uses of *The Federalist*," in *Saving the Revolution* (235–236) (Charles R. Kesler ed. 1987); Frank B. Cross, *The Failed Promise of Originalism* 68 (2013).

80 Charles Fried, *Order and Law* 66 (1991).

81 Mitchell N. Berman, "Originalism Is Bunk," 84 *New York University Law Review* 1, 62 (2009), quoting Keith E. Whittington, *Constitutional Interpretation: Textual Meaning, Original Intent, and Judicial Review* 62–65 (1999).

82 Leonard W. Levy, *Original Intent and the Framers' Constitution* (1988). A study of Madison and his note taking concluded that Madison revised his notes both to alter the tone of the debate and to make them more compatible with his later thinking. Mary Sarah Bilder, *Madison's Hand* 89, 96–103, 141, 188, 216–220, 226, 245–247, 253–254 (2015). *But see* Robert N. Clinton, "Original Understanding, Legal Realism, and the Interpretation of 'This Constitution,'" 72 *Iowa Law Review* 1177, 1197–1208 (noting references to participants' recollection of Convention in early congressional debates).

83 *The Federalist* No. 52; James Madison in Congress, April 6, 1796.

84 Hylton v. United States, 3 U.S. (3 Dall.) 121 (1796) (deciding what is a "direct tax" under Art. 1, § 9).

85 Rakove, "Fidelity through History (or to It)," 65 *Fordham Law Review* 1587, 1604–1605 (1997); *see* Powell, "The Original Understanding of Original Intent," 98 *Harvard Law Review* 885 (1985); Paul Brest, "The Misconceived Quest for the Original Understanding," 60 *Boston University Law Review* 236 (1980).

86 Manning, "The Role of the Philadelphia Convention in Constitutional Adjudication," 80 *George Washington Law Review* 1753, 1758–1760 (2012). Manning gave examples of the care with which the Convention reached certain compromises, including the Electoral College and the impeachment process. *Id.* at 1786–1791. But those debates and resolutions say little that helps decide the major constitutional issues of today.

87 To a smaller extent, the situation is the same for multiclause constitutional amendments.

88 Maier, *Ratification*. Major differences among the states were also reflected in the diversity of proposed amendments to the Constitution. *See* Maeva Marcus, "The Adoption of the Bill of Rights," 1 *William & Mary Bill of Rights Law Review* 115 (1988).

89 *E.g.*, Rakove, 65 *Fordham Law Review* at 1600–1601.

90 Rakove, *Original Meanings* at 353–354.

91 *E.g.*, Cohens v. Virginia, 19 U.S. (6 Wheat.) 264, 418 (1821) (Marshall, C.J.) ("The opinion of the *Federalist* has always been considered as of great authority."); *but see* McCulloch v. Maryland, 17 U.S. (4 Wheat.) 316, 433 (1819) (rejecting defense counsel's use of *The Federalist*); *see* Bailyn, *To Begin the World Anew* 126–130 (2003) (*The Federalist* cited sparingly until New Deal litigation).

92 Alison L. LaCroix, *The Ideological Origins of American Federalism* 217 (2010).

93 Levy, *Original Intent and the Framers' Constitution* at 48; Jeffrey A. Segal & Harold J. Spaeth, *The Supreme Court and the Attitudinal Model* 59 (1993) (*The Federalist* was "political propaganda"); William N. Eskridge, Jr., "The New Textualism," 37 *U.C.L.A. Law Review* 621, 683 (1990) (same); Eskridge, "Should the Supreme Court

Read *The Federalist* but Not Legislative History?," 66 *George Washington Law Review* 1301 (1998); Jamal Greene, "The Case for Original Intent," 80 *George Washington Law Review* 1683, 1693–1694 (2012); Rakove, "Early Uses of *The Federalist*," in *Saving the Revolution* at 248 ("it had been written originally as a partisan tract)."

94 David F. Epstein, "The Case for Ratification: Federalist Constitutional Thought," in *The Framing and Ratification of the Constitution* 293 (Levy & Mahoney eds. 1987).

95 The Bill of Rights was a departure from previous recitations of rights by omitting declarations of eternal principles. Daniel J. Elazar, "How Present Conceptions of Human Rights Shape the Protection of Rights in the United States," in *Old Rights & New* 41 (Robert A. Licht ed. 1993).

96 *See* Reid, *The Authority of Rights* 227–237 (1986).

97 Madison, initially no fan of a bill of rights, switched positions to win election to the House of Representatives over James Monroe. Levy, *Origins of the Bill of Rights* 32, 38–39 (1999).

98 Levy, *Original Intent* at 163–168, 292–293; *see* Fergus M. Bordewich, *The First Congress* 116–120 (2016).

99 "[S]ome legal theorists defined the word 'constitution' to mean security of rights." Reid, *The Authority of Rights* at 6.

100 Cornell, *The Other Founders* at 159–164; Robert A. Rutland, *The Birth of the Bill of Rights, 1776–1791* at 198, 213 (1955).

101 *Id.* at 166–187.

102 Wood, "The Supreme Court and the Uses of History," 39 *Ohio Northern University Law Review* 435, 443 (2013).

103 Eisgruber, *Constitutional Self-Government* 43 (2001); *see* Joel Alicea & Donald Drakeman, "The Limits of New Originalism," 15 *University of Pennsylvania Journal of Constitutional Law* 1161 (2013) ("Broadly speaking, the question is what to do with too much evidence pointing in too many directions.").

104 Cornell, 82 *Fordham Law Review* at 721–724, 752; *see* Powell, 71 *North Carolina Law Review* at 957–964.

105 Rakove, "Joe the Ploughman Reads the Constitution, or, the Poverty of Public Meaning Originalism," 48 *San Diego Law Review* 575, 577, 584–588 (2011).

106 Flaherty, 95 *Columbia Law Review* at 553. In Missouri v. Holland, 252 U.S. 416, 433–434 (1920), a case involving state power in the context of a treaty, Justice Holmes stated that the Framers "have called into life a being the development of which could not have been foreseen completely by the most gifted of the begetters.... [I]t has taken a century and cost their successors much sweat and blood to prove that they have created a nation. The case before us must be considered in the light of our whole experience and not merely in that of what was said a hundred years ago.... We must consider what this country has become in deciding what [the Tenth] Amendment has reserved." *See generally* James Willard Hurst, *Justice Holmes on Legal History* (1964).

107 Jonathan Gienapp, "Historicism and Holism: Failures of Originalist Translation," 84 *Fordham Law Review* 935, 942–943, 955 (2015).

108 Bailyn, *Sometimes an Art* 22 (2015); *id.* at 14 ("History ... is the critical, skeptical, empirical source-bound reconstruction of past events, circumstances, and people based on the belief that the past is not only distant from us but also different.

Historians look for differences in the past and for how those differences changed and evolved to create the world we know, which contains, however deeply buried, the residues of those past worlds.").

109 Posner, "What Is Obviously Wrong with the Federal Judiciary, Yet Eminent Curable, Part I," 19 *Green Bag 2d* 187, 200 (2016).

110 One scholar called Scalia's use of 200-year-old treatises and histories "specious." L. Benjamin Young, Jr., "Justice Scalia's History and Tradition: The Chief Nightmare in Professor Tribe's Anxiety Closet," 78 *Virginia Law Review* 581, 590 (1991); *see* James J. Brudney & Lawrence Baum, "Oasis or Mirage: The Supreme Court's Thirst for Dictionaries in the Rehnquist and Roberts Eras," 55 *William & Mary Law Review* 483 (2013); Frank B. Cross, *The Failed Promise of Originalism* 56 (2013). John Adams was especially hostile to English dictionaries, which he declared were vestiges of the same British tyranny that the American Revolution destroyed forever. "We are no more bound by Johnson's Dictionary than by the Cannon [*sic*] Law of England." Joseph J. Ellis, *Founding Brothers* 226 (2000). Judge Learned Hand noted that "it is one of the surest indexes of a mature and developed jurisprudence not to make a fortress out of the dictionary." Cabell v. Markham, 148 F.2d 737, 739 (2d Cir. 1966); *but see* Stephan G. Calabresi & Andrea Matthews, "Originalism and *Loving v. Virginia*," 2012 *Brigham Young Law Review* 1393, 1396 (2013) ("The best indicia of original public meaning come from dictionaries and grammar books that are widely in use at the time a law is passed.").

111 Charles A. Miller, *The Supreme Court and the Uses of History* 111 (1969).

112 Cornell, 56 *U.C.L.A. Law Review* at 1099.

113 Flaherty, "History 'Lite' in Modern American Constitutionalism," 95 *Columbia Law Review* 523, 525–526, 529, 553, 557–567 (1995) ("constitutional discourse is replete with historical assertions that are at best deeply problematical and at worst, 'howlers'"; Epstein erroneously conflated Locke, Blackstone, and the Takings Clause in the Constitution); David Dow, "When Words Mean What We Believe They Say: The Case of Article V," 76 *Iowa Law Review* 1 (1990); Treanor, "Taking Text Too Seriously: Modern Textualism, Original Meaning, and the Case of Amar's *Bill of Rights*," 106 *Michigan Law Review* 487 (2007) (criticizing Amar for drawing inferences from the order of Bill of Rights, which were placed in the order convenient for insertion seriatim into the Constitution).

114 Sunstein, "The Idea of a Usable Past," 95 *Columbia Law Review* 601, 605 (1995).

115 Wood, 39 *Ohio Northern University Law Review* at 449.

116 Involving historians in litigation tends to create "an awkward and possibly corrupting role to have them start to play the part of advocates in a particular case." Reena Raggi, "A Dialogue with Federal Judges on the Role of History in Interpretation," 80 *George Washington Law Review* 1889, 1907 (2012); *see* Rakove, *Original Meanings* 9–10 (1996).

117 Miller, *supra* at 111.

118 Cornell, "'To Assemble Together for Their Common Good': History, Ethnography, and the Original Meanings of the Rights of Assembly and Speech," 84 *Fordham Law Review* 915, 918–919 (2015).

119 Nelson, "Emerging Notions of Modern Criminal Law in the Revolutionary Era: An Historical Perspective," 42 *N.Y.U. Law Review* 450, 451 (1967).

120 Moreover, given the diversity of laws and practices in the thirteen states and the limited communication among them, it is far, far less likely that there would be consensus in the late-eighteenth-century United States than among the nine Justices

of the Supreme Court, whose cultures are very similar and who communicate constantly.

121 The complex relationship between English law and colonial law, especially Rhode Island's, was the subject of Bilder, *The Transatlantic Constitution; Colonial Legal Culture and the Empire* (2004). Historians, including Cornell, have rejected the assumption, moreover, that the populace listened to lawyers on the meaning of the Constitution the same way they listened to lawyers on practical law. Another study went further, stating that "a thoroughgoing popular revolt against professional lawyers and the laws on which they relied convulsed nearly all the states in the decade after Independence." Aaron T. Knapp, "Law's Revolutionary: James Wilson and the Birth of American Jurisprudence," 29 *Journal of Law & Politics* 189, 234 (2013).

122 Cornell, "The People's Constitution versus the Lawyers' Constitution: Popular Constitutionalism and the Original Debate over Originalism," 23 *Yale Journal of Law & Humanities* 295, 301 (2011).

123 48 *San Diego Law Review* 575 (2011); *see* Ilya Somin, "Originalism and Political Ignorance," 97 *Minnesota Law Review* 625 (2012).

124 Cornell, "Originalism on Trial: The Use and Abuse of History in *District of Columbia v. Heller*," 69 *Ohio State Law Review* 625, 631 (2008).

125 Scalia, "Originalism: The Lesser Evil," 57 *University of Cincinnati Law Review* 849, 856 (1989).

126 *Id.* at 860–861.

127 *Id.* at 856–861.

128 *Id.* at 856–857.

129 Scalia, *A Matter of Interpretation* 45 (1997).

130 554 U.S. 570 (2008).

131 505 U.S. 833, 970 (1992).

132 *E.g.*, Arizona v. Hicks, 480 U.S. 321 (1987) (what constitutes a search and seizure); Morrison v. Olson, 487 U.S. 654 (1988) (separation of powers); Employment Div., Dept. of Human Resources of Oregon v. Smith, 494 U.S. 872 (1990) (free exercise of religion); Printz v. United States, 521 U.S. 898 (1997) (federal government commandeering state employees to enforce federal statute); Crawford v. Washington, 514 U.S. 36 (2004) (right to confront witnesses); McCreary County v. ACLU, 545 U.S. 844 (2005) (public displays of religious symbols); Citizens United v. FEC, 558 U.S. 350 (2010) (unfettered independent campaign spending); McDonald v. City of Chicago, 561 U.S. 742 (2010) (state gun-control statute); Brown v. Entertainment Merchants Ass'n, 131 S.Ct. 2729 (2011) (violent video games). During the twenty-one years of the Rehnquist Court, *The Federalist* was cited in 112 cases; in 21 of those, or 18 percent, it was cited by opinions that disagreed with one another. Matthew J. Festa, "Dueling Federalists: Supreme Court Decisions with Multiple Opinions Citing *The Federalist*, 1986–2007," 31 *Seattle Law Review* 75, 96–97 (2007).

133 Dallin H. Oaks, "Legal History in the High Court – Habeas Corpus," 64 *Michigan Law Review* 451, 472 (1966).

134 William G. Merkel, "*The District of Columbia v. Heller* and Antonin Scalia's Perverse Sense of Originalism," 13 *Lewis & Clark Law Review* 349, 364 (2009); *see* Killenbeck, 16 *University of Pennsylvania Journal of Constitutional Law* at 293–299 ("Justice Anthony Kennedy's clever but misleading embrace of the notion that the Founders 'split the atom of sovereignty,' [is] a theoretical device that is wrong, wrong, wrong as a matter of science, history, and constitutional policy").

135 Davies, 13 *Lewis & Clark Law Review* at 658.
136 Davies, "The Fictional Character of Law-and-Order Originalism: A Case Study of the Distortions and Evasions of Framing-Era Arrest Doctrine in *Atwater v. Lago Vista*," 37 *Wake Forest Law Review* 239, 245 (2002). Souter wrote for the Court that the arrest, replete with handcuffs and detention, of a "soccer mom" for driving without a seatbelt did not violate the Fourth Amendment and was supported by history.
137 Davies, 13 *Lewis & Clark Law Review* at 667–668.
138 Matthew D. Bunker & Clay Calvert, "Contrasting Concurrences of Clarence Thomas: Deploying Originalism and Paternalism in Commercial and Student Speech Cases," 26 *Georgia State Law Review* 346 (2010); *see* Mark A. Graber, "Clarence Thomas and the Perils of Amateur History," in *Rehnquist Justice* 89 (Earl M. Maltz ed. 2003).
139 Levy, *Original Intent and the Framers' Constitution* at 300. Easterbrook said that lawyers use history terribly. Raggi, 80 *George Washington Law Review* at 1890. Tushnet criticized the historical work of Raoul Berger, an icon of an earlier generation. Tushnet, *Red, White, and Blue* 37 n. 55 (1988).
140 Powell, "Rules for Originalists," 73 *Virginia Law Review* 659, 661 (1987); *see, e.g.*, Andrew Koppelman, "Phony Originalism and the Establishment Clause," 103 *Northwestern University Law Review* 727, 749 (2009) ("the 'originalism' that one now finds on the Supreme Court is a phony originalism which is opportunistically used to advance substantive positions that the judges find congenial").
141 Morgan Cloud, "A Conclusion in Search of a History to Support It," 43 *Texas Tech Law Review* 29, 32 (2010).
142 Powell, *supra* at 664–665; *see* Calabresi, "The Tradition of the Written Constitution: Text, Precedent, and Burke," 57 *Alabama Law Review* 635 (2006); David A. Strauss, "Originalism, Conservatism, and Judicial Restraint," 34 *Harvard Journal of Law & Public Policy* 137 (2010).
143 Davies, "Selective Originalism: Sorting Out Which Aspects of *Giles*'s Forfeiture Exception to Confrontation Were or Were Not 'Established at the Time of the Founding,'" 13 *Lewis & Clark Law Review* 605, 609–611 (2009).

CHAPTER 23 FUNDAMENTALS RECONSIDERED: OTHER DOCTRINES

1 Robert A. Burt, "Precedent and Authority in Antonin Scalia's Jurisprudence," 12 *Cardozo Law Review* 1685, 1710–1711 (1991).
2 Jack Rakove, "Fidelity through History (or to It)," 65 *Fordham Law Review* 1587, 1608–1609 (1997).
3 Michael J. Klarman, "*Brown*, Originalism, and Constitutional Theory: A Response to Professor McConnell," 81 *Virginia Law Review* 1181 (1995), criticizes originalists' inconsistency in defending Brown v. Board of Education by turning to a broad concept of tradition and broad reading of the Civil War Amendments, including Scalia's defense of *Brown* in Rutan v. Republican Party of Illinois, 497 U.S. 62, 96 n. 1 (1990) (the Fourteenth Amendment when read in conjunction with the Thirteenth "leaves no room for doubt that laws treating people differently because of their race are invalid"); *see* Burt, *supra* at 1712.
4 *See* John F. Manning, "Federalism and the Generality Problem in Constitutional Interpretation," 122 *Harvard Law Review* 2003 (2009); Manning, "Separation of Powers as Ordinary Interpretation," 124 *Harvard Law Review* 1939, 2006–2013 (2011).

Other versions of this approach have been advanced. *E.g.*, Charles A. Miller, *The Supreme Court and the Uses of History* 161–167 (1969) (discussing, *e.g.*, Felix Frankfurter's "two-clause" theory, which posits that specific clauses and general clauses require different approaches).

5 Steven R. Greenberger, "Justice Scalia's Due Process Traditionalism Applied to Territorial Jurisdiction: The Illusion of Adjudication without Judgment," 33 *Boston College Law Review* 981, 1023–1026 (1992).

6 *Id.* at 1032; Richard A. Champagne, Jr., "The Problem of Integrity, Tradition and Text in Constitutional Interpretation," 72 *Nebraska Law Review* 78, 97 (1993).

7 Laurence Tribe & Michael C. Dorf, "Levels of Generality in the Definition of Rights," 57 *University of Chicago Law Review* 1057, 1087, 1091, 1100–1101 (1990); *see* Frank Michelman, *Brennan and Democracy* 15 (1999) (customary law is majoritarian).

8 Richmond Newspapers, Inc. v. Virginia, 448 U.S. 555, 589 (1980) (Brennan, J., concurring in the judgment).

9 Michelman, *supra* at 99–112. Michelman also described Scalia's use of tradition as communitarian. *Id.* at 104.

10 Thomas has not respected Everson v. Board of Education, 330 U.S. 1 (1946), an originalist opinion that established the "wall of separation" standard. If *Everson* was not followed because it was wrong as a matter of original understanding, there is truly nothing left to *stare decisis* as practiced by uncompromising originalists.

11 *See* Stephen B. Presser, *Recapturing the Constitution* (1994). Concurring in McDonald v. Chicago, 561 U.S. 742 (2010), Thomas found that gun ownership was a privilege of citizenship guaranteed directly by the Fourteenth Amendment. This position was broadly challenged on historical and textual grounds in Philip Hamburger, "Privileges or Immunities," 105 *Northwestern University Law Review* 61, 145 n. 305 (2011). Hamburger said that Thomas distorted history, misread documentary evidence that contradicted his opinion, ignored the distinction "between the privileges or immunities of *citizens* and the rights of persons," and relied on racist sources. *See generally* Kurt T. Lash, *The Fourteenth Amendment and the Privileges and Immunities of American Citizenship* (2014).

12 Kathleen M. Sullivan, "The Justice of Rules and Standards," 106 *Harvard Law Review* 22, 113 (1992). The precise scope of *stare decisis* at the founding is not clear. One historian wrote: "[A]ccording to Blackstone [and others], a precedent that did not conform with what a judge thought the law to be should or could be ignored." Holly Brewer, "Age of Reason? Children, Testimony, and Contract in Early America," in *The Many Legalities of Early America* 328 (Christopher L. Tomlins & Bruce H. Mann eds. 2001), citing, *e.g.*, Blackstone, I *Commentaries* *69–*71, *76–*77. Others have found the application of *stare decisis* more complex. *E.g.*, Zachariah Chaffee, Jr., "Delaware Cases, 1790–1800," 57 *Harvard Law Review* 407–426 (1944), book review of *Delaware Cases, 1792–1830* (Daniel Boorstein ed. 1943, 3 vols.).

13 Based primarily on the number of times Justices voted to hold statutes unconstitutional, Judge Frank Easterbrook published a study in 2002 on whether conservative judges were more or less activist than liberal judges and concluded that there was no difference. His analysis put Scalia in the middle of the pack. Easterbrook, "Do Liberals and Conservatives Differ in Judicial Activism?," 73 *University of Colorado Law Review* 1403 (2002).

14 Scalia, *A Matter of Interpretation* 83 (1997) (comment by Tribe).

15 *See* Powell, "The Political Grammar of Early Constitutional Law," 71 *North Carolina Law Review* 950, 973–974 (1993).

16 Scalia, *supra* at 139.

17 LaCroix, *The Ideological Origins of American Federalism* 89–108 (2010). There were precedents, such as the relationship between England and Scotland. *Id.* at 24–29, 120–124. There were also some earlier discussions of a multilayered government in the 1760s.

18 *See* Joel Alicea & Drakeman, "The Limits of New Originalism," 15 *University of Pennsylvania Journal of Constitutional Law* 1161 (2013). John Manning argued that this fact supports a textual reading of the Constitution rather than a search for broad principles. Manning, "The Role of the Philadelphia Convention in Constitutional Adjudication," 80 *George Washington Law Review* 1753 (2012).

19 Lance Banning, "The Constitutional Convention," in *The Framing and Ratification of the Constitution* 124 (Levy & Dennis J. Mahoney eds. 1987).

20 Bailyn, *To Begin the World Anew* 131 (2003); *see* Mark R. Killenbeck, "The Original (?) Public (?) Meaning of 'Commerce,'" 16 *University of Pennsylvania Journal of Constitutional. Law* 289, 293–399 (2013) (quoting framing-era letters); *see generally* Purcell, *supra*.

21 Louis Hartz, *The Liberal Tradition in America* 137 (1955).

22 Nelson, *Marbury v. Madison* 34 (2000). *Reading Statutes* by Scalia and Bryan A. Garner vigorously disputed many of the arguments and conclusions that follow.

23 Bernard Bailyn, *The Origins of American Politics* 66–70 (1969). Other encroachments on separation of powers, mostly involving patronage, were common. *Id.* at 72–78.

24 Donald S. Lutz, "The First Constitutions," in *The Framing and Ratification of the Constitution* 75 (Leonard Levy & Dennis J. Mahoney eds. 1987); *see* Levy, "Introduction: American Constitutional History, 1776–1789," in *id.* at 17.

25 Bailyn, *The Ideological Origins of the American Revolution* 301 (1967).

26 Bailyn, *Origins of American Politics* at 79.

27 Flaherty, "The Most Dangerous Branch," 105 *Yale Law Journal* 1725, 1791–1792 (1996). The unsettled nature of separation of powers at the founding can be seen from John Jay's simultaneously holding the position of Secretary of Foreign Affairs and Chief Justice of the United States between Oct. 19, 1789, and March 22, 1790, and John Marshall's serving as both Secretary of State and Chief Justice of the United States from February 4, 1801, to March 4, 1801. The Constitution, Art. I, § 6, cl. 2, prohibits a member of Congress from holding other federal office, but nothing specifically barred someone from holding positions in the other two branches.

28 While the founding generation was committed to popular or republican government, prevention of tyranny, which included the revocation of fundamental rights, was critical. Changing the charter of a colony or company, such as the East India Company, was the exercise of arbitrary power and tyranny. Colonists regarded the coercive acts that Parliament passed in the wake of the Boston Tea Party, affecting Massachusetts and Quebec, despotic and unconstitutional. The first Continental Congress asserted that "the legislature of Great Britain is not authorized by the constitution to . . . erect an arbitrary form of government in any quarter of the globe." Following the Glorious Revolution of 1688, an articulate minority was concerned that parliamentary despotism, rather than the triumph of representative democracy, would replace the despotism of the crown. Reid, *Constitutional History of the American Revolution; The Authority of Law* 30–36, 58–60 (1993).

29 Only one state, Massachusetts, gave the governor the right to veto legislation. 2 *The Debate on the Constitution* 1091 (Bailyn ed. 1993).

30 This is an abbreviated list. *See, e.g.,* Manning, 124 *Harvard Law Review* at 1978–1985.

31 The role of Congress in appointing government employees was removed at the last minute, along with other modifications in the roles of the three Branches. Flaherty, "The Most Dangerous Branch," 105 *Yale Law Journal* 1725, 1737, 1755–1756, 1776, 1781 (1996); *see* Wood, *The Creation of the American Republic, 1776–1787*, at 153–154 (1969).

32 Maier, *Ratification* at 364–365, quoting XXII *The Documentary History of the Ratification of the Constitution* 1953 (Merrill Jensen, John P. Kaminski *et al.* eds.1976–). Twenty-seven volumes have been published, with four more forthcoming.

33 Stephen E. Sachs, "Constitutional Backdrops," 80 *George Washington Law Review* 1813, 1860–1861 (2012) (quoting Madison).

34 Rossum, *Federalism, the Supreme Court, and the Seventeenth Amendment: The Irony of Constitutional Democracy* 74–77 (2001); *see* Judith A. Best, "The Presidency and the Executive Power," in *The Framing and Ratification* at 215–220.

35 Manning, 124 *Harvard Law Review* at 1947–1948, 1993–1995.

36 Ackerman, *The Decline and Fall of the American Republic* 248–249 (2010); *see* Rakove, 65 *Fordham Law Review* at 1589 ("by 1787 American thinking was moving well past the rigid Montesquieuian axioms that early state constitutions had endorsed"). Article VIII of Madison's Virginia Plan proposed that "the Executive and a Convenient number of the National Judiciary, ought to compose a Council of revision with authority to examine every act of the National Legislature before it shall operate. . . . " Scalia told me that he considered *Mistretta* less objectionable than *Morrison*.

37 Barry Friedman, "Dialogue and Judicial Restraint," 91 *Michigan Law Review* 577, 581 (1993).

38 Edwin Chemerinsky, "Foreword, Vanishing Constitution," 103 *Harvard Law Review* 44, 65–76 (1989). There were exceptions, including Patrick Henry, George Mason, and Elbridge Gerry. In the founding era the right to vote was denied to blacks, women, and many white males based on state property-ownership requirements.

39 The legislatures of all but two original states chose their governors and most state legislatures selected presidential electors. Douglass C. North, John J. Wallis & Barry R. Weingast, *Violence and Social Orders* 231 (2009).

40 G. Edward White, "The Arrival of History in Constitutional Scholarship," 88 *Virginia Law Review* 485 (2001); *see* Bailyn, *To Begin the World Anew* 47–48 (2003) (Madison "believed that legislative majoritarianism could quickly lead to the destruction of rights of minorities").

41 *E.g., The Federalist*, No. 15 at 110–111 (Hamilton); *id.*, No. 51 at 322 (Madison); Treanor, "Judicial Review before *Marbury*," 58 *Stanford Law Review* 455, 558 (2005).

42 As a delegate to the Virginia constitutional convention, John Marshall endorsed judicial review of federal statutes. Maier, *Ratification* at 290–291 (2010); Maeva Marcus, "The Effect (or Non-Effect) of Founders on the Supreme Court Bench," 80 *George Washington Law Review* 1794, 1800–1801 (2012) (Justices stated support of judicial review when addressing grand juries and petit juries when sitting as trial judges). Jefferson wrote to Madison that a bill of rights was "the legal check which it puts into the hands of the judiciary" to rein in Congress, Levy, *Origins of the Bill of Rights* 33 (1999), although some founding-era leaders, including Jefferson, were hostile to the judiciary, *see, e.g.,* Daniel Boorstein, *The Lost World of Thomas Jefferson* 202–203 (1948). Professor Louis Hartz stated that judicial review was accepted because "the moral unanimity of a liberal society nourishes a legalistic frame of mind and an acquiescence in restraint on the part of the majority." Hartz, *The Liberal Tradition in America* 46 n.*, 47–50 (1955). In a word, revolutionary-era Americans were legalistic

and litigious, although resort to the courts varied from community to community. Nelson, *Plymouth County* 4 (1981); Peter Charles Hoffer, *Law and People in Colonia America* xii (rev. ed. 1998).

43 5 U.S. (1 Cranch) 137 (1803).

44 Treanor, 58 *Stanford Law Review* at 455, 457, 555, 556; Treanor, "Process Theory, Majoritarianism, and the Original Understanding," 75 *Fordham Law Review* 2989 (2007). Treanor found that courts invalidated mostly statutes that limited the right to a jury trial or implicated judicial power, which was not part of the legislative process. *Id.* at 2991–2993. Some scholars said that Treanor overstated the role of the judiciary in this period. *E.g.*, Larry Kramer, *The People Themselves: Popular Constitutionalism and Constitutional Review* 4, 99 (2001).

45 LaCroix, *The Ideological Origins of American Federalism* at 161–174. LaCroix traces the replacement of Madison's proposal that gave Congress a negative veto over state legislation that violated the Constitution by judicial review by virtue of the Supremacy Clause. "[C]ourts and judges would be the mediating agents between the national and state governments, ensuring the supremacy of the general government in its particular areas of competence while minimizing the size of the shadow that national; oversight cast on the states." *Id.* at 171.

46 *The Anti-Federalist Papers and the Constitutional Convention Debates* 124 (Ralph Ketcham ed. 1986). Opposing ratification, Anti-Federalist pamphleteer "Brutus" argued in February 1788, that "the courts are vested with the supreme and uncontrollable power, to determine in all cases that come before them, what the constitution means; they cannot, therefore, execute a law, which, in their judgment, opposes the constitution. . . . " *Id.* at 299. The Privy Council rejected colonial law antithetical to the British constitution, a precedent for judicial review. A form of judicial review seems to have existed under the Articles of Confederation. Mary Sarah Bilder, *The Transatlantic Constitution* 188–190 (2004).

47 *The Federalist* No. 78 at 466; *see id.*, No. 80; Breyer, *Making Our Democracy Work* 6–9 (2010). Moreover, during the immediately post-framing era, federal judges generally accepted, though not without vigorous dispute, that federal courts had the power to create common-law crimes, a legislative function, which was not rejected until Hudson v. Goodwin, 11 U.S. (7 Cranch) 32 (1812); *see* Morton Horwitz, *Transformation of American Law, 1780–1860*, at 11–12 (1977); Presser, *Recapturing the Constitution* 97–101, 122–123 (1994); Presser, *The Original Misunderstanding* 67–99 (1991).

48 LaCroix, "Federalists, Federalism, and Federal Jurisdiction," 30 *Law & History Review* 205, 210 (2012).

49 Rossum, "James Wilson and the Pyramid of Government," in *The American Founding; Politics, Statesmanship, and the Constitution* 73 (Rossum & Gary L. McDowell eds. 1981); Renée Lettow Lerner, "Judicial Review Before *Marbury*," 72 *George Washington Law Review* 45, 48 (2003). James Wilson was a prominent member of the Philadelphia Convention, a lecturer on the Constitution, and later a Supreme Court Justice. "Wilson's lectures gave birth to American jurisprudence as such." Aaron T. Knapp, "Law's Revolutionary: James Wilson and the Birth of American Jurisprudence," 29 *Journal of Law & Politics* 189, 194 (2013). He was a Federalist, but of a different stripe than Madison and certainly Hamilton. A strong proponent of the common law, he favored direct election of the President and Senators. Wilson was a controversial figure. "Although respected by many, Wilson was not well regarded by all Pennsylvanians. Anyone familiar with ratification in Pennsylvania would know that Wilson was mocked, denounced, and burned in effigy because of his status as

a member of the state's legal elite." Cornell, "Meaning and Understanding in the History of Constitutional Ideas: The Intellectual History Alternative to Originalism," 82 *Fordham Law Review* 721, 738 (2013).

50 Scalia, *Interpretation* at 52, 54 (comment by Wood). Cornell and Konig disagreed in part and cited the passionate fight for juries, largely by Anti-Federalists, as proof. Cornell, *The Other Founders* 60, 126–138 (1999); Konig, 56 *U.C.L.A. Law Review* at 1320–1324. William Nelson emphasized another aspect of the role of judges in the mid and late eighteenth century. "Because there was no modern bureaucracy, the judiciary and the officials, such as sheriffs responsible to it, were the primary link between a colony's central government and its localities. . . . The courts, as a vital part of the government, maintained order, protected life and property, apportioned and raised taxes, supervised the construction and maintenance of highways, issued licenses, and regulated licensees' businesses." Nelson, *Marbury v. Madison* 12–13 (2000); Nelson, *The Common Law in Colonial America (Vol. III)* 119 (2016). Following independence, and especially in the early nineteenth century, the role of courts as the resolver of disputes and the frequency of commercial litigation increased. *See* Nelson, *Plymouth County* 76–77, 91–121 (1981).

51 135 S.Ct. 2584, 2629 (2015).

52 Rakove, 65 *Fordham Law Review* at 1589.

53 Martin T. Redish & Elizabeth J. Cisar, "If Angels Were to Govern: The Need for Pragmatic Formalism in Separation of Powers Theory," 41 *Duke Law Journal* 449, 501 (1991). Courts can sometimes more accurately mirror the will of the people than legislatures, such as in the case of Terri Schiavo, who was in a vegetative state; legislators were pandering to political fringes by preventing her death while over 80 percent of the public sided with the judges who permitted the removal of feeding tubes that kept her alive. Jeffrey Rosen, *The Most Democratic Branch* 2–3 (2006). Posner objects to the use of the term "political branches" to exclude the courts, which he argues are political. Posner, "What Is Obviously Wrong with the Federal Judiciary, Yet Eminent Curable, Part II," 19 *Green Bag 2d* 257, 264–265 (2016).

54 Stephen Macedo, *The New Rights vs. the Constitution* 28 (1986).

55 133 S.Ct. 2612 (2013). Earlier, Scalia joined a liberal majority in City of Pleasant Grove v. United States (1987) (6–3), to enforce the preclearance procedure.

56 *Id.* at 2629.

57 Tushnet stated that the Court's "skeptical examination of Congress's fact-finding processes is particularly illuminating in suggesting that the Court regards Congress not as a partner but as something of a recalcitrant subordinate whose actions have to be looked at with great care so that the Court can insure itself that Congress is acting responsibly." Tushnet, *The New Constitutional Order* 51 (2003).

58 495 U.S. 385 (1990).

59 *Id.* at 409–410. The dissent did not cite *Munoz-Flores*. The Court does evaluate the procedures in Congress but is ordinarily highly deferential. *E.g.*, N.L.R.B. v. Canning, 134 S.Ct. 2550 (2014) (Scalia, J., concurring) (Congress decides what is or is not a recess in context of President's power to make recess appointments).

60 Bendix Autolite Corp. v. Widvestco Enterprises, Inc., 486 U.S. 888, 897 (1988) (Scalia, J., concurring in judgment).

61 Presser, *Recapturing the Constitution* at 49–58.

62 Aleinikoff, "Constitutional Law in the Age of Balancing," 96 *Yale Law Journal* 943–944, 949 (1987). Liberal Tushnet, like conservative Scalia, rejected balancing on nonoriginalist grounds: it "really does not constrain the judges. . . . The more general

problem is that the sociological defense of balancing assumes that all insiders agree on certain fundamental points and assumes that there are no fundamental differences between insiders and outsiders." Tushnet, *Red, White, and Blue* 183–185 (1988). Balancing by fundamentalists differs from balancing by liberals.

CHAPTER 24 CONSERVATIVE OPINIONS RECONSIDERED:
INDIVIDUAL RIGHTS

1 David T. Konig, "Why the Second Amendment Has a Preamble: Original Public Meaning and the Political Culture of Revolutionary America," 56 *U.C.L.A. Law Review* 1295, 1317, 1321 (2009).
2 Harry A. Shain, *The Nature of Rights at the American Founding and Beyond* 2 (Shain ed. 2007). A principal reason was the limited social and political prerogatives of many white males, not to mention slaves and married women. *See* Charles A. Miller, *The Supreme Court and the Uses of History* 49 (1969) ("The framers did not believe that the welfare of the state was essentially different from the welfare of the people.").
3 Saul Cornell, "'To Assemble Together for Their Common Good': History, Ethnography, and the Original Meanings of the Rights of Assembly and Speech," 84 *Fordham Law Review* 915, 930–934 (2015); *cf.* John R. Bowen, *Religions in Practice; An Approach to the Anthropology of Religion* 253 (1998).
4 Gordon S. Wood, "The Supreme Court and the Uses of History," 39 *Ohio Northern University Law Review* 435, 446, 448 (2013); *see* Mary Sarah Bilder, *The Transatlantic Constitution* 146–147, 158–159, 166 (2004).
5 Thomas Drakeman, *Church, State, and Original Intent* 326 (2010).
6 Note, "Forgetting to Weight: The Use of History in the Supreme Court's Establishment Clause," 102 *Georgetown Law Journal* 845, 847–848 (2014); *see* William E. Nelson, *Americanization of the Common Law; The Impact of Legal Change on Massachusetts Society, 1760–1830*, at 108 ("Although the religious establishment officially lingered on until 1833, the Religious Freedom Act of 1811 in effect destroyed it" in Massachusetts); *see id.* at 146–147.
7 Robert A. Rutland, *The Birth of the Bill of Rights, 1776–1791*, at 127, 166–167 (1955).
8 E.g., Nelson, *The Common Law in Colonial America (Vol. III): The Chesapeake and New England Colonies* 74–77, 84–90, 99–107 (2016).
9 Philip Hamburger, *Separation of Church and State* 19–64 (2002); *see* Everson v. Board of Education of Ewing, 330 U.S. 1, 16 (1947). According to some scholars, Jefferson's and Madison's views were extreme and not within mainstream thinking. *E.g.*, Stephen B. Presser, *Recapturing the Constitution* 163–166 (1994).
10 Kent Greenawalt, *Religion and the Constitution – Establishment and Fairness* 76 (2008); *see* Dennis J. Goldford, *The Constitution of Religious Freedom* 51–56 (2012).
11 Eric R. Claeys, "Justice Scalia and the Religion Clauses: A Comment on Professor Epps," 21 *Washington Journal of Law & Politics* 349, 351–352 (2006); Anthony Barone Kolenc, "Mr. Scalia's Neighborhood: A Home for Minority Religions?," 81 *St. John's Law Review* 819, 829 (2007), quoting Scalia, "On Making It Look Easy by Doing It Wrong: A Critical View of the Justice Department," in *Private Schools & the Public Good* 175 (Edward Gaffney ed. 1981).
12 Chad Flanders, "Can We Please Stop Talking about Neutrality? Koppelman between Scalia and Rawls," 39 *Pepperdine Law Review* 1139, 1141 (2013); *see* Thomas J. Curry, *The First Freedoms: Church and State in America to the Passage of the First Amendment*

216–218 (1986); Dennis J. Goldford, *The Constitution of Religious Freedom* 51, 117 (2012). Leonard W. Levy disagreed in *Original Intent and the Framers' Constitution* 320 (1988): "The establishment clause, Rehnquist urged [in *Wallace v. Jaffree*, 472 U.S. 38 (1985)], did not prohibit Congress 'from providing nondiscriminatory aid to religion.' Rehnquist was flat wrong." *See* Levy, *The Establishment Clause: Religion and the First Amendment* 94–111 (1985); Michael W. McConnell, "Free Exercise Revisionism and the *Smith* Decision," 57 *University of Chicago Law Review* 1109, 1115 (1990). A. Gregg Roeber, "The Limited Horizons of Whig Religious Rights," in *The Nature of Rights* 203, 206–209 (Shain ed. 2007).

13 *Id.* at 203–204, 211–220.

14 *E.g.*, Bilder, *The Transatlantic Constitution* at 5 (Because refugees from the religious and governmental practices of Puritan Massachusetts settled there, "Rhode Island's governing structure and a significant portion of its population retained an agnostic, at times hostile, attitude toward religious establishment and neighboring colonies."). Puritanism in Massachusetts dominated almost all aspects of society deeply into the eighteenth century, when it coexisted with the common law. Nelson, *The Common Law in Colonial America (Vol. III): The Chesapeake and New England Colonies* 87–112 (2016). To a lesser extent this was true of other New England colonies. *Id.* at 113–131.

15 Massachusetts, Connecticut, and New Hampshire had established churches, although they disagreed on what constituted establishment of religion. Joel Alicea & Drakeman, "The Limits of New Originalism," 15 *University of Pennsylvania Journal of Constitutional Law* 1161, 1216–1218 (2013); Carl H. Esbeck, "Uses and Abuses of Textualism and Originalism in Establishment Clause Interpretation," 2011 *Utah Law Review* 489, 492–493; Robert A. Rutland, *The Birth of the Bill of Rights, 1776–1791*, at 59 (1955).

16 "According to one tally, 11 of the 13 states had religious qualifications for office holding." Akhil Amar, *The Bill of Rights* 33 (1998). Goldford, *The Constitution of Religious Freedom* 51–56 (2012); Wood, 39 *Ohio Northern University Law Review* at 443; Greenawalt, *supra* at 76.

17 Aaron Phelps Stokes III, *Church and State in the United States* 154 (1950).

18 Steven D. Smith, "Discourse in the Dusk; The Twilight of Religious Freedom," 122 *Harvard Law Review* 1968, 1898 (2009); Smith, "The Jurisprudential Establishment Clause: A Reappraisal," 81 *Notre Dame Law Review* 1843 (2006); Esbeck, 2011 *Utah Law Review* at 493–494; Matthew P. Harrington, "Regulatory Takings and the Original Understanding of the Takings Clause," 45 *William & Mary Law Review* 2053 (2004); McConnell, "Neutrality under the Religion Clauses," 81 *Northwestern University Law Review* 146, 152, 161 (1986).

19 William R. Hutchison, book review of Hamburger, *Separation of Church and State* (2002), 23 *Law & History Review* 201, 204 (2005).

20 Roeber, *The Nature of Rights* at 202–205.

21 Lee v. Weisman, 505 U.S. 507, 641 (1992).

22 542 U.S. 1, 49–50 (2004) (Thomas, J., concurring).

23 134 S.Ct. 1811, 1835 (2014).

24 545 U.S. 844 (2005).

25 *E.g.*, Andrew Koppelman, "Phony Originalism and the Establishment Clause," 103 *Northwestern University Law Review* 727, 734–737.

26 Bernard Schwartz, I *The Bill of Rights: A Documentary History* 256–379 (1971).

27 *E.g.*, Roeber, *The Nature of Rights* at 202–205 ("The assault on the devisal of individual property, perverse sexual mores, and corrupt religious dogma followed in Catholicism's train, logically and inevitably.").

28 Pauline Maier, *Ratification* 186 (2010).

29 *Id.* at 420.

30 O'Connor stated in *McCreary*, 545 U.S. at 882: "[T]he goal of the [Religion] Clauses is clear: to carry out the Founders' plan of preserving religious liberty to the fullest extent possible in a pluralistic society. By enforcing the Clauses, we have kept religion a matter for the individual conscience, not for the prosecutor or bureaucrat. At a time when we see around the world the violent consequences of the assumption of religious authority by government, Americans may count themselves fortunate: Our regard for constitutional boundaries has protected us from similar travails, while allowing private religious exercise to flourish."

31 For an earlier discussion of the issue of standing in establishment cases, *see* Arthur Sutherland, "Establishment According to *Engel*," 76 *Harvard Law Review* 25 (1962).

32 Posner, *Reflections* on *Judging* 121 (2013).

33 132 S.Ct. 2492, 2511 (2012) (Scalia, J., dissenting).

34 *Id.* at 2522. Scalia also relied on consequences in Babbitt v. Sweet Home Chapter of Committee for a Greater Oregon, 515 U.S. 687, 714 (1995) (Scalia, J., dissenting): "The Court's holding that the hunting and killing provision incidentally preserves habitat on private lands imposes unfairness to the point of financial ruin – not just upon the rich, but upon the simplest farmer who finds his land conscripted to national zoological use."

35 561 U.S. at 750, 767, 775.

36 Sullivan v. Finkelstein, 496 U.S. 617, 632 (2990) (Scalia, J., concurring in part).

37 554 U.S. 570, 651 (2008).

38 Sunstein, "Justice Breyer's Democratic Pragmatism," 115 *Yale Law Journal* 1719, 1726 (2006).

39 Breyer's dissent argued that the appropriate standard to review the District of Columbia statute was the "rational basis" standard with interest balancing, which has a substantial contemporary component. 561 U.S. at 687–723.

40 J. Harvie Wilkinson III, "Of Guns, Abortions, and the Unraveling Rule of Law," 95 *Virginia Law Review* 253, 263 (2009).

41 Richard A. Posner, "In Defense of Looseness," *The New Republic*, Aug. 27, 2008, www.tnr.com/article/books/defense-looseness.

42 Marcia Coyle, *The Roberts Court; The Struggle for the Constitution* 124 (2013).

43 William M. Treanor, "Process Theory, Majoritarianism, and the Original Understanding," 75 *Fordham Law Review* 2989, 2993 (2007). Much of this material was presented to the Court in amicus briefs by leading historians whose credentials far outweighed those of the authors of the amicus briefs on which the majority relied.

44 Konig, 56 *U.C.L.A. Law Review* at 1309–1310.

45 Jack N. Rakove, "Thoughts on *Heller* from a 'Real Historian,'" June 27, 2008, Balkanization, http://balkin.Blogspot.com/2008/06.

46 Paul Finkelman, "The Living Constitution and the Second Amendment: Poor History, False Originalism, and a Very Confused Court," 37 *Cardozo Law Review* 623 (2015).

47 Cornell, "The Original Meaning of Original Understanding: A Neo-Blackstonian Critique," 67 *Maryland Law Review* 150, 152–158 (2007).

48 Wood, "The Supreme Court and the Uses of History," 39 *Ohio Northern University Law Review* 435, 443 (2013). Cornell agreed. "The early debate over gun control does not fit the modern individual/collective rights dichotomy.... The right belonged to citizens who exercised it when they acted collectively for public defense." The concept drew on republican constitutionalism and "English common law jurisprudence, particularly its conception of rights as obligations." Cornell, "The Early American Origins of the Modern Gun Control Debate: The Right to Bear Arms, Firearms Regulation, and the Regulation of History," 17 *Stanford Law & Policy Review* 567, 568 (2006). Lawrence B. Solum wrote, "meaning is not just a function of the meaning of individual words and phrases; it is also the function of syntax (or grammar)." Solum, "The Fixation Thesis: The Role of Historical Fact in Original Meaning," 91 *Notre Dame Law Review* 1 (2015).

49 Miller, *The Supreme Court* at 94.

50 Finkelman, *supra* at 628.

51 Martin Flaherty, "Can the Quill Be Mightier than the Uzi?: History 'Lite,' 'Law Office,' and Worse Meets the Second Amendment," 37 *Cardozo Law Review* 663, 672 (2015); see Reva B. Siegel, "Dead or Alive: Originalism as Popular Constitutionalism in *Heller*," 122 *Harvard Law Review* 191 (2008).

52 Michael Waldman, *The Second Amendment, a Biography* 97–98, 100–101 (2014).

53 Cornell, "*Heller*, New Originalism, and Law Office History: 'Meet the Boss, Same as the Old Boss,'" 56 *U.C.L.A. Law Review* 1095, 1101–1110 (2009); *see* Cornell, *A Well-Regulated Militia; The Founding Fathers and the Origins of Gun Control in American* 137–165 (2006); Rakove, "Joe the Ploughman Reads the Constitution, or, the Poverty of Public Meaning Originalism," 48 *San Diego Law Review* 575 (2011).

54 Another instance was the closer relationship between the individual citizen and the presidency, caused by the partisan presidential race between Jefferson and Aaron Burr and Jefferson's "Revolution of 1800." *See* Ackerman, *The Failure of the Founding Fathers* 3–35 (2005).

55 Rakove, 48 *San Diego Law Review* at 595; Cornell, "The Ironic Second Amendment," 1 *Albany Government Law Review* 292, 295 (2008) ("most leading historians of the Founding Era reject the individual rights model"); Brief of Amici Curiae Jack N. Rakove, Saul Cornell, David T. Konig, Lois G. Schwoerer, *et al.*, in Support of Petitioners in *Heller*, reprinted in *The Second Amendment on Trial; Critical Essays on District of Columbia v. Heller* 53 (Cornell & Nathan Kozuskanich eds. 2013), argued, "Anglo-American political tradition . . . never treated private ownership of firearms as an individual right." Early state constitutions did not provide for an individual right, with the arguable exception of Virginia. The arms issue arose largely because the 1789 Constitution assigned Congress power over the militia in Art. I, § 8, coupled with a provision for a federal army and navy. Ratification debate focused on militias not on individual rights. Brief in *The Second Amendment on Trial* at 54, 60–66, 72–73; Levy, *Origins of the Bill of Rights* 133–135 (1999); see Bailyn, *To Begin the World Anew* 115 (2003).

56 Cornell, "A New Paradigm for the Second Amendment," 22 *Law & History Review* 161, 164–167 (2004); *see* Cornell, "Commonplace or Anachronism: The Standard Model, the Second Amendment, and the Problem of History in Contemporary Constitutional Theory," 16 *Constitutional Commentary* 221–246 (1999); Cornell, 17 *Stanford Law & Policy Review* at 592 ("a genuinely historical coconut of the early history of gun regulation demonstrates that the simplistic claims made by the modern opponents of gun regulation have little basis in the historical record"). History contradicts many

originalist arguments. For example, under eighteenth-century law, the notion of self-defense did not entitle citizens to use deadly force against attackers in most cases, and Pennsylvania Anti-Federalists "accepted a level of gun regulation that far exceeds anything modern gun control groups have advocated." Cornell, 29 *Northern Kentucky Law Review* at 671–673, 680.

57 Cornell, "Meaning and Understanding in the History of Constitutional Ideas: The Intellectual History Alternative to Originalism," 82 *Fordham Law Review* 721, 724 (2013).

58 *Id.* at 740–747, 752; *see* Cornell, 17 *Stanford Law & Policy Review* at 575–577. Cornell entitled a section of his article on *Heller*, "Originalism as Constitutional Scam."

59 Merkel, "Uncoupling the Constitutional Right to Self-Defense from the Second Amendment: Insights from the Law of War," 45 *Connecticut Law Review* 1809, 1825 (2013); *see* Merkel, "*The District of Columbia v. Heller* and Scalia's Perverse Sense of Originalism," 13 *Lewis & Clark Law Review* 349 (2001); Cornell, 67 *Maryland Law Review* at 153–158.

60 Cornell, 82 *Fordham Law Review* at 724. Cornell also said that Scalia cherry-picked dictionaries.

61 Michael A. Bellesiles, "Gun Laws in Early America: The Regulation of Firearms Ownership, 1607–1794," 16 *Law & History Review* 567, 576 (1998).

62 Cornell, 82 *Fordham Law Review* at 746–747; *see* John O. McGinnis & Michael B. Rappaport, *Originalism and the Good Constitution* 119 (2013) ("originalism requires modern interpreters to follow the original interpretive rules used by the enactors of the Constitution as much as the original word meanings or grammatical rules").

63 Konig, 56 *U.C.L.A. Law Review* at 1325, 1331; *see* Konig, "The Second Amendment: A Missing Transatlantic Context for the Historical Meaning of 'the Right of the People to Keep and Bear Arms," 22 *Law & History Review* 119 (2004); H. Jefferson Powell, "The Original Understanding of Original Intent," 98 *Harvard Law Review* 885, 898–899 (1985). According to Cornell, Scalia relied on a discredited source, Eugene Volokh, who in turn relied on mid-nineteenth-century sources, while ignoring Joseph Story and his colleagues as well as Blackstone. Cornell, "Originalism on Trial: The Use and Abuse of History in *District of Columbia v. Heller*," 69 *Ohio State Law Review* 625, 632–639 (2008).

64 Konig, *supra* at 1331; *see* William G. Merkel, "The Second Amendment in Context: The Case of the Vanishing Predicate," 76 *Chicago-Kent Law Review* 403 (2000); Cornell, "'Don't Know Much about History'; The Current Crises in Second Amendment Scholarship," 29 *Northern Kentucky Law Review* 657, 662–664 (2002).

65 Tushnet, *Out of Range* xvi, 10, 15, 25–28 (2007).

66 Amar, *The Bill of Rights* 51–57 (1998).

67 *The Second Amendment; A Biography* xii–xiii (2014) (second ellipses in original). Waldman also demonstrated that precedent was against Scalia and the conservatives. *Id.* at 80, 82–83, 123, discussing, *inter alia*, United States v. Miller, 307 U.S. 174 (1939).

68 521 U.S. 507, 544 (Scalia, J., concurring).

69 *Id.*

70 561 U.S. 742 (2010).

71 Despite its strong pedigree, the Seventh Amendment has not been strictly applied to the states, *e.g.*, Jackson v. Wood, 2 Cow. 819 (N.Y. 1824), which allowed state courts to initiate certain practices, *e.g.*, summary procedures such as directed verdict, judgment notwithstanding the verdict, and summary judgment, as well as summary proceedings for collection of taxes and for banks to collect debts. State courts "have

permitted legislatures to alter the jury right until it has become unrecognizable." Renée Lettow Lerner, "The Failure of Originalism in Preserving Constitutional Rights to Civil Jury Trial," 22 *William & Mary Bill of Rights Journal* 811, 841–860 (2014).

72 Scalia, *A Matter of Interpretation* 137 n. 13 (1997).

73 Despite overwhelming evidence against Scalia's interpretation of the Second Amendment, he characterized the evidence as indisputably in *his* favor in conversations with me.

74 Scalia, *supra* at 66 (statement of Tribe). Colonies and then states reduced the number of crimes punishable by death.

75 Nelson, *Americanization of the Common Law* at 100.

76 Alan Rogers, "'A Sacred Duty': Court Appointed Attorneys in Massachusetts Criminal Cases, 1780–1980," 41 *American Journal of Legal History* 237–238 (1997); Nelson, "Emerging Notions of Modern Criminal Law in the Revolutionary Era: An Historical Perspective," 42 *N.Y.U. Law Review* 450, 480 (1967).

77 "'Benefit of Clergy' in Maryland and Virginia," 34 *American Journal of Legal History* 49–50 (1990). The procedure in the mid eighteenth century had become totally separated from its ecclesiastic origins. *See* John H. Langbein, Renée Lattow Lerner & Bruce P. Smith, *History of the Common Law; The Development of Anglo-American Legal Institutions* 618–620 (2009); Nelson, *The Common Law in Colonial America (Vol. III)* 45 & n. 31 (2016); Mullaney v. Wilbur, 421 U.S. 684, 692–693 (1975); McGauda v. California, 402 U.S. 183, 197–198 (1971).

78 John Perry, "Textualism and the Discovery of Rights," in *Philosophical Foundation of Language in the Law* 126 (Andrei Marmor & Scott Soames eds. 2011).

79 Scalia, *supra* at 120 (comment by Dworkin).

80 Levy, *Origins of the Bill of Rights* 321–333 (1999).

81 Langbein, "The Historical Origins of the Sanction of Imprisonment for Serious Crime," 5 *Journal of Legal Studies* 35 (1976).

82 Thomas A. Greene, "The English Criminal Trial Jury and the Law-Finding Traditions on the Eve of the French Revolution" in *The Trial Jury in England, France, Germany 1700–1900,* at 50–52 (Antonio Padoa Schioppa ed. 1987).

83 Mark E. Kann, *Punishment, Prisons, and Patriarchy; Liberty and Power in the Early American Republic* 131 (2005).

84 Nelson, "Emerging Notions of Modern Criminal Law in the Revolutionary Era: An Historical Perspective," 42 *N.Y.U. Law Review* 450, 460 (1967).

85 Levy, *supra at* 240. One scholarly article ascribed a somewhat different meaning to the word "unusual" in the Eighth Amendment. "As used in the Eighth Amendment, the word 'unusual was a term of art that referred to government practices that are contrary to 'long usage' or 'immemorial usage.'" John V. Stinneford, "The Original Meaning of 'Unusual'; The Eighth Amendment as a Bar to Cruel Innovation," 102 *Northwestern University Law Review* 1739 (2008); *see* Stinneford, "Rethinking Proportionality under the Cruel and Unusual Punishment Clause," 97 *Virginia Law Review* 899 (2011). This is another example of new scholarship challenging originalist dogma.

86 497 U.S. 639, 671 (1990); *see* Morgan v. Illinois, 504 U.S. 719 (1992) (Scalia, J., dissenting).

87 Levy, *supra* at 185.

88 David N. Mayer, *Liberty of Contract; Rediscovering a Lost Constitutional Right* 20–21 (2011).

89 Levy, *supra* at 248. Nathan S. Chapman & Michael W. McConnell, "Due Process as Separation of Powers," 121 *Yale Law Journal* 1672 (2012) ("Due process of law . . . [f]undamentally . . . was about securing the rule of law.").

90 *See* Wood, "The History of Rights in Early America," in *The Nature of Rights* at 248, quoting Edwin S. Corwin, *Basic Doctrine of American Constitutional Law* 254 (1914) ("Blackstone had agreed that one of the absolute rights of an individual was 'the right of property: which consists in the free use, enjoyment and disposal of all his acquisition, without any control or diminution, *save only by the law of the land.*'").

91 Chapman & McConnell, *supra* at 1807; *see* Mayer, *supra* at 20.

92 Ronald Dworkin, "The Arduous Virtue of Fidelity: Originalism, Scalia, Tribe, and Nerve," 65 *Fordham Law Review* 1249, 1254 n. 6 (1997).

93 Jack M. Balkin, "Abortion and Original Meaning," 24 *Constitutional Commentary* 291, 304 (2007). The natural antonym of substance seems to be procedure, not process. Processes involve content, such as the mid-nineteenth-century "Bessemer Process" for mass-producing steel, which included introducing precise amounts of carbon and manganese. No more than "domestic tranquility" can the modern meaning of "due process" be assumed. From the start there was uncertainty and disagreement about the scope of the Due Process Clause.

94 Jeffrey Rosen, "Originalist Sin," *New Republic*, May 5, 1997.

95 Mayer, *supra* at 11–21; *see* Calder v. Bull, 3 U.S. (3 Dall.) 386 (1798). David E. Bernstein, *Rehabilitating Lochner: Defending Individual Rights against Progressive Reform* 9–10 (2011), traced the judicial acceptance of substantive due process to the 1830s. Robert Bork and Professor David Currie dated substantive due process from the horrific *Dred Scott* decision, Scott v. Sandford, 60 U.S. (19 How.) 393 (1857). Bork, *The Tempting of America* 32–33 (1987). This is a minority position. E.g., Nelson, *The Fourteenth Amendment* 198 (1988) ("In *Lochner v. New York*, the majority of the Court in an alternative holding started off in uncharted directions authorized neither by a uniformly shared original understanding of the Fourteenth Amendment nor by the three decades of case law following it.").

96 *See generally* Randy E. Barnett, *Restoring the Lost Constitution; The Presumption of Liberty* (rev. ed. 2014).

97 Bernstein, *Rehabilitating Lochner* at 8 & n. 3 (2011).

98 Levy, *Origins* at 183–185.

99 538 U.S. 760 (2003). Scalia joined Thomas's opinion for the Court and filed a concurring opinion. Kennedy, Stevens, and Ginsburg dissented in part.

100 Davies, "Farther and Farther from the Original Fifth Amendment: The Recharacterization of the Right against Self-Incrimination as a 'Trial Right' in *Chavez v. Martinez*," 70 *Tennessee Law Review* 987 (2003).

101 526 U.S. 314, 335 (1999).

102 Levy, *Origins* at 196.

103 There is even some framing era evidence supporting the decision in Miranda v. Arizona in the form of a prohibition on pretrial interrogation of prisoners in Middlesex County, Massachusetts. Nelson, "Emerging Notions of Modern Criminal Law in the Revolutionary Era: An Historical Perspective," 42 *N.Y.U. Law Review* 450, 478–479, 481 (1967).

104 542 U.S. 507 (2004).

105 Joshua Stein, "Historians before the Bench: Friends of the Court, Foes of Originalism," 25 *Yale Journal of Law & Humanities* 359, 374–380 (2013), quoting historians' brief in Rasul v. Bush. Two law professors questioned Scalia's opinion in *Hamdi*

on both originalist and pragmatic grounds: "Apart from what we think are its dubious historical roots, this view would straightjacket the government without regard to changing conditions.... Not only is [suspension of the writ of habeas corpus] a draconian remedy, but if invoked it might be far more destructive of civil liberties than a judicially defined solution." Daniel A. Farber & Suzanna Sherry, *Judgment Calls; Principles and Politics in Constitutional Law* 137 (2009).

106 Edwin Chemerinsky, "The Jurisprudence of Justice Scalia, a Critical Appraisal," 22 *Hawaii Law Review* 385, 392 (2000); Stephen A. Siegel, "The Federal Government's Power to Enact Color Conscious Laws: An Originalist Inquiry," 92 *Northwestern University Law Review* 477 (1998).

107 Schnapper, "Affirmative Action and the Legislative History of the Fourteenth Amendment," 71 *Virginia Law Review* 753, 754, 791 (1985).

108 *See, e.g.*, Cornell, 82 *Fordham Law Review* 721.

109 Randall Kennedy, *For Discrimination* 150–151 (2013); Nelson, *The Fourteenth Amendment* 101–104 (1988).

110 *See, e.g.*, Garrett Epps, *Democracy Reborn: The Fourteenth Amendment and the Fight for Equal Rights in Post-Civil War America* (2006); *see* Nelson, *supra* at 197; Epps, "Interpreting the Fourteenth Amendment: Two *Don'ts* and Three *Dos*," 16 *William & Mary Bill of Rights Journal* 433, 442–443, 450, 452 (2007); Richard H. Fallon, Jr., "Are Originalist Constitutional Theories Principled, or Are They Rationalizations for Conservatism?," 34 *Harvard Journal of Law & Public Policy* 5, 17 (2010).

111 Powell, "Rules for Originalists," 73 *Virginia Law Review* 659, 668 (1987); *see* Koppelman, "Phony Originalism and the Establishment Clause," 103 *Northwestern University Law Review* 727, 744 (2009) ("If the Framers had intended to address only a specific problem, they could have said so."); Nelson, *supra* at 81 (some Congressmen asserted that the Fourteenth Amendment incorporated the first eight amendments to the Constitution). In the North as well as the South racist and federalism arguments fueled opposition to granting rights to former slaves. *Id.* at 96–109.

112 *Id.* at 93–96.

113 *Id.* at 143.

114 *Id.* at 125–133.

115 *Id.* at 61–63. Much of the rhetoric supporting the principles embedded in the amendment was derived, albeit with some qualifications, from natural or higher law. *Id.* at 64–74, 82–87. Added to the complexity was that the amendment threatened to upset the federalism balance in favor of the national government. The rebuttal to challenges on these grounds was primarily that all the amendment did was require states to treat all citizens equally. *Id.* at 74–80, 87–93.

116 McConnell, "Originalism and the Desegregation Decisions," 81 *University of Virginia Law Review* 947, 953 (1995).

117 *Id.* at 1140. McConnell's scholarship on the Fourteenth Amendment has been challenged. Mark A. Graber, "Clarence Thomas and the Perils of Amateur History," in *Rehnquist Justice* 89–90 (Earl M. Maltz ed. 2003).

118 Nelson, *supra* at 133. Some early originalists relied on the purpose and text of the Fourteenth Amendment to challenge *Brown*. Robert Bork, *The Tempting of America* 82 (1990) ("The purpose that brought the fourteenth amendment into being was equality before the law, and equality, not separation, was written into the text.").

119 Steven G. Calabresi & Michael W. Perl, "Originalism and *Brown v. Board of Education*," 2014 *Michigan State Law Review* 428.

120 163 U.S. 537 (1896).

121 Berman, "Originalism Is Bunk," 84 *New York University Law Review* 1, 92 (2009); *see* Schnapper, "Affirmative Action and the Legislative History of the Fourteenth Amendment," 71 *Virginia Law Review* 753, 754 (1985) ("From the closing days of the Civil War until the end of civilian Reconstruction some five years later, Congress adopted a series of social welfare programs whose benefits were expressly limited to blacks."); *see* Randall Kennedy, *For Discrimination* 26 n.*, 150–151 (2013); *see* Posner, "The *DeFunis* Case and the Constitutionality of Preferential Treatment of Racial Minorities," 1974 *Supreme Court Review* 1, 21–22; Terrence Sandalow, "Racial Preferences in Higher Education: Political Responsibility and the Judicial Role," 42 *University of Chicago Law Review* 653, 654 (1974). Moreover, Harlan employed the color-blind language in the context of depriving rights to blacks and was not addressing the correction of past discrimination. Barring affirmative action does not necessarily level the playing field. For example, while not without legal challenges, many universities favor children of alumni, a form of affirmative action for middle- and upper-class whites.

122 At Virginia's ratification convention, Madison said that "a solemn declaration of our essential rights" would be "unnecessary and dangerous." It was dangerous because "an enumeration which is not complete, is not safe." Maier, *Ratification* 297 (2010). At Pennsylvania's ratifying convention, James Wilson argued that the federal constitution, unlike state constitutions, requires that "every thing which is not given, is reserved," because the national government is one of limited, articulated powers. *Id.* at 77–80. After his election to the House of Representatives, Madison pushed for a bill of rights largely to forestall a second convention that might undo the Constitution. Herbert J. Storing, "The Constitution and the Bill of Rights," in *The American Founding* 32 (Rossum & McDowell eds. 1981). Madison's proposed constitutional amendments provided rights to people versus the national government, but did not weaken the national government in relation to the states, which Anti-Federalists wanted. The Senate rejected his proposed amendment that would have weakened the states, "no state shall violate the equal right of conscience, or the freedom of the press or the trial by jury in criminal cases."

123 Cornell, *The Other Founders* 160 (1999); Paul C. Peterson, "The Problem of Consistency in the Statesmanship of James Madison," in *The American Founding* at 127.

124 *See* Nelson, *supra* at 112–123.

125 Scalia argued that once you favor someone on the basis of race, you automatically disfavor someone else on the basis of race; it is a zero-sum game. That was not true in *Lucas*.

126 Fergus M. Bordewich, *The First Congress* 225–226, 243–252, 290–293, 297–300 (2016); *see* Powell, *A Community Built on Words* 30 (2002) ("The bank question for [Jefferson and Hamilton] was a war over the meaning of the Republic, and not merely a debate over the just interpretation of the constitutional text."); Powell, *Languages of Power* 37–54 (1991). In a debate in Massachusetts in 1773, those most unhappy with England argued that Britain's power did not extend to its colonies but that its liberties (rights) did; Loyalists like Massachusetts Governor Thomas Hutchison argued the opposite. Bernard Bailyn, *Sometimes an Art* 156–165 (2015).

127 Frederick M. Gedicks, "An Originalist Defense of Substantive Due Process: Magna Carta, Higher-Law Constitutionalism, and the Fifth Amendment," 58 *Emory Law Journal* 585, 669 (2009).

128 517 U.S. 620 (1996).

129 *Id.* at 653 (emphasis added).

130 Jane S. Schacter, "*Romer v. Evans* and Democracy's Domain," 50 *Vanderbilt Law Review* 361, 388 (1997).

131 S.I. Strong, "Justice Scalia as a Modern Lord Devlin: Animus and Civil Burden in *Romer v. Evans,*" 71 *Southern California Law Review* 1, 27–28, 35–41 (1997) (the only legal support for Scalia's position was Dronenburg v. Zech, 741 F.2d 1388 (D.C. Cir. 1984), where a conservative three-judge panel of Bork, Scalia, and Stephen Williams sustained the Navy's discharge of a homosexual).

132 Rosen, "Originalist Sin," *New Republic,* May 5, 1997. Scalia did not write an opinion in Boy Scouts of America v. Dale, 530 U.S. 640 (2000) (Rehnquist, C.J.). The Court's opinion, which he joined, when read literally, reversed decades of precedent and eliminated all antidiscrimination laws by holding that the First Amendment's right of association permitted members of the group to exclude minorities. Many commentators pointed out that the opinion contradicted Employment Div., Dept. of Human Resources of Oregon v. Smith, 494 U.S. 872 (1990), and other decisions. Andrew Koppelman, *A Right to Discriminate? How the Case of Boy Scouts of America v. James Dale Warped the Law of Free Association* (2014) (the law of freedom of association in "disarray"); Stephen Clark, "Judicially Straight? *Boy Scouts v. Dale* and the Missing Scalia Dissent," 76 *Southern California Law Review* 521, 597 (2003); Edwin Chemerinsky & Catherine Fisk, "The Expressive Interest of Associations," 9 *William & Mary Bill of Rights Journal* 595, 612–616 (2001); Daniel A. Farber, "Foreword, Speaking in the First Person Plural: Expressive Associations and the First Amendment Symposium: The Freedom of Expressive Association," 85 *Minnesota Law Review* 1483, 1494–1495 (2001); Dale Carpenter, "Expressive Association and Anti-Discrimination Law after *Dale*: A Tripartite Approach," *id.* at 1515 (2001). The opinion was indefensible.

133 539 U.S. 558 (2003).

134 Stein, 25 *Yale Journal of Law & Humanities* at 372; *but see* Rosen, *The Most Democratic Branch* 107 (2006) (thirty-two out of the thirty-seven states had criminal sodomy laws in 1868); Louis Crompton, "Homosexuals and the Death Penalty in Colonial America," 1 *Journal of Homosexuality* 277 (1976) ("it appears that in 1776 male homosexuals in the original 13 colonies were universally subject to the death penalty"). Sexual relations between women were subject to lesser punishment, if any. "No doubt this reflected the fact that the Old Testament proscribed the death penalty for male homosexuality but made no reference to lesbianism." *Id.* at 278. There were some instances of prosecution for homosexual conduct in the colonial era. Nelson, *The Common Law in Colonial America (Vol. III)* 106 (2016) (Massachusetts).

135 Congress's action on polygamy was constitutional because the Constitution's Art. IV, § 3, allows Congress to establish conditions for admission of states into the Union.

136 517 U.S. at 642–643. Scalia defended his stance: "A State 'does not violate the Equal Protection Clause merely because the classifications made by its laws are imperfect.' . . . Just as a policy barring the hiring of methadone users as transit employees does not violate equal protection simply because some methadone users pose no threat to passenger safety. . . . Amendment 2 is not constitutionally invalid simply because it could have been drawn more precisely so as to withdraw special antidiscrimination protections only from those of homosexual 'orientation' who actually engage in homosexual conduct," i.e., did something that violated the law.

137 550 U.S. 81, 108, 122 (2007).

138 135 S.Ct. 2584 (2015) (Kennedy, J.).

139 Brown v. Board of Education, 347 U.S. 483, 492–493 (1954), stated: "In approaching this problem, we cannot turn the clock back to 1868 when the [Fourteenth] Amendment was adopted, or even to 1897 when *Plessy v. Ferguson* was written. We must consider public education in the light of its full development and its present place in American life throughout the Nation." *Brown* rejected *Plessy*'s preposterous position that separation of the races did not mark blacks with "a badge of inferiority."

140 497 U.S. 261 (1990). Scalia also joined Rehnquist's paternalistic opinion for the Court.

141 Susan R. Martyn & Henry J. Bourguignon, "Coming to Terms with Death: The *Cruzan* Case," 42 *Hastings Law Journal* 817, 832, 837, 855 (1991) (the right of Nancy Cruzan rests on "analogous precedents of the Supreme Court, but also on a long-standing tradition of the role of the family in American society"); James E. Fleming, "Constitutional Tragedy in Dying: Or Whose Tragedy Is It Anyway?," in *Constitutional Stupidities, Constitutional Tragedies* 163 (William N. Eskridge, Jr., & Sanford Levinson eds. 1998) (*Cruzan* "entails that the Constitution sanctions a grievous wrong, a horrible form of tyranny: allowing the state to impose upon some citizens, against the grain of their consciences, considered convictions about dying with dignity, what they regard as a ruinous, tragic ending of their lives").

142 Benjamin C. Zipursky, "The Pedigrees of Rights and Powers in Scalia's *Cruzan* Concurrence," 56 *Pittsburgh Law Review* 283 (1994) (Scalia analyzed the problem from the standpoint of the state's historical power to stop suicide as opposed to his normal approach of examining the historical right of individuals to engage in specified conduct.).

143 Nelson, *The Common Law in Colonial America (Vol. III)* at 117.

144 530 U.S. 57, 92 (2000). O'Connor, joined by Rehnquist, Breyer, and Ginsburg, with Souter and Thomas concurring separately.

145 Because of its focus on property rights, the Takings Clause is discussed in the next chapter.

CHAPTER 25 CONSERVATIVE OPINIONS RECONSIDERED: OTHER

1 Mary Sarah Bilder, *The Transatlantic Constitution* 168–175, 183–185 (2004).

2 Resistance to the Tea and Sugar Acts was not based on British regulation of commerce but on lack of colonial participation in the legislative process. Alison L. LaCroix, *The Ideological Origins of American Federalism* 40–44 (2010).

3 *Id.* at 54–56, 60–65, 69.

4 After 200 years or so, courts are still facing some of the complex international governing issues that mid-eighteenth-century colonials faced. *See* Breyer, *The Court and the World; American Law and New Global Realities* (2015).

5 William E. Nelson, *The Common Law in Colonial America (Vol. III)* 3, 13 (2016).

6 Some early court decisions by judges who participated in the framing adopted expansive concepts of commerce, including a case involving a 1790 Act regulating seamen's working conditions, United States v. The William, 28 Fed. Cases 614 (D. Mass. 1808) (No. 16 700) (David, J.) ("Further, the power to regulate commerce is not to be confined to the adoption of measures, exclusively beneficial to commerce itself, or tending to its advancement; but, in our national system, as in all modern sovereignties, it is also to be considered as an instrument for other purposes of general policy and interest. The mode of its management is a consideration of great delicacy and importance; but the national right, or power, under the constitution,

to adopt regulations of commerce to other purposes, than the mere advancement of commerce, appears to me to unquestionable."); *see* Case of the Brig Wilson, 1 Brockenbrough's Rep. 423, 431 (Va. Cir. 1820) (Marshall, C.J.) ("There is not, in the Constitution, one syllable on the subject of navigation. And yet, every power that pertains to navigation has been uniformly exercised, and, in the opinion of all, been rightfully exercise, by congress."); Gibbons v. Ogden, 22 U.S. (9 Wheat.) 195, 203–204 (1824) (Marshall, C.J.); United States v. Coombs, 37 U.S. (12 Pet.) 72 (1838) (Story, J.).

7 Jack T. Valauri, "Originalism and the Necessary and Proper Clause," 39 *Ohio Northern University Law Review* 773 (2013). Conservative Circuit Judge Lawrence Silberman upheld the ACA on the ground that "to 'regulate' can mean to require action, and nothing in the definition appears to limit that power only to those already active in relation to an interstate market," which disagreed with Scalia on the reading of the constitutional text. Seven-Sky v. Holder, 661 F.3d 1, 16 (D.C. Cir. 2011).

8 Robert J. Purshaw, Jr., & Grant S. Nelson, "A Critique of the Narrow Interpretation of the Commerce Clause," 96 *Northwestern University Law Review* 695, 696, 718 (2001).

9 George Mason of Virginia "feared that congress would pass laws that allowed merchants of the Northern states to demand exorbitant freight costs and to monopolize the purchase of commodities, paying prices that served their interest 'to the great injury of the landed interests' and the 'impoverishment of the people.'" Pauline Maier, *Ratification* 46 (2010); *see* Murray Dry, "The Case against Ratification: Anti-Federalist Constitutional Thought," in *The Framing and Ratification of the Constitution* 290 (Leonard W. Levy & Dennis J. Mahoney eds. 1987) ("it is hard to imagine the major arguments of *The Federalist* # 10, which refers to regulating 'various and interfering interests,' supporting anything but a strong government and a broad commerce power"); Mark R. Killenbeck, "The Original (?) Public (?) Meaning of 'Commerce,'" 16 *University of Pennsylvania Journal of Constitutional Law* 289 (2013) (a broad commerce power meant that it extended to any offense that interferes with, obstructs, or prevents trade and navigation); Killenbeck, "Pursuing the Great Experiment: Reserved Powers in a Post-Ratification Compound Republic," 1999 *Supreme Court Review* 8 (whole purpose of the Constitutional Convention was to restrict the states and create a viable national government).

10 E.g., Leo Marx, *The Machine in the Garden: Technology and the Pastoral Ideal in America* 148–149 (1964).

11 *See* Killenbeck, *supra*. One scholar focused on the pro-debtor proclivities of state legislatures and the resulting negative effect on raising capital for the new country, abroad as well as at home. Those concerns led to a stronger national government, particularly in the economic spheres, including the power to tax, the sole power to issue currency, and the payment of bonds that funded the Revolutionary War debt at par (mostly to well-off speculators with taxes levied on farmers). Woody Holton, *Unruly Americans and the Origins of the Constitution* (2007).

12 196 U.S. 375, 398 (1905); *see* Frank H. Easterbrook, "Federalism and Commerce," 36 *Harvard Journal of Law & Public Policy* 935, 936–937 (2013).

13 Gordon Wood, *The Idea of America* 138, 266 (2011).

14 Grant Nelson & Purshaw, "Rethinking the Commerce Clause: Applying First Principles to Uphold Federal Commercial Regulations but Preserve State Control over Social Issues," 85 *Iowa Law Review* 1 (1999); *see* Joseph Biancalona, "Originalism and the Commerce Clause," 71 *University of Cincinnati Law Review* 383, 388, 398, 402–403 (2002) ("The original, the enduring, principle of the Commerce Clause is

that Congress has the power to regulate economic activities that realistically take place on interstate markets.").

15 *See* Jeffrey Toobin, *The Oath* 278 (2012).

16 545 U.S. 1 (2005). Law Professor Michael S. Greve, a nonoriginalist conservative, gave high grades to Scalia's opinion in Gonzales v. Raich, 545 U.S. 1 (2005): "By reintroducing the Necessary and Proper Clause, the Scalia analysis clears the decks of *Wickard*'s inanities and reverts to an intelligible Commerce Clause that extends only to matters that are (a) commerce, meaning the voluntary exchange of goods and services; and (b) 'among the several statues' (including ... the first and last leg of any interstate transaction). . . . In John Marshall's words, the congressional *end* must be legitimate and within the scope of the Constitution. . . . [N]either the Gun Free School Zones Act in *Lopez* nor the civil remedies provision at issue in *Morrison* was plausibly related, let alone necessary, to anything having to do with interstate commerce." Greve, *The Upside-Down Constitution* 346 (2012). Relying on the complexity of the issues and relative expertise in *Lopez*, Breyer deferred to Congress and voted to uphold the law. *See* Breyer, *Making Our Democracy Work* 127–128 (2010).

17 Many law professors argued that the Commerce Clause challenge to the ACA was unprecedented and baseless. *E.g.*, Andrew Koppelman, "Did the Law Professors Blow It in the Health Care Case?," 2014 *University of Illinois Law Review* 1273 (2014).

18 ACA, 132 S.Ct. at 2646.

19 A vote to strike down the Affordable Care Act arguably requires a vote to strike down federal laws restricting abortion. In Gonzales v. Carhart, 550 U.S. 124, 169 (2007) (federal partial-birth abortion law), the concurrence by Thomas joined by Scalia noted the parties did not brief the Commerce Clause issue.

20 Wood, *The Idea of America* 258 (2011); *see* Arthur Schlesinger, Jr., *The New York Review of Books*, Dec. 21, 2000 ("Hamilton's enthusiasm over the dynamics of individual acquisition was always tempered by a belief in government regulation and control.").

21 Nelson, *The Common Law in Colonial America (Vol. III)* 133 (2016). The text omits reference to the dormant (or negative) Commerce Clause, which limits state power over interstate commerce in the absence of federal government regulation. John Marshall suggested the doctrine in Wilson v. Black-Bird Creek Marsh Co., 27 U.S. (2 Pet.) 245 (1829), it was expanded upon in Cooley v. Board of Wardens, 53 U.S. 299 (12 How.) (1851), and was first applied to strike down a state law in Reading R.R. v. Pennsylvania, 82 U.S. (15 Wall.) 232 (1873). Despite its impressive pedigree, Scalia rejected the dormant Commerce Clause on the basis of textualism ("Congress shall have Power ... to regulate Commerce ... among the several States"), the role of judicial power, and originalism. Scalia called the Dormant Commerce Clause "an unjustified judicial invention." "The historical record provided no grounds for reading the Commerce Clause to be other than what it says – an authorization for Congress to regulate commerce." Tyler Pipe Ind., Inc. v. Washington Dept. of Revenue, 483 U.S. 232, 263 (1987) (Scalia, J, concurring in part, dissenting in part); *see, e.g.*, American Trucking Ass'n v. Smith, 496 U.S. 167, 202–203 (2002) (Scalia, J., concurring in judgment); Comptroller of the Treasury of Maryland v. Wynne, 135 S.Ct. 1787 (2015) (Scalia, J., dissenting). Scalia's view was pro-state and libertarian; it was also a minority view and controversial. Mark Tushnet, "Scalia and the Dormant Commerce Clause: A Foolish Formalism?," 12 *Cardozo Law Review* 1717, 1724 (1991); *see* Breyer, *Making Our Democracy Work* 129–131 (2010). Finally, complicating the effort to understand the concept is that courts were little involved in enforcing the Commerce Clause until the mid nineteenth century. William M. Treanor, "Process

Theory, Majoritarianism, and the Original Understanding," 75 *Fordham Law Review* 2989, 2991–2992, 2994 (2007).

22 505 U.S. 1003, 1028 n. 15 (1992), where Scalia observed that the Bill of Rights Madison presented to the first Congress in June 1789 included: "No person shall be . . . obliged to relinquish his property, where it may be necessary for public use, without a just compensation." That language was limited to physical takings. That language was also legislative history.

23 *Id.* at 1055–1060, citing, *e.g.*, M'Clenahan v. Curwin, 3 Yeates 362, 373 (Pa. 1802) (citizens "were bound to contribute as much of [land], as by the laws of the country, were deemed necessary for the public convenience"); Mugler v. Kansas, 123 U.S. 623, 664 (1887) (upholding ordinance that effectively prohibited operation of a previously lawful brewery, although the "establishments will become of no value as property").

24 John T. Noonan, Jr., *Narrowing the Nation's Power; The Supreme Court Sides with the States* (2002). The (liberal) New York Times editorial, Aug. 21, 2002, stated: "The Supreme Court's conservative justices say they practice judicial restraint and accuse their liberal colleagues of activism. But a conservative judge has just written a blistering book arguing that the court's conservatives are actually engaged in a huge power grab, under the banner of respect for the states, that seriously erodes the rights of ordinary Americans."

25 *Compare* Gary S. Gildin, "The Supreme Court's Legislative Agenda to Free Government from Accountability for Constitutional Deprivation," 114 *Penn State Law Review* 1333, 1383 (2010) (Court's conduct "suggest[s] the Court is pursuing an agenda at odds with the intent of the legislature that enacted Section 1983 to provide a broad remedy to citizens deprived of their constitutional rights"), *with* Kurt T. Lash, "Leaving Aside the *Chisholm* Trail: The Eleventh Amendment and the Background Principle of Strict Construction," 50 *William & Mary Law Review* 1577, 1697 (2009) (the original understanding of Articles I and III, along with the Ninth, Tenth, and Eleventh Amendments required preservation of state sovereign immunity; "the federal separation of powers is itself premised on the existence of independent sovereign people(s) in the states"); *see* Erwin Chemerinsky, "Against Sovereign Immunity," 53 *Stanford Law Review* 1201, 1216 (2001) (separation of powers cuts against sovereign immunity).

26 Treanor, "Against Textualism," 103 *Northwestern University Law Review* 983, 992 (2009).

27 Treanor, "The Origins and Significance of the Just Compensation Clause of the Fifth Amendment," 94 *Yale Law Journal* 694, 708 (1985).

28 *Id.* at 695, 708.

29 Ely, "'That due satisfaction may be made:' the Fifth Amendment and the Origins of the Compensation Principle," 36 *The American Journal of Legal History* 1, 4 (1992).

30 *Id.* at 12, 14, 17–18. Originalists Thomas and Scalia took a narrow view of the eminent-domain power in Kelo v. New London, 545 U.S. 489 (2002), and voted to hold the Connecticut statute unconstitutional.

31 John F. Hart, "Takings and Compensation in Early America: The Colonial Highway Acts in Social Context," 40 *American Journal of Legal History* 253 (1996).

32 John P. Reid, *The Concept of Liberty* 25 (1988). Reid entitled a subchapter, "The Centrality of Property." *Id.* at 29. The right to security was tied to the protection of property. Reid, *Constitutional History of the American Revolution; The Authority of Rights* 34–38 (1986). "Property rights" was a concept that also included the historic birthright or inheritance of an Englishman, akin to other constitutional rights.

It was a shared right, but it was very real. *Id.* at 99–106, 109–110. Madison wrote that property "embraces every thing to which a man may attach value and have a right, . . . [including] his opinions and the free communication of them" and that "conscience is the most sacred of all property." *The Complete Madison* 267–269 (Saul K. Padover ed. 1953).

33 *Id.* at 69, 72; *see* Bruce Ackerman, *We the People; Foundations* 116 (1991) ("For the first 150 years [after the founding], few doubted that the Founding Federalists placed a high constitutional value on private property and market freedom.").

34 521 U.S. 902 (1997).

35 Scalia also argued that the President's obligation to take care that the laws be faithfully executed cannot be delegated to state officials. *Id.* at 922. The Constitution does not deny the President that power and Scalia cited no authority for his position beyond the provisions themselves.

36 *Id.* at 940, 955–962.

37 Merkel, *"The District of Columbia v. Heller* and Antonin Scalia's Perverse Sense of Originalism," 13 *Lewis & Clark Law Review* 349, 363 (2009).

38 Wesley J. Campbell, "Commandeering and Constitutional Change," 122 *Yale Law Journal* 1104, 1171–1179 (2013).

39 LaCroix, *The Ideological Origins of American Federalism* at 196.

40 Siding with a number of constitutional historians, including Samuel Beer, Edward S. Corwin, and H. Jefferson Powell, one scholar accused Scalia of "finding a novel anticommandeer principle in the recesses of the Constitution." James B. Staab, *The Political Thought of Justice Antonin Scalia* 288–293, 307 n. 198 (2006); *see* Frank B. Cross, *The Failed Promise of Originalism* 98–99 (2013) (in *Plaut,* Scalia took evidence from the framing era that was not identical to the current controversy and found it analogous. In *Printz,* Scalia took evidence from the framing era that was not identical to the current controversy and distinguished it.). Scalia's argument that early Congresses rarely exercised commandeering powers can also be answered both by the point that "the failure of the early Congresses to address the scope of federal power in a particular area or to exercise authority was not an argument against its existence," 521 U.S. at 949 (Stevens, J.), and by the fact that the Senate was appointed by state legislatures and would be unlikely to commandeer states, Gene R. Nichol, "Justice Scalia and the *Printz* Case: The Trials of an Occasional Originalist," 70 *University of Colorado Law Review* 953, 971 (1999). A nonoriginalist point is that the balance of power has changed since 1789. Then, there were strong states and a weak national government. Now, the opposite is true. *See generally* Greve, *The Upside-Down Constitution.*

41 LaCroix, *supra* at 201.

42 135 S.Ct. 2652 (2015).

43 *E.g., The Anti-Federalist Papers and the Constitutional Convention Debates* 275–277 (Ralph Ketcham ed. 1986) (statement of "Brutus" on Oct. 18, 1787); Bruce Ackerman, *We the People: Foundations* 6 (1991) ("the distinctive spirit of the American Constitution . . . seeks to distinguish between two different decisions that may be made in a democracy. The first is a decision by the American people; the second, by their government"); Wood, "The History of Rights in Early America," in *The Nature of Rights at the American Founding and Beyond* 245 (Barry A. Shain ed. 2007) ("The American people, unlike the English, retained an actual law-making authority. They could make fundamental laws or constitutions, whereas their legislative representatives could make only ordinary statutes.").

44 Raoul Berger, "Standing to Sue in Public Actions: Is It a Constitutional Requirement?," 78 *Yale Law Journal* 816, 827 (1969); *see* F. Andrew Hessick, "Standing, Injury in Fact, and Private Rights," 93 *Cornell Law Review* 275, 279–286 (2008).

45 Scalia, "The Doctrine of Standing as an Essential Element of the Separation of Powers," 17 *Suffolk University Law Review* 881 (1983).

46 *See, e.g.*, Ferguson v. City of Charleston, 532 U.S. 67, 93 (Scalia, J., dissenting).

47 Jefferson Powell wrote: "When the Massachusetts Senate accused the Virginia legislature of usurping the interpretive authority of the federal courts, Madison's *Report of 1800* responded first by pointing out that not all 'instances of usurped power' could eventuate in justiciable cases. . . . " Powell, "The Political Grammar of Early Constitutional Law," 71 *North Carolina Law Review* 949, 983 (1993); see Powell, *Languages of Power* 139–148 (1991) (reproducing full text).

48 529 U.S. 765, 773–778 (2000) (also holding that a *qui tam* civil action does not lie against a state); *see* Steven L. Winter, "What If Justice Scalia Took History and the Rule of Law Seriously?," 12 *Duke Environmental Law & Policy Forum* 155, 165 (2001).

49 Cass R. Sunstein, "What's Standing after *Lujan*? Of Citizen Suits, 'Injuries,' and Article III," 91 *Michigan Law Review* 163, 177–178 (1992).

50 Note, "The Appellate Jurisprudence of Justice Antonin Scalia," 54 *University of Chicago Law Review* 705, 714–715 (1987).

51 *See* Note, "The Mischaracterization of Justice Scalia as Environmental Foe: What Harm to Standing Following the Court's Stance in *Laidlaw Environmental Services (TOC), Inc. v. Friends of the Earth*," 10 *Widener Law Review* 561 (2000). Scalia was more sanguine of the judiciary's role before he was a judge. Writing in 1980 about judicial enforcement of unconstitutional delegation, he noted that "even those who do not relish the prospect of regular judicial enforcement of the unconstitutional delegation doctrine might well support the Court's making an example of one – just one – of the many enactments that appear to violate the principle. The educational effect on Congress might well be substantial." Scalia, "A Note on the Benzene Case," 20 *Regulation* 28 (July/Aug. 1980).

52 133 S.Ct. 2675 (2013).

53 James E. Pfander & Daniel D. Birk, "Article III Judicial Power, the Adverse-Party Requirement, and Non-Contentious Jurisdiction," 124 *Yale Law Journal* 1346 (2015).

54 Powell, *A Community Built on Words* 66–73 (2002).

55 *See id.* at 71–73. Powell noted: "One of the many ironies of U.S. constitutional history is the identification of John Marshall with the view of constitutional interpretation that locates it almost exclusively in the judicial branch." *Id.* at 73. Powell noted that another irony wrongly credited Marshall with the creation of judicial review. *Id.*

CHAPTER 26 LIBERAL OPINIONS RECONSIDERED

1 New York Times v. United States, 403 U.S. 713 (1971) (the *Pentagon Papers Case*); H. Jefferson Powell, *A Community Built on Words* 61 (2002).

2 Leonard W. Levy, *Original Intent and the Framers' Constitution* 195–220 (1988). There were instances in the colonial era of truth being accepted as a defense in a libel case. William E. Nelson, *The Common Law in Colonial America (Vol. III): The Chesapeake and New England Colonies* 88 (2016).

3 Walter Berns, *The First Amendment and the Future of American Democracy* 89–101 (1985). Before he was appointed Chief Justice, John Marshall, a strong Federalist, defended the constitutionality of the Alien and Sedition Acts. *Address of the Minority*

in the Virginia Legislature to the People of that State; Containing a Vindication of the Constitutionality of the Alien and Sedition Laws 2, 14 (1799).

4 John P. Reid, *The Concept of Liberty in the Age of the American Revolution* 117 (1988).

5 Texas v. Johnson, 491 U.S. 397 (1989); Chaplinsky v. State of New Hampshire, 315 U.S. 568 (1942). Laurence Tribe called the analysis "constitutionally suspect." Scalia, *A Matter of Interpretation* 81–82 (1997) (comment by Tribe).

6 Eugene Volokh, "Symbolic Expression and the Original Meaning of the First Amendment," 97 *Georgetown Law Journal* 1057, 1060 (2009).

7 *See* Geoffrey R. Stone, "Content Regulation and the First Amendment," 25 *William & Mary Law Review* 189 (1983).

8 Texas v. Johnson, *supra*; Chaplinsky v. State of New Hampshire, *supra*.

9 491 U.S. 397 (1989).

10 505 U.S. 377 (1992).

11 Amar, "The Case of the Missing Amendments: R.A.V. v. City of St. Paul," 106 *Harvard Law Review* 124, 127 (1992); Robert Austin Ruescher, "Saving Title VII: Using Intent to Distinguish Harassment from Expression," 23 *Review of Litigation* 349, 359 (2004) ("R.A.V. established a new standard for determining the constitutionality of laws restricting speech with 'slight social value.'").

12 Kagan, "Regulation of Hate Speech and Pornography after R.A.V.," 60 *University of Chicago Law Review* 873, 878 (1993).

13 *Id.* at 882–883.

14 *E.g.*, Anthony G. Amsterdam, "Perspectives on the Fourth Amendment," 107 *Harvard Law Review* 349 (1974).

15 Amar, *The Bill of Rights* 68–74 (1998). Three cases in England and Massachusetts in the 1760s, all well known in the colonies, have been credited with being the spark for the Fourth Amendment. All three involved searches pursuant to general warrants. William J. Stuntz, "The Substantive Origins of Criminal Procedure," 105 *Yale Law Journal* 393, 396–402 (1995).

16 Thomas Y. Davies, "Recovering the Original Fourth Amendment," 98 *Michigan Law Review* 547, 657–660, 745 (1999); Davies, 43 *Texas Tech Law Review* at 85–90.

17 *Id.* at 551. In Maryland v. King, 133 S.Ct. 1958, 1980–1982 (2013), discussed in Chapter 8, Scalia equated the search of an arrestee without a warrant with a search pursuant to a general warrant. However, the backgrounds and rationales of the two types of searches differ, *e.g.*, the latter is an abuse of judicial power, identified with the Crown; there was no public police force as we know it. Scalia also stated that, "I doubt that the proud men who wrote the charter of our liberties would have been so eager to open their mouths for royal inspection." *Id.* at 1989. But King was in custody pursuant to a lawful arrest and those holding him were the free citizens of the United States, not the British monarch.

18 Davies, 98 *Michigan Law Review* at 745; *see* Robert A. Rutland, *The Birth of the Bill of Rights* 1776–1791, at 20–21 (1955); David E. Steinberg, "High School Drug Testing and the Original Understanding of the Fourth Amendment," 30 *Hasting Constitutional Law Quarterly* 263 (2003).

19 Davies, 98 *Michigan Law Review* at 551, 554. The amendment that Madison proposed to the First Congress, modified by the Select Committee, more clearly made the point: "The rights of the people to be secured in their persons, their houses, their papers, and their other property, from all unreasonable searches and seizures, shall not be violated by warrants issued without probable cause, supported by oath or affirmation, or not particularly describing the places to be searched, or the persons or things to

be seized." The Select Committee changed the wording. Leonard W. Levy, *Origins of the Bill of Rights* 282, 285 (1999). Reid noted that the general-warrant problem was more severe in Britain than in America, although the practice was well publicized in America. Reid, *Constitutional History of the United States; The Authority of Rights* 194–195 (1986).

20 Davies, 98 *Michigan Law Review* at 551, 554.

21 267 U.S. 132 (1925).

22 Davies, "The Supreme Court Giveth and the Supreme Court Taketh Away: The Century of Fourth Amendment Search and Seizure Doctrine," 100 *Journal of Criminal Law and Criminology* 933, 965–971 (2010).

23 California v. Acevedo, 500 U.S.565, 581 (1991). Scalia cited only Akhil R. Amar, "The Bill of Rights as a Constitution," 100 *Yale Law Journal* 1131, 1171–1178 (1991) (who had relied on Scalia) and the case of Huckle v. Money, 95 Eng. Rep. 768 (K.B. 1763), which involved a general warrant (not a warrantless search), where the issue was the propriety of the substantial damages awarded for the unlawful search.

24 Davies, "The Fictional Character of Law-and-Order Originalism: A Case Study of the Distortions and Evasions of Framing-Era Arrest Doctrine in *Atwater v. Lago Vista*," 37 *Wake Forest Law Review* 239, 263 n. 64 (2002); Davies, 100 *Journal of Criminal Law and Criminology* at 937, 952; Davies, 98 *Michigan Law Review* at 547.

25 Davies, 37 *Wake Forest Law Review* at 250; Davies, "Independent State Ground: Should State Courts Depart from the Fourth Amendment in Construing Their Own Constitutions, and If So, on What Basis beyond Simple Disagreement with the United States Supreme Court's Result? Correcting Search-and-Seizure History: Now-Forgotten-Common Law Warrantless Arrest Standards and the Original Understanding of 'Due Process of Law,'" 77 *Mississippi Law Journal* 1, 6–11 (2007); Davies, 98 *Michigan Law Review* at 594; Richard M. Re, "The Due Process Exclusionary Rule," 127 *Harvard Law Review* 1887 (2014).

26 Davies, "Can You Handle the Truth? The Framers Preserved Common-Law Criminal Arrest and Search Rules in 'Due Process of Law' – 'Fourth Amendment Reasonableness' Is Only a Modern, Destructive, Judicial Myth," 43 *Texas Tech Law Review* 51, 132–133 (2010).

27 Davies, 77 *Mississippi Law Journal* at 54–56; Davies, 100 *Journal of Criminal Law and Criminology* at 943–944.

28 Davies, 37 *Wake Forest Law Review* at 248, 250.

29 Davies has argued that the Supreme Court simply invented a new rule in Carroll v. United States, 267 U.S. 132, 156–159 (1925), namely, that law-enforcement officers could make a warrantless search of automobiles on the basis of probable cause. Davies, 100 *Journal of Criminal Law and Criminology* at 967. The division between felony and misdemeanor was different at common law than now – there were fewer felonies. Horace L. Wilgus, "Arrest without a Warrant," 22 *Michigan Law Review* 541, 572–573 (1924).

30 358 U.S. 307 (1959); *see* Davies, 98 *Michigan Law Review* at 679; Davies, 100 *Journal of Criminal Law and Criminology* at 979–980; Davies e-mail to author, Dec. 3, 2014.

31 358 U.S. at 315.

32 The Supreme Court's expansion of the Fourth Amendment dated from Boyd v. United States, 116 U.S. 616 (1886), which created a privilege for producing documents that themselves were unprivileged. Davies called *Boyd* "a classic example of unbridled judicial activism conducted under the cover of 'history.'" Davies, 77 *Mississippi Law Journal* at 203.

33 *Id.* at 80.

34 *Id.* at 61.

35 Writing earlier, Levy said: "The Fourth Amendment would not emerge from colonial precedent; rather it would repudiate them.... The ideas comprising the Fourth Amendment reversed rather than formalized colonial precedents. Reasonable searches and seizures in colonial America closely approximated whatever the searcher thought reasonable. Levy, *Original Intent and the Framers' Constitution* 224 (1988); *see* William Cuddihy, "Warrantless House-to-House Searches and Fourth Amendment Originalism: A Reply to Professor Davies," 44 *Texas Tech Law Review* 997, 998 (2012); *see generally* Cuddihy, *The Fourth Amendment: Origins and Original Meaning*, 602–1791 (2009). Cuddihy's evidence suggests that Massachusetts may have been a special case with somewhat different problems than other colonies and early states, which further complicates the picture for originalists. Davies disputed Cuddihy's broader arguments, including that warrantless searches were a major concern at the founders. Davies, 43 *Texas Tech Law Review* at 89 n. 189.

36 Scalia's opinions have been criticized on other grounds. While noting that Scalia's claim for coherence was strong, one commentator observed: "The shortcomings of the textualist methodology applied by Justice Scalia in criminal procedure cases are not hard to see. Inflexible, pedantry, lack of sensitivity to the needs of law enforcement (or to deter illegal law enforcement), the absence of a role for decent moral sympathies – these and other obvious limitations only begin the familiar catalogue. Scholars have already criticized such tendencies at length...." George Kannar, "The Constitutional Catechism of Antonin Scalia," 99 *Yale Law Journal* 1297, 1342 (1990).

37 132 S.Ct. 945 (2012).

38 3 Blackstone, *Commentaries* 208–215 (1st American ed. 1772).

39 *Restatement of Torts* § 218, Comments b & c (1935). Scalia's discussion of trespass was not extensive. The distinction may also cast doubt on Scalia's originalist analysis in *Hicks* (movement of stereo equipment). See Susan Staves, "Chattel Property Rules and the Construction of Englishness," 12 *Law & History Review* 123, 124 (1994) ("Early property law was much more concerned with real property than with chattel property; in the eighteenth century, lawyers played a kind of catch-up game in which effort was expended to develop (or, less sympathetically, to complicate) the law of chattels.").

40 Posner, *Reflections* at 216.

41 508 U.S. 366 (1993).

42 Eric J. Segall noted a problem. Scalia said that "even if a 'frisk' prior to arrest would have been considered impermissible in 1791 ... perhaps it is only since that time that concealed weapons capable of harming the interrogator quickly ... have become common – which might alter the judgment of what is 'reasonable' under the original standard." 508 U.S. at 382. Segall asks, "But if, according to Justice Scalia, the interpretation of the word 'unreasonable' to a given set of facts can change, why can't the meaning of phrases like 'cruel and unusual punishments,' 'equal protection,' 'liberty,' and 'due process,' also change?" http://wakeforestlawreview.com/2015/09/will-the-real-justice-scalia-please-stand-up/.

43 Davies, 98 *Michigan Law Review* at 629 n. 216; Davies, 37 *Wake Forest Law Review* at 304 n. 22.

44 David H. Flaherty, *Privacy in Colonial New England* 195 (1972).

45 *See* Edwin J. Butterfoss, "Bright Line Breaking Point: Embracing Justice Scalia's Call for the Supreme Court to Abandon as Unreasonable Approach to Fourth Amendment Searches and Seizures Law," 82 *Tulane Law Review* 77, 88 nn. 75, 76 (2007).

46 National Treasury Employees Union v. Von Raab, 489 U.S. 646, 681 (1989).

47 *Id.*

48 John H. Langbein, Renée Lettow Lerner & Bruce P. Smith, *History of the Common Law* 613 (2009) ("A large part of the business of administering the so-called Bloody Code [in 19th century England] was the selection of those who were hanged as examples.").

49 Reid, *The Authority of Rights* 39–40 (1986). The first few Congresses were more nationalistic than the ratifiers. Thornton Anderson, *Creating the Constitution* 174–183 (1993).

50 Davies, 77 *Mississippi Law Journal* at 222.

51 Shapiro, *"Beyond Reasonable Doubt" and "Probable Cause"; Historical Perspectives on the Anglo-American Law of Evidence* 24 (1991).

52 *Id.* at 1–41.

53 Aaron T. Knapp, "Law's Revolutionary: James Wilson and the Birth of American Jurisprudence," 29 *Journal of Law & Politics* 189, 271 (2013). There was no standard practice in the thirteen states with respect to many aspects of civil juries, which was one reason for its absence from the original Constitution. Lerner, "The Failure of Originalism in Preserving Constitutional Rights to Civil Jury Trial," 22 *William & Mary Bill of Rights Journal* 811, 825–828 (2014); *see* Nelson, *The Common Law in Colonial America (Vol. II): The Middle Colonies and the Carolinas* 3 (2013).

54 Nelson, *Marbury v. Madison* 16–22 (2000).

55 Frank Warren Hackett, "Has a Trial Judge of a United States Court the Right to Direct a Verdict?," 24 *Yale Law Journal* 127 (1914); Lerner, *supra* at 868–878. Colonial Virginia seems to have given judges greater powers. Nelson, *The Common Law in Colonial America (Vol. III)* at 40–41 (2016). There were variations within colonies, especially in Virginia. *Id.* at 48–49.

56 The conventional understanding that all felonies were punishable by death applied more to England than to the colonies or states. But there was little judicial discretion in any event. Kathryn Preyer, "The Criminal Law, and Reform in Post-Revolutionary Virginia," in *Blackstone in America; Selected Essays of Kathryn Preyer* 147 (Mary Sarah Bilder, Maeva Marcus & R. Kent Newmyer eds. 2009).

57 Mark DeWolf Howe, "Juries as Judges of Criminal Law," 52 *Harvard Law Review* 582 (1939); Albert W. Alschuler & Andrew G. Deiss, "A Brief History of the Criminal Jury in the United States," 61 *University of Chicago Law Review* 867 (1994); Stephanos Bibas, "Two Cheers, Not Three, for Sixth Amendment Originalism," 34 *Harvard Journal of Law & Public Policy* 45, 46–47 (2010); *see* Stephen B. Presser, *The Original Misunderstanding; The English, the Americans and the Dialectic of Federalist Jurisprudence* 105–111 (1991).

58 Nelson, *The Common Law in Colonial America (Vol. III)* at 7–8.

59 *Id.* at 124.

60 Langbein, "The English Criminal Trial Jury on the Eve of the French Revolution," in *The Trial Jury in England, France, Germany 1700–1900*, at 38 (Antonio Padoa Schioppa ed. 1987). Nelson paints the same picture in America. Nelson, *Marbury v. Madison* at 22.

61 Nelson, "The Province of the Judiciary," 37 *John Marshall Law Review* 325 (2004).

62 Langbein, Lerner & Smith, *supra* at 624.

63 Langbein, *Trial Jury* at 37.

64 Nelson, "The Lawfinding Power of Colonial American Juries," 71 *Ohio State Law Journal* 1003 (2010); *see* Stephanos Bibas, "Two Cheers, Not Three, for Sixth Amendment Originalism," 34 *Harvard Journal of Law & Public Policy* 45 (2010); Kathryn Turner Preyer, "*U.S. v. Callender*, Judge and Jury in a Republican Society," in *Origins of the Federal Judiciary: Essays on the Judiciary Act of 1789*, at 173 (Maeva Marcus ed. 1992); *see* Preyer, "Two Enlightened Reformers of the Criminal Law: Thomas Jefferson of Virginia and Peter Leopold, Grand Duke of Tuscany," in *Blackstone in America* at 173. Stevens's opinion for the Court in *Apprendi* focused on the role of the judge: "[W]ith respect to the criminal law of felonious conduct, 'the English trial judge in the late 18th century had very little explicit discretion in sentencing. The substantive criminal law tended to be sanction-specific; it prescribed a particular sentence for each offense. The judge was meant simply to impose that sentence (unless he thought in the circumstances that the sentence was so inappropriate that he should invoke the pardon power to commute it).'" 530 U.S. at 479, quoting Langbein, *Trial Jury*.

65 In Yates v. Evatt, 500 U.S. 391 (1991), the Justices assumed that the operative standard in criminal trials was guilt beyond a reasonable doubt. But even that fundamental requirement cannot be established with certainty as existing in 1791. Langbein, Lerner & Smith, *supra* at 607 ("the beyond-reasonable-doubt standard . . . would not be articulated until the late eighteenth century and did not become broadly accepted until the nineteenth century").

66 *See* Robert L. Jones, "Finishing a Friendly Argument: The Jury and the Historical Origins of Diversity Jurisdiction," 82 *New York University Law Review* 997 (2007) (the prospect of more sophisticated jurors in federal courts who were more sympathetic to creditors and more understanding of commercial litigants was a factor in creating diversity jurisdiction).

67 Lerner, 22 *William & Mary Bill of Rights Journal* 811; *see* Lerner, "The Rise of Directed Verdict: Jury Power in Civil Cases before the Federal Rules of 1938," 81 *George Washington Law Review* 448 (2013).

68 *Id.* at 457.

69 Lerner, 22 *William & Mary Bill of Rights Journal* at 878–880. In the colonies "jury trial was denied not by abolishing the right to a jury, but by shifting special types of cases from common law courts to the vice-admiralty court, which sat without juries." Reid, *The Authority of Rights* at 191. The operation of the vice-admiralty court became a major grievance leading to the Revolution. *Id.* at 177–183.

70 Edith Guild Henderson, "The Background of the Seventh Amendment," 80 *Harvard Law Review* 289 (1966).

71 541 U.S. 36 (2004).

72 448 U.S. 56, 66 (1980).

73 *See* Davies, "What Did the Framers Know and When Did They Know It? Fictional Originalism in *Crawford v. Washington*," 71 *Brooklyn Law Review* 105, 114–116 (2005).

74 Davies, "Not 'the Framers' Design': How the Framing-Era Ban against Hearsay Evidence Refutes the *Crawford-Davis* 'Testimonial' Formulation of the Scope of the Original Confrontation Clause," 15 *Brooklyn Journal of Law & Policy* 349 (2007).

75 *See* Richard D. Friedman, "No Link: The Jury and the Origins of the Confrontation Right and the Hearsay Rule," in *"The Dearest Birth Right of the People of England": The Jury in the History of the Common Law* 93–100 (John Cairns and Grant McLeod eds. 2002).

76 Davies, 15 *Brooklyn Journal of Law & Policy* at 304. Another commentator raised an objection that has also been applied to the Fourth Amendment. Scalia "gives no explanation why it can be concluded that the Confrontation Clause constitutionalized common law as stated in English decisions when other parts of the Sixth Amendment expressly rejected English common law. . . . What *Crawford's* historical inquiry ignores is that America's criminal procedure during the framing generation was simply not the same as England. . . . It had shifted towards an adversary system." Randolph N. Jonakait, "The Too-Easy Historical Assumptions of *Crawford v. Washington*," 71 *Brooklyn Law Review* 219, 224 (2005).

77 Davies, 15 *Brooklyn Journal of Law & Public Policy* at 349.

78 *Id.* at 351, 352; Davies, "Selective Originalist: Sorting Out Which Aspects of *Giles's* Forfeiture Exception to Confrontation Were or Were Not 'Established at the Time of the Founding,'" 13 *Lewis & Clark Law Review* 605, 634–642 (2009).

79 Unsworn hearsay statements could be used to corroborate or impeach testimony given by another witness at the trial or to prove a background fact. Davies, 15 *Brooklyn Journal of Law & Policy* at 349.

80 *Id.* at 436.

81 Friedman, in *"The Dearest Birth Right"* at 96.

82 Davies, 71 *Brooklyn Law Review* at 108; Davies, "Revisiting the Fictional Originalism in *Crawford's* 'Cross-Examination Rule': A Reply to Mr. Ky," 72 *Brooklyn Law Review* 557 (2007). Opportunity to cross-examine became a requirement in the nineteenth century. Davies, 13 *Lewis & Clark Law Review* at 645–646.

83 15 Davies, 15 *Brooklyn Journal of Law & Policy* at 398. English judges viewed the Marian rule as a settled exception to the cross-examination aspect of the confrontation right. *Id.*

84 Nelson, *Americanization of the Common Law* 26–26, 114 (1975); *see* Gavin Francis, *Adventures in Human Beings* 203 (2015) ("in Genesis, chapter 24, Abraham asks his servant to swear an oath by touching him in the hollow of the thigh – a reference to the ancient custom of swearing by the testes (hence, 'testify')").

85 Davies, 13 *Lewis & Clark Law Review* at 643.

86 Davies, 15 *Brooklyn Journal of Law & Policy* at 369–371.

87 *Id.* at 418.

88 *See* Bibas, 34 *Harvard Journal of Law & Public Policy* at 50–52.

89 Bibas, "The Limits of Textualism in Interpreting the Confrontation Clause," 37 *Harvard Journal of Law & Public Policy* 737, 741(2014). Scalia turned the ambiguous word "witness" into "testimony" without adequate analysis or foundation. *Id.* at 740. He similarly equated confrontation with the right to cross-examination. They are not identical, *e.g.*, Richard II, Act I, Scene 1: "Then call them to our presence – face to face, and frowning bow to bow, ourselves will hear the accuser and the accused freely speak." Coy v. Iowa, 487 U.S. 1012, 1016 (1988) (Scalia, J.). More research will clarify the relationships.

90 554 U.S. 353 (2008).

91 Davies, 13 *Lewis & Clark Law Review* at 609–610.

92 *Id.* at 612.

93 Ellen Liang Yee, "Forfeiture of Confrontation Rights in *Giles*: Justice Scalia's Faint-Hearted Fidelity to the Common Law," 100 *Journal of Criminal Law & Criminology* 1495, 1508, 1512, 1517 (2010); *see* Davies, 13 *Lewis & Clark Law Review* at 654.

94 Richard D. Friedman, "The Confrontation Clause Re-Rooted and Transformed," 2003–2004 *Cato Supreme Court Review* 439, 466.

95 *E.g.*, Friedman, *"Giles v. California,* A Personal Reflection," 13 *Lewis & Clark Law Review* 733 (2009).
96 *See* Jay Sigler, "A History of Double Jeopardy," 7 *American Journal of Legal History* 283, 290–298 (1963).
97 *Id.* at 299–306.
98 *Id.* at 298, 307–308.

CHAPTER 27 CONFLICTED OPINIONS RECONSIDERED

1 425 U.S. 1 (1976).
2 Gordon S. Wood, *The Creation of the American Republic, 1776–1787,* at 32–34, 107–114 (1969).
3 Zephyr Teachout, *Corruption in America; From Benjamin Franklin's Snuff Box to Citizens United* 38–39 (2014). The English concept of corruption included bribery, largely because of the crown's enormous power to dispense jobs and favors in contrast to colonial governors. Bernard Bailyn, *The Origins of American Politics* 43–51 (1969); *see* Shelley Burtt, "Ideas of Corruption in Eighteenth-Century England," in *Private and Public Corruption* 101, 115 (William C. Heffernan & John Klenig eds. 2004).
4 Teachout, *Corruption* at 50. Fear of corruption permeated many debates, including over federal appointments, the size of the House of Representatives, qualifications to hold office, and the frequency of elections. *Id.* at 56–80.
5 Brief of Amicus Curiae Professor Lawrence Lessig in McCutheon v. FEC, No. 12–536, Sup. Ct., which discussed various constitutional provisions designed to protect the country from corruption. The government's brief did not discuss the original public understanding.
6 Teachout, *supra* at 211.
7 *Id.* at 120, 232–233, 237. "Prior to *Buckley,* quid pro quo was not part of any definition of corruption." *Id.* at 239.
8 *See* Lessig, "Originalists Making It Up Again: *McCutcheon* and 'Corruption,'" www .thedailybeast.com/articles/2014/02 ("the Framers' view of corruption would have been enough to justify most campaign finance laws"); James D. Savage, "Corruption and Virtue at the Constitutional Convention," 56 *Journal of Policy* 174, 181 (1994) ("When the delegates spoke of corruption at the convention they did so in a manner that reflected classical republican concerns about dependency, cabals, patronage, unwarranted influence, and bribery."); Wood, *The Idea of America* 259 (2011) ("in the opposition language of the Anglo-American world, Hamilton set out to 'corrupt' American society to use monarchical-like governmental influence to tie existing commercial interests to the government and to create new hierarchies of interest and dependency"); Douglass C. North, John J. Wallis & Barry R. Weingast, *Violence and Social Orders* 307 (2009).
9 *E.g., The Federalist* No. 63 (Madison) (the Constitution's structure impedes "the danger of combining in pursuit of unjust measures"); Woody Holton, *Unruly Americans and the Origins of the Constitution* 237 (2007) (Anti-Federalists feared that "'the natural aristocracy' would 'easily unite their interests' behind slates of like-minded candidates").
10 In challenging the exemption for media corporations, Scalia acknowledged the problem. "Amassed corporate wealth that regularly sits astride the ordinary channels of information is much more likely to produce the New Corruption (too much of one point of view) than amassed corporate wealth that is generally busy making

money elsewhere." Austin v. Michigan Chamber of Commerce, 494 U.S. 652, 691 (1990). Actually, it was more like the Old Corruption. Scalia also pointed out that the campaign-finance laws favored incumbents. There has been a consistent anti-incumbency strain in American political life, although its relevance to constitutional law is unclear.

11 Wood, *supra* at 192.

12 *Id.* at 313. The Supreme Court rejected Jefferson's view, but not until 1819 in the *Dartmouth College Case*, 17 U.S. (4 Wheat.) 519 (1819). At the founding, the public, along with John Adams, Jefferson, and Madison, distrusted banks, which states chartered. Ron Chernow, *Alexander Hamilton* 346–348 (2004).

13 Laurence H. Tribe, "Dividing *Citizens United*: The Case V. the Controversy," 30 *Constitutional Commentary* 463 (2015) (bare result probably correct, but analysis wrong); *see generally* Lessig, *Republic Lost; How Money Corrupts Congress* (2011); Robert C. Post, *Citizens Divided; Campaign Reform and the Constitution* (2014).

14 Bruce Ackerman, *We the People: Foundations* 179 (1991). Ackerman read *The Federalist* No. 78 as relying on judicial review to curb factions: "When factional politicians break through constitutional constraints, the judges should invalidate their proposed statutes and expose them for what they are: mere stand-ins for '*the people themselves.*' Only the People can change the Constitution. . . . " Ackerman, *supra* at 192.

15 "Of course, in contemporary America, elected officials typically are most responsive not to actual (demographic) majorities but to shifting alliance of influential or well-financed pressure groups." H. Jefferson Powell, *The Moral Tradition of American Constitutionalism* 11 n. 24 (1993).

16 Frank H. Easterbrook, "The State of Madison's Vision of the State: A Public Choice Perspective," 107 *Harvard Law Review* 1328, 1331–1332 (1994).

17 *The Federalist* No. 51.

18 *Id.; see id.*, No. 10. While the cost of organizing a majority faction is large, so, too, are the benefits. *See* Mark Tushnet, "*The Federalist* and the Institutions of Fundamental Rights," in *The Framers and Fundamental Rights* 127 (Robert A. Licht ed. 1992).

19 *See* Easterbrook, *supra* at 1346–1347; Ackerman, *supra* at 246.

20 Brisbin, "Antonin Scalia, William Brennan, and the Politics of Expression: A Study of Legal Violence and Repression," 87 *American Political Science Review* 912, 918 (1993).

21 Eric J. Segall, "The Constitution According to Justices Scalia and Thomas: Alive and Kickin,'" 91 *Washington Law Review* 1663, 1665 (2014).

22 P. M. Vasudev, "Corporate Law and Its Efficiency; A Review of History," 50 *American Journal of Legal History* 237, 242–243 (2008–2010).

23 Wood, "The History of Rights in Early America," in *The Nature of Rights at the American Founding and Beyond* 250–251 (Barry A. Shain ed. 2007); *see* First National Bank v. Belotti, 435 U.S. 765, 828 (1978) (corporations do not have First Amendment free-speech rights where political expression is not a necessary component of their business).

24 Bailyn, *To Begin the World Anew* 50 (2003).

25 North *et al.*, *Violence and Social Orders* at 192, 197. Concern over the influence of stock corporations was reflected in England's Bubble Act of 1720, directed at the South Sea Bubble, and Adam Smith's *Wealth of Nations* (1776). "As late as 1776, the founder of modern economics [Smith] viewed corporations largely . . . as tools for the political manipulation of the economy." North *et al.*, *supra* at 205. In *The*

Liberal Tradition in America, Louis Hartz pointed out that at the founding America was economically underdeveloped and unsophisticated.

26 Limited liability did not develop as an attribute of corporations until the nineteenth century. Stephen B. Presser & Jamil S. Zainaldin, *Law and Jurisprudence in American History* 415 (8th ed. 2012).

27 From a textualist standpoint, the treatment of students and corporations should be the same, yet Scalia's concern for corporate rights was greater than for students' rights. He allowed inroads on the rights of students in Veronia School District 47J v. Acton, 515 U.S. 646, 654 (1995): "Traditionally at common law, and still today, unemancipated minors lack some of the most fundamental rights of self-determination . . . even as to their physical freedom. . . . " Embryos also have less rights that are less than plenary. Another difficult issue is the First Amendment rights of political parties. Washington State converted its open primary system to one in which candidates self-designated party preference on ballots, voters could vote for any candidate, and the top two vote getters advanced to the general election. The Republican Party challenged the law on its face, arguing that it violated a party's constitutional right to nominate its own candidates. Writing for the Court in Washington State Grange v. Washington State Republican Party, 552 U.S. 442 (2008), Thomas stated that the Court could not resolve the constitutionality of the statute on its face and that additional facts were needed. Scalia, joined by Kennedy, dissented that the statute unconstitutionally impaired the First Amendment rights of political parties. *Id.* at 462. Interestingly, neither Thomas's nor Scalia's opinion mentioned the absence of political parties at the founding or their negative image. "No one thought the emergence of parties was a good thing." Wood, *The Idea of America* 245 (2011). The founders "viewed parties, or 'factions' as they termed them, as monarchical vestiges that had no place in a true republic." Chernow, *Alexander Hamilton* at 390; *see* George Kannar, "Strenuous Virtues, Virtuous Lives, the Social Vision of Antonin Scalia," 12 *Cardozo Law Review* 1845, 1858–1859 (1990).

28 558 U.S. at 427, 430, 432.

29 *Id.* 430. The crime of conspiracy is an example of special treatment for group activities. In *Active Liberty; Interpreting Our Democratic Constitution* 43–50 (2005), Breyer focused on the purpose of the First Amendment, which sought "primarily to encourage the exchange of information and ideas necessary for citizens themselves to shape that 'public opinion which is the final source of government in a democratic state.'" Breyer relied on proportionality: "Does the statute strike a reasonable balance between electoral speech-restricting and speech-enhancement? Or does it instead impose restrictions on speech that are disproportionate when measured against their electoral and speech-related benefits, taking into account the kind, the importance, and the extent of those benefits, as well as the need for the restriction in order to secure them." *See* Teachout, *Corruption in America* at 241 ("While corruption has narrowed to quid pro quo, free speech has expanded to encompass all money spent on communication.").

30 Scalia argued that money is speech, since restricting any cog in the machine restricts speech, *e.g.*, limiting the sale of books or what newspapers can pay their staffs. But that does not mean money = speech; it enables speech and may warrant a different analysis. Nixon v. Shrink Mo. Gov't PAC, 528 U.S. 377, 400 (1999) (Breyer, J., concurring); Breyer, *Active Liberty* 46 (2005).

31 It was also naïve. The idea that barring limits on campaign speech will simply result in more speech without serious side effects, including major distortions, was unrealistic.

The Court ignored similar considerations in Morrison v. Olson, 487 U.S. 654 (1988), and Jones v. Clinton, 520 U.S. 681 (1997) (9–0) (attending to a civil suit would not unduly distract a President). Clinton made the scrutable mistake of lying to his lawyer, a state of affairs that was beyond the resources of the Constitution to remedy.

32 Unlimited spending also reduced the claimed superiority of the democratic branches. If big money controlled elected officials, less reason existed to respect their judgments as the will of the people. The political imbalance created by campaign-finance decisions resembles the political imbalance recognized and addressed in Baker v. Carr, 369 U.S. 186 (1962), and Reynolds v. Sims, 377 U.S. 533 (1964) (one person, one vote). Both reflected undue influence or, in other words, corruption as it was understood by the founders.

33 514 U.S. 334, 360–371 (1995).

34 States were the dominant force regarding the practice, and the First Amendment did not then apply to the states. Thomas alone dissented in Doe v. Reed, 561 U.S. 186 (2010), on the ground that "compelled disclosure of signed referendum and initiative petitions . . . severely burdens those rights and chills citizen participation in the referendum process." Scalia's concurring opinion in the case argued that, in colonial times, voting, like legislating was a public act, with both usually accompanied by a show of hands, citing historical sources. *Id.* at 228. Secret ballots gradually took over starting in the 1890s. Teachout, *supra* at 178–180.

35 Nelson, "Emerging Notions of Modern Criminal Law in the Revolutionary Era: An Historical Perspective," 42 *N.Y.U. Law Review* 450, 470 (1967).

36 Powell, *A Community Built on Words* 61 (2002).

37 Scalia's dissent stated that "to prove that anonymous electioneering was used frequently is not to establish that it is a constitutional right. . . . Evidence that anonymous electioneering was regarded as a constitutional right is sparse, and as far as I am aware evidence that it was *generally* regarded as such is nonexistent." *Id.* at 373. In other contexts Scalia did not insist that a tradition must have been regarded as a constitutional right to receive protection. E.g., Rutan v. Republican Party of Illinois, 497 U.S. 62, 95–96 (1990) (Scalia, J., dissenting) ("when a practice not expressly prohibited by the text of the Bill of Rights bears the endorsement of a long tradition of open, widespread, and unchallenged use that dates back to the beginning of the Republic, we have no proper basis for striking it down"). Moreover, Scalia's position in *McIntyre* would make all evidence of traditions prior to 1789 irrelevant.

38 *See generally The Press & the American Revolution* (Bernard Bailyn & John B. Hench eds. 1980).

39 Saul Cornell, *The Other Founders* 76 (1999); Murray Dry, "Anti-Federalism in *The Federalist*: A Founding Dialogue on the Constitution, Republican Government, and Federalism," in *Saving the Revolution* 42 (Charles R. Kesler ed. 1987) ("The eighteenth-century practice of writing under pseudonyms was intended to highlight the importance of reasoned argument.").

40 Scalia was intrigued by my point but never mentioned it in an opinion. From one perspective Scalia's position supporting the constitutionality of a ban on anonymous speech was inconsistent with his other campaign-financing positions. First, the practice had a history going back at least to the ratification debates. Second, a ban restricted speech. Third, a ban allied him with good-government people, mostly liberal, who opposed him in campaign-financing cases.

41 Jerome Hellerstein, "Picketing Legislation and the Courts," 10 *North Carolina Law Review* 158, 160–163 & n. 11 (1931).

42 Truax v. Corrigan, 257 U.S. 312, 323 n. 26 (1921) (Brandeis, J.).

43 257 U.S. 312 (1921).

44 *Id.* at 323.

45 *Id.* at 348–349 (Pitney, J., dissenting). "In the constitutional law of the late nineteenth and early twentieth centuries, labor boycotts, strikes, and pickets were simply understood not as speech but rather as conduct. At the beginning of the nineteenth century, labor unions seeking what would today be considered routine objectives would have been considered criminal conspirators." Ken I. Kersch, "How Conduct Became Speech and Speech Became Conduct: A Political Development Case Study in Labor Law and the Freedom of Speech," 2 *University of Pennsylvania Journal of Constitutional Law* 255, 273 (2006).

46 Hellerstein, *supra* at 168, 177.

47 Note, "Picketing by Labor Unions in the Absence of a Strike," 40 *Harvard Law Review* 896, 898 (1927).

48 310 U.S. 88 (1940). Nondisruptive expressive boycotts have a more respectable pedigree than picketing and appear to go back to the founding. *See* FTC v. Superior Court Trial Lawyers' Ass'n, 493 U.S. 411, 447–451 (1990) (Brennan, J., concurring in part, dissenting in part).

49 Scalia chastised Justices who cited Brandeis for the right to be let alone, stated it was "a right the Constitution 'conferred *as against the* government." That was not entirely accurate. Brandeis included as threats to privacy both assault and defamation, which are exclusively or at least primarily individual, not government, activity. *See* Nathaniel L. Nathanson, "The Philosophy of Mr. Justice Brandeis and Civil Liberties Today," in *Six Justices on Civil Rights* 146–148 (Ronald D. Rotunda ed. 1983).

50 494 U.S. 872 (1990).

51 McConnell, "Free Exercise Revisionism and the *Smith* Decision," 57 *University of Chicago Law Review* 1109, 1129–1152 (1990). McConnell also discussed (and rejected) other defenses of *Smith*, including the difficulty of applying the prior balancing test. He rejected Scalia's claim of anarchy: there was no lawlessness, the courts would decide based on a written Constitution, just like it decides other questions of equality and inequality.

52 Wood, *Empire of Liberty* 468 (2009).

53 Jay S. Bybee, "Common Ground: Robert Jackson, Antonin Scalia, and a Power Theory of the First Amendment," 75 *Tulane Law Review* 251, 253–254 (2000).

54 Richard A. Brisbin, Jr., "Antonin Scalia, William Brennan, and the Politics of Expression: A Study of Legal Violence and Repression," 87 *American Political Science Review* 912, 916 (1993).

55 Garrett Epps, "Some Animals Are More Equal than Others: The Rehnquist Court and 'Majority Religion,'" 21 *Washington Journal of Law & Politics* 212, 325 (2006).

56 Kent Greenawalt, "Religion and the Rehnquist Court," 99 *Northwestern University Law Review* 145, 151 (2004).

57 John T. Noonan, Jr., *Narrowing the Nation's Power* 15–40 (2002).

58 McConnell, 57 *University of Chicago Law Review* at 1116–1119. E.g., Brian Leiter, *Why Tolerate Religion* (2013); Andrew Koppelman, *Defending American Religious Neutrality* (2013); Vincent Phillip Munoz, "The Original Meaning of the Free Exercise Clause: The Evidence from the First Congress," 31 *Harvard Journal of Law & Public Policy* 1083 (2009) ("Despite the vast quantity of research devoted to understanding

religion and the American Founding, the original meaning of the First Amendment's Free Exercise Clause remains a matter of significant dispute.").

59 319 U.S. 624 (1943).

60 406 U.S. 205 (1972). Noonan explained: "*Yoder* was fought and decided on the meaning of Free Exercise. A religious practice, central to the religion, was allowed to displace the general law of the state. [*Smith*] held that couldn't be done and added another point: a court couldn't even tell what a central religious belief was." Noonan, *The Lustre of Our Country; The American Experience of Religious Freedom* 192 (1998).

61 McConnell, "Neutrality under the Religion Clauses," 81 *Northwestern University Law Review* 146, 151 n. 26 (1986). Scalia noted that McConnell was far from conclusive and said only that his reading was "within the contemplation of the framers and ratifiers." *Boerne*, 521 U.S. at 537–538.

62 41 Stat. 305, 308–309 (Oct. 28, 1919).

63 10 U.S.C. § 744 (exemption for religious apparel).

64 Noonan, *Narrowing the Nation's Power* at 38–41.

65 521 U.S. 597 (1997).

66 *Id.* at 546, 559, 561. Breyer joined O'Connor's opinion except for overruling *Smith*.

67 Ruth Colker, "The Supreme Court's Historical Errors in *City of Boerne v. Flores*," 43 *Boston College Law Review* 783, 784, 817 (2002); *see* Colker, "The Section Five Quagmire," 47 *U.C.L.A. Law Review* 653 (2000).

68 134 S.Ct. 2751 (2014).

69 There also may be tension with Citizens United v. FTC, 558 U.S. 310 (2010), which provided corporations with independent rights. Empowering organizations, albeit nonprofits, was a characteristic of the desegregation struggle. *E.g.*, NAACP v. Button, 371 U.S. 416 (1963) (Brennan, J.) (invalidating state laws that restricted organizations' efforts to promote law suits).

70 Doe v. Reed, 561 U.S. 186, 228 (2010).

71 455 U.S. 252, 261 (1982).

72 Koppelman & Frederick M. Gedicks, "Is *Hobby Lobby* Worse for Religious Liberty than *Smith*?," 9 *University of St. Thomas Journal of Law & Public Policy* 223, 224 (2015).

73 *See* Gedicks & Koppelman, "Invisible Women: Why an Exemption for Hobby Lobby Would Violate the Establishment Clause," 67 *Vanderbilt Law Review En Banc* 51 (2014).

74 Giannella, "Religious Liberty, Nonestablishment, and Doctrinal Development Part I, The Religious Liberty Guarantee," 80 *Harvard Law Review* 1381, 1386 (1967); *see* James Madison, *Memorial and Remonstrance against Religious Assessments* (1785), reprinted in Everson v. Board of Education, 330 U.S. 1, 72 (1947).

75 Corbin, "Corporate Religious Liberty," 30 *Constitutional Commentary* 277, 281–282 (2015).

76 134 S.Ct. at 2797–2799 (Ginsburg, J., dissenting). *See* Douglas Nejaime & Reva Siegel, "Conscience Wars: Complicity-Based Conscience Claims in Religion and Politics," 124 *Yale Law Journal* 100 (2015). The application of the law to Hobby Lobby interfered with no traditional religious practices. S. I. Strong, "Religious Rights in Historical, Theoretical, and International Context: *Hobby Lobby* as a Jurisprudential Anomaly," 48 *Vanderbilt Journal of Transnational Law* 813, 859 (2015).

77 Corbin, *supra* at 293–294.

78 134 S.Ct. at 2796–2797.

PART VI SCALIA'S NONCONSTITUTIONAL OPINIONS

1 490 U.S. 504, 528 (1989).
2 Eskridge & Frickey, *Cases and Materials on Legislation* (1988).
3 Eskridge, "Textualism, the Unknown Ideal?," 96 *Michigan Law Review* 1509, n. *a* (1998).
4 Eskridge, Frickey, Elizabeth Garrett & James J. Brudney, *Cases and Materials on Legislation & Regulation* 590–591 (5th ed. 2014). Plain meaning is more circumscribed than the new textualism, which permits resolving linguistic ambiguities using context, canons, and other statutes. *Id.* In the late 1950s Harvard Professors Henry M. Hart, Jr., and Albert M. Sachs wrote: "The hard truth of the matter is that American courts have no intelligible, generally accepted, and consistently applied theory of statutory interpretation." Hart & Sacks, *The Legal Process: Basic Problems in the Making and Application of Law* 1169 (Eskridge & Frickey eds. 1994).
5 *Id.* at 1125. The use of legislative history is relatively modern. "The notion that legislative debates could be the vehicle of communicating extra-statutory commands to subsequent interpreters was quite foreign to eighteenth-century and nineteenth-century lawyers, and a similar latitude toward pre-ratification discussions prevailed in constitutional discourse at least until the 1830's." H. Jefferson Powell, "Rules for Originalists," 73 *Virginia Law Review* 659, 685–687 (1987).
6 Breyer, *Making Our Democracy Work* 92 (2010). Judge Henry J. Friendly recounted then–Harvard Professor Felix Frankfurter's Cardozo lecture, "Mr. Justice Brandies and the Constitution," 45 *Harvard Law Review* 33 (1931): "'Though we may not end with the words in construing a disputed statute,' he said in his lecture, paraphrasing one of his opinions, 'one certainly begins there.' It was to enforce this 'hoary platitude' that, as a teacher, he had developed his threefold imperative to law students: (1) Read the statute; (2) read the statute; (3) read the statute!" Friendly, "Mr. Justice Frankfurter and the Reading of Statutes," in *Benchmarks* 201–202 (1967).
7 Breyer, *supra* at 102.
8 Manning, "Separation of Powers as Ordinary Interpretation," 124 *Harvard Law Review* 1939, 1971–1972 (2011). Thus, the legislature adopted both a purpose and the means by which the purpose was to be implemented, which is resolved by looking at the level of generality of the provision. *Id.* at 1972–1973.
9 Posner, *Divergent Paths* 174 (2016).
10 This summary is taken primarily from Eskridge, "The New Textualism," 37 *U.C.L.A. Law Review* 621 (1990); Eskridge, 96 *Michigan Law Review* 1509.
11 Blackstone's *Commentaries on the Laws of England* ∗61–∗62.
12 William M. Treanor, "Against Textualism," 103 *Northwestern University Law Review* 984, 997 (2009); *see* Treanor, "Judicial Review before *Marbury*," 58 *Stanford Law Review* 455, 457, 555, 556 (2005); Matthew P. Harrington, "Judicial Review before John Marshall," 72 *George Washington Law Review* 51 (2003); Maeva Marcus, "Is the Supreme Court a Political Institution?," 72 *George Washington Law Review* 95 (2003).
13 Eskridge, "The New Textualism," 37 *U.C.L.A. Law Review* 621, 679 (1990) ("Everyone knows that [the assumption that Congress is aware of judicial of judicial interpretations of provisions that a statute borrows or reenacts and of the cannons of construction] have virtually no basis in reality.").
14 Mikva, "Reading and Writing Statutes," 48 *University of Pittsburgh Law Review* 627, 629 (1987).

15 Purpose-oriented judges and scholars do not use legislative history willy-nilly. "The [legislative] history should be examined for the light it throws on general purpose. Evidence of specific intention with respect to particular applications is competent only to the extent that the particular applications illuminate the general purpose and are consistent with other evidence of it." Hart & Sacks, *supra* at 1379.

16 Robert A. Katzmann, *Judging Statutes* 47–49 (2012); Brudney, "Intentionalism's Revival," 44 *San Diego Law Review* 1991, 1009–1010 (2007); Jonathan R. Segal, "The Use of Legislative History in a System of Separated Powers," 53 *Vanderbilt Law Review* 1457, 1480 (2000); Manning, "Textualism as a Nondelegation Doctrine," 97 *Columbia Law Review* 673, 698 (1997).

17 Victoria Nourse & Jane Schacter, "The Politics of Legislative Drafting: A Congressional Case Study," 77 *New York University Law Review* 575, 590–600, 614–616 (2002); Abbe Gluck & Lisa Schultz Bressman, "Statutory Interpretation from the Inside – An Empirical Study of Congressional Drafting, Delegation, and the Canon: Part I," 65 *Stanford Law Review* 65 (2013); *id.*, Part II, 66 *Stanford Law Review* 725 (2014) (employing empirical data from congressional sources). Congress's use of legislative history is sophisticated and useful in some areas of the law, including tax. Brudney & Cory Dislear, "The Warp and Woof of Statutory Interpretation: Comparing Supreme Court Approaches in Tax Law and Workplace Law," 2008 *Duke Law Review* 1231.

18 Eskridge, "Should the Supreme Court Read *The Federalist* but Not Legislative History?," 66 *George Washington Law Review* 1301 (1998) (*The Federalist* is old, it was propaganda, and it went far beyond the issues dealt with in the Constitution).

19 Eskridge stated that "the new textualism opens up a tension between the rule of law and democracy than softer versions of textualism – follow the text but check it against legislative history – avoid. Majority-based choices in that event would more often be trumped by dictionary-toting, grammar-minded judges holding Congress to the letter of what it writes. If so, the new textualism is less responsive to democratic desires than the faithful agent, the statutory interpreter who tries to figure out what the principal would have her do under the circumstances." Eskridge, 96 *Michigan Law Review* at 1548; *see* Breyer, *Making Our Democracy Work* (2010); Brudney, "Faithful Agency versus Ordinary Meaning Advocacy," 57 *St. Louis University Law Journal* 975 (2013).

20 Koppelman & Gedicks, "Is *Hobby Lobby* Worse for Religious Liberty than *Smith?*," 9 *University of St. Thomas Journal of Law & Public Policy* 223, 245 (2015); Brudney & Dislear, "Liberal Justices' Reliance on Legislative History: Principle, Strategy, and the Scalia Effect," 29 *Berkeley Journal of Employment & Labor Law* 117 (2008) (survey of more than thirty years of Supreme Court labor-law opinions found judges were less likely to vote their ideological preferences when they consider legislative history).

21 467 U.S. 837, 842–845 (1984).

22 Robert Katzmann, *Judging Statutes* 27 (2014); Breyer, "Judicial Review of Questions of Law and Policy," 38 *Administrative Law Review* 363 (1986). A statute may be applied differently depending on whether a court of appeals hears a case on appeal from the district court or from an administrative agency.

23 Eskridge argued that Scalia's dissent from Stevens's opinion in Babbitt v. Sweet Home Chapter of Communities for a Greater Oregon, 515 U.S. 687 (1995) (the case of the spotted owl), was, like Stevens's majority opinion, replete with normative components. Eskridge, "Nino's Nightmare: Legal Process Theory as a Jurisprudence of Toggling between Facts and Norms," 57 *St. Louis University Law Journal* 865 (2013). Eskridge also analyzed the dueling canons of construction relied on by Stevens and Scalia, which, he argued, provided strong evidence of the futility of a theory of

interpretations based on canons. Eskridge, "The New Textualism and Normative Canons," 113 *Columbia Law Review* 531 (2013).

24 Scalia & Garner, *Reading Law* (2012).

CHAPTER 28 FOUR LIBERAL SPECIAL CASES

25 Successor Attorney General Richard Thornburgh affirmed the order.

26 502 U.S. 314 (1992).

27 Scalia likened Doherty to an unsuccessful applicant for Social Security benefits who reapplied. Stevens and Souter joined Scalia.

28 Scalia pointed out that the regulation on which the majority relied was applicable only to asylum cases. *Id.* at 336–337.

29 *Id.* at 343.

30 543 U.S. 371 (2005).

31 *Id.* at 378.

32 *Id.* at 386. Thomas and Rehnquist dissented.

33 Kungys v. United States 485 U.S. 759 (1988). Stevens, joined by Marshall and Blackmun, would have imposed a greater burden on the government on remand, while White joined in material part by O'Connor would have granted the government's petition for denaturalization, which made the dissent more conservative than Scalia's opinion.

34 INS v. Cardoza-Fonseca, 480 U.S. 421, 452 (1987). Scalia did not join the majority opinion because it relied heavily on legislative history.

35 Clinton v. Jones, 520 U.S. 681 (1997).

36 Comment, 1994 *Brigham Young Law Review* 663, 661–662; Comment, 18 *Nova Law Review* 1919 (1993).

37 Burns v. Reed, 500 U.S. 478, 481–482 (1991).

38 *Id.* at 482 n. 1.

39 *Id.* at 481–483.

40 *Id.* at 478.

41 *Id.* at 498–499.

42 Scalia acknowledged that current § 1983 law differed from 1791 common law. Kalina v. Fletcher, 522 U.S. 118, 132–135 (1997) (Scalia, J., concurring). Absolute prosecutorial immunity did not exist when § 1983 was enacted. In fact, it appears that qualified immunity did not exist either. Thomas Y. Davies, "The Supreme Court Giveth and the Supreme Court Taketh Away: The Century of Fourth Amendment Search and Seizure Doctrine," 100 *Journal of Criminal Law and Criminology* 933, 1030 (2010).

43 509 U.S. 259 (1993).

44 *Id.* at 271–278.

45 *Id.* at 280–281.

46 Kennedy, joined by Rehnquist, White, and Souter.

47 Scalia supported limited immunity from damages for federal law-enforcement agents whose searches violated the Fourth Amendment, a conservative position. Anderson v. Creighton, 483 U.S. 635 (1987) (Scalia, J.). Scalia rejected adherence to the common law – "Although it is true that we have observed that our determinations as to the scope of official immunity are made in the light of the 'common law tradition,' . . . we have never suggested that the precise contours of official immunity can and should be slavishly derived from the often arcane rules of the common law." *Id.* at 644–645. Stevens, Brennan, and Marshall favored no immunity.

48   518 U.S. 1 (1996).

49   *Id.* at 11.

50   *Id.* at 19.

51   *Id.* at 22. Scalia questioned whether licensed social workers had any clinical experience. State rules often limited the privilege further, *e.g.*, by mandating a balancing test.

52   *Id.* at 36. Rehnquist joined Scalia's opinion in large part.

53   Williamson v. United States, 512 U.S. 594 (1994).

54   Rehnquist, Kennedy, and Thomas.

55   *See* Wiggins v. Smith, 539 U.S. 510 (2003); Smith v. Spisak, 558 U.S. 139 (2010).

56   135 S.Ct. 793 (2015).

57   *Id.* at 806–807.

58   28 U.S.C. § 2253(c)(1)(A).

59   Day v. McDonough, 547 U.S. 198 (2006).

60   Breyer and Thomas joined Scalia.

61   Wilkinson v. Dotson, 544 U.S. 74, 86 (2005). Kennedy alone dissented on the ground that habeas corpus was the sole remedy.

CHAPTER 29   LIBERAL CRIMINAL STATUTORY OPINIONS

1   United States v. R.L.C., 503 U.S. 291, 307 (1992) (Scalia, J., concurring in part and concurring in the judgment).

2   United States v. Santos, 553 U.S. 507, 514, 519 (2008).

3   William N. Eskridge, Jr., Phillip P. Frickey, Elizabeth Garrett & James J. Brudney, *Cases and Materials on Legislation and Regulation* 693–696 (5th ed. 2014). The rule of lenity appeals to civil libertarians and separation-of-powers formalists. *Id.* at 709.

4   553 U.S. at 514, 519; *see* Joanmarie Ilaria Davoli, "Justice Scalia for the Defense?," 40 *University of Baltimore Law Review* 687, 742–749 (2011). "Under a fair warning rationalization, the rule of lenity is most appropriately applied to criminal statutes that create offenses that are *malum prohibitum* (bad only because they are prohibited) rather than *malum in se* (bad by their very nature)." Eskridge, Frickey & Garrett, *Cases and Materials on Legislation* 886 (4th ed. 2007).

5   Moncrieffe v. Holder, 133 S.Ct. 1678 (2013).

6   Conservative Thomas predictably favored white-collar criminals. He was 5–2 with Scalia on white-collar cases while 1–5 on blue-collar cases. Liberal Stevens predictably favored blue collars. He was 3–7 with Scalia on white collar and 5–1 on blue collar. Liberal Ginsburg was 4–2 and 4–2.

7   Carr v. United States, 560 U.S. 438 (2010) (Sotomayor, J.).

8   *Id.* at 458. Alito, Thomas, and Ginsburg dissented.

9   526 U.S. 1 (1999).

10   *Id.* at 3.

11   *Id.* at 13.

12   *Id.* at 14.

13   *Id.* at 20–21. Thomas's one-paragraph dissent seconded Scalia.

14   131 S.Ct. 2045 (2011).

15   18 U.S.C. § 1512(a)(1)(C).

16   131 S.Ct. at 2048.

17   *Id.* at 2050.

18   *Id.* at 2052.

19 *Id.* at 2053.
20 Scalia did not discuss another confusing section of the statute: "In a prosecution [under the statute], no state of mind need be proved with respect to the circumstance . . . that the law enforcement officer is an officer or employee of the Federal Government." In other words the statute required "intent" but not a "state of mind." Alito construed that provision as requiring nothing more to convict than the commission of a federal crime and "the recipient of the communication (a law enforcement officer or judge who turns out to be a federal officer or judge)." *Id.* at 2059–2060. However, the statute did not require a recipient to convict, just an intent.
21 Abramski v. United States, 134 S.Ct. 2259 (2014).
22 Scalia criticized the Court for not applying the rule of lenity. *Id.* at 2280–2281.
23 Schmuck v. United States, 489 U.S. 705, 715 (1989).
24 Kann v. United States, 323 U.S. 88 (1944).
25 United States v. Maze, 414 U.S. 395 (1974).
26 489 U.S. 705 (1989).
27 *Id.* at 707.
28 *Id.* at 711–712.
29 *Id.* at 723 (joined by Brennan, Marshall, and O'Connor).
30 18 U.S.C. § 2314.
31 498 U.S. 103 (1990).
32 *Id.* at 119–126. To the argument that "falsely made" would be redundant in his formulation, Scalia responded that "forged" and "counterfeited" meant the same thing. Moderates O'Connor and Kennedy joined the dissent.
33 *Id.* at 129–130, 131.
34 348 U.S. 503 (1955).
35 514 U.S. 695 (1995).
36 *Id.* at 716–717.
37 Rehnquist, joined by O'Connor and Souter, dissented on the basis of *stare decisis*, citing a number of cases in which the government had proceeded under § 1001 in judicial proceedings as evidence of a reliance interest in the old law. *Black's Law Dictionary* 816 (7th ed. 1999) defined "reliance interest" as "[t]he interest a nonbreaching party has in recovery costs stemming from that party's reliance on the performance of a contract." *See* Lon L. Fuller & William R. Purdue, Jr., "The Reliance Interest in Contract Damages I," 46 *Yale Law Journal* 52 (1936). Past prosecutions are not a reliance interest. What difference did they make?
38 500 U.S. 257 (1991).
39 *Id.* at 272–274.
40 *Id.* at 278–280; *see generally* Steven L. Winter, "The Meaning of 'under Color of Law,'" 91 *Michigan Law Review* 323 (1992).
41 500 U.S. at 281.
42 513 U.S. 64 (1994).
43 18 U.S.C. § 2255(a)(1) (1988 & Supp. V) (emphasis added).
44 513 U.S. at 81–82, 85.
45 483 U.S. 350 (1987).
46 561 U.S. 358 (2010).
47 *Id.* at 404. The issue in *Skilling* was the subject of a petition for a writ of *certiorari* two years earlier in Sorich v. United States, 555 U.S. 1204 (2009). When the Court denied Sorich's petition, Scalia alone dissented: "It may be true that petitioners here, like the defendants in other 'honest services' cases, have acted improperly. But '[b]ad

men, like good men, are entitled to be tried and sentenced in accordance with the law.'" *Id.* at 1208.

48 561 U.S. at 365, 408.

49 *See* Pamela Mathy, "Honest Services Fraud after *Skilling*," 42 St. Mary's Law Review 645, 685–686 (2011).

50 561 U.S. at 422–423 (joined by Thomas and in large part by Kennedy); *cf.* Chisom v. Roemer, 501 U.S. 380 (1991) (pre-amendment content clear). The same days as *Skilling*, Scalia concurred in part in Black v. United States, 561 U.S. 465, 474 (2010), a factually similar case that the Court reversed because of a defect in the instructions to the jury. Scalia wrote: "In my view, the error lay not in instructing inconsistently with the theory of honest-services fraud set forth in *Skilling*, but in instructing the jury on honest-services fraud *at all.*" He would dismiss the case rather than remand for a new trial.

51 Cheek v. United States, 498 U.S. 192, 205 (1991) (White, J.).

52 *Id.* at 207–208.

53 *Id.* at 209–210.

54 524 U.S. 184 (1998).

55 18 U.S.C. § 922(a)(1)(A) made it unlawful for anyone to deal in firearms without a federal license; § 924 imposed punishment on anyone who "willfully" violated a provision of the chapter.

56 524 U.S. at 200–202 (joined by Rehnquist and Ginsburg).

57 *Id.* at 205.

58 United States v. Murdock, 290 U.S. 389, 394 (1933) (citations omitted).

59 *Id.* at 652.

60 521 U.S. 642 (1997).

61 *Id.* at 679. Thomas, joined by Rehnquist, also concurred in part and dissented in part while voting to reverse the conviction.

62 United States v. Santos, 553 U.S. 507 (2008). Souter, Thomas, and Ginsburg joined Scalia entirely or in principal part. Stevens concurred in the result.

63 Fraud Enforcement and Recovery Act of 2009, 123 Stat. 1617 (2009), § 2(f)(1).

64 Enhancement of sentences based on convictions for committing three violent felonies appears in Chapter 26.

65 508 U.S. 223 (1993).

66 *Id.* at 225.

67 *Id.* at 242 (joined by Stevens and Souter). Perhaps a better example would be someone who used a cane as a pool cue, since someone who exhibited a cane would not clearly be *using* the cane.

68 *Id.* at 241–246. In Watson v. United States, 552 U.S. 74 (2007) (Souter, J.), the Court unanimously held that the *purchaser* of the gun for narcotics did not "use" the gun.

69 18 U.S.C. § 5037(c)(1)(B).

70 503 U.S. 291 (1992).

71 *Id.* at 307 (Scalia, J., concurring in part and concurring in the judgment). *R.L.C.* was the first opinion to expand the rule of lenity to sentencing. *See* Eskridge, Frickey, Garrett & Brudney, *Cases and Materials on Legislation* 710 (5th ed. 2014).

72 503 U.S. at 307–311. Dissenting, Blackmun and O'Connor voted for the longer sentence.

73 511 U.S. 39 (1994).

74 *Id.* at 59–60 (joined by Kennedy).

75 529 U.S. 694 (2000) (Souter, J.).

76 *Id.* at 715–716, 718.
77 *Id.* at 726.

CHAPTER 30 LIBERAL CIVIL STATUTORY OPINIONS

1 135 S.Ct. 2480 (2015).
2 135 S.Ct. 2652 (2015).
3 545 U.S. 967 (2005).
4 *Id.* at 1005. Scalia relied on the delivery of pizzas to explain the internet. "It is therefore inevitable that customers will regard the competing cable-modem service as giving them *both* computing functionality *and* the physical pipe by which that functionality comes to their computer – both the pizza and the delivery service that nondelivery pizzerias require to be purchased from the cab company. . . . After all is said and done, after all the regulatory cant has been translated, and the smoke of agency expertise blown away, it remains perfectly clear that someone who sells cable-modem service is 'offering' telecommunications. For that simple reason set forth in the statute, I would affirm the Court of Appeals." Scalia rejected the Court's (per Thomas, J.) use of dictionaries to establish that the word "offer" was ambiguous. *Id.* at 1009, 1014.
5 499 U.S. 187 (1991).
6 But it's not clear that there would be any *discrimination* if Johnson Controls treated men and women the same, however paternalistically.
7 554 U.S. 84 (2008).
8 *Id.* at 103. It is debatable whether Scalia's opinion was more or less liberal than the Court's, but it was clearly more liberal than Thomas's dissent: "I continue to believe that disparate-impact claims are not cognizable under the Age Discrimination in Employment Act of 1967." *Id.* at 104. Thomas rejected *stare decisis.* Scalia was also bracketed in E.E.O.C. v. Arabian American Oil Co., 499 U.S. 244, 259 (1991), where the majority held that antidiscrimination provisions of Title VII of the Civil Rights Act of 1964 did not operate extraterritorially. Concurring, he distanced himself from the majority's refusal to give deference to the EEOC. Three liberal Justices dissented.
9 135 S.Ct. 2028 (2015). The case involved a Muslim who wore a head scarf to employ-ment interviews. While she was never asked whether she wore the head scarf for religious reasons, the interviewer correctly surmised that was the fact. The employer had a policy against sales personnel wearing hats or caps of any kind.
10 *Id.* at 2037–2042. Scalia wrote conservative employment-discrimination opinions. *E.g.*, Young v. UPS, 135 S.Ct. 1338, 1361 (2015).
11 Pauley v. BethEnergy Mines, Inc., 501 U.S. 680 (1991).
12 *E.g.*, Sullivan v. Everhart, 494 U.S. 83 (1990); General Dynamics Land Systems v. Cline, 540 U.S. 581, 602 (2004) (Scalia, J., dissenting); United States v. Mead Corp., 533 U.S. 218, 239 (2001); Scalia, "Judicial Deference to Administrative Interpretations of the Law," 1989 *Duke Law Journal* 511–521; Andrew M. Grossman, "*City of Arlington v. FCC*: Justice Scalia's Triumph," 2013 *Cato Supreme Court Review* 331.
13 501 U.S. at 706, 708; *see* David C. Vladeck & Alan B. Morrison, "The Roles, Rights, and Responsibilities of the Executive Branch," in *The Rehnquist Court* 174–175 (Her-man Schwartz ed. 2002).
14 Pittston Coal Group v. Stebben, 488 U.S. 105 (1988).
15 *See* Stephen Wizner, "Judging in the Good Society: A Comment on the Jurisprudence of Justice Scalia," 12 *Cardozo Law Review* 1831, 1836–1837, 1864–1874 (1991).

16 Chicago v. Environmental Defense Fund, 511 U.S. 328 (1994). Stevens and O'Connor dissented.

17 Utility Air Regulator Group v. EPA, 134 S.Ct. 2427 (2014).

18 42 U.S.C. §§ 7401–7671q.

19 481 U.S. 681 (1987) (Powell, J.).

20 340 U.S. 135 (1950).

21 481 U.S. at 686–692.

22 *Id.* at 696–698 (joined by Brennan, Marshall, and Stevens).

23 Letter from Scalia to Justice Marshall, June 12, 1989, quoted in Bernard Schwartz, "'Shooting the Piano Player'? Justice Scalia and Administrative Law," 47 *Administrative Law Journal* 1, 50 (1995). Along with Dick Cheney and Donald Rumsfeld, Scalia had opposed liberalizing amendments to FOIA when he worked as head of the Office of Legal Counsel in the Ford Administration. Joan Biskupic, *American Original* 46–47 (2009).

24 493 U.S. 146 (1989) (Blackmun, J.).

25 *Id.* at 153.

26 *Id.* at 160–164. Stevens dissented separately.

27 15 U.S.C. § 13(a).

28 496 U.S. 543 (1990).

29 *Id.* at 556–559.

30 *Id.* at 561–571.

31 *Id.* at 578–579. Kennedy joined Scalia's concurrence.

32 504 U.S. 621 (1992).

33 *Id.* at 633, 638.

34 *Id.* at 640–641.

35 15 U.S.C. §§ 1601 *et seq.*

36 Koons Buick Pontiac GMC, Inc. v. Nigh, 543 U.S. 50 (2004).

37 *Id.* at 76.

38 Jerman v. Carlisle, McNellie, Rini, Kramer & Ulrich LPA, 559 U.S. 573 (2010).

39 Hamilton v. Lanning, 560 U.S. 505 (2010).

40 11 U.S.C. § 707(b)(2)(A)(ii)(I).

41 Ransom v. FIA Card Services, N.A., 131 S.Ct. 716 (2011).

42 Merck & Co. v. Reynolds, 559 U.S. 633 (2010). Thomas joined Scalia's opinion. Plaintiffs still won because they could not have discovered their claim with the exercise of ordinary diligence.

43 Shady Grove Orthopedic Assoc. v. Allstate Ins. Co., 559 U.S. 393 (2010).

44 304 U.S. 64 (1938). The case basically held that federal courts must apply state substantive law when deciding claims and defenses founded on state law.

45 Scalia supported standing in United States v. Williams, 514 U.S. 527, 541 (1995) (Scalia, J. concurring), over dissents by Rehnquist, Kennedy, and Thomas. The majority granted standing to someone other than the taxpayer to challenge the imposition of a tax against a claim that the United States waived immunity only for suits by "taxpayers." Scalia argued that denying standing to someone who was the subject of a lien was "implausible." "The exemption of the sovereign from suit involves hardship enough where consent has been withheld. We are not to add to its rigor by refinement of construction where consent has been announced."

46 Scalia & Garner, *Reading Law* 290 (2012).

47 California Federal Savings & Loan Ass'n v. Guerra, 479 U.S. 272 (1987).

48 *Id.* at 296. Brennan, Blackmun, and O'Connor joined Marshall's opinion. Stevens and Scalia concurred separately. Rehnquist, White, and Powell dissented.

49 Rose v. Rose, 481 U.S. 619 (1987).

50 Scalia wrote: "I know of no precedent for the proposition . . . that compatibility with the purpose of a federal statute can save a state law that violates its text. Such a doctrine in effect asserts a power to narrow statutory texts, insofar as their pre-emptive effect is concerned, so as to make them more precisely tailored to the purpose that the Court perceives." *Id.* at 640.

51 42 U.S.C. §§ 1973gg *et seq.*

52 Arizona v. Inter Tribal Council of Arizona, Inc., 133 S.Ct. 2247, 2255 (2013).

53 508 U.S. 223, 242 (1993) (Scalia J., dissenting).

54 133 S.Ct. at 2261, 2270.

55 Beneficial Nat'l Bank v. Anderson, 539 U.S. 1 (2003). Thomas sided with Scalia.

56 This book does not discuss Scalia's opinions in federal tax cases, which are often highly technical. (An exception is United States v. Williams, *supra*, which involved standing.) In general, a vote for the government would be a liberal vote and a vote for the taxpayer would be a conservative vote, since the definition of liberal supposes generally larger government and greater equality in wealth. A study reviewed Justices' votes through 2002. Scalia voted for the taxpayer 31.8 percent, which placed him ninth in votes for the taxpayer among the eleven Justices included and near the liberal end of the spectrum. In contrast, Thomas, the Court's other textualist/originalist, placed first with his conservative vote for the taxpayer 66.7 percent of the time. Stephen T. Black & Katherine D. Black, "Justice Scalia's Tax Jurisprudence," 34 *University of Toledo Law Review* 509, 511 (2003).

CHAPTER 31 CONSERVATIVE STATUTORY OPINIONS

1 Toby Golick, "Justice Scalia, Poverty and the Good Society," 12 *Cardozo Law Review* 1817 (1991) (citing seven cases); *see* James G. Wilson, "Constraints of Power: The Constitutional Opinions of Judges Scalia, Bork, Posner, Easterbrook, and Winter," 40 *University of Miami Law Review* 1171, 1182 (1986) ("diffuse groups are frequently vulnerable to well-organized interest groups, who can easily capture administrative agencies that regulate their activities"). Statistical analyses, including a study of voting patterns involving judicial review of federal administrative agency statutory interpretations between 1984 and 2006, supported the conclusion that originalist/textualist Scalia (and Thomas) usually endorsed conservative statutory interpretations. Richard H. Fallon, Jr., "Three Symmetries between Textualist and Purposovist Theories of Statutory Interpretation – and the Irreducible Roles of Values and Judgments within Both," 99 *Cornell Law Review* 685, 724–726 (2014), had Scalia affirm agency decisions 71.6 percent of the time when the decisions were conservative, but only 53.8 percent of the time when the decisions were liberal. The differential for Thomas was even greater. Breyer, a nontextualist pragmatic liberal, agreed with conservative rulings 64.9 percent of the time and liberal rulings 79.4 percent of the time. *See* William N. Eskridge, Jr., & Lauren E. Baer, "The Continuum of Difference: Supreme Court Treatment of Agency Statutory Interpretations from *Chevron* to *Hamden*," 96 *Georgetown Law Journal* 1083, 1154 (2008) (presenting statistics showing less disagreement and greater deference to agencies).

2 42 U.S.C. § 1973.

3 501 U.S. 380 (1991) (Stevens, J.).

4 *Id.* at 398–399. Later, Stevens would write: "Elected judges, no less than appointed judges, occupy an office of trust that is fundamentally different from that occupied by elected officials." Republican Party of Minnesota v. White, 536 U.S. 765, 797 (2002).

5 *Id.* at 404–405, 411(joined by Rehnquist and Kennedy) Gordon S. Wood wrote six years later: "At the same time more and more Americans began looking to the once-feared judiciary as a principal means of restraining these wild and rampaging popular legislatures.... Hamilton implied, and others drew out the implication more fully in subsequent years, that the judges, although not elected, resembled legislators and executives in being agents or servants of the people with a responsibility equal to that of the other two branches of government to carry out the people's will, even to the point of sharing in the making of law." Scalia, *A Matter of Interpretation* 52–54 (1997) (comment by Wood).

6 532 U.S. 661 (2001).

7 42 U.S.C. § 12101.

8 532 U.S. at 705. The case was reminiscent of Chaney v. Heckler, 718 F.2d 1174 (D.C. Cir. 1983) (Scalia, J., dissenting), where Scalia rejected the claim that prisoners under death sentence were protected by the FDA as consumers of lethal drugs. The Supreme Court reversed, but on the ground that the FDA's decision was nonreviewable. Heckler v. Chaney, 470 U.S. 821 (1985).

9 532 U.S. at 699–701. Scalia joined Alito's conservative opinion in Ledbetter v. Goodyear Tire & Rubber Co., 550 U.S. 618 (2007), a Title VII case that limited employees' rights.

10 561 U.S. 247 (2010).

11 *E.g.*, Leasco Data Processing Equip. Co. v. Maxwell, 468 F.2d 1326, 1336 (2d Cir. 1972) (Friendly, J.).

12 § 10(b), 15 U.S.C. § 78j(b).

13 David M. Dorsen, *Henry Friendly, Greatest Judge of His Era* 253–254 (2012).

14 *Id.* at 255, 266 (internal quotation marks omitted). Stevens and Ginsburg dissented. *See* Thomas A. Dubbs, "Textualism and Transnational Securities Law: A Reappraisal of Justice Scalia's Analysis in *Morrison v. National Australia Bank*," 20 *Southwestern Journal of International Law* 227 (2014) (judgment for Morrison was eminently warranted even under Scalia's textualism).

15 135 S.Ct. 2480 (2015).

16 *Id.* at 2497–2504.

17 SCOTUS is a standard abbreviation for Supreme Court of the United States.

18 *Id.* at 2505.

19 *See generally* John F. Manning, "The Absurdity Doctrine," 116 *Harvard Law Review* 2387, 2454–2476 (2003). Scalia confined the doctrine to "scrivener's error," when the error was a typographical error or something similar. Scalia, *A Matter of Interpretation* 20 (1997). Pragmatic and generally purposivist appeals-court judge Henry J. Friendly utilized the doctrine broadly in tax cases. Dorsen, *supra* at 260–261.

20 Posner, *The Federal Courts: Crisis and Reform* 281 (1985).

21 Scalia told me that King v. Burwell upset him considerably. He was outraged and depressed over the Court's inventing a statute in the image of its personal preferences. But he was more upset over Arizona State Legislature v. Arizona Independent Redistricting Comm'n,135 S.Ct. 2652 (2015), decided the same week, which upheld congressional redistricting by an independent referendum-created commission despite the Constitution's giving the task to state "legislatures." King v. Burwell was more important, but the linguistic distortion was greater in the Arizona case.

22 In Comcast Corp. v. Behrend, 133 S.Ct. 1426 (2013), a case charging illegal monopolization, Scalia, writing for a conservative five-Justice majority, rejected a class certification because the plaintiffs failed to show "that damages are capable of measurement on a classwide basis." The four dissenters accused the majority of misreading antitrust law and rewriting the facts. In Amgen Inc. v. Connecticut Retirement Plans & Trust Funds, 133 S.Ct. 1184 (2013), a class action seeking money damages for alleged violations of §10(b) and Rule 10b–5a, Scalia and Thomas dissented when the Court held that plaintiffs did not have to demonstrate materiality of the common question of law or fact to obtain class certification, when the rule did not mention materiality. Scalia voted to sustain a class action in Chadbourne & Parke, LLP v. Troice, 134 S.Ct. 1058 (2014).

23 In West Virginia University Hospitals, Inc. v. Casey, 499 U.S. 83 (1991), the hospital prevailed against Pennsylvania in a civil-rights action over Medicaid reimbursements. The hospital sought $100,000 for expert services under a statute that permitted the award of "a reasonable attorney's fee." 42 U.S.C. § 1988. Rejecting the award, Scalia's opinion relied heavily on statutes that provided for the prevailing party to recover for expert witnesses or "costs" in addition to attorney's fees. It was a highly textualist analysis. Marshall's quintessentially purposivist dissent said: "As Justice Stevens demonstrates, the Court uses the implements of literalism to wound, rather than minister to, congressional intent in this case. That is a dangerous usurpation of congressional power when any statute is involved. It is especially troubling for special reasons, however, when the statute at issue is clearly designed to give access to the federal courts to persons and groups attempting to vindicate vital civil rights." 499 U.S. at 102.

24 Scalia was instrumental in shunting plaintiffs to arbitration based on contractual terms dictated by corporations. AT&T Mobility LLC v. Concepcion, 131 S.Ct. 1740 (2011); *see* American Express Co. v. Italian Colors Restaurant, 133 S.Ct. 2304 (2013). Scalia rejected arguments based on federalism and accepted the argument that the Federal Arbitration Act of 1925 preempted state laws permitting consumer class actions. E.g., Jill I. Gross, "Justice Scalia's Hat Trick and the Supreme Court's Flawed Understanding of Twenty-First Century Arbitration,"112 *Brooklyn Law Review* 111, 115 (2015) (Scalia's decisions enforcing arbitration had corporate counsel "cheering on the sidelines"); Christopher R. Drahozal, "Federal Arbitration Act Preemption," 79 *Indiana Law Journal* 393 (2004); Katherine Van Wezel Stone, "Rustic Justice: Community and Coercion under the Federal Arbitration Act," 77 *North Carolina Law Review* 931 (1999).

25 Sikes v. United States, 131 S.Ct. 2267, 2288 (2011). Kagan and Ginsburg dissented in a more traditional opinion. *See generally* Pamela S. Karlan, "Democracy and Disdain," 126 *Harvard Law Review* 1 (2011); Ruth Colker & James J. Brudney, "Dissing Congress," 100 *Michigan Law Review* 80 (2001).

CHAPTER 32 THE OTHER ORIGINALIST JUSTICE

1 Richard H. Fallon, Jr., "Are Originalist Constitutional Theories Principled or Are They Rationalizations for Conservatism?," 34 *Harvard Journal of Law & Public Policy* 5, 22 (2010).

2 Neder v. United States, 527 U.S. 1, 30 (1999).

3 Almendez-Torres v. United States, 523 U.S. 224 (1998); Apprendi v. New Jersey, 530 U.S. 466 (2000); Oregon v. Ice, 555 U.S. 160 (2009); United States v. Gaudin, 515 U.S.

506 (1993); Ring v. Arizona, 536 U.S. 584 (2002); Sullivan v. Louisiana, 508 U.S. 275 (1993). The exception was *Neder*, where Scalia dissented from the Court's decision that failure to submit the issue of materiality to the jury in a tax case was harmless error.

4 R.A.V. v. City of St. Paul, Minn., 505 U.S. 377 (1993) (agree); Virginia v. Black, 538 U.S. 343 (2003) (disagree); United States v. Stevens, 559 U.S. 460 (2010) (agree); Brown v. Entertainment Merchants Ass'n, 131 S.Ct. 2729 (2011) (disagree); Borough of Duryea, Pa. v. Guanieri, 131 S.Ct. 2488 (2011) (disagree).

5 Bailey v. United States, 133 S.Ct. 1031 (2013) (disagree); Florida v. Jarnines, 133 S.Ct. 1409 (2013) (agree); Kyllo v. United States, 533 U.S. 27 (2001); Maryland v. King, 133 S.Ct. 1958 (2013) (disagree); Thornton v. United States, 541 U.S. 615 (2004) (disagree); United States v. Jones, 132 S.Ct. 945 (2012) (unanimous opinion) (agree); Arizona v. Gant, 556 U.S. 332 (2009) (agree); Minnesota v. Dickerson, 508 U.S. 366 (1993) (disagree).

6 Indiana v. Edwards, 554 U.S. 164 (2008) (agree); Martinez v. Court of Appeals of California, 528 U.S. 152 (2000) (disagree); United States v. Gonzalez-Lopez, 548 U.S. 140 (2006) (disagree).

7 Johnson v. United States, 529 U.S. 694 (2000) (disagree); Monge v. California, 524 U.S. 721 (1998) (disagree); Smith v. Massachusetts, 543 U.S. 462 (2005) (agree); United States v. Dixon, 509 U.S. 443 (1993) (disagree).

8 Crawford v. Washington, 541 U.S. 36 (2004) (agree); Davis v. Washington, 547 U.S. 813 (2006) (disagree); Giles v. California, 554 U.S. 353 (2008) (agree) (Melendez-Diaz v. Massachusetts, 557 U.S. 305 (2009) (agree); Michigan v. Bryant, 131 S.Ct. 1143 (disagree).

9 City of Bourne v. Flores, 521 U.S. 507 (1997) (agree).

10 Rogers v. Tennessee, 532 U.S. 451 (2001) (agree).

11 Hamdi v. Rumsfeld, 542 U.S. 507 (2004) (agree).

12 United States v. Resendez-Ponce, 549 U.S. 102 (2007) (disagree).

13 United States v. Rodriquez-Moreno, 526 U.S. 275 (1999) (disagree).

14 Gonzales v. Raich, 545 U.S. 1 (2005) (disagree). In United States v. Lopez, 514 U.S. 519 (1995), Thomas, concurring separately, argued that federal regulation of manufacturing and agriculture was unconstitutional under the originalist Commerce Clause.

15 Virginia Office for Protection & Advocacy v. Stewart, 131 S.Ct. 1632 (2011) (agree).

16 514 U.S. 519 (1995).

17 545 U.S. 1 (2005).

18 Other instances are McIntyre v. Ohio Elections Comm'n, 514 U.S. 334, 370 (1995) (Thomas, J., concurring); Mitchell v. United States, 526 U.S. 314, 343 (1991) (Thomas, J., dissenting); Morse v. Frederick, 551 U.S. 393, 410 (2007) (Thomas, J., concurring); *see* Joel K. Goldstein, "Calling Them as He Sees Them: The Disappearance of Originalism in Justice Thomas's Opinions on Race," 74 *University of Maryland Law Review* 79 (2014).

19 Bradley P. Jacob, "Will the Real Constitutional Originalist Please Stand Up?," 40 *Creighton Law Review* 595 (2007).

20 Eric A. Posner & Adrian Vermeule, "Originalism and Emergencies: A Reply to Lawson," 87 *Boston University Law Review* 313, 319 (2007).

21 David L. Hudson, Jr., "Clarence Thomas: The Emergence of a Commercial Free-Speech Protector," 35 *Creighton Law Review* 485, 487 (2002); *see* Matthew D. Bunker & Clay Calvert, "Contrasting Concurrences of Clarence Thomas: Deploying

Originalism and Paternalism in Commercial and Student Speech Cases," 26 *Georgia State Law Review* 321 (2010) (Thomas would effectively eliminate free-speech rights for students).

22 Randy E. Barnett, "Scalia's Infidelity: A Critique of 'Faint-Hearted' Originalism," 75 *University of Cincinnati Law Review* 7, 14–15 (2006); *but see* Goldstein, *supra* (Thomas not originalist in race opinions).

23 Bruce Ackerman, "Symposium: Fidelity to Constitutional Theory: Fidelity as Synthesis – A Generation of Betrayal," 65 *Fordham Law Review* 1519, 1522 (1997).

24 538 U.S. 343 (2003). Concurring, Scalia agreed that "a State may, without infringing the First Amendment, prohibit cross burning carried out with the intent to intimidate." *Id.* at 368.

25 *Id.* at 388. Scalia made the same point in his confirmation hearings. Hearings, Sen. Jud. Comm., 99th Cong., 2d Sess., Aug. 5, 1986, on Nomination of Judge Antonin Scalia, to be Associate Justice of the Supreme Court of the United States 52.

26 538 U.S. at 394–395. Thomas discussed cases where a mandatory presumption was upheld in contexts not involving the First Amendment, such as statutory rape and possession of drugs with intent to distribute. *Id.* at 377–398.

27 131 S.Ct. 2729 (2011).

28 *Id.* at 2751, 2755.

29 Kelo v. City of New London, 545 U.S. 469, 523 (1995).

30 *E.g.*, Mark Tushnet, *A Court Divided* 93–95, 97, 99 (2005). Thomas's reading of the Declaration of Independence and his use of natural rights are subject to serious challenge. While an oversimplification, natural rights are the approach of John Locke and the Declaration of Independence, with their emphasis on the innate rights of individuals. Thomas wrote that "a 'plain reading' of the Constitution . . . puts the fitly spoken words of the Declaration in the center of the frame formed by the Constitution." Thomas, "Toward a 'Plain Reading' of the Constitution – The Declaration of Independence in Constitutional Interpretation," 30 *Howard Law Journal* 983 (1987); *see, e.g.*, Scott Douglas Gerber, *First Principles; The Jurisprudence of Clarence Thomas* 43–47 (1999). However, the inalienable rights endorsed by the document were applicable only in a state of nature or to a new political state, and not to an established country where duties accompanied rights. Constitutional Convention Delegate James Wilson, a major figure, explained that "the right of individuals to their private property, to their personal liberty, to their health, to their reputation, and to their life, flow[s] from a human establishment, and can be traced to no higher source. The connection between man and his natural rights is intercepted by the institution of civil society . . . [and] he can claim nothing but what the society provides." American intellectual John Dewey proclaimed that "natural rights and natural liberties" existed "only in the kingdom of mythical social zoology." Rogers M. Smith, "The Politics of Rights Talk, Then and Now," in *id.* at 317. John Reid argued that colonists were primarily asserting the rights of Englishmen, not abstract concepts of natural law. Reid, "The Nature of Rights at the Founding," in *id.* at 90. Reid also pointed out that "aside from the rhetoric in the preamble, the Declaration of Independence does not contain claims of natural rights. All rights asserted in the Declaration were English rights. . . . " Reid, *The Authority of Rights* 5 (1986). Excepted was the right of one's religious conscience and perhaps the corporate right of people to govern themselves. Barry A. Shain, "Rights Natural and Civil in the Declaration of Independence," in *The Nature of Rights at the American Founding and Beyond* 130, 136, 139–143 (Shain

ed. 2007); *see generally id.* at 116–162. Daniel T. Rogers observed: "[T]he Constitution's drafter had already carefully deleted every instance of the term 'rights' from the Constitution in favor of a more cautious reference to 'immunities' and 'privileges.' "Rights Consciousness in American History," in *id.* at 263.

31 Reid, *The Authority of Rights* at 89–94.

32 Stephen T. Black & Katherine D. Black, "Justice Scalia's Tax Jurisprudence," 34 *University of Toledo Law Review* 509, 511 (2003).

CHAPTER 33   CONCLUSION

1 While originalists reject the wall-of-separation standard as ahistorical, others disagree. *See, e.g.*, Mark Tushnet, *Red, White, and Blue* 33 (1988).

2 *See* Tushnet, *Taking the Constitution Away from the Courts* 156 (1999) ("Overall, the justices seem to pick the theories that lead them to where they want to go anyway, and drop a theory pretty quickly if it seems to force them to unacceptable conclusions.").

3 Scalia faltered at least once by using legislative history. In Department of Revenue of Montana v. Kurth Ranch, 511 U.S. 767, 798 (1994) (Scalia, J., dissenting), he challenged the majority's reading of the Double Jeopardy Clause: "'To be put in jeopardy' does not remotely mean 'to be punished,' so by its terms this provision prohibits, not multiple punishments, but only multiple prosecutions. Compare the proposal of the House of Representatives, for which the Senate substituted language similar to the current text of the Clause: 'No person shall be subject, except in cases of impeachment, to more than one punishment or one trial for the same offense.'"

4 Solum, "The Fixation Thesis: The Role of Historical Fact in Original Meaning," 91 *Notre Dame Law Review* 1, 31 (2015).

5 Cass R. Sunstein, "Justice Scalia's Democratic Formalism," 107 *Yale Law Journal* 529, 565–566 (1997); *cf. King James Bible* (2000, 2003) (Job 38:11: "Thus far shall you come, but no farther: and here shall your proud waves be stayed."); *Bible, International Standard Version* (1996–2006) ("You may come only this far and no more. Your majestic waves will stop here.").

6 *See* Jeffrey Rosen, "Economic Freedoms and the Constitution," 35 *Harvard Journal of Law & Public Policy* 15–16 (2012).

7 515 U.S. at 549, 585–586.

8 Rosen, *The Most Democratic Branch* 152 (2006). For example, no judge presiding at prosecutions brought under the Sedition Act questioned the constitutionality of the law. *Id.* at 154.

9 Powell, "On Not Being 'Not an Originalist,'" 7 *St. Thomas Law Journal* 259, 272 (2010).

10 Breyer, *Active Liberty; Interpreting Our Democratic Constitution* (2005). Active liberty "refers to a sharing of a nation's sovereign authority among its people." "[I]nstitutions and methods of interpretation must be designed in a way such that this form of liberty is both sustainable over time and capable of translating the people's will into sound principles." It is pragmatic; it looks at consequences. *Id.* at 15–16, 18. Passive liberty "protects[s] the individual citizen from the tyranny of the majority"; it is the material of the Bill of Rights, along with separation of powers, federalism, and an independent judiciary. *Id.* at 4.

11 Of course, clerks can also write questions for the Justice, but there is often a give or take that reveals the thought process of the Justice.

12 The imprecise standard is the number of cases since Scalia's death in which Thomas voted to the right of Alito. Welch v. United States, 136 S.Ct. 1257 (2016) (Thomas, J., dissenting); Green v. Brennan, 136 S.Ct. 1769 (2016) (Thomas, J., dissenting); Foster v. Chatman, 136 S.Ct. 1737 (2016) (Thomas, J., dissenting); United States v. Bryant, 136 S.Ct. 1954 (2016) (Thomas, J., concurring); Williams v. Pennsylvania, 136 S.Ct. 1899 (2016) (Thomas, J., dissenting); Taylor v. United States, 136 S.Ct. 2074 (2016) (Thomas, J. dissenting); Birchfield v. North Dakota, 136 S.Ct. 2160 (2016); but see Mathis v. United States, No. 15-6092 (2016). Even more speculative is the possibility that the removal of Scalia's vitriolic pen will encourage other Justices to take liberties.

APPENDIX C

1 Unanimous opinions, including United States v. Jones, 132 S.Ct. 945 (2012) (GPS search-and-seizure case), are not listed unless the opinions differ as to liberality.
2 Chief Justice Rehnquist's entries are in italics, Chief Justice Roberts's are in roman typeface.
3 Cases in boldface are constitutional cases; those in roman are statutory or common law. Cases underlined are criminal cases. "(C)" indicates a concurring opinion, "(D)" indicates a dissenting opinion, and "(C, D)" indicates an opinion that concurs in part and dissents in part. Not counted in the statistics are those Scalia concurring opinions that only noted that he did not join the Court's opinion because it relied on legislative history; to be included an opinion had to comment on the relevant issue.
4 Also contains constitutional elements.
5 This case, implicating Miranda v. Arizona, is treated as a constitutional decision.
6 "?" signifies that no valid comparison can be made.
7 See note 4, supra.

Table of Cases

Index

Comments on